# World of
# a Slave

# World of a Slave

## ENCYCLOPEDIA OF THE MATERIAL LIFE OF SLAVES IN THE UNITED STATES

### Volume 2: J–Z

MARTHA B. KATZ-HYMAN

*and*

KYM S. RICE, EDITORS

## GREENWOOD

AN IMPRINT OF ABC-CLIO, LLC
Santa Barbara, California • Denver, Colorado • Oxford, England

**Library of Congress Cataloging-in-Publication Data**

World of a slave : encyclopedia of the material life of slaves in the United States /
Martha B. Katz-Hyman and Kym S. Rice, editors.
    p. cm.
   Includes bibliographical references and index.
   ISBN 978-0-313-34942-3 (set : acid-free paper) — ISBN 978-0-313-34943-0
(set : ebook)— ISBN 978-0-313-34944-7 (v. 1 : acid-free paper) — ISBN 978-0-313-34945-4
(v. 1 : ebook) — ISBN 978-0-313-34946-1 (v. 2 : acid-free paper) — ISBN 978-0-313-34947-8
(v. 2 : ebook)
   1. Slavery—United States—History—Encyclopedias. 2. African Americans—
Material culture—History—Encyclopedias. 3. Material culture—United States—History—
Encyclopedias. I. Katz-Hyman, Martha B. II. Rice, Kym S.
   E441.W895    2011
   306.3'620973—dc22        2010037597

ISBN: 978-0-313-34942-3
EISBN: 978-0-313-34943-0

15  14  13  12  11    1  2  3  4  5

This book is also available on the World Wide Web as an eBook.
Visit www.abc-clio.com for details.

Greenwood
An Imprint of ABC-CLIO, LLC

ABC-CLIO, LLC
130 Cremona Drive, P.O. Box 1911
Santa Barbara, California 93116-1911

This book is printed on acid-free paper ∞

Manufactured in the United States of America

# Contents

Preface     vii

Acknowledgments     ix

Introduction     xi

Alphabetical List of Entries     xix

Topical List of Entries     xxi

Dance and Music     1

Literacy and Orality     11

**The Encyclopedia**     17

Selected Bibliography     553

Index     561

About the Editors and Contributors     577

# Preface

Human beings spend their lives surrounded by things. Sometimes these objects are utilitarian, such as the cars we drive, the beds we sleep on, or the shoes we wear. Others may represent something more unique and personal, like a gift from a beloved friend or relative. Still others reflect the society in which we live or our value systems and beliefs. Whether we are considering the objects that help us to do our work or those that reflect our choices, passions, and decisions, we all understand that these things say something about us and our identity, often more powerfully than words. This encyclopedia tries to capture the material culture of slavery. Until recently, scholars, museums, and the general public thought that little tangible evidence remained from those 200-plus years of U.S. history, other than a detailed documentary record that reflects almost entirely the slaveholders' perspective. Thanks largely to recent archaeological investigations conducted across the plantation South, the Chesapeake, the Upper South, and sites in New England and the Mid-Atlantic, new museum collecting practices, and a renewed interest in and access to the oral histories collected from former slaves by the Federal Writers' Project of the Works Progress Administration in 1936–1938, we know more about what slaves surrounded themselves with than ever before. The entries collected here use objects as a prism for understanding both the complex institution that was American slavery and the individual experiences of the people trapped within it. The items that brought joy and preserved culture get as much attention as those that inflicted cruel punishments or extracted long hours of backbreaking labor.

As much as possible, it is the story of the enslaved that we try to tell, and it is their world that we explore throughout the encyclopedia. The focus is on the enslaved in all of the areas where slavery was to be found, from the North to the South, and west to Texas, and from the 17th century through Emancipation. In addition, many entries discuss how the West and Central African traditions and customs brought by those torn from their homelands continued to manifest themselves in the everyday lives of African Americans even through the difficult years of slavery. This melding of cultural traditions and influences resulted in new practices and beliefs, called creolization, which enabled enslaved Africans to use the objects they found in their new locations and the ideas that they learned to make sense out of experiences that were demeaning and painful, and lives that were marked by unrelenting labor and unpredictability.

Although thousands of books have been published about slavery, this is the first encyclopedia to focus on the material culture of slaves in the United States. It covers the everyday lives of the enslaved: what they wore, saw, and looked at; played and played with; ate and drank and smoked; worked on and in; heard, read, used, made, touched, hid away, lived in, built, were given, slept on, carried, raised, and cultivated; were sold on; and much more. The experiences of the enslaved are the principal topic, but a great deal is revealed about the white and slaveholding society as well. Much of the information contained in the entries has not been published before in this format. Hopefully, this reference will serve as a springboard for future investigations and new discoveries about this important subject.

The encyclopedia includes more than 170 entries arranged alphabetically. Readers also will find a topical list of entries at the front of the book so that they can quickly find topics of interest. Two broad essays on music and dance and on literacy and orality appear before the encyclopedia entries as necessary context for readers to understand the wider material culture. The individual entries include suggestions for further reading, and cross-references are given to related entries, either as bolded topics in the entries or following "*See also*" at the end of the entry. The volume ends with a selected bibliography that will lead readers to substantive books and articles as well as Web sites. Contributors are experts drawn from academia, historical archaeology, museums, and public history who work in this field.

The encyclopedia boasts a large number of images selected from museum and library collections to illustrate the entries. The photographs of now-vanished slave quarter houses, the watercolor portraits of the enslaved, and the archaeological survivals from slave-related sites chosen for this encyclopedia are but a sample of what has survived and been documented for posterity. We have tried to be as wide-ranging as possible, realizing that examples from archives of material slave life are anything but generic; architecture and objects were as varied as the plantations and states in which enslaved African Americans lived. For example, slave housing looked very different in Virginia, New Orleans, and Tennessee and even from plantation to plantation to less grand slaveholdings, depending on local vernacular and resources, degree of wealth, and architectural ambitions.

Many entries are accompanied by sidebars that offer complementary testimony from the Federal Writers' Project slave narratives. The narrative excerpts taken from interviews with former slaves usually were transcribed in vernacular speech with unusual spelling and grammar, and they use language that some modern readers may find offensive. As many historians note, these interviews are problematic in that the individuals who were interviewed for the project were mostly young children as slaves. Their memories were also shaped by the era in which the interviews were conducted, the Great Depression. Many of the people interviewed in 1936–1938 were old, hungry, and living in poverty. The interviewers, most of whom were white, asked leading questions and frequently patronized their subjects. Nonetheless, these accounts often are detailed, and they offer the most direct record that we have of the world of a slave. Fisk University Social Science Institute staff member Ophelia Settle Egypt was a rare example of an African American interviewer. When she interviewed a former slave in 1929 or 1930, she was told, "If you want Negro History, you will have to get [it] from somebody who wore the shoes."[*] This encyclopedia offers readers a chance to put on those shoes.

---

[*]In Rawick, George P. *The American Slave: Oklahoma and Mississippi Narratives*, Vol. 7 (Westport, CT: Greenwood Press, 1972), pp. 45–46.

# Acknowledgments

Putting together a reference work of this size takes time, patience, and the contributions and assistance of many people. Our thanks first go to our editor, Wendi Schnaufer, who first approached Kym about this project more than four years ago. Kym then recruited Martha to help her, and all along the way, Wendi has been there to encourage, help, and push this encyclopedia to completion. We are most grateful. Our thanks, as well, to Michael Millman, who became our editor during the production of the encyclopedia and smoothed the way to its conclusion.

We acknowledge the contributions of our advisory board: Fath Davis Ruffins, curator, Division of Home and Community Life, National Museum of American History; Theresa Singleton, associate professor of anthropology, the Maxwell School of Syracuse University; and John Michael Vlach, professor of American studies and anthropology at the George Washington University. They reviewed the initial list of entries and made good suggestions regarding topics that the encyclopedia needed to cover.

Our thanks to the following for allowing us to use images from their collections: Roddy Moore, director, Blue Ridge Institute & Museum, Ferrum College; Daniel Ackermann, associate curator, Museum of Early Southern Decorative Arts and the Old Salem Toy Museum; Jill Slaight, rights and reproductions, New-York Historical Society; Leah Stearns, digital services coordinator, Monticello, Thomas Jefferson Memorial Foundation; and especially, Marianne Martin, visual resources librarian, Colonial Williamsburg Foundation, who worked with her colleagues across the Foundation to get us the images we wanted.

We are especially grateful to all of our contributors, many of whom wrote more than one entry—some at the last minute. Many of them responded directly to our personal requests; others responded to our call for contributors. Without their enthusiasm, support, and writing, this project never would have been completed. Their names and affiliations are found in the list of contributors.

Our deepest thanks is reserved for our families. At times this project has taken over our dining rooms, living rooms, and family rooms, not to mention our lives, and they have been very understanding. Tsvi and Mark: thank you.

Martha B. Katz-Hyman
Kym S. Rice

# Introduction

The study of human experience through objects and their context is called material culture. According to the pioneering scholar of material culture, Thomas Schlereth, the methodology that underlies the study of material culture is that "objects made or modified by humans, consciously or unconsciously, directly or indirectly, reflect the belief patterns of individuals who made, commissioned, purchased, or used them, and, by extension, the belief patterns of the larger society of which they are a part."[1] In the case of enslaved African Americans, these objects can be as large as a house that survives from the 1800s or as small as a fragment from a ceramic plate recovered from a slave quarter after being buried for more than a century. Some objects are more ephemeral: while they might have survived slavery, their meanings have slipped away in modern life, and archaeologists are only now beginning to unravel them.

This encyclopedia takes a broad look at enslaved experiences over the more than 250 years between the establishment of the first colonial settlements and the Civil War that ended chattel slavery in the United States. The work concentrates on the American South. This is where the largest enslaved African American populations resided, over the longest period of time. By 1861, some 4 million enslaved individuals lived in the region, about half the total population of the South. Our entries try to cover everything used by slaves, whether that is the goods found in their dwellings; their work tools; the furniture, textiles, and other goods used by them in the course of their day; or the houses in which they lived and worked as well as the landscapes in which they were situated; the clothing they wore and how they wore it; their food and how they prepared it; even their hairstyles and oral traditions. From the emerging field of slave archaeology, we find tantalizing evidence that some things, which remained largely invisible to whites, reflected the belief systems that accompanied captive Africans to the Caribbean and Americas, but often were adapted or changed in the face of their altered circumstances. Slaves came into contact with other objects too, ones that we associate with the oppression that marked their chattel status, including those that were used to inflict the cruel punishments that many slaves feared or experienced. For all its bleakness, slavery was far from monolithic. We know that enslaved African Americans were able to purchase fashionable items at stores as consumers as well as make or repurpose objects for themselves. These modest endeavors suggest the ways that material goods added richness and color to an individual's life and contributed in no small measure to creating and maintaining personal and collective identity. All this was a part of "the World of a Slave."

Although the characteristics of enslavement varied from place to place and changed over time, all slaves occupied two distinctive and complex worlds: the one that was dictated to them and controlled by whites, which they needed to traverse and survive daily, and the one that they fashioned for themselves within their families and their communities that existed apart from whites. Our contributors address both the ways that particular objects functioned in these two worlds, and the different kinds of meaning that those items might have embodied for enslaved people.

Nearly 200 years stretch between 1619, when the first Africans arrived in the Virginia colony, and the official end of the U.S. slave trade by Congress in 1807. Although estimates by scholars vary, more than 12 million captive Africans were transported to the Caribbean, South America, and mainland North America over this time span. Still others were brought illegally, despite the ban, right up until the Civil War. This movement of Africans to the Americas has been called the largest forced migration in world history. Some African captives were themselves the victims of tribal wars in their own countries; others were people who had been kidnapped either by slave traders or their African agents and sold into slavery. Most could trace their origins to the wide swath of what is identified in the 21st century as West and Central Africa, although individuals were transported to coastal slave markets from locations much farther away. To a large extent, the Africans who came to what became the United States were from West Central Africa. Yet they spoke assorted different languages and dialects and held many different beliefs and traditions. In fact, it is thought that some already knew a version of the creolized form of English learned from Europeans that is preserved in the Gullah language found in the Georgia and South Carolina Sea Islands. Seeking agricultural workers for their colonial holdings, and especially valuing individuals with experience in the crops that they hoped to exploit like tobacco, sugar, or rice, many European countries, including Great Britain, Holland, France, and Portugal, participated in the African slave trade until well into the 18th century. According to the Trans-Atlantic Slave Trade Database, more than 40,000 voyages from Africa by slave-trading vessels are documented.[2]

Those individuals who survived the terrible trip across the Atlantic known as the Middle Passage spent upward of 45 days together below deck in close quarters with inadequate food, water, and exercise. On some ships, even while outfitted in heavy chains, slaves were forced to dance, sing, or drum for the crew's amusement—and were whipped if they refused. Some captives carried out mutinies against their captors and others jumped overboard in desperation. The trip, too, was subject to the vagaries of weather, including terrible storms. By a recent estimate, some 10.5 million Africans probably survived the Middle Passage.[3] After arriving in the Caribbean or North America, individuals could be sold several times over and travel considerable distances before they reached their final destinations.

The brutality associated with the African slave trade makes it relatively certain that few, if any, enslaved individuals transported personal belongings with them to the New World. Although most captives reportedly were stripped of their clothing before the voyage, a cowry shell tucked away in hair or perhaps a bead necklace might have traveled across the Atlantic Ocean on a slave ship and thus into the colonial South. It is more likely that slaves acquired such items on board ship. Slavers often carried goods for trading that included glass beads. The *Henrietta Marie*, which sunk off the coast of present-day Florida in 1701, had thousands of glass beads in its cargo hold, along with shackles and chains. African women possibly were given beads on board ship as a diversion. James Penny, an English slave trader in the 1770s and 1780s, reported that he furnished captives with pipes and tobacco as well as musical instruments. He noted that "the women are supplied with beads, which they make into ornaments."[4]

With the exception perhaps of some scattered trinkets recovered by archaeologists at different sites associated with slavery, what nearly all Africans brought with them stayed alive only in their memories, perhaps later reinforced by oral traditions that were repeated and passed down within the groups or communities that colonial enslavement created. This included information on how to grow and harvest certain African crops; what foods were preferred and how to cook them; medical and health practices; the shapes and materials that composed once familiar household objects; the perpetuation of sacred forms that were imbued with spiritual meaning and power; and traditions related to the built environment. These were all they had to help them make sense of their lives in a very foreign place, under circumstances that, by and large, robbed them of their names, families, and societies. This process, which, in fact, occurs with all people who move to a new culture, was continuous and changing. Second-, third-, fourth-, and even fifth-generation people of African descent became more and more acculturated, and they were as familiar with their material environment as people in the 21st century are with theirs. Throughout the 18th century, newly arrived Africans brought reminders of old traditions to their new homes, but they soon learned the ways of the European colonists who now owned them and became accustomed within several generations to their new environments.

The material objects that are the easiest to associate directly with American slavery across its entire time span are those related to work. They are the hoes, plows, and other implements that worked the fields, the looms that made cloth, the needles and thread that sewed or repaired clothes, the pots that cooked food and the plates that it was served on, the variety of tools that crafted everything from silver cups to manacles, the chamber pots that had to be emptied each morning, the saddles that needed cleaning or repair—the list goes on and on. Although building techniques and forms varied across the region, from shotgun houses to one-room cabins, enslaved individuals constructed both the buildings in which they lived and those in which they worked.

Slaves used a diverse range of objects to perform work that varied in terms of quality and quantity, depending on their owners' economic level. A farm where two or three slaves resided presented a different living situation and level of material comfort than a plantation with several hundred workers in residence. Similar modifications are found in Southern cities, where most enslaved individuals lived in proximity to their owners. In some cases, enslaved African Americans not only used these objects to do the jobs required of them by whites, but crafted them as part of their labors as trades workers. The domestic workforce handled different objects than did the field hands. Yet, even given these many distinctions, doing work day in and day out for someone else, without choice or precious little recompense, was a condition that all slaves shared. Regardless of location or time period, the white and the black worlds intersected over work. Through their daily use of the implements that performed every type of job imaginable, enslaved African Americans learned much of what they knew about the world of their white masters. And whenever possible or desirable, they acquired or replicated these objects for themselves. The pallets, benches, stools, and iron pots that furnished many slave quarters were homemade or readily available and looked the same as those used by lower-class whites or free blacks.

To many readers, the notion that enslaved people slept in beds, lived in houses with wood floors, cooked with a variety of equipment, and wore clothing that spanned the range from coarse linen shirts and trousers for work in the fields to dresses of printed cottons or suits of fine livery may seem strange. After all, being a slave implies that someone owns not only one's physical body but also anything else that one might have, from the clothing one wears to the food one puts into one's mouth to the bed one sleeps in—whatever that bed might be—to the utensils one cooks with. It implies a material status so low that only the most basic of food, shelter, and clothing is provided. Yet the evidence we have, both archaeological and documentary, shows time and time again that slaves in the 18th century and 19th century lived within a fairly wide range of material levels, from those who truly did have only the most basic of the necessities of life, to those who managed to acquire goods that were equal to or better than those that poor to middling whites could obtain.

How did slaves accumulate these goods? Were they yet another facet of the negotiation historians described that occurred regularly between master and slave that characterizes other aspects of enslavement? If slaves had no legal right to own these items, why were they not required to give them up to their owners? And if American slavery was not denoted by having few, if any, possessions of one's own, then how was it characterized?

The last question is probably the easiest to answer: simply, that these people of African descent were slaves by virtue of laws, enacted beginning in the late-17th century, that delineated their status and reflected long-time prejudices, not because these laws dictated levels of material goods. The law said they were chattel, and the law provided the ways in which they could cease being slaves. Over time, these laws were modified, repealed, and reenacted. Sometimes they specified what slaves could and could not possess, like guns, liquor, or dogs. In these cases, the laws reflect what enslaved individuals actually did possess or had access to and, therefore, what slave owners were unhappy about them possessing and wished to prohibit. But, by and large, these laws were enacted to regulate behavior and legal status, not consumption.

How slaves acquired goods is also relatively easy to answer, because of the wealth of primary sources—letters, diaries, business records, legal records, runaway slave advertisements—that provide the information. Masters issued clothing, blankets, and food on a semiregular schedule: clothing was issued in the spring/summer and fall/winter or once a year on New Year's Day, blankets usually in the fall, and food was distributed weekly as well as seasonally. It appears from the available documentation that, once these goods were issued, masters as well as slaves considered these goods to be the slaves' property. Masters also supplied slaves with the tools necessary to do their jobs, although these remained the property of the master and are the items most likely to be found listed in probate inventories of slaveholders as the property of the deceased's estate.

Although not well documented, some slaves received hand-me-down cooking utensils, furniture, and clothing from their masters. This, however, was not a usual practice. They also picked up items discarded by whites, repaired them and put them to their own purposes. They obtained goods by theft, usually from their owners, a crime for which, if discovered, they were punished and sometimes legally prosecuted. That many masters or overseers kept a close eye on the tools and supplies used by their enslaved workers, scrutinized their return carefully, and kept them under lock and key suggests that stealing was a widespread problem. On the other hand, enslaved individuals understandably displayed little remorse over these appropriations, thinking perhaps that they had earned these items.

Slaves made things for themselves and bartered and sold these goods to their masters, to white neighbors, and on the open market. Especially on rural plantations, slaves had their own plots of land called "patches" and grew their own produce, and they also took advantage of nearby streams, rivers, and woodlands to catch fish and trap animals. Slaves acquired goods by purchasing them with money they earned from tips or gifts, from the sale of produce or animals, primarily chickens, from the sale of their own products, like baskets, or from their own labor. In urban settings, greater opportunities existed for enslaved individuals to earn money, including by selling produce or other items at city markets. By the end of the antebellum period, the hiring-out system had evolved in such a way that many enslaved individuals were permitted to keep some part of their wages. With cash accumulated over many years, some slaves hoped to buy their freedom or that of family members, but many others used their money more immediately, to purchase a variety of goods, ranging from fabrics and ribbons to tools, liquor, and food. These purchases are well documented in surviving store account books; in both early Maryland and Virginia, for instance, these records often appear as credit accounts in the slave's own name. All of these goods were the same types of things bought by whites and free blacks.[5]

As for why slave owners allowed their slaves to keep their goods, one answer may be found in a principle derived from ancient Roman law, called the *peculium*, that was well understood by most slave owners. According to this principle, slaves were allowed to accumulate property but that property was subject to appropriation by the master at any time, although in practice, the appropriation of the goods may have happened infrequently, if at all. Thomas Jefferson makes it clear that he understood this principle in a letter that he wrote to his son-in-law, Thomas Mann Randolph, in 1798, thanking Randolph "for putting an end to the cultivation of tobacco as the peculium of the Negroes. I have ever found it necessary to confine them to such articles as are not raised on the farm. There is no other way of drawing a line between what is theirs and mine."[6] Historian Orlando Patterson writes that the peculium

> solved the most important problem of slave labor: the fact that it was given involuntarily. It was the best means of motivating the slave to perform efficiently on his master's behalf. It not only allowed the slave the vicarious enjoyment of the capacity he most lacked—that of owning property—but also held out the long-term hope of self-redemption for the most diligent slaves. The master lost nothing, since he maintained an ultimate claim on the peculium, and he had everything to gain.[7]

From the point of view of the slave owners' self-interest, allowing slaves to accumulate goods made good management sense: slaves who stood to lose a lot materially by rebelling might think twice about doing so if it meant losing the property they had worked long and hard to accumulate. Therefore, for all practical purposes, it is most likely that slaves' personal goods were considered by both blacks and whites to belong to the slaves and therefore not subject to inventory or other accounting as part of the possessions of the slaves' owner, although the real possibility exists that white slave owners, at least initially, felt that the items owned by their slaves were of no real value.

In the antebellum period, when the institution of slavery came under greater threat, some slaveholders did express concerns about whether enslaved individuals should be allowed to spend the money they earned as they pleased and choose their own possessions. Not only did slaveholders wish to reinforce their control and authority over their slaves whenever possible, but they increasingly perceived that any means by which enslaved individuals could carve out some measure of autonomy for themselves was dangerous to the entire system. "Money is power," an Alabama planter astutely observed in 1858. He suggested "cram[ming] negroes' pockets with strings, old buckles, nails, &c. instead of silver dollars."[8] But by the 1850s, enslaved individuals certainly were too sophisticated as consumers to be satisfied with any old castoffs. Even if the amount of money that slaves had was not great, it still permitted them the ability to acquire possessions that they could use in any way they saw fit. Through goods, enslaved African Americans found one means with which to thwart the threadbare life accorded them by whites and craft a distinctive identity.

While archaeological excavations have found evidence of guns and other weapons in slave quarters, the objects associated with reading and writing that have been uncovered might be considered more seditious. By the outbreak of the Civil War, because Southern whites were increasingly fearful of anything that might provoke dissention or violence among their slaves, enslaved people were legally prohibited from learning to read and write. By these laws, whites hoped to limit slaves' access not only to books, but also to newspapers, auction posters, and the rare anti-slavery tract. Some slaveholders, who were motivated by their religious beliefs, taught their slaves to read the Bible regardless, but undoubtedly some individuals, such as Frederick Douglass, who escaped from slavery in Maryland and went on to become one of the most famous black abolitionists, learned on their own. The pens, pencils, ink bottles, and slates found by archaeologists tucked behind walls and secreted in other locations on slave-occupied sites offer a tantalizing clue that some enslaved individuals pursued these skills, regardless of the risk. It is significant that in their testimony given before the Freedmen's Bureau at the Civil War's end, many former slaves declared emphatically that their first act in freedom was to learn to read and write.

In the words of an ancient Yoruba proverb, "However far the stream flows, it never forgets its sources."[9] Although the Africans who came to the New World as slaves possessed backgrounds as different as the languages that they spoke, they sought and found areas of common ground. Africa clearly provided a critical element that shaped enslaved material culture over several generations. To have some stability in their lives, enslaved people had to make some sense of the chaos around them. One way they did this was to take the objects they had, both manufactured and natural, and impose upon them the usages and meanings that similar objects carried in Africa. They also made objects with materials found in the United States that in form and function resembled those that they knew from their homelands. Archaeological evidence suggests that even as they acculturated, enslaved individuals retained some cultural traditions. While the form and meaning changed over time, ideas about the innate power of certain objects—pierced coins worn as charms, crystals placed under kitchen floors, or pottery marked with cosmogram symbols—and their ability to protect and transform were preserved and handed down to descendants. African elements likewise remained alive in many facets of slave life: in the music they played, the songs they sang, the dances they performed, the food they ate, the stories they told, the hairstyles and adornments they wore, and the ways in which they buried their dead. In areas such as the Sea Islands of South Carolina and Georgia, where enslaved African Americans lived together in large groups with limited contact with whites, these traditions and practices stayed intact into the 20th century.

Many 21st-century Americans recognize that this country is far richer for the contributions made to it by enslaved African Americans. This powerful legacy has transformed American culture. We can see, hear, and taste it every day, through the foods we eat, the landscape that surrounds us, the words we hear, and the music, art, and dance that we enjoy. It is harder to experience enslaved material culture, although it forms a distinctive element in this story of survival and change. While slavery is interpreted at many museums and historic sites in the 21st century, original objects with enslaved provenance are few, and archaeological materials are seldom displayed. Whether they purchased, found, or appropriated them, African Americans adopted the familiar objects that signified the white world and brought them into their lives. Despite the fact that these items made their lives more comfortable and bearable, they must have served as poignant reminders of what free people could possess. At the same time, as terrible as slavery was, it did not truly rub out what enslaved African Americans were as a people. Archaeology in slave sites across the South shows that the old ways persisted in secret, not only because whites found them subversive but also because enslaved individuals thought it was important to preserve them at any cost.

## NOTES

1. Thomas Schelereth, *Material Culture Studies in America* (Lanham, MD: AltaMira Press, 1982), 3.

2. Trans-Atlantic Slave Trade Database (www.slavevoyages.org). The number of Africans taken on the voyages documented in the database represents approximately 80 percent of those actually transported.

3. Trans-Atlantic Slave Trade Database (www.slavevoyages.org).

4. Jerome S. Handler, "On the Transportation of Material Goods by Enslaved Africans During the Middle Passage: Preliminary Findings from Documentary Sources," *The African Diaspora Archaeology Newsletter*, 2006. (http://www.diaspora.uiuc.edu/news1206/news1206 .html#1). Also, Jerome S. Handler, "The Middle Passage and the Material Culture of Captive Africans," *Slavery & Abolition* 30, no. 1 (March 2009): 1–26.

5. Ann Smart Martin, *Buying into the World of Goods: Early Consumers in Backcountry Virginia* (Baltimore, MD: Johns Hopkins University Press, 2008).

6. Thomas Jefferson to Thomas Mann Randolph Jr., June 14, 1798, Library of Congress, Washington, DC.

7. Orlando Patterson, *Slavery and Social Death: A Comparative Study* (Cambridge, MA: Harvard University Press, 1982), 185–186.

8. Quoted in James O. Breeden, ed., *Advice Among Masters: The Ideal in Slave Management in the Old South* (Westport, CT: Greenwood Press, 1980), 274.

9. Quoted in Charles Joyner, *Down By The Riverside: A South Carolina Slave Community* (Urbana: University of Illinois Press, 1986), xiii.

# Alphabetical List of Entries

Abolition Imagery
Accordions
African Free School
Animal Traps
Armories
Auction Advertisements
Auction Blocks
Balafons
Banjos
Barter Goods
Baskets and Basket Making
Beads
Beds
Bells and Horns
Benevolent Associations
Bible
Blacksmith Shops
Blankets
Boats
Books
Bottle Trees
Brands
Bray Schools
Brooms
Buttons
Canoes
Caricatures
Cast Iron Pots
Cemeteries
Chamber Pots and Privies
Charms
Chickens
Churches and Praise Houses
Clocks and Watches
Cloth
Clothing Allotments
Clothing and Footwear

Coffins and Caskets
Coffles
Coins and Currency
Collards
Colonoware
Conjure Bags
Contraband Camps
Cooking and Cooks
Cooperage
Corn
Corn Cribs
Cosmograms
Cotton and Cotton Plantations
Courthouses
Credit Accounts
Crosses
Dairies
Dependencies
Dogs
Dogtrot Houses
Dolls
Dormitories
Double-Pen Houses
Dovecoats
Drums
Emancipation Proclamation
Faunal Remains
Fences
Ferries
Fetishes
Fiddles
Firearms
Fish and Shellfish
Fishing Poles
Flutes
Food and Foodways
Freedom Papers

# ALPHABETICAL LIST OF ENTRIES

Free Produce
French Horns
Furnishings
Gardens
Gourds
Graves
Guineas
Guitars
Gumbo
Hair and Hairstyles
Headwraps, Tignons, and Kerchiefs
Herbs
Hoecakes
Hoes
Hominy
Hoppin' John
Horses
Indigo
Ironwork
Jew's Harps
Kitchens
Koran
Laundries
Legal Documents
Linen Textiles
Liquor
Livery
Locks and Keys
Lofts
Marbles
Markets
Master's House
Medicine
Military Equipment
Mines and Mining
Mirrors
Mules
Nails
Negro Cloth
Nets and Seines
Nurseries and Nursemaids
Okra
Pallets
Passes
Peanuts
Personal Objects
Pigs and Pork
Pot Likker
Pottery
Pounders
Punkahs and Fly Brushes
Quilts

Rations
Razors
Ribbons
Rice and Rice Fields
Runaway Slave Advertisements
Sale Notices
Scarification
Sculleries
Servants Halls
Sesame
Sewing Items and Needlework
Shells
Shipyards
Shoes
Shotgun Houses
Shrines and Spirit Caches
Skin
Slave Badges
Slave Collars
Slave Drivers
Slave Galleries
Slave Hospitals
Slave Housing
Slave-Made Objects
Slave Narratives
Slave Pens, Slave Jails, and Slave Markets
Slave Quarters
Slave Ships
Spinning Houses
Spring Houses
Stews
Subfloor Pits
Sugar
Tabby
Tar, Pitch, and Turpentine
Textiles
Thumb Pianos
Tobacco
Tobacco Barns
Tobacco Factories
Tobacco Pipes
Two Rooms over Two Rooms Houses
Underground Railroad
Watermelons
Wheat
Whips
Woodworking Tools
Wool Textiles
Work Routines
Writing Tools
Yams and Sweet Potatoes
Yards

# Topical List of Entries

## DOCUMENTS
Abolition Imagery
Auction Advertisements
Caricatures
Courthouses
Emancipation Proclamation
Freedom Papers
Legal Documents
Passes
Runaway Slave Advertisements
Sale Notices
Slave Narratives

## ECONOMY
Barter Goods
Baskets and Basket Making
Bells and Horns
Blacksmith Shops
Canoes
Chickens
Clocks and Watches
Cloth
Clothing Allotments
Clothing and Footwear
Coins and Currency
Colonoware
Cooperage
Corn
Corn Cribs
Cotton and Cotton Plantations
Credit Accounts
Ferries
Firearms
Fish and Shellfish
Gardens
Guineas
Hoes
Horses

Indigo
Ironwork
Linen Textiles
Markets
Mules
Nails
Negro Cloth
Pigs and Pork
Pottery
Razors
Ribbons
Slave Badges
Slave-Made Objects
Sugar
Tar, Pitch, and Turpentine
Textiles
Tobacco
Tobacco Factories
Wheat
Wool Textiles

## EDUCATION AND LITERACY
African Free School
Bible
Books
Bray Schools
Koran
Qur'an (*see* Koran)
Writing Tools

## FOOD AND DRINK
Animal Traps
Benne (*see* Sesame)
Cast Iron Pots
Chickens
Collards
Colonoware
Cooking and Cooks

Cooperage
Corn
Dairies
Faunal Remains
Fish and Shellfish
Fishing Poles
Food and Foodways
Gardens
Gourds
Gumbo
Herbs
Hoecakes
Hominy
Hoppin' John
Kitchens
Liquor
Markets
Medicine
Nets and Seines
Okra
Peanuts
Pigs and Pork
Pot Likker
Pounders
Rations
Rice and Rice Fields
Sesame
Spring Houses
Stews
Subfloor Pits
Sugar
Watermelons
Wheat
Yams and Sweet Potatoes

**HOME**
Banjos
Beds
Chamber Pots and Privies
Cloth
Colonoware
Faunal Remains
Fiddles
Furnishings
Jew's Harps
Kalimba (*see* Thumb Pianos)
Pallets
Thumb Pianos

**MUSIC**
Accordians
Balafons
Banjos
Drums

Fiddles
Flutes
French Horns
Guitars
Jew's Harps
Kalimba (*see* Thumb Pianos)
Thumb Pianos
Xylophones (*see* Balafons)

**PERSONAL ITEMS**
Animal Traps
Banjos
Barter Goods
Baskets and Basket Making
Beads
Beds
Bible
Blankets
Books
Bottle Trees
Brooms
Buttons
Cast Iron Pots
Charms
Coins and Currency
Cloth
Clothing Allotments
Clothing and Footwear
Colonoware
Conjure Bags
Cosmograms
Credit Accounts
Crosses
Dogs
Dolls
Fetishes
Fiddles
Fishing Poles
Furnishings
Guitars
Hair and Hairstyles
Headwraps, Tignons, and Kerchiefs
Linen Textiles
Livery
Marbles
Markets
Mirrors
Negro Cloth
Nets and Seines
Nkisi (*see* Fetishes)
Pallets
Personal Objects
Pottery
Quilts

Razors
Ribbons
Sewing Items and Needlework
Shoes
Slave Badges
Slave-Made Objects
Slave Narratives
Subfloor Pits
Textiles
Tobacco Pipes
Wool Textiles
Writing Tools
Yards

## PLACES
Abolition Imagery
African Free School
Armories
Auction Blocks
Cemeteries
Churches and Praise Houses
Contraband Camps
Graves
Kitchens
Lofts
Mines and Mining
Servants Halls
Shipyards
Slave Galleries
Slave Housing
Slave Pens, Slave Jails, and Slave Markets
Slave Quarters
Subfloor Pits
Underground Railroad
Yards

## RELIGION
Beads
Benevolent Associations
Bible
Bottle Trees
Buttons
Cast Iron Pots
Cemeteries
Charms
Chickens
Churches and Praise Houses
Coffins and Caskets
Colonoware
Conjure Bags
Cosmograms
Crosses
Faunal Remains
Fetishes

Gourds
Graves
Herbs
Koran
Marbles
Medicine
Mirrors
Nails
Nkisi (*see* Fetishes)
Qur'an (*see* Koran)
Scarification
Sewing Items and Needlework
Shells
Shrines and Spirit Caches
Slave Galleries
Subfloor Pits
Tobacco Pipes
Yards

## RITES OF PASSAGE
Benevolent Associations
Brooms
Cemeteries
Churches and Praise Houses
Coffins and Caskets
Cosmograms
Fetishes
Graves
Nkisi (*see* Fetishes)
Scarification

## SLAVERY
Abolition Imagery
Armories
Auction Advertisements
Auction Blocks
Bells and Horns
Bible
Books
Brands
Coffles
Colonoware
Contraband Camps
Cotton and Cotton Plantations
Emancipation Proclamation
Ferries
Free Produce
Guineas
Liquor
Livery
Locks and Keys
Passes
Punkahs and Fly Brushes
Rations

Rice and Rice Fields
Runaway Slave Advertisements
Sale Notices
Skin
Slave Badges
Slave Collars
Slave Drivers
Slave Galleries
Slave Hospitals
Slave Housing
Slave Narratives
Slave Pens, Slave Jails, and Slave
    Markets
Slave Quarters
Slave Ships
Sugar
Tobacco
Tobacco Factories
Underground Railroad
Whips
Work Routines

**STRUCTURES**
Armories
Blacksmith Shops
Churches and Praise Houses
Corn Cribs
Courthouses
Dairies
Dependencies
Dogtrot Houses
Dormitories
Double-Pen Houses
Dovecoats
Fences
Kitchens
Laundries
Locks and Keys
Lofts
Master's House
Sculleries
Servants Halls
Shotgun Houses
Slave Galleries
Slave Hospitals
Slave Housing
Slave Pens, Slave Jails, and Slave Markets
Slave Quarters
Spinning Houses
Spring Houses
Tabby
Tobacco Barns
Tobacco Factories
Two Rooms over Two Rooms Houses

**WORK**
Barter Goods
Baskets and Basket Making
Bells and Horns
Blacksmith Shops
Boats
Canoes
Clocks and Watches
Cloth
Clothing Allotments
Clothing and Footwear
Coins and Currency
Cooking and Cooks
Cooperage
Corn
Cotton and Cotton Plantations
Credit Accounts
Dairies
Dogs
Ferries
Fiddles
Firearms
Fish and Shellfish
Fishing Poles
Flutes
French Horns
Gardens
Hoes
Horses
Indigo
Ironwork
Kitchens
Laundries
Linen Textiles
Livery
Markets
Master's House
Medicine
Military Equipment
Mines and Mining
Mules
Nails
Nets and Seines
Nurseries and Nursemaids
Pottery
Pounders
Punkahs and Fly Brushes
Quilts
Razors
Rice and Rice Fields
Servants Halls
Sewing Items and Needlework
Shipyards
Shoes

Slave Badges
Slave-Made Objects
Slave Ships
Spinning Houses
Spring Houses
Subfloor Pits
Sugar
Tar, Pitch, and Turpentine
Textiles

Tobacco
Tobacco Barns
Tobacco Factories
Wheat
Whips
Woodworking Tools
Wool Textiles
Work Routines
Yards

# J

**JEW'S HARPS.** The Jew's or jaw harp is an ancient, small, mouth-resonated single-reed instrument found in many cultures throughout Europe and Asia. It most likely originated in Asia. The "Jew's harp" is an English term, and it became the name most commonly used in America. Globally, more than 1,000 names are used for this instrument. "Jew's harp" first appeared in English in 1595, in editions of Richard Hakluyt's (1552–1616) *Principal Navigations, Voyages, Traffiques and Discoveries of the English Nation*. It is not known why the English name associates the instrument with Judaism; no other name for it does.

The Jew's harp is relatively simple to make despite the fact that it is capable of producing sophisticated music. The instrument is in the shape of a hoop and down the center is a flexible tongue (lamella). There are two principal types. The idioglot variety has a vibrating tongue cut from a single piece of wood, bone, or metal. The hetroglot style has a metal or cast frame, to which is affixed a separate metal reed. These two basic types have many variations. In either case, the musician holds the frame in the mouth and manually plucks or manipulates the free end of the tongue to produce sound. It is possible for the musician to shift the instrument's tone by adjusting the mouth shape and to adjust volume by changing the velocity of breath.

Most likely the Jew's harp was brought to Africa by the earliest traders and adapted for use by northern and west African societies, in particular. African versions are of the hetroglot style. The instrument has strong traditions in western African nations, particularly in Mali, Niger, and Cameroon, regions that were targeted for the slave trade. Before the 18th century, the Songhai society, from Mali, Niger, and Benin, extended use of the Jew's harp, called the *bamboro*, to the Hausa and Fulani societies, most heavily located in northern Nigeria and southeastern Niger. However, use of the instrument can also be found in African societies as far away as Madagascar.

Enslaved Africans carried their own traditional use of the instrument to Caribbean and American plantations, where at first it probably had similar usage and purpose in dance music and ceremonial rituals as it did in Africa. Accounts from former slaves indicate that the Jew's harp also was used for personal recreation and entertainment. In America, the Jew's harp might well have promoted cultural transmission of African and European musical styles because it was an instrument familiar to and quite popular with white Americans.

FURTHER READING

Wright, Michael. "The Search for the Origins of the Jew's Harp." *The Silk Road: The Silk Road Foundation Newsletter* 2 (Nov. 2004): 49–55. At www.silkroadfoundation.org/newsletter/srvol2num2.pdf.

LINDA E. MERIANS

# K

**KITCHENS.** Enslaved cooks lived, managed, and worked in their kitchens. Southern hospitality drove their labor and was central to their world. The kitchens were the stage for their culinary skills and the production of Southern plantation **food**. During the 18th century, entertainment was a critical part of plantation culture, but the growth in large-scale plantations created an isolated atmosphere that fostered local socialization. Neighboring plantations became a community as each took turns hosting dinners and balls. The kitchen became a distinct space in which the performance of such traditional customs manifested itself in the production of food, catering, and social entertaining.

The rise in hospitality within these microcommunities called for increased attention to culinary fare. Whereas in the 17th century food was seen more as a necessity for survival, the formalization of kitchen spaces coincided with an increased desire to produce noteworthy meals as part of the entertaining platform. This in turn, made kitchens, ballrooms, and enslaved **cooks** a more valuable commodity, as they were the center of food production. The cooks' role in the kitchen promoted the performance of a particular kind of presentation of wealth and custom that made the South known for its hospitality.

## Plantation Kitchens

Plantations varied in size, function, order, and location. The larger the plantation was, the more specialized roles and buildings it housed. For example, Shirley plantation in Charles City County, Virginia, has a large external kitchen and a separate external formal laundry. Shirley was one of Virginia's most prominent plantations, and the cook had a dwelling separate from the laundress. On many smaller plantations, the kitchens tended to be combined with the laundry, and the enslaved house servants shared the living space. The grander the property, the more formal plantation service buildings became, as they closely mirrored the aspirations of their planter owners.

The main house had its own set of public, semipublic, and private spaces. The heart of the planter's order was his hall, which in turn became the nucleus of his world. It was the center of entertaining, of public displays of wealth, and the meeting point

### Sleeping in the Kitchen

Mark Discus, a former Missouri slave, slept in the kitchen:

Married folks lived in log cabins, but the single folks lived in the big house. I slept on a pallet on the floor in the kitchen and every mornin' the ol' master would holler, "Mark, Mark, light that fire." And If I didn't git right up I got a cane over my head.

*Source:* George P. Rawick, ed. "Missouri." *The American Slave: Arkansas, Colorado, Minnesota, Missouri, and Oregon and Washington Narratives,* Supp. Ser. 1, Vol. 2. Westport, CT: Greenwood Press, 1978.

between the inside and outside worlds. It was in this space that planters performed the elite activities that defined their Anglo-American world, including balls, dinners, and social gatherings. By the middle of the 18th century, formal "dining rooms" were standard in these houses. Georgian-style house plans suggested ways to incorporate new spaces into traditional homes and ways to control their interior circulation, leading to an architectural response to specific social requirements.

The kitchen was the heart of the slaveholding mistress's order and in some instances closely reflected her purpose. The kitchen and the enslaved cook who worked in it became the mistress's responsibility, directed by the domestic ideals of the day. Thus,

Robinson-Aiken slave building and kitchens, Charleston, South Carolina. (Library of Congress.)

the kitchen arose as an essential part of the cultural landscape. The vast majority of 18th-century real estate sale advertisements for Virginia properties, for example, list the kitchen directly after the main house, as it was seen as the second most important building on a plantation.

## Home and Work Place

Most enslaved cooks lived in the external kitchens that lay outside the main house, and their quarters and living conditions differed from those of field hands and other unskilled workers. Kitchen quarters could be seen as a microcosm of the Big House, with private space created by constructing an upstairs sleeping quarters. This provided a clear division of work and home space that was unique to the enslaved cooks and their families. However, on larger plantations, the kitchens were reserved exclusively for food production.

## Domestics' Quarters

The domestic slaves lived and worked within the white landscape. Many house servants slept inside the mansion. The cook's living space depended on the location of the kitchen, however. By the 18th century, most large-scale Virginia plantations constructed external kitchens, but some kept their internal kitchens and continued to house the cook(s) within the main house, in a room adjacent to the kitchen. This was a departure from the detached kitchen arrangement known to have prevailed on the landscape of 18th-century Tidewater Virginia. This internal kitchen type is among the four general styles of kitchen and homes that enslaved cooks lived and worked in through the 18th and 19th centuries.

The most common, the external kitchen, usually sat adjacent to the main house, sometimes among the rows or streets formed with other **dependencies**, all visible from the main house. Their exteriors resembled the main house in style but differed in construction. These external kitchens generally came in three forms. The first was a small one-room cabin, with a chimney that varied in size.

In some cases, within this type of kitchen, large hearths encompassed one entire wall of the kitchen building. Given the width of the hearth and the adjacent fireplaces, this type of building was most likely used as both a kitchen and laundry. The sleeping quarter would be located in a loft opposite the fireplace. Some kitchens also accommodated weaving rooms, where the kitchen was on the first floor and the weaving room sat upstairs, presumably within the space of the cook's or weaver's sleeping area, and away from the mess of food preparation.

The second common external kitchen building was a two-room dwelling with a central chimney. The fireplace was located either along the back of the dwelling or in the middle of the kitchen space, dividing the space in two. If the chimney stood along the backside of the kitchen, the enslaved cook usually would have a ladder or stairs along the internal sidewall leading to a loft above. If the fireplace sat as a divider between the two rooms, the space typically was split in multiple ways. Similarly, a third kitchen variation had fireplaces on the gable ends of the kitchen.

Although separate from the main house, the kitchen was placed where its windows or openings faced the main house. This allowed the mistress to "watch over" the cook, or at least enforce the notion of her eyes staring into the kitchen at all times. The main kitchen door usually was placed toward the dining area to promote a direct flow of service from kitchen to table. The placement of the windows and doors encouraged a constant association between the main house and kitchen and between mistress and cook. By the beginning of the 19th century, architectural developments began transforming this virtual connection into actual constructed spaces. Enclosed colonnades, hidden walkways, "all-weather" passageways, and "whistling walks" began to appear.

### The Passageway

Architectural trends continued to shift into the early 19th century. In the 17th century, enslaved spaces were separated from those of whites; the 18th century saw this partitioning formalized as part of what were highly structured working landscapes. The vast majority of kitchens remained outside in ancillary buildings, while the plantation homes became highly functional producers of domestic entertainment. Balls and banquets became synonymous with Southern culture, and its hospitality became renowned.

By the early 19th century, many plantations had constructed an all-weather passageway that stretched from the kitchen to the main house. These covert walkways were purportedly built to keep the enslaved cooks from having to walk through rain and snow. The construction of these passageways, however, coincided with a changing ideological view of enslavement and public displays of wealth and servitude that allowed the planter to directly and individually control circulation to every room in the house. The introduction of an all-weather passageway, which made some aspects of slavery invisible, began appearing throughout the South, especially in Virginia, just as slavery and anti-slavery became a more significant subject of international dialogue. With the close of the trans-Atlantic slave trade in 1808, some planters found new ways to deemphasize their direct connection to enslaved servitude and labor on the landscape.

### Furnishings

While 18th- and 19th-century field **slave quarters** had little in the way of built-in furniture and storage, kitchens had comparatively more **furnishings**. Enslaved field hands often installed furnishings privately and found areas under the floor to hide and store their belongings. Kitchens were unique in that they had all the amenities available at the time, but the cook's enslaved status often limited their accessibility. White mistresses "carried the keys" and kept **sugar**, knives, and other valuable and dangerous items locked in the kitchen safe. Food, especially butter, sugar, **liquor**, and other valuable ingredients, were stored and locked in the main house. This **lock and key** relationship intensified during the mid-18th century, as some enslaved cooks and field hands began "stealing" these items for their personal consumption. This temptation must have been overwhelming for the cooks as they had to smell, taste, and work with these items on a regular basis.

### Aesthetics

Most external kitchens resembled the main house, both in style and material. Most fireplaces were made of brick, rather than sticks and mud, and the floors usually were plain compressed clay, brick, or oyster shell in lieu of wooden planks. White wash was often applied to the interior of the kitchen to promote a "finished" or "visually clean" look. Kitchens usually were proportional to the main house and larger than most other outbuildings. They most often sat adjacent to the main house and near the kitchen **garden**. The interior varied as much, if not more, than the exterior. The furnishings changed drastically between the late 17th and 19th centuries. Whereas 17th-century cooking technology consisted of an iron pot over open flame, the 18th century saw the spread of kitchen technology and equipment specialization that included the use of Dutch ovens, salamanders, and more sophisticated tools. With the invention of the stove in the mid-19th century, the material culture of kitchens became increasingly technical. What had been reserved in Virginia for the Governor's Palace kitchen during the 18th century now made its way into plantation kitchens. These elite kitchens were stocked with fat skimmers, **fish and shellfish** forks, trivets, mortars, and countless other elaborate tools.

### Work Space
The kitchen furnishings varied, yet most had the basic necessities. Along with the usual hearth cooking area, some had formal dressers (built-in shelves) for rolling bread and baked goods, and these also served as storage for plates, pots, pans, and utensils. This marks the importance of the kitchen's presentation as a "visually clean space" and suggests the mistress had close control over the presentation of this particular ideal. While the kitchen space was kept visually clean, some kitchens had the formality of an adjacent scullery. Many **sculleries** included "slop drains" for the washing of food items, dishes, pots, and so forth. These sculleries helped the flow of kitchen work, separating the business of cleaning from the production of food.

### Home Space
The cooks usually slept on the second floor of the kitchen, either in a loft or a separate room. Their **beds** varied in size and quality, ranging from a basic straw mat and a wool **blanket** to mattresses laid on wooden frames. Regardless of the bedding's quality, the cook's family typically was allowed to live in this area as a nuclear family, without having to share with other slaves. This was drastically different from the situation in field quarters and even the domestic **dormitories**, where the sleeping arrangements sometimes disregarded family bonds.

The cook's life was not as privileged as it might seem. The field hands sometimes slept in dormitories with as many as 25 other people, but they did not have to sleep close to a burning hot oven. The field hands often cooked outside in the house-yard during hot days and nights. In contrast, the cook had to use the hearth regardless of the weather. This consistent use of the kitchen as workplace regularly interfered with the cook's comfort in bed, as sleeping outside in the summer was a way to keep cool.

Yet just as field hands found innovative ways to make their cabins "home," enslaved cooks also made their kitchens home and were just as connected to their roots as the field hands were. Cooks carved pictures into the walls of the second floor and persevered for the sake of their families and themselves. Although they were housed away from the rich cultural space of the house-yards and slave cabins, they nonetheless remembered their origins and displayed their cultural symbolism within the white landscape of the plantation. For whites and blacks alike, kitchens represented the wealth and pride that came to characterize what was termed Southern hospitality.

*See also* Cast Iron Pots; Laundries; Subfloor Pits; Yards.

FURTHER READING

Bullock, Helen Claire Duprey. *Kitchens in Colonial Virginia.* Williamsburg, VA: Colonial Williamsburg Research Series RR-102, 1931.

Hole, Donna C. *Architectural Fittings in Colonial Kitchens,* Vol. 1. Colonial Williamsburg Research Series RR-16, 1980.

Upton, Dell, and John Michael Vlach, eds. *Common Places: Readings in American Vernacular Architecture.* Athens: University of Georgia Press, 1986.

Vlach, John Michael. *Back of the Big House: The Architecture of Plantation Slavery.* Chapel Hill: University of North Carolina Press, 1993.

KELLEY DEETZ

**KORAN (QUR'AN).** Muslims believe the Koran (Qur'an, literally "the Recitation" in Arabic) to be the unmediated, unaltered, and final word of God as revealed to the Prophet Muhammad in the seventh century CE. As such, it is the scripture of Muslims. By the start of the Atlantic slave trade, Islamic traditions had spread throughout a substantial part of the African continent because of trade, exploration, and conquest. As a result, although statistics are difficult to pinpoint, somewhere between 7 and 20 percent of slaves who undertook the involuntary voyage to North America were Muslims. Although few African Koran copies made it to the United States, the Koran nevertheless played a significant role in the lives of many slaves in antebellum America.

Compared with non-Muslim slaves, enslaved Muslims tended to be literate when they arrived in North America and some of them transcribed portions or even entire reproductions of the Koran in Arabic, a few of which still exist. For example, Job Ben Solomon Jallo (1701–1773), also known as Ayuba Suleiman Diallo, a Senegalese Muslim of aristocratic birth enslaved for a brief period in Maryland, composed three separate copies of the Koran solely from memory. Abdulrahman Ibrahim Ibn Sori (1762–1829), also known as Abd ar-Rahman, the famous West African prince enslaved for 40 years in Mississippi, occasionally delighted audiences by telling them he was writing out "The Lord's Prayer" in Arabic, when in actuality he had transcribed the first *sura*, or chapter, of the Koran, known as the *fatiha*. Omar Ibn Said (1770–1864), a Muslim scholar from Senegal enslaved in the Carolinas until his death in his mid-90s, recorded in Arabic many passages and prayers from the Koran as well as excerpts from the Christian Bible that include invocations to Allah and the Prophet Muhammad. Bilali Mohammed (ca. 1770–1857), a Georgian slave originally from Timbo, Fouta Djallon (Guinea, West Africa), where he may have been an *imam*, or religious leader, was buried with his own copy of the Koran.

Although Islamic law and tradition allowed for limited forms of slavery—Muhammad and his companions owned slaves, for example—the Koran's verses dealing with slavery tend to emphasize the humanity of the enslaved and grant them legal rights (for instance, suras 2, 4, 9, 16, 23, 24, 30, 33, 58, and 70). By contrast, the **Bible** espoused by most European American slave owners contains certain passages commanding slaves to obey their masters "in everything . . . whatever your task" (Colossians 3:22–25). Furthermore, the Koran has no evidence of prejudice against blacks as sometimes found in the Bible, such as the Curse of Ham in Genesis 9:18–27. For these reasons, the Koran often was an attractive alternative to the Bible for religious slaves as well as a source of opposition to the abuses of chattel slavery.

FURTHER READING

Austin, Allan D. *African Muslims in Antebellum America: A Sourcebook*. New York: Garland Publishing, 1984.

Turner, Richard B. *Islam in the African-American Experience*. 2nd ed. Bloomington: Indiana University Press, 2003.

DANIEL C. DILLARD

# L

**LAUNDRIES.** Until mechanization and the introduction of crude washing machines began to offer some relief later in the 19th century, washing clothes, bedding, and other fabrics was a difficult, labor-intensive, and arduous task that had to be performed regularly by women. In the urban and rural slave South, enslaved or free black women did the laundry.

Even as stricter standards of cleanliness began to take hold in early America, garments and bedding were aired frequently, rather than washed. Because many individuals owned just a few garments, **clothing** was worn and reworn many times before it was laundered. Shirts, undergarments, and other types of body **linen** were likely to be washed more regularly. Laundry was a regular chore that had to be done year-round; however, because of its onerous nature, by the 1800s, most white Americans came to rely on either hired help or enslaved workers to do the washing.

Typically, dirty clothes were washed in a series of steps. First rips and tears were mended and missing **buttons** replaced. Then, large quantities of water had to be lifted, hauled, or carried from the well or stream in buckets for the main laundry production. Firewood had to be collected and put at the ready. Equipment that included a variety of different size washtubs was set out. The colonial Virginia governor Lord Botetourt's 1770 probate inventory details the assorted laundry equipment needed in his household: "2 Linnen Baskets, 3 washing Tubs, 3 Rensing [rinsing] tubs, 2 pails, 1 Large Iron pot, 1 Large Boyling Copper."

Clothes usually were soaked in a tub for one or two days, during which time they were scrubbed to remove stains, using different remedies depending on what caused the stain. The clothing was then transferred to large vats of heated water, in large iron or copper pots or even waterproofed wooden vats, to which soap had been added for the washing. Delicate fabrics such as silk, those prone to shrinkage like felt and **wool**, or yellowing and fading like calico were not boiled. After picking the clothes out of the tubs with sticks, they were beaten with flat bats, identified as battling sticks by former slaves, sometimes against a wooden battling block or a bench, to get the dirt out. The clothes were boiled again to remove any remaining vermin such as lice and then rinsed first with hot, then cold water. When finished, the clothes were dried on trees, bushes, laid flat on the grass or placed on racks or ropes near the **kitchen** fire or

## Washing Clothes

Marie Askin Simpson, enslaved in Missouri, remembered the time-consuming effort necessary to wash clothes and the equipment that it required:

Mother did most of the cooking and washing and ironing. In those days they did the washing with battlin' sticks and boards. They layed the clothes on this board and battled them with battlin' sticks. We had little "piggins" to carry the water, a little thing, made of ceder, with little handles. Much smaller than the regular water buckets. It could be carried anywhere, easily. They were pretty little things, with bright brass bindings, and they kept them brightly polished, too.

We boiled our clothes in big iron kettles, over a fire in the yard. We made our own lye and soap. The ash-hopper was made of boards, a sort of trough that was set slant-wise over a big iron kettle. The wood ashes from the fire place were dumped in this hopper. Hot water was poured over the ashes and they drained down into the kettle. It dripped slowly. When we thought the lye was strong enough, we got a turkey feather, (a chicken feather won't do, 'cause it would eat up too quick) and if the lye from the hopper was strong enough it would eat up the turkey feather. Then a fire was started under the kettle.

Into this big kettle of boiling ash-lye, we stirred in "cracklin." This was the fried out fats left over from hog killin'. Old meat rinds, old meats that had turned strong, any kind of fat meat that was not used to eat, was thrown into this hot boiling lye. When the meat did not melt anymore we know that there was enough fat in the lye to make soap.

This was boiled down until it got "ropey". We tested it by dripping some of it in cold water. If it floated on top, it wasn't done. If it sunk to the bottom, we pulled the fire from under it and let it get cold. That was called hard soap. Next day, it was cut into chunks, placed on boards and put in the smoke house or attic to dry. If a body wanted soft soap, they just didn't let it "cook" so long. Soft soap was jelly like and looked like molasses. Nobody had any other soap but home made soap, to wash, scrub or use on their bodies. Soft soap was a little handier to use to boil the clothes with. Some folks made as much as a barrel and a half, owing to the old grease they had.

The ironing was done with hand wrought flat irons. They were kept hot by setting them up before the fireplace and heaping nice clean hot coals to them.

*Source:* George P. Rawick, ed. "Missouri." *The American Slave: Arkansas, Colorado, Minnesota, Missouri, and Oregon and Washington Narratives,* Supp. Ser. 1, Vol. 2. Westport, CT: Greenwood Press, 1978.

Sally Brown, a former Georgia slave, cleaned clothes by pounding them with a "battlin" stick:

I used battlin' blocks and battlin' sticks to help clean the clothes when we wuz washin'; we all did. We took the clothes out'n the suds, soaped 'em good and put 'em on the block and beat 'em with a battlin' stick, which wuz made lak a paddle. On wash days you could hear them battlin' sticks poundin' every which way. We made our own soap; used ole meat and grease, and poured water over wood ashes, which was kept in a rack-lak thing, and the water would drip through the ashes. This made strong lye.

*Source:* George P. Rawick, ed. *The American Slave: Georgia Narratives*, Supp. Ser. 1, Vol. 3, Part 1. Westport, CT: Greenwood Press, 1978.

outside. At the point at which the garments still were slightly damp, they were ironed on tables in the kitchen with a metal iron that had been heated in the fire. As part of their job, enslaved laundresses made the soap used for the washing, usually by boiling tallow and lye together with a small amount of lime, although by 1800 ready-made laundry soap might be purchased in cities. Sometimes urine was added to the soap as a bleaching agent. Many enslaved laundresses bore scars from burns caused by soap lye, boiling washing water, or hot irons and had chapped hands and arms.

In the 18th century, laundries frequently shared spaces with kitchens, but by the early 19th century, on larger plantations or among the urban slaveholding elite, free-standing laundries were included among the **dependencies**. Virginia planter John Tayloe III, who built the elaborate Octagon town house in the new capital city of Washington, D.C., in 1801, included a two-story laundry with servant housing within a complex of work buildings that also incorporated a stable, an icehouse, and a **dairy**. On most plantations or farms, however, laundry usually was done outside in the service **yard** because it required work space and that a steady fire be maintained.

Old laundry and kitchen, Mrs. Hugh Foster House, 201 Kennon Street, Union Springs, Bullock County, Alabama. (Library of Congress.)

Enslaved domestic workers who spent their days around slaveholders were expected to look presentable, and they undoubtedly did their laundry on a regular basis. Field hands had little time to wash their meager wardrobes, but by the antebellum period, slaveholders increasingly equated clean clothes and bodies with better health and good work habits. In 1848, a planter writing in the *Southern Cultivator and Monthly Journal* recommended that field hands be allowed one hour on Saturday evening "for the purpose of washing their clothes." Another suggested dividing the workers into "companies" that would take turns doing the mending and the laundry for the group. University of Louisiana professor James Debow (1820–1867), writing about plantation management in 1852, noted that he gave "all females half of every Saturday to wash and clean up, my cook washing for young men and boys through the week." A former Texas slave, Mary Reynolds confirmed, "once in a while they'd give us a li'l piece of Sat'day evening to wash our clothes in the branch [creek]. We hanged them on the ground in the woods to dry."

After the American Revolution, slaveholders manumitted (freed) significant numbers of enslaved African Americans, and those newly freed individuals migrated to cities like Baltimore, Richmond, and Washington, D.C., where they entered into the service economy—in some cases, performing the same jobs that they had held in slavery. Early city directories for Washington, D.C., published in the 1820s indicate that many free African American women had established independent business there as laundresses.

*See also* Cast Iron Pots; Cooperage.

FURTHER READING

Breeden, James O., ed. *Advice among Masters: The Ideal in Slave Management in the Old South*. Westport, CT: Greenwood Press, 1980.

Olmert, Michael. *Kitchens, Smokehouses and Privies: Outbuildings and the Architecture of Daily Life in the Eighteenth-Century Middle Atlantic*. Ithaca, NY: Cornell University Press, 2009.

Olmert, Michael. "Laundries, Largest Buildings in the Eighteenth-Century Backyard," *Colonial Williamsburg Journal*. At www.history.org/Foundation/journal/Autumn09/laundries.cfm.

"Slave Narratives: A Folk History of Slavery in the United States from Interviews with Former Slaves Georgia Narratives, Part 4," from the Federal Writers' Project, 1936–1938, Library of Congress. At http://www.gutenberg.org/files/18485/18485-h/18485-h.htm.

Vlach, John Michael. *Back of the Big House: The Architecture of Plantation Slavery*. Chapel Hill: University of North Carolina Press, 1993.

KYM S. RICE

**LEGAL DOCUMENTS.** Legal documents were essential to the institution of American slavery. During the 17th and 18th centuries, legislators in Britain's North American colonies passed laws that established slavery within their particular colony. Colonists relied on statutes to control the actions and lives of the men, women, and children whom they enslaved. Laws gave owners the power to exploit enslaved people for their own economic benefit and the authority to punish any behavior deemed a challenge to the master's position. Beginning in the last quarter of the 18th century and continuing until 1865, Americans used legal documents to both end slavery in some states and continue slavery in other states.

Because slave laws—including those passed during the colonial period and those approved after the end of the American Revolution—defined enslaved men, women,

## Fate of Slaves When the Master Died

Historians estimate that most slaves were sold at least once in their lives. In this recounting of the settlement of a Missouri slaveholder's estate in 1855, the slaves' fate rested in the hands of his widow:

Hiram L. Sloan, a wealthy resident, had his home and farm along the banks of the little stream. He had a number of slaves and much other property at the time of his death during the spring of 1855.

By an order of the Court of Common Pleas, Judge Ranney presiding, a public sale of all his property was issued on the 12th day of October, the sale to take place on December 3rd and 4th, 1855, in order that the division of his property could be made for his heirs.

This story will begin on the night of December 2nd, just before the sale to be held on the following day, on which night the twenty-four slaves appeared at the Sloan residence to bid farewell to their mistress, the widow of Hiram Sloan, before they were transferred to other owners. The slaves lived in cabins a short distance from the Sloan residence which was called by them the "Big House."

The colored people had known for some time of the approaching sale and were much cast down, not knowing to whom they would be transferred nor if families would be scattered among different owners.

On this evening, preceding the sale, the colored folks came to the "Big House," led by Uncle Nelson, the patriarch among the slaves. Uncle Nelse was a leader among his people, an exhorter in their religious gatherings, an example of industry and loyalty, so they followed him trustfully in their last visit to the "Big House."

Standing just inside the door, his white hair showing through the gathering gloom of the winter evening, with twenty other blacks, old and young, just behind him, Uncle Nelse twisted his battered hat and tried to speak. But words would not come.

"Come in, Uncle Nelse. Come inside, all of you who can find room," said Mrs. Sloan.

Slowly the blacks came into the room to stand near the wall on either side of the door. They were of all ages from Uncle Nelse to the babe in arms. On the faces of all could be read a story of tragedy—of fear for the future.

"Old Miss, please 'scuse us for botherin' you, but we are mighty pestered in our minds an' we know you'll be kind to us when we's about to be parted from you. We just had a gatherin' at our quarters. We prayed and sung some hymns. We prayed that you all would keep as many as you can, and we prayed from our hearts that none of us would be sold down the river. Please, Old Mis' won't you try and keep any of us from going down the river?"

"Uncle Nelse, and all of you—you must know it grieves me to lose you and I hope you will all find good homes. I hope you will always remember kindly your old home here. I wish I were able to keep you all, but this I can't do as I have not enough money. But I promise you this, and Marshall Clarke, who will conduct the sale, promises, when possible that husband and wife will not be separated and babies will not be taken from their mothers."

"Thank you, Old Mis', thank you kindly. But we's also skeered that some of us will be sold down the river. A boat done landed here tonight and Tom was down at the landing. He says four or five germans, lookin' lack the Missip or Loozan got off the boat.

"Do you rackon they is aimin' to buy some of us?" asked Uncle Nelse, the others waiting breathlessly, for the answer.

"I don't know, Uncle Nelse," Old Mis' replied, "It is a public auction and they can bid if they want to. But if they do make bids I'll try to get my friends to outbid them. It is the best I can promise you."

"Thank you, Old Mis', thank you. I done tole 'em you'd not fergit us in this time of awful sorrer."

Early in the morning of December 3, the slaves in the Sloan Negro quarters were astir. Uncle Nelse called them to the largest cabin for sunrise prayer. It was a pathetic scene.

"Good Lord, once mo' we gather at Thy footstool an for the last time we are meet in prayer. Some of us may go nawth, some of us will go west, but, Good Lord, we pray that none of us will go down the river, where black folks ain't held much account. The Good Book tells us 'Thou art the Resurrection an' the Life'. If we live 'cordin' to the book we will be saved in everlastin' happiness in the Good Lan' where black skins ain't held against a body." "Amen."

After a hearty breakfast and the distribution of well-filled pokes to be carried for later consumption, Uncle Nelse went to the bank of Sloan Creek, muddy from recent rains. But in his memory he could see the Sloan Creek of other days—The Sloan Creek of Spring and Summer.

He remembered the dog-wood blossoms that told him that fishing time had come. His mind went back to the Sweet Williams, Johnny-Jump-ups that grew in profusion along the banks of the stream.

"Oh, Good Lord, why ain't Marster Hiram here to keep his black folks from bein' scattered lack chaff before the wind. Where at kin we find pleasant waters and green pastures lack the waters of this crick and the green fields of Marster Hiram's farm?"

Then, later, came Marshall Clarke, who was to conduct the sale, with an inventory of the slaves to be sold, and a sad procession started for the courthouse. They were led into the courthouse and left in the corridor to be inspected by prospective buyers, then to be called one by one to the auction block.

Old Mis' was there and went slowly through the corridors stopping and speaking to each one in passing. She stopped before Charlotte, a young woman with an infant in arms, "I am going to try and bid you in, Charlotte," she said.

"God bless you, Old Mis' and kin I keep my baby?" cried the young mother with tears of happiness running down her cheeks when she was told that she would not lose her child.

James Stalcup and Dr. Franklin Cannon, friends of Mrs. Sloan were there. Mrs. Julia Sherman, another friend, was also present—all passing slowly down the corridor inspecting the slaves.

Learning that each of her friends expected to buy slaves she urged them to buy without separating husband and wife or mother and child and was made happy by their promises to respect her wishes.

On the morning of December 3, 1855, His Honor, Mayor Cale was present. Judge Ranney of the Court of Common Pleas, giant of brawn and brain, greeted all whom he met.

By the report of Marshall Clarke we learn to whom and for what prices the slaves were sold. It is a satisfaction that the friends of Mrs. Sloan had made their purchases without separating families and that Old Mis' was able to keep her promise to Charlotte.

*Source:* George P. Rawick, ed. "Missouri." *The American Slave: Arkansas, Colorado, Minnesota, Missouri, and Oregon and Washington Narratives,* Supp. Ser. 1, Vol. 2. Westport, CT: Greenwood Press, 1978.

and children as property, individual masters could use legal documents to manage their laborers and to transfer these people to new owners. These documents included deeds, indentures or letters of agreement, lawsuits, wills, probate inventories, and manumissions. These records are a valuable source for historians because they contain details about the lives of colonial and American slaves.

## Deeds

Slave owners used a written conveyance known as a "deed" to convey one or more enslaved laborers to a new master. A deed began by noting the name of the first person—the "grantor"—and then the name of the person who would gain ownership of

Receipt given to Judge S. Williams of Eufaula by Eliza Wallace in payment of $500 for a black man, January 20, 1840. (Library of Congress.)

the slave or slaves—the "grantee." Next, the grantor specified the names of the slave or slaves to be transferred to the new owner. Often, deeds included details about the ages, family connections, and skills of these enslaved laborers. In the case of a female slave, the grantor noted that the grantee also gained ownership of any children whom she might have during her lifetime. The grantor specified the amount of money that the grantee agreed to pay for the slave or slaves as well as the length of time the grantee had to make this payment. In some cases, the local court required a grantor's wife to give her consent to the sale. A wife's agreement was necessary if the deed conveyed a slave or slaves who were part of her "dower"—the portion of property that a husband left to a wife to use during the time she was a widow. The deed concluded with the signatures of the grantor and the people who witnessed the transaction. Both the grantor and the grantee ensured that the clerk of the local court recorded the deed in the record book, so there was a legal record of the transfer of title to a slave or slaves.

Additional details in some deeds explain a master's reason for conveying one or more enslaved laborers to another person. A number of owners sold individual slaves as punishment for what the master saw as "bad behavior." The sale of an enslaved laborer also showed other slaves what would happen to them if they challenged the control of a master. Also, by the third quarter of the 18th century, some planters did not have enough work for all of the slaves on their plantations. These planters sold slaves to middling planters who wanted to expand their labor forces and to planters who needed slaves to create new plantations in the western part of the colony. Soon after the turn of the 19th century, planters along the Atlantic coast began to convey thousands of enslaved men, women, and children to plantation owners in the cotton-producing areas in the Deep South and to slave traders who moved enslaved laborers to this region.

Grantors used a specific type of deed to transfer ownership of slaves to family members and friends. In a "deed of gift," the grantor transferred legal title to one or more slaves to a grantee without receiving any payment from the grantee. Many grantors in deeds of gifts were parents who wanted to give an enslaved laborer to a child. Slave owners gave enslaved laborers to sons so they would have workers for their plantations. Many daughters received domestic slaves as their "dowry"—the property that a female took to her marriage.

Whether a slave owner used a deed or a deed of gift to transfer ownership of an enslaved laborer, the grantor used a written document to convey a slave because it would benefit the white family. Deeds enabled masters to sell slaves to assert their power and control over their labor force or to make money. Transfers through deeds of gift gave owners a way to convey enslaved laborers to their family members and friends.

## Wills

From the first half of the 17th century until the end of slavery in 1865, slaveholders included instructions in their wills that detailed the transfer of enslaved laborers to new masters after their deaths. In many instances, the author of the will—the "testator"—conveyed workers to his or her spouse and children. Masters also left slaves to people in their extended families and to close friends and neighbors.

By law, a male testator left a specified portion—often one-third—of his labor force to his wife, and she controlled these slaves during the rest of her lifetime. The widow had a "life right" to this portion of her husband's enslaved men, women, and children. The testator also noted the person who would gain possession of these "dower" slaves—enslaved laborers whom a husband left to his wife during her widowhood—after her death. Some men gave their wives full ownership of a portion of their labor force, and, as a result, these women could bequeath these slaves to their heirs.

Next, the slave owner—whether male or female—divided the remaining enslaved men, women, and children among family and friends. The testator included descriptions of individual slaves to ensure that each heir received a specific enslaved laborer or laborers. The details included a slave's name, gender, approximate age, racial background (negro, mulatto, mustee, or octoroon), place of birth, family connections, and skills.

Testators considered the skills of their enslaved laborers when they made their bequests. Sons who inherited plantations needed agricultural laborers to tend, harvest, and transport crops to **markets**. Future plantation owners also required skilled slaves, including carpenters, blacksmiths, and wheelwrights who could repair agricultural tools and wagons. As the wives of planters, daughters received domestic slaves trained to cook, do laundry, and look after children. In the case of urban slaveholders, the slaves whom they bequeathed to their sons and daughters possessed skills that could be used in small towns and large cities. These enslaved men, women, and children worked in taverns, stores, and factories.

Whether they lived in urban areas or on plantations, testators had one goal when they planned bequests of slaves to their heirs: to provide for the financial future of their families and friends. Many testators did not take the wishes of their enslaved laborers into account when they wrote their wills, although a few might leave a favored slave a favorite possession or even grant freedom to a favored slave in their wills. It was more often the case that the provisions that benefited white families often separated enslaved husbands from wives and enslaved parents from their children. The act of dividing slave families was a sign of the control that slave owners exerted over their enslaved laborers.

After listing the bequests of slaves and any other personal property, a testator appointed someone—usually a family member or a close friend—to serve as the "executor" of the will. The executor was responsible for taking a decedent's will to the local court, ensuring that the clerk copied this document in the record book, and distributing the various legacies to the heirs. If a slave owner died without making a will, the court appointed a person to serve as the "administrator" of the estate. The administrator had the same responsibilities as an executor. When the executor or administrator transferred slaves to their new owners, the enslaved men, women, and children gathered any **clothing**, **blankets**, tools, and personal possessions they might have to take to their next home.

### Probate Inventories

After an executor presented a decedent's will in court and the clerk copied this document in the locality's record book, the court frequently appointed a small group of individuals—usually three or four people known as "appraisers"—to compile a handwritten list of the deceased person's possessions. This record, known as a "probate inventory," included a decedent's enslaved men, women, and children.

The local officials chose the appraisers carefully because it was important to have an accurate legal record of a person's estate and the value of the property owned by the decedent. In many instances, the members of the court selected individuals who were friends of the decedent and who were of a similar social and economic standing. As a result, most appraisers were knowledgeable about the value of a decedent's possessions and slaves because they had similar items and laborers in their own homes.

Once the appointed men agreed to serve as appraisers, the local officials instructed them to write down each item they found, to add any necessary description of an item so as to distinguish it from similar objects, and to note the value of the item. After the appraisers completed the probate inventory, they gave the document to the executor or administrator who then took it to the local **courthouse**. The clerk copied the probate inventory in the record book and gave the original back to the executor or administrator who used this list to keep track of the bequests to be transferred to the decedent's heirs.

As an executor or administrator examined a probate inventory, this person paid attention to the details that the appraisers recorded when it was time to divide the enslaved laborers among a decedent's heirs. This information included the name and gender of each slave. Many appraisers wrote down a slave's approximate age and racial background (negro, mulatto, mustee, or octoroon). In addition, some appraisers noted a slave's place of birth, family connections, and skills.

Probate inventories also included lists of objects that shaped the lives of enslaved men, women, and children. Appraisers recorded items that slaves used each day as they worked. These objects ranged from agricultural tools to **kitchen** equipment and utensils. Often, appraisers noted the presence of material to be made into clothing for slaves as well as **shoes** and socks for the decedent's laborers. Through the appraisers' descriptions of a decedent's real property and the buildings that stood on the land, it is possible to learn about the physical environment in which enslaved men, women, and children lived and worked.

### Lawsuits

During the first half of the 17th century, a small number of Africans used their knowledge of colonial laws to initiate "lawsuits"—legal actions heard by members of the local court. Both African men and women traveled to their local court in the role of the "plaintiff"—the person who brought a lawsuit against another individual. They sued their master for their freedom and the freedom of their spouses and children. The slave owner—the "defendant"—appeared in court to answer the legal action. Extant records from several colonies indicate that some African men and women were successful in their attempts to gain their independence.

The opportunities for slaves to initiate lawsuits disappeared as various colonies, and later states, established legal slavery. Enslaved men and women lost the chance to appear in court as plaintiffs because slave laws defined these enslaved individuals as property, not as people who had the right to take someone to court. In addition, slaves could not appear in court as defendants or to provide testimony against a white man or woman. After the American Revolution, "freedom suits" initiated by enslaved African Americans again appeared among court cases heard in Upper South courtrooms, but only a few of these cases resulted in slaves winning their freedom. Some Maryland slaveholders bargained with their slaves and promised to manumit (free) their slaves after they had "served" for a term of several years rather than face a lawsuit.

Although statutes classified enslaved men, women, and children as property, in one instance, the law treated slaves as people who were responsible for their own actions. An enslaved man or woman accused of committing a capital crime stood trial as a person in a court of "oyer and terminer"—a French legal term that means "to hear and to determine." In an oyer and terminer trial, the local officials heard the evidence against the accused individual and decided the fate of this person. Slaves were denied the right to a jury trial that white men and women had.

During the proceedings, the accused slave could testify and have other enslaved people serve as witnesses. Having heard the testimony of the accused slave and all witnesses, the officials discussed the evidence and reached a verdict. Slaves found guilty of a capital offence received a death sentence.

### Indentures of Apprenticeship

During the 17th, 18th, and 19th centuries, some slave owners decided to have one or more of their enslaved laborers trained as artisans. A master entered into an "indenture of apprenticeship"—an agreement in which each of the parties agreed to reciprocal obligations—with an artisan. A slave owner—the grantor in the indenture of apprenticeship—agreed to allow an enslaved laborer to live and work with an artisan. In return, the artisan—the grantee in the indenture of apprenticeship—promised to teach the slave a specified trade, art, or occupation. The agreement also detailed the length of time that the apprenticeship would last and any other training that a slave would receive. In some colonies and states, laws allowed an artisan to teach reading, writing, and arithmetic to enslaved apprentices.

### Slave Hiring

From the 17th century until the end of the Civil War, some slave owners hired out enslaved laborers to others. If a slaveholder did not have enough work to keep each slave busy, the master might hire out a worker. Others leased their skilled slaves to increase their income. People hired slaves because they needed extra help to tend or harvest crops. Individuals also rented slaves because they could not afford to purchase an enslaved laborer.

Once an owner found someone willing to hire a slave, the two parties negotiated an agreement that outlined how long the enslaved worker would be hired. The contracts included deals for short-term labor—from a day to few months—as well as arrangements for as long as a year. Many localities set aside January 1st as the day to negotiate annual contracts that ran from New Year's Day until Christmas. Written agreements also specified what the person who hired the slave would provide—food, clothing, shelter, and any necessary medical care during the term of service.

Many contracts detailed the work that the slave would perform. Hired slaves labored on both large and small plantations, produced naval stores, worked in factories and on the railroad, dug canals, repaired tools, and constructed buildings. In urban areas, leased slaves cooked and served food in taverns, ran errands, and worked in stores. The practice of hiring slaves—whether in rural or urban settings—enabled whites to adapt their labor force to their needs.

Hiring out offered some precious autonomy for slaves. In antebellum cities like Richmond, Virginia, or Washington, D.C., the hiring-out system evolved such that enslaved individuals negotiated their own terms for their hires, paid some of their wages back to their owners, and made their own independent living arrangements.

## Manumissions

Although many slave owners used legal documents to maintain power and control over their enslaved laborers, some masters used a specific type of legal document—a "manumission"—to free one or more of their slaves from the institution of slavery. The total number of slaves manumitted was a small portion of the enslaved men, women, boys, and girls who labored for others. Between the 17th century and 1865, a series of colonial statutes and state laws often limited a master's ability to release individuals from slavery.

When a master decided to free an enslaved laborer, the master could use either a deed or a will to do so. In the case of a deed, the owner—the grantor—gave freedom to the former slave, the grantee. The grantor specified the name and gender of this laborer and often included information about the person's age. Next, the deed of manumission stipulated the date a slave was to become free and any financial assistance that a master agreed to provide. Some manumission agreements also contained details about the family connections and skills of the freed person.

Slave owners also used the instructions in wills to end slavery for some of their enslaved laborers. The author of the will—the testator—noted the name of the person who would become free as well as this individual's gender. Next, the testator specified the date that the slave would gain freedom. Some testators noted the names of family members and any special skills that the former slave possessed.

Whether a slave gained freedom in a deed or a will, the resulting written document was an important legal document. For the owner, the manumission provided a way to release people from the institution of slavery. For the recently freed person or persons, the manumission changed their lives and gave them the opportunity, although limited by legal restrictions on free people of color, to labor for their own benefit.

*See also* Blacksmith Shops; Cotton; Freedom Papers; Slave Tags and Badges.

FURTHER READING

"Africans in America," PBS Online. At www.pbs.org/wgbh/aia/home.html.

Berlin, Ira. *Generations of Captivity: A History of African-American Slaves.* Cambridge, MA: Belknap Press of Harvard University Press, 2003.

Finkelman, Paul. *Slavery, Race, and the American Legal System, 1700–1872.* New York: Garland, 1988.

Morris, Thomas D. *Southern Slavery and the Law: 1619–1860.* Chapel Hill: University of North Carolina Press, 1996.

"Slaves and the Courts, 1740–1860," American Memory, Library of Congress. At http://memory .loc.gov/ammem/sthtml/sthome.html.

JULIE RICHTER

**LINEN TEXTILES.** Made from the processed inner fibers of the flax plant, linens of medium to coarse quality were used to make slaves' summer **clothing**, some of their winter clothing, and bedding. Depending on the extent and type of processing, linen textiles

Detail from "Industry and Idleness" handkerchief, England, 1770–1785, copper plated-printed linen. An enslaved man and an indentured servant wear identical linen clothing. (The Colonial Williamsburg Foundation.)

ranged from unbleached, coarse, and scratchy goods for use as sails, grain sacks, mattress ticks, and worker's clothing to gossamer laces and fine bleached white fabrics used by wealthy individuals for underwear, decorative clothing ruffles, tablecloths, and **bed** sheets.

Although finer grades of linen were bleached white in the sun, less expensive varieties remained their natural grayish-brown unbleached color. The transformation of the flax fibers into linen was a lengthy process that began by pulling up the plants by the roots to preserve the fiber length. The stems were then put through a series of steps that released the soft fibers from the straw-like stem portions of the flax plant. After the flax seeds were removed with a flail, the stems were softened by exposing them to water, either by laying them out to absorb moisture from the air or by submerging them in water. The outer stems then were broken mechanically with a flax break and then beaten by hand with a special wooden hand tool to further break down the outer layer. Once the stems were sufficiently broken, they were pulled again and again through a hackle, which was a wooden board with **nails** or spikes that acted like a comb, pulling out the rough outer stems and leaving the softer inner fibers. The shorter tow fibers, left in the hackle tool during processing, were spun and used to make coarse textiles. Tow linen typically was filled with slubs and sometimes adulterated with incompletely removed stem pieces of the flax plant.

Linen had many advantages as a utility fabric. It was strong, absorbent, and washable, getting softer with each washing. Linens encompassed a wide variety of fabric names, including lawn, sheeting, holland, garlix, crocus, canvas, osnaburg, and numerous other varieties. Linen was relatively inexpensive and widely available as an import from the British Isles and northern Europe. Linen also was produced in America in areas where climate and soil favored flax production.

Osnaburg, also spelled osnabriggs or oznabig, was a variety of linen widely used for laborers' clothing, including that of slaves. Originally named for the German city of Osnabrück, osnaburg was later copied in Scotland from the 1740s on. Although 18th-century osnaburg was coarse unbleached or brown linen, osnaburg made from the **cotton** plant became prevalent by the early 19th century, spurred by developments in ginning and **spinning** that made cotton goods faster and more economical to produce. Cotton osnaburg eventually supplanted the linen version of the textile for the clothing of free laborers and slaves. Nineteenth-century cotton osnaburgs, often woven in America, came in stripes, checks, and solid colors.

Osnaburg was used for summer clothing and underwear. Male slaves wore shirts and pants made of linen osnaburg, while female slaves had osnaburg shifts and petticoats. Before the 1820s, workingmen's linen pants were made in several different styles: breeches constructed with tight buckled bands below the knees, or loose-fitting trousers that ended anywhere from the calf to the shoe tops, similar to modern cutoffs or trousers. During the first quarter of the 19th century, knee-length breeches ceased to be worn in favor of long pants, or pantaloons. Workingwomen's linen clothing included shifts or chemises and petticoats. Styled similar to plain knee-length dresses, shifts served as underwear but sometimes were worn as outerwear while women performed heavy manual labor in hot conditions. Petticoats were full skirts tied around the waist over the shifts.

The textile called "rolls" was a related material used for laborer's clothing, especially in the 18th century. Made from either flax or hemp, the fabric probably was named because it came on rolls, rather than on bolts or as folded yard goods. In the 18th century, slaves' trousers, aprons, and petticoats were made from rolls.

FURTHER READING

Baumgarten, Linda. "'Clothes for the People': Slave Clothing in Early Virginia." *Journal of Early Southern Decorative Arts* 14, no. 2 (November 1988): 26–70.

Baumgarten, Linda. "Common Dress, Clothing for Daily Life." In *What Clothes Reveal: The Language of Clothing in Colonial and Federal America*, edited by Linda Baumgarten, 106–139. New Haven, CT: Yale University Press, 2002.

Costa, Tom. "Virginia Runaways," Virginia Center for Visual History, University of Virginia. At http://people.uvawise.edu/runaways/index.html.

Montgomery, Florence. *Textiles in America, 1650–1870*. New York: W. W. Norton and Company, 1984, reissued 2007.

Rump, Elizabeth. "A Brief Introduction to Flax Processing," History Online, Chadds Ford Historical Society. At www.chaddsfordhistory.org/history/flax.htm.

Windley, Lathan A., comp. *Runaway Slave Advertisements: A Documentary History from the 1730s to 1790*. I: Virginia and North Carolina. II: Maryland. III: South Carolina. IV: Georgia. Westport, CT: Greenwood Press, 1983.

LINDA BAUMGARTEN

**LIQUOR.** Liquor and other intoxicating beverages were central to the history of enslavement in the Americas. Rum and other hard liquors were used to **barter** for enslaved people in West and Central Africa, some of whom would be shipped to the Americas to grow sugarcane and other raw materials for the manufacture of liquor that in turn would be used through the so-called Triangle (or Triangular) Trade to acquire more enslaved Africans. Although some varieties of traditional alcoholic beverages were known in Africa, religious and social taboos curtailed the consumption of alcohol before the introduction of Western liquors. Both in Africa and the Diaspora, Western-style liquors, alongside traditional folk wines and other intoxicants, became entrenched. Alcoholic beverages were a common part of enslaved people's lives and often were used as an easy escape from the hardships of daily life. Although alcohol consumption among enslaved people, the home manufacture of alcohol, and the sale of alcoholic beverages to the enslaved were regulated highly by state and county authorities as well as by individual slaveholders, it was an everyday part of early African American lives, whether legal or contraband. This aspect of enslaved material life left its mark on the archaeological record, oral histories, and religious life and left a heritage of alcoholism in many early African American communities.

Several types of alcoholic beverages were known in West and Central Africa during the time of the trans-Atlantic slave trade. Palm wine, the fermented sap of the raffia or oil palm, was known throughout both regions. Less potent were weak beers brewed from millet, sorghum, and other traditional cereals, and meads made from wild honey. Palm wine was incredibly time-consuming to make and demanded both skill and courage to tap the tall trees or to carefully fell them and draw the sap through the crown. Traditional liquors also were made from indigenous fruit, notably that of the ebony family, cousin to the American persimmon. With the coming of sugarcane, bananas, and other plants from Asia and the Mediterranean, other folk beverages were brewed in villages using ceramic vessels. Eventually, with the introduction of pineapples and other tropical American crops, a wide variety of folk liquors were available in the traditional societies from which enslaved Africans came.

Liquor use was regulated by traditional social and religious taboos. Those West Africans who adopted Islam either temporarily refrained from or outright abandoned the consumption of intoxicating drink. In those societies that retained more traditional beliefs, individuals younger than a certain age, women, and persons being initiated into adulthood or in training for a secret society also were forbidden from consuming alcohol. If an individual had a special relationship with a deity or ancestor, this could also be grounds for an alcohol taboo. For all other individuals, alcohol consumption and use were important parts of festival rites, celebrations, funerals, and the regular propitiation of deities or ancestral forces. Virtually every community practiced some ritual requiring strong liquor to feed the other world, perhaps by pouring a little on the ground.

Much like the introduction of **cast iron pots** and manufactured **cloth**, the introduction of Western liquors eliminated time-consuming and dangerous work associated with collecting palm sap, honey, and fermenting beverages. Along with gunpowder, weaponry, trinkets, **beads**, and other items, rum, whiskey, and other liquors became central in the purchase and sale of enslaved peoples destined for the Western Hemisphere. Once these enslaved Africans arrived in the Americas, they became aware of an astonishing variety of Western liquors, including red wine, which some, including the people of Kongo-Angola, originally rejected on the grounds that it was the blood of their people. The colonial world—often devoid of clean water—relied on weak alcoholic beverages for liquid intake because of the sanitizing elements of

## Wine

In Mississippi, one of the older women on Charlie Davenport's plantation made homemade wine:

> Ole mammy nearly allus made a heap of dewberry en simmon (persimmon) wine. En us little tykes would gather black walnuts in de woods en store 'em under de cabins to dry. At night when de work wuz all done en de candles out we'd set around de dyin embers en eat a pan of cracked walnuts pickin de meat out wid horseshoe nails. Den mammy would pour herself en her ole man a cup ob wine. We nevah got to taste hit lessen us got sick. Den she'd mess hit up wid wild cherry bark en say "drink dat down". Hit nearly strangled us but us gulped hit down.

*Source:* George P. Rawick, ed. *The American Slave: Mississippi Narratives*, Supp. Ser. 1, Vol. 7, Part 2. Westport, CT: Greenwood Press, 1978

On the South Carolina plantation where George Fleming lived, liquor was not reserved just for special holidays:

> We got a lil' extra liquor and brandy on de holidays, but cose we had some all along enduring de whole entire year. Marse had three stills on de place and dar was plenty liquor, but he didn't let anybody git drunk. He call de lil' niggers, too, sometimes and give 'em a drink, and he give 'em jelly biscuits. He call everybody up to de big house on Christmas and make a speech; den he give everybody some good brandy.

*Source:* George P. Rawick, ed. "South Carolina." *The American Slave: North Carolina and South Carolina Narratives*, Supp. Ser. 1, Vol. 11. Westport, CT: Greenwood Press, 1978.

brewing and fermentation. Beer, cider, **corn**, and rye whiskey, and alcoholic beverages mixed with milk were primary, not secondary, drinks in early America. Wealthier slaveholders, who could afford more variety, imbibed Madeira, port, rum, spiced rum, gin, and other wines and spirits. Some enslaved Africans would become specialized workers charged with the production of these liquors at urban or plantation-based distilleries. Through this contact and social intercourse with indentured servants, the earliest African Americans became connoisseurs in their own right of this newfound relationship with alcohol.

In the archaeological record, shards of bottles used for liquor have been found in the grounds of former **slave quarters**. Indeed, alcoholic beverages such as rum, whiskey, and the like occasionally were distributed by slaveholders at harvest time or holidays as a reward and incentive. In some areas, people developed various recipes for harvest beer—light spirits meant to serve as a stimulant as harvesting pushed into the wee hours of the morning and late hours of the night. George Washington noted that "others are getting out of the practice of using spirits at harvest," and yet he retained the custom of purchasing a hogshead of rum for the same purpose. Those enslaved workers who produced **chickens**, **garden** produce, and other products often bartered for liquor at **markets** or purchased it from taverns or stores in town. Landon Carter, an 18th-century Virginia plantation owner, exerted patriarchal control over his enslaved population by attempting to discourage the purchase of alcohol. He limited their cloth allowance so that they would "buy **linen** to make their other shirt instead of buying liquor with their fowls."

For others, liquor invited theft from plantation storage and cellars. Liquor consumption was largely limited to Saturdays and Sundays when some enslaved people were granted half or full days of rest. Jim Allen, a former slave in Mississippi, said, "On Sat'day night, we mostly had fun playin' and drinkin' whiskey and beer—no time to fool around in the de week time." Not surprisingly the resulting fights and being too hungover to attend to daily chores led to laws forbidding the sale of liquor to slaves and to slave owners banning alcohol entirely from their slave quarters. Other slaveholders feared that alcoholic consumption might foment revolt. Although a great deal of these spirits were enjoyed recreationally, archaeological evidence of alcoholic residues from burial sites points to the continued practice of pouring libations as a gift to the ancestors. At other times, spirits were used as flavoring for certain foods or more often as a solvent for an array of traditional **medicines**.

Enslaved blacks often produced their own homemade wines. On George Mason's Virginia plantation, Gunston Hall, a specific group of enslaved workers were charged with the making of apple cider, peach liquor, and persimmon brandy. The last was a common beverage in the enslaved community, often brought to the fields in a **gourd** as refreshment. The recipes for persimmon liquor have some similarity to both European and African beverages, because they were prepared from a fruit from the same botanical family that is almost identical to the persimmon that is native to West and Central Africa. Another botanical cognate—the honey locust pod—was used in similar ways. Any fruit (berries and orchard fruit) or grain (corn, rye, and the like) were mixed with sugars and left to ferment in crocks. Former slave Charles Ball noted that a pint of hard cider was regularly disbursed to enslaved workers in Maryland and Virginia, probably because of the surplus of apples and other orchard fruit used for that purpose. Some enslaved people grew and sold hops, suggesting that they had adopted European traditions of the brewer's trade. In coastal South Carolina and Georgia, several varieties of palm wine were made from the native palmetto. Palm cabbage full of palmetto sap or the berries from the top of the tree were fermented into a beverage that reminded Low Country blacks of similar tastes from their African homelands.

If rum was the key beverage provided to the enslaved communities during the colonial period because of the Triangular Trade, corn whiskey took its place in enslaved life in the antebellum period. Whiskey was not merely a drink but a painkiller as well as an ingredient in **medicine**. Alcohol, in the form of "moonshine," became part of an underground economy between whites and blacks. The Fourth of July, harvest time, the autumn corn shucking, and Christmas often were times of drinking for those slaveholders who allowed it. However, the presence of alcohol did not impress all enslaved people. Yarrow Mamout, enslaved in Maryland and what became the Georgetown district of Washington, was a Muslim of the Fulbe people whose orthodox approach to Islam forbade alcohol consumption. He was quoted as saying,

"Whiskey, very bad!" Abolitionist and former slave Frederick Douglass (ca. 1818–1895) thought the practice of free-flowing Christmas-week alcohol was nothing more than a ruse on the part of slave owners, when hiring day, January 1, was right around the corner. Families might be split up and men might be forced to leave for a year or two, and drunkenness might detract from attempts to run away from slavery or from remembering the coming tragedy. Douglass also thought that drunkenness was another way in which slaveholders sought to demonstrate the inability of enslaved blacks to control and monitor themselves. On some plantations, because of the influence of the Baptist church or because of the temperance of the slaveholder, no alcohol at all was consumed, and fresh cider and other nonalcoholic beverages were offered at times of celebration or as refreshment during harvest time.

## FURTHER READING

Ball, Charles. *Slavery in the United States: A Narrative of the Life and Adventures of Charles Ball, a Black Man, who lived Forty Years in Maryland, South Carolina and Georgia.* New York: John S. Taylor, 1837. "North American Slave Narratives," Documenting the American South Collection, University Library of the University of North Carolina at Chapel Hill. At http://docsouth.unc.edu/neh/ballslavery/ball.html.

Covey, Herbert C., and Dwight Eisnach. *What the Slaves Ate: Recollections of African American Foods and Foodways from the Slave Narratives.* Santa Barbara, CA: Greenwood Press, 2009.

Douglass, Frederick. *Life and Times of Frederick Douglass: His Early Life as a Slave, His Escape from Bondage, and His Complete History to the Present Time.* 2nd ed. New York: Bedford/St. Martin's, 2002.

Doumbia, Adama, and Naomi Doumbia. *The Way of the Elders: West African Spirituality and Tradition.* St. Paul, MN: Llewellyn, 2004.

Georgia Writer's Project. *Drums and Shadows: Survival Studies among the Georgia Coastal Negroes.* Athens: University of Georgia Press, 1986.

Joyner, Charles. *Down by the Riverside: A South Carolina Slave Community.* Urbana: University of Illinois Press, 1984.

Morgan, Philip D. *Slave Counterpoint: Black Culture in the Eighteenth-Century Chesapeake and Lowcountry.* Chapel Hill: University of North Carolina Press, 1998.

Walsh, Lorena S. "The Chesapeake Slave Trade: Regional Patterns, African Origins, and Some Implications." *The William and Mary Quarterly.* 3rd ser. 58, no. 1 (2001): 139–170.

MICHAEL W. TWITTY

**LIVERY.** Livery was a specific distinctive uniform worn by mid-level male servants of an elite household with a large staff, usually more than eight. Intended to enhance the employer's status, livery gradually fell out of use in early 19th-century America. Upper servants—butlers, tutors, and housekeepers—wore their own clothes even when seen by the public. Housemaids, cooks, scullery workers, and so forth generally worked behind the scenes. Doormen, footmen, waiters, and carriage attendants wore dirty clothes in the early morning when they polished silver plate and cleaned iron-bladed knives, laid fires, and prepared candlesticks and lamps. When in the public eye, they changed into fancy dress provided by their employers, or in the case of slaves, their owners.

Livery suits usually were made of **wool** in two colors and trimmed with "livery lace." In 1755, George Washington ordered two enslaved servants' suits of scarlet and

---

### Suiting up to Become a Footman

Former Texas slave Willis Woodson wore livery as a footman:

De mostest fun I ever got was when Marse Isom 'lows me to be footman. He gits me [Not readable] uniform, most like a sojer's, 'ceptin' mine an red with black stripes down de pants. I 'member it jist like yesterday, de first time I puts it on. Marse give a cel'bration at he house and de doorman am sick, so I has to be it. He give me dat suit and say to hurry put it on. Den he make me come to de front door and let him in over and over, so as to git de hang of it. He told me to take his hat and cane and put dem up, and to say. 'Thank you,' and 'Dis way, please,' and not to say no more to nobody, and I didn't. After dat night I opens de door lots of times, but mostest I wears dat suit when I takes de white folks to church, while dey listens to preachin' and I holds de hosses.

*Source:* George P. Rawick, ed. *The American Slave: Texas Narratives*, Vol. 5, Parts 3 & 4. Westport, CT: Greenwood Press, 1972.

---

off-white to be trimmed with scarlet. He further ordered "Silver lac'd hats for the above Livery's." He placed subsequent orders in 1764 and 1784. During his presidency, Thomas Jefferson wrote that blue coats with scarlet **cloth** were to be worn over waistcoats of scarlet. The trimmings were to be silver. Less elaborate was the livery that Jacob Read's (1752–1816) runaway slave, Mungo, took with him from Charleston, South Carolina. It was of "brown Yorkshire cloth lined with white, with a scarlet cape [collar]."

Attitudes toward livery varied from place to place and changed over time. Livery was worn less in the North and decreased in use during the early republic. In the early 19th century, Margaret Hall, an English traveler, wrote home to her family that until she reached the South she had seen liveried servants in only two Philadelphia houses. She approved of Charles Carroll (1737–1832) who had "no less than three servants in livery" at his Maryland estate. The author of an unpublished novel of about the same date and set in Washington, D.C., wrote about an invitation to a servants' party where "Gentlemen with livery not admitted." In 1827, Robert Roberts (ca. 1780–1860), the free African American butler to Gov. Christopher Gore of Massachusetts, advised young male servants to be dressed in a clean shirt collar and cravat, "with a clean round jacket, white linen apron and clean shoes." For dinner they were to "look neat and tidy, but not foppish" in "good superfine blue body coat, blue cassimere trowsers, and a yellow cassimere vest." Roberts did not mention livery.

FURTHER READING

Baumgarten, Linda. *What Clothes Reveal: The Language of Clothing in Colonial and Federal America*. Williamsburg, VA: Colonial Williamsburg Foundation in association with Yale University Press, 2002.

Carson, Barbara G., Ellen Kirven Donald, and Kym S. Rice. "Household Encounters: Servants, Slaves, and Mistresses in Early Washington." In *The American Home: Material Culture,*

Black servant William Lee in livery in the background, with George Washington, Martha Washington, and her two Custis grandchildren. Engraving by Edward Savage, London, 1798. (Library of Congress.)

*Domestic Space, and Family Life*, edited by Eleanor McD. Thompson, 71–93. Winterthur, DE: Henry Francis du Pont Winterthur Museum, 1998.
Roberts, Robert. *The House Servant's Directory*. Boston, 1827.

Barbara G. Carson

**LOCKS AND KEYS.** Masters often suspected their slaves of stealing from them—and evidence suggests that enslaved individuals did pilfer food and other items from whites, sometimes out of necessity. The former North Carolina slave Louisa Adams remembered, "We were so hungry we were bound to steal or perish." Kentucky slave Peter Bruner echoed, "The white people had plenty of the best of food but we never got any unless we stole it." In other instances, slaves stole as a kind of quid pro quo for their treatment. In every case, slaves knew that if caught stealing, they would be severely punished.

To prevent thefts, slaveholders methodically locked up their expensive foodstuffs, **liquor**, and any other items that might prove too alluring. Even the outbuildings, which could not be patrolled closely at night, sometimes were padlocked to prevent theft. Whenever possible, slaveholders maintained control of the keys to these locks. They locked and unlocked all doors, storage boxes, trunks, closets, and rooms themselves when needed. As a Virginia planter warned in 1834, "Never put temptations in their way by leaving keys or money carelessly about." Regardless of slaveholders' vigilance, things nevertheless still disappeared. In 1801, at Thomas Jefferson's Monticello, the theft of "80 gallons of Coles best cider, in 3 days exactly, under 2 locks & keys" was noted.

Because the slaveholder's wife or daughters supervised the household, it often fell to them to hold the keys that controlled the locked spaces and to closely monitor the daily access to these spaces by enslaved domestic workers. Jefferson's daughters performed that role at Monticello and carried the keys to the storage areas and wine cellar. On the plantation, all outbuildings and storage spaces, including those that adjoined the work areas under the house, were locked. Jefferson even locked the privy nearest the house to prevent anyone outside his immediate family from using it.

Evidence suggests that at least some slaveholders or the overseers that they employed recognized the rights of slaves to acquire personal possessions and protect them. At Poplar Forest, Jefferson's retreat in Bedford County, Virginia, and at Carter's Grove plantation near Williamsburg, Virginia, archaeologists have recovered several metal locks from the **slave quarters**. Other individuals observed that slaves used wooden locks with keys that they made themselves. When noted landscape architect Frederick Law Olmsted (1822–1903) visited a Savannah, Georgia, plantation in the 1850s, he noticed individual slave cabins were equipped with closets that locked with a key. He further observed, "The people were nearly all absent at work, and had locked their outer doors, taking the keys with them."

***See also*** Chamber Pots and Privies; Dependencies; Personal Objects; Subfloor Pits.

FURTHER READING

Heath, Barbara J. "Slavery and Consumerism: A Case Study from Colonial Virginia." *African-American Archaeology: Newsletter of the African-American Archaeology Network* 19 (Winter 1997). African Diaspora Archaeology Network. At www.diaspora.uiuc.edu/A-AANewsletter/newsletter19.html.

Olmsted, Frederick Law. *The Cotton Kingdom: A Traveller's Observations on Cotton and Slavery in the American Slave States*, edited by Arthur M. Schlesinger. New York: Da Capo Press, 1996.

Stein, Susan R. "Restoration Focuses on 'Working' Monticello." *Monticello Newsletter* 14, no. 2 (Winter 2003): 1–5. Monticello. At www.monticello.org/press/newsletter/2003/winter/dependencies03.pdf.

KYM S. RICE

**LOFTS.** A significant number of slaves lived in log cabins with one-room lofts. Many of the lofts measured about 12 by 14 feet squared or as a rectangle with similar dimensions. Other lofts were larger, with a size of a one and one-half story structure. They were made of tree timbers and had roofs made of pine slabs. Cabins had wood chimneys and dirt floors, and contained root cellars dug into floors for storing vegetables. They could house 8 to 12 people.

**Slave quarters** typically were located on streets behind the Big House where the owner or overseer could see the slaves. At times, the size of a loft was a factor in its location. A few masters were benevolent enough to keep large "families" together in one spot.

**Slave housing** varied over time and space and was dictated by the slave masters' preferences, but according to most descriptions, the loft, as a living quarter, was a particular favorite among slaves, because it gave them the feeling of having their own home. The loft was sometimes a structure whose only luxury was hinged shutters, and it often was built without a fireplace. It was warmed only by the heat rising from a fireplace on the first floor. On some occasions, the loft was lighted by a window on each wall, even when the room below did not have windows.

In many lofts some occupants slept on **beds** while other slept on the floor, boards, straw mats, or **pallets**, or simply wrapped themselves with **blankets**. Even under such conditions, the concept of "family" and "home" was created and had a valuable psychological effect on the slave.

Some slave quarters had half lofts. Enslaved families could store items and use them as sleeping quarters for children. After more slaves were brought to North America's mainland, housing space and the need to shelter slaves became more critical, and the slaves and the masters built more lofts.

Slave owners discovered early that they had to separate field and domestic slaves and with that discovery came separate housing. Slaves who worked in the fields lived in housing commonly called slave quarters or slave cabins. Domestic slaves or servants often lived in lofts above the **kitchen**, in designated locations within the Big House, or in **dependencies** attached or near the main house.

Early slave housing was makeshift and flimsy. Whenever, the slaveholder found "an extra room" a slave was placed there, usually with little or no regard to structure or preferences. In the Mid-Atlantic region, where small farms were the rule, a relatively small number of slaves lived in these "extra" buildings, with detached kitchens, in attics, or in basements of a main dwelling. Extra rooms or lofts continued to be of use on plantations even after slavery was abolished in some areas.

*See also* Subfloor Pits.

FURTHER READING

Blassingame, John. *The Slave Community: Plantation Life in the Antebellum South.* New York: Oxford University Press, 1972.

Morgan, Phillip. *Slave Counterpoint: Black Culture in the Eighteenth Century Chesapeake and Lowcountry.* Chapel Hill: University of North Carolina Press, 1998.

"Voices from the Days of Slavery: Former Slaves Tell Their Stories," American Memory, Library of Congress. At http://memory.loc.gov/ammem/collections/voices/.

FRED LINDSEY

# M

**MARBLES.** The game of marbles had special significance in the lives of slave children. For some, it was a favorite game, but for others, the significance of the game was more than child's play. Some former slaves recalled trading marbles for lessons and for **passes** to visit family at other plantations. Archaeological excavations at a number of plantation **slave quarters** illustrate the types of marbles with which the children played. Marbles and **doll**'s heads are among the objects known to have been placed on African American **graves** as offerings.

Many slave children had no other playthings besides marbles. In **slave narratives** gathered by the Federal Writers' Project (1936–1938), 67 of the former slaves interviewed recall playing marbles as children, and for many, this was the only game they played. Some recalled playing marbles with white children on their plantations. Rev. Squire Dowd in North Carolina remembered that if the master would not give them passes to visit other plantations at Christmas, they could obtain them from the white children with whom they played.

Slave narratives described a game in which a square was drawn in the dirt, with a marble in each corner and one in the middle. Some slave children played for fun or to win marbles; others gambled for money. John Smith in North Carolina said that they did not have money, so they played for **watermelons**. A Florida slave, Lindsey Moore, was taken into town by his master to compete against slaves from other plantations, with the masters betting on the winners. Moore used pennies tossed by the spectators to place small wagers of his own.

In the antebellum period, most commercially produced marbles—of stone, clay, porcelain, and glass—were imported from Germany. The slave narratives and archaeological evidence both point to the use of handmade clay marbles and store-bought marbles of stone, porcelain, or clay. Several former slaves described making marbles of lumps of clay, baked in the sun or hardened in the fireplace. The esteemed educator Booker T. Washington (1856–1915) wrote in his memoirs that he rolled marbles out of red clay and put them in the ashes in the fireplace. He learned to gradually increase the heat so that the marbles would not crack, and wrote, "This lesson was of great value to me in beginning to burn brick at our school." Washington and others also owned store-bought marbles. One former slave recalled running footraces against

---

### Playing with Marbles

In North Carolina, former slave Charlie Barbour played with marbles and little else: "I 'minds me of de days when as a youngn' I played marbles an' hide an' seek. Dar wuzn't many games den, case nobody ain't had no time fer 'em."

*Source: George P. Rawick, ed.* The American Slave: North Carolina Narratives, *Vol. 14. Westport, CT: Greenwood Press, 1972.*

George Fleming, a former South Carolina slave, amused himself with marbles, too:

> Us lil' kids played lots of games den, some of dem like what dey plays now, but we had a better time. Befo' we was big enough to work, 'cept tote water and de like of dat, we played sech things as marbles. We had purty red and blue marbles dat Marse Lyntt brung frum de store.

*Source: George P. Rawick, ed. "South Carolina."* The American Slave: North Carolina and South Carolina Narratives, *Supp. Ser. 1, Vol. 11. Westport, CT: Greenwood Press, 1978.*

---

slaves from other plantations and being rewarded with a jackknife or a bag of marbles.

Noted abolitionist Rev. John Sella Martin (1832–1876) recalled that he had been an expert player with a large stock of marbles. A white boy, Eaton Bass, asked to partner with him. In exchange, Martin insisted that Bass teach him the alphabet. Although he had been taught not to teach slaves to read, Bass eventually consented,

Clay marbles found at the Nicholas-Tyler House site in Williamsburg, Virginia. (The Colonial Williamsburg Foundation.)

giving Martin a book and lessons. Methodist minister Richard Parker (b. 1808–ca. 1879) collected old **nails** as a child and exchanged them for marbles. Then he would give marbles to white boys in exchange for teaching him a letter. Parker continued to trade marbles for lessons until he could read words of two syllables. James Forten (1766–1842), another abolitionist, claimed that a game of marbles saved him from a life of West Indian servitude. Born free, he was serving in the Continental Army at age 14 when his ship was captured by the English in 1780. He played marbles with the captain's son, and they became good friends. The boy saved him from being captured and sold as a slave.

Archaeologists have found marbles in excavations of slave quarters at a number of plantation sites, including Mount Vernon, George Washington's Virginia estate; the Hermitage, the Nashville home of Andrew Jackson; and Poplar Forest, Thomas Jefferson's retreat near Lynchburg, Virginia. Homemade clay marbles were most common, although striped porcelain marbles were recovered at the Hermitage along with those of local clay. Homemade marbles also were found at slave quarters of Kingsley plantation in Jacksonville, Florida, and at North End plantation in the Georgia Sea Islands. At Ashland-Belle Helene plantation in Louisiana, where historical records show that marbles were the only toy sold in the Ashland store, archaeologists found marbles of glass, limestone, and clay. A hand-blown glass marble and a clay marble were found at the slave barracks of the Bruin Slave Jail in Alexandria, Virginia.

FURTHER READING

Blassingame, John W., ed. *Slave Testimony: Two Centuries of Letters, Speeches, Interviews and Autobiographies*. Baton Rouge: Louisiana State University Press, 1977.

"Born in Slavery: Slave Narratives from the Federal Writers' Project, 1936–1938," American Memory, Library of Congress. At http://memory.loc.gov/ammem/snhtml/.

Harlan, Louis R., and Raymond W. Smock, eds. *The Booker T. Washington Papers*, Vol. 12. Champaign: University of Illinois Press, 1982, 266.

Randall, Mark E. "Early Marbles." *Historical Archaeology* 5 (1971): 102–105.

BARBARA MAGID

**MARKETS.** For thousands of years, consumers throughout the world regularly have patronized markets to purchase fresh produce and other foodstuffs that were destined for their kitchens and tables. Markets served as important locations for the exchange of news and gossip between buyers and sellers, and for social gatherings by residents of all races.

As customers, workers, and most important, entrepreneurial vendors and hucksters, free and enslaved African Americans participated in this economic system, which in particular gave slaves critical access to cash. According to travelers' descriptions, account books, and other sources, African Americans sold several items at markets, including vegetables, fruits, butter, eggs, prepared **food**, **chickens**, and other animals that they gathered in the wild or raised themselves in their **yards** and **gardens**.

Slaveholders frequently allowed slaves to grow food in their spare time and sell the surplus. Because the individuals who shopped at produce markets usually paid with cash or engaged in some sort of **barter**, the market took on a special significance among African Americans as an income source. In early Washington, D.C., President

Market scene in Macon, Georgia. Engraving of sketch by A. R. Waud, 1867. (Library of Congress.)

Thomas Jefferson regularly patronized Alethia Browning Tanner's (d. 1864) vegetable stand located near the White House grounds. Reportedly, Tanner made enough money from her produce sales that she was able to purchase her freedom in 1810 and eventually that of several other family members.

Wherever they occurred, most often in towns or cities, markets typically were informal open-air gatherings, held seasonally on particular weekdays. Engravings of early Philadelphia and New York illustrate markets that took place there on street corners where hucksters sold items out of carts, wagons, **baskets**, and other containers: anyone with surplus goods to sell or trade could participate. In the precapitalist "walking city," historians single out food markets as important settings where transactions occurred among individuals who conducted face-to-face business.

By the 18th century, municipal authorities began to regulate American markets: they built market houses and collected license fees from vendors who rented stalls in these buildings. At the same time, some Southern localities also sought to control what slaves could buy and sell both door-to-door as well as in markets. In cities like Baltimore, Maryland, some market regulations were tightened in response to white complaints about sales practices by African Americans, whom they accused of selling food at lower prices, in off-hours, or outside established locations. Some even went so far as to accuse black vendors of stealing food from whites to enhance their inventories.

FURTHER READING

Junior League of Washington. *The City of Washington: An Illustrated History.* New York: Alfred A. Knopf, 1977.

Tangires, Helen. *Public Markets and Civil Culture in Nineteenth-Century America*. Baltimore, MD: Johns Hopkins University Press, 2003.

Upton, Dell. "The City as Material Culture." In *The Art and Mystery of Historical Archaeology: Essays in Honor of James Deetz*, edited by Anne Yentsch and Mary C. Beaudry, 51–74. Boca Raton, FL: CRC Press, 1992.

Walsh, Lorena, Ann Smart Martin, and Joanne Bowen. "Provisioning Early American Towns. The Chesapeake: A Multidisciplinary Case Study; Final Performance Report." National Endowment for the Humanities Grant RO-22643-93, 1997. Research Division, Historical Research, Reports, Colonial Williamsburg Foundation. At http://research.history.org/Files/HistRes/Provisioning.pdf.

KYM S. RICE

**MASTER'S HOUSE.** The master's house was the primary domestic space for a slave-holding family. The house could be large or small, but typically it was the most comfortable and well-appointed building on the property in either a rural or an urban context. The master's house was physically distinct from the work buildings, the food preparation, **garden** cultivation, or livestock raising structures, and the enslaved peoples' cabins. The master communicated distinctiveness by distancing the master's house from the other buildings, by giving it a more ornamented appearance, and by situating it at the center or at the highest point of the property. Roads and paths generally led to and from the master's house, so any entrance to or egress from the property encountered it.

From the slaveholders' perspective, the master's house was the center of the property. Slaveholding families identified the master's house as their family seat, a place for rituals and celebrations such as marriages and funerals to take place. For many

---

### Christmas at the Big House

As John Sneed from Texas described, field slaves only approached the slaveholder's house on special holidays like Christmas:

> On Christmas all us go to de big house and crowd 'round massa. He a li'l man and some black boys'd carry him 'round on dere shoulders. All knowed dey gwine git de present. Dere a big tree with present for everyone, white and black. Lots of eggnog and turkey and baked hawgs and all kind good things. Dere allus lots of white folks company at massa's house and big banquets and holidays and birthdays. Us like dem times, 'cause work slack and food heavy. Every las' chile have he birthday celebrate with de big cake and present and maybe de quarter in silver from old massa, bless he soul. Us play kissin' games and ring plays and one song am like dis:
>> "I'm in de well,
>> How many feet?
>> Five. Who'd git you out?"
> Iffen it a man, he choose de gal and she have to kiss him to git him out de well. Iffen a gal in de well, she choose a man.

*Source:* George P. Rawick, ed. *The American Slave: Texas Narratives*, Vol. 5, Parts 3 & 4. Westport, CT: Greenwood Press, 1972.

---

Drayton Hall plantation, in the Carolina Low Country near Charleston, South Carolina, is one of the most handsome examples of Palladian architecture in North America. The house was built for John Drayton, begun in 1738 and completed in 1742, using both free and slave labor. (Library of Congress.)

slaveholding families, the master's house represented expressions of their sophistication, wealth, and power. From the perspective of the enslaved people, the master's house was the center from which they received their working orders, **food rations**, and punishments. For all enslaved people, the master's house was a physical and unavoidable symbol of the slaveholder's presence.

Enslaved laborers usually built the master's house, following accepted local building practices, or the directions of a carpenter, a housewright, or, rarely, an architect. Construction varied, depending on the size of the enslaved population, the ambitions of the master, and the availability of materials, inspiration, skilled craftsmen, and capital to finance the project. For the large, showplace master's houses, a planter typically hired carpenters and craftsmen who brought their own forces of skilled enslaved workers to the project with them. Particularly for houses outside of urban centers, these crews would set up temporary housing on site and remain there until their portion of the work was finished. In a few cases, masters demanded a specific kind of house and hired free white construction workers from great distances, only relying on enslaved labor for menial construction assistance and work on secondary buildings.

Because of the ravages of time, wind, fire, and weather, only a small percentage of master's houses still exist. Most of the extant houses give a biased view into the kinds of houses slaveholders occupied, skewing contemporary viewers' perceptions that all masters' houses were large and comfortable. Granted, even the poorest master's house probably was of higher quality than the other living spaces on the property, but most small and middling master's houses have vanished from the landscape. This is particularly true for master's houses from the 17th and 18th centuries, for which the survival of any building is rare. Extant buildings tend to be the largest, the most architecturally notable, made of the most permanent materials, and to have been maintained by a family or a continuous series of owners. Scholars have discovered that since the beginning of English settlement in North America at Jamestown in 1607, cultural preferences for personal square footage have grown exponentially. In the 17th and early 18th centuries, a prosperous slaveholding planter might have lived in an approximately 500-square-foot house. The planter and his family lived in that house, and, particularly in the 17th century, also included some of his enslaved and indentured workers. As indenture became less common in favor of lifetime servitude and pro-slavery legislation gained power during the 17th century, more workers were likely to be enslaved and to live separately from their owners. A surviving small wood-frame planter's house called "Pear Valley" in Northampton County, Virginia, has a footprint of about 21 by 16.5 feet, for a total of approximately 350 square feet. The building has a single room on the ground floor, with access to a **loft** under the roof provided by a ladder through a hole in the ceiling. Notwithstanding the building's modest size, the owner of Pear Valley was an upper-middle-class planter in the county. Upon his death, the value assigned to his estate placed him securely in the most affluent quarter of the population. Pear Valley is an extremely rare example of what many scholars think was a common building type and size until the mid-18th century.

Technological advancements generated much larger crops and greater financial returns, and as enslaved populations stabilized and grew, slaveholders began building larger houses. At the turn of the 19th century, a common form of master's house for prosperous planters in the American South was the "I-house." I-houses had side gables, one room to either side of a central passage, as well as a symmetrical façade, and rose two stories high. This type of house was quick and economical to build and easy to enlarge, either with shed additions or by adding two rooms, front and back, to each side of the passage under an expanded roof, in what is commonly called a double-pile arrangement. These houses were so ordinary that few scholars paid attention to them until the study of vernacular architecture emerged in the 1980s. Another common house type, particularly in the coastal South, was the planter's cottage, a variation on the English cottage. Usually one story high with an attic and side chimneys, the cottage was one room deep and two rooms wide, with an entrance directly into one of the rooms. These houses often expanded to incorporate a central passage with two flanking rooms. Single-room, 20- by 16-foot structures such as Pear Valley became the prototype for enslaved peoples' cabins.

Historians make the distinction that while most enslaved people lived in groups of 50 or more, most masters owned from one to five enslaved persons. Most slaveholders were not wealthy planters, and their houses were small, modest, and often impermanent. Particularly when settling new land in the parts of Mississippi, Alabama, Georgia, and Louisiana, which became known as the **Cotton** Belt, most people's priorities were to clear the land, plant a crop, and start making profits. Hence, the vast majority of master's houses began as single-room log cabins, expanded, and enclosed under a layer of clapboards as the slaveholding family established themselves on a property. Travelers' descriptions from the 1830s describe fine silver and ceramic on display in a log building with unglazed windows and large cracks between the logs. The grand, white-pillared mansions that figure so prominently in modern conceptions of the master's house were relatively uncommon features on the landscape.

Thinking about the landscape in gendered terms provides context for understanding how the master's house functioned in the lives of slaveholding families and enslaved persons. The master's house, together with outbuildings like the **kitchen**, smokehouse, icehouse, and **dairy**, and vegetable and flower gardens were predominantly female spaces, whereas the fields, barns, and crop-processing structures were male spaces. Considering the master's house as a female space gives insight into how both slaveholding and enslaved women thought about, organized, and controlled their worlds. The mistress, or dominant slaveholding woman who was usually the wife or a relative of the male head of the household, ran the house, issuing orders for **clothing** to be cleaned, mended, and made; for food preparation and storage; and for care and maintenance of valuable family goods like china, silver or silverplated ware, spices, and **liquor**. An enslaved domestic servant, typically a woman, often served her mistress as a housekeeper. The person who filled this role delegated the various tasks to the corps of enslaved domestics, managed their output and performed quality control to the mistress' standards, and was an expert on the requirements of the domestic economy. Depending on the household, the enslaved housekeeper sometimes effectively took over the duties of the mistress. Only households with a large enslaved population had specified domestic servants. On smaller farms with one to five enslaved persons, typically a single enslaved woman performed domestic work like cooking and washing for the slaveholding family and the other enslaved laborers or split her time between domestic and field duties.

Enslaved domestic servants spent most of their working lives in the master's house, and personal servants such as maids and valets often lived in the house with the slaveholding family. Especially in urban master's houses, visitors observed that enslaved domestics would sleep in the hallways or in the attics. In the past, many historians of slavery have argued that enslaved domestics reaped material benefits such as better, more nutritionally diverse foods, better housing, and more substantial clothing than the enslaved field workers. More recently, historians have questioned this argument, asserting that these material gains came at high costs. Close contact with slaveholders often exposed domestic servants to challenging demands, mood swings, and sometimes violent reactions, and physically separated these domestic servants from the community of other enslaved workers who lived together in the cabin settlements, some of whom may have been family members, friends, or spouses. In addition, domestic servants had fewer opportunities than other enslaved people to make money on the side. Skilled artisans could be hired out or hire themselves out for tasks, and field hands could grow and sell more vegetables or **chickens**. Enslaved domestic servants' duties were personal and specific, and it was difficult for them to capitalize on their skills, although they frequently received monetary tips for their duties from their masters as well as from visitors.

Especially on larger farms, the master's house had a series of support buildings close by, including the kitchen, dairy, washhouse, smokehouse, carriage house, and stables. Enslaved domestic servants, such as the cook and assistants, the laundresses, and seamstresses, who typically were female, and the grooms and carriage drivers, who were typically male, often lived in rooms in the buildings associated with their work. Through the antebellum period, as slaveholders' fears about emancipation increased, the design of houses and the situation of outbuildings included more opportunities for slaveholders to scrutinize the work of the enslaved.

It is more common to think about the master's house in a rural farming context, in terms of a plantation, but many of its characteristics remained consistent in an urban context. In a town or city, the master's house occupied the optimal position on the lot, featured more refined architectural details and higher quality building materials than the other structures on the property, and existed as a primarily female space. Private homes were among the few socially acceptable places for slaveholding women to gather and visit in cities and towns, and reports and censuses suggest that more enslaved women than men lived and worked in domestic urban environments. Smaller property sizes and high population density meant that enslaved domestic servants lived in close quarters with the slaveholding family, but urban homemaking duties such as going to the **markets** and running errands offered domestic servants a small amount of time and space that was not directly supervised. Close quarters and a large urban enslaved domestic servant population also presented possibilities for social interaction with other enslaved persons, sometimes in the form of religious meetings or unsanctioned outings. Urban town houses often had gardens and work **yards** separated one from the other by **fences** and alleys, which could operate as communication points between properties and across neighborhoods.

In a rural context, the master's house typically occupied a site separated from the quarters but positioned in a way that allowed the slaveholder some level of supervision over the living and working spaces of enslaved people. The overseer's house was a proxy for the master's house, an outpost of surveillance and control over the lives and relationships of the enslaved. On large properties with large enslaved populations, slaveholders employed overseers to stand in for the master and organize, direct, monitor, and often punish the labor force. Slaveholders considered supervision necessary to control enslaved persons, tacitly acknowledging that enslaved people were not mindless workers but had meaningful lives and relationships beyond their situations as chattel property. Enslaved persons often knew their home plantations and the surrounding properties intimately, and recognized ways to use and inhabit the landscape, including the fields, woods, swamps, and water sources, for social, ritual, and spiritual purposes. Any free time found many slaves traveling to surrounding properties, visiting friends and family, with their master's approval or, as was more often the case, without it. For many enslaved persons, the domestic ideals of home and home place extended far beyond the confines of their cabins and out of sight of the master's house. To reinforce the slaveholders' position of power, overseers stood in as secondary masters, and often their houses were situated near the slave quarters to represent secondary master's houses. Overseers' houses were smaller and less refined than the master's house, although they were significantly more commodious than the quarters cabins. The slaveholders' fallacy lay in thinking that observation of the quarters would encompass all facets of enslaved persons' lives and communities.

Typically, large plantations had several enslaved men trained as carpenters, coopers, and brick makers and layers who maintained the master's house and agricultural buildings. On smaller building projects, a master probably assigned a group of enslaved men from his own labor force to assist a carpenter or to build according to local practices. Masters often hired enslaved workers from neighbors and family members to work on construction projects. Hiring enslaved workers was a common practice, particularly for masters who owned few enslaved workers or did not want to allocate manpower away from crop cultivation.

*See also* Cooks; Dependencies; Kitchens.

FURTHER READING

Barrow, James C. "Plantation Architecture of the Lower South on the Eve of the Civil War." *The Journal of Southern History* 11 (1945): 370–388.

Carson, Cary, Norman F. Barka, William M. Kelso, Garry Wheeler Stone, and Dell Upton. "Impermanent Architecture in the Southern American Colonies." *Winterthur Portfolio* 16 (1981): 135–196.

Ellis, Clifton. "The Mansion House at Berry Hill Plantation: Architecture and the Changing Nature of Slavery in Antebellum Virginia." *Perspectives in Vernacular Architecture* 13 (2006): 22–48.

Fazio, Michael W. "The Idea of the Southern Plantation." PhD diss., Cornell University, 1987.

Kniffen, Fred. "Folk Housing: Key to Diffusion." *Annals of the Association of American Geographers* 55 (1965): 549–577.

Upton, Dell. "White and Black Landscapes in Eighteenth-Century Virginia." In *Material Life in America, 1600–1860*, edited by Robert Blair St. George, 357–369. Boston: Northeastern University Press, 1988.

Vlach, John Michael. *Back of the Big House: The Architecture of Plantation Slavery*. Chapel Hill: University of North Carolina Press, 1993.

EMILIE JOHNSON

**MEDICINE.** The poor living and working conditions experienced by enslaved African Americans took a daily as well as a long-term toll on their bodies. Not only was their life expectancy lower than that of whites, but also they were more susceptible to different maladies that included recurrent intestinal, respiratory, skin, and parasitic diseases. Enslaved individuals endured work-related injuries that ranged from minor conditions like hemorrhoids or arthritis to more serious maladies: internal damage from beatings; burns from boiling **sugar**; and fingers, hands, or arms amputated or crushed in mechanical equipment. Although archaeological excavations have revealed tooth brushes in **slave quarters**, both males and females experienced dental problems. Female slaves suffered, too, from complications of pregnancy, and the infant mortality rate among slaves was high. Large numbers of early Americans, including slaves, fell victim to yellow fever, smallpox, and malaria.

In both modern and contemporaneous terms, slave quarters were unsanitary. Few privies (outhouses) were available for slaves to use; instead daily waste and other trash was dumped outside in the quarter **yard**, where sewage contaminated the soil and the water and attracted vermin. Consequently, intestinal parasites were especially widespread. Slaves of all ages, both male and female, and especially young children who played outside, were treated regularly by their owners for worms that sometimes infected the victim's internal organs and caused severe pain.

Poor nutrition was another cause of health problems. By one estimate, 80 percent of the calories consumed by slaves came from **corn** and pork, which meant that, on

---

### Homemade Remedies

James Bolton remembered some homemade remedies in Georgia:

> Gyarlic was mos'ly to kyore wums. They roastid the gyarlic in the hot ashes an' squez the juice outen it, an' made the chilluns take it. Sometimes they made poultices outen gyarlic for the pneumony."
>
> We saved a heap er bark from wile cherry, an' poplar an' black haw, an' slip'ry ellum trees, an' we dried out mullein leaves. They was all mixed an' brewed to make bitters. When-some-ever a nigger got sick, them bitters was good fer, well, Ma'am, they was good fer whut ailed 'im. We tuk 'em fer rheumatiz, fer fever, an' fer the mis'ry in the stummick, an' fer mos' all sorts er sickness. Red oak bark tea was good fer so' th'oat.

As Sally Brown related, sometimes slaves in Georgia relied on folk remedies for pain:

> We jest had our babies and had a granny to ketch 'em. We didn't have all the pain-easin' medicine then. The granny would put a rusty piece of tin or a ax under the straw tick and this would ease the pains. Us didn't have no mattresses in them days, but filled a bed tick with fresh straw after the wheat wuz thrashed, and it wuz good sleepin' too. Well, the granny put a ax under my straw tick once. This wuz to cut off the after-pains and it sho did too, honey. We'd set up the fifth day and after the 'layin'-in' time wuz up we wuz 'lowed to walk outdoors and they tol' us to walk around the house jest once and come in the house. This wuz to keep us from takin' a lapse.

*Source:* George P. Rawick, ed. *The American Slave: Georgia Narratives.* Part 1, Supp. Ser. 1, Vol. 3. Westport, CT: Greenwood Press, 1978.

---

average, enslaved individuals consumed meals that were high in fat and carbohydrates and low in iron, calcium, and desirable vitamins. As a result, many enslaved individuals were chronically malnourished, even if they had their own **gardens** or were able to hunt game or **fish** to supplement their diets.

Because slaveholders' economic well-being relied entirely on their workers' productivity, they usually took sickness among their enslaved population seriously. Nevertheless, many blamed the slaves themselves for getting sick, comparing them with troublesome children or animals that needed supervision and guidance. A Mississippi planter complained in 1847 that "Negroes are a thriftless, thoughtless people, and have to be restricted in many points essential to their constitutions and health. Left to themselves they will over eat, unseasonably eat, walk half the night, sleep on the ground, out of doors, anywhere." To prevent illness and to protect their self-interest, antebellum planters aimed to establish healthier living and working conditions for slaves. In Southern agricultural journals, they published essays that touted various preventive measures, such as prohibiting slaves from working in the rain or other bad weather, cooking all meat including pork thoroughly, and initiating regular inspections of enslaved housing for cleanliness. They discussed building cabins with better air circulation and assigning smaller groups to live in them.

In the case of illness, slaveholders routinely first treated their sick slaves themselves. The diary of 18th-century Virginia plantation owner Landon Carter (1710–1778) reflects his constant worry over his slaves' various illnesses and his relentless efforts to treat them. He, like most slaveholders in his time and into the 19th century, turned to physicians for advice or to acquire medicines only if his own remedies were unsuccessful, the symptoms proved mysterious, or the situation turned into a real emergency. On the whole, medical care by physicians in the 18th and 19th centuries was rudimentary.

Physicians routinely treated sick people by bleeding or purging them—and sometimes did both. Irrespective of race or class, many individuals suffered—and died—under a physician's care. Like other whites, slaveholders availed themselves of a combination of folk remedies and drugs, usually procured from a doctor without examination, to treat illnesses. Records for an early 19th-century Fredericksburg, Virginia, physician indicate that slaveholders sent him notes that briefly described their slaves' sickness and asked for medicine to treat them. Only rarely did they require the doctor to directly treat slaves who were seriously ill.

For many illnesses, slaveholders dispensed quinine, the antimalarial drug that reduces fever, and various emetics to induce vomiting or purging. On occasion, they tried bloodletting. Most frequently, they treated a variety of complaints with calomel, a mercury-based purgative that kills bacteria but also is highly toxic because the mercury remains permanently in the body. Archaeologists working at Andrew Jackson's Hermitage plantation near Nashville, Tennessee, uncovered in the slave quarter a series of medicine bottles that originally contained calomel. Accounts for Pierce Butler's (1806–1867) plantation on Butler's Island, Georgia, indicate that slaves there were treated for arthritis with patent medicines and rum. Slaves may have even dosed themselves on occasion. Patent medicine bottles have been recovered in several different slave quarters sites, but they perhaps were used for their high alcoholic content.

Often the slaveholding mistress, or in some cases, the overseer's wife, was given charge of sick slaves. As Tines Kendrick, a former Georgia slave described her mistress:

> Ole Miss, she generally looked after the niggers when they sick and give them the medicine. And, too, she would get the doctor iffen she think they real bad off. . . . Howsoever, it was hard sometime to get her to believe you sick when you tell her that you was, and she would think you just playing off from work.

Slaveholders frequently suspected that slaves claimed sickness as a way to get off work, and slaves did feign illness as a method of resistance.

Consequently, slaveholders let their slaves get very sick before calling a doctor. Tines Kendrick recounted the time that a little boy was very sick for about a week. His mother begged the mistress to get a doctor but she refused, "She say Mose ain't sick much." In fact, the child died shortly thereafter in some agony.

Some slave owners, particularly those who owned significant numbers of individuals built special **slave hospitals** or sick houses on their properties. Ideally, pregnant slaves delivered their children in these buildings, and sick slaves recovered there. More important, from the slaveholder's perspective, a separate facility kept contagious diseases from spreading through the entire population. Slave owners sometimes put an older enslaved woman who was past manual work in charge of the sick at the hospital.

In reality, whenever possible, the enslaved community turned to its own healers for medical care. Slaveholders tacitly acknowledged this by permitting slaves to use slave healers (also called "root doctors") for treatments, and even sometimes used these cures themselves, although most whites feared poisoning at the hands of slaves. Their therapies usually involved teas or potions made from **herbs** or plants they gathered or grew. As former slave Vinnie Brunson explained, "We had de remedies dat wuz handed down to us from de folks way back befo' we wuz born." Poke root, for example, in either poultice and salve form, was used to relieve pain or reduce sores or as a laxative. Many treatments prescribed by slave healers reportedly worked. Enslaved individuals trusted them over the medicines haphazardly dispensed to them by white slaveholders or physicians.

Other slave healers included midwives who delivered the children within the slave community. Just as slaves did, slaveholders seem to have recognized and respected their abilities. Elsey, a midwife on Alexander Telfair's Georgia plantation, not only helped with slave births but also assisted the births of the white women who lived in the neighborhood. Unknown to most owners, although sometimes suspected, midwives also mixed and administered the botanical remedies that could induce an abortion.

Among the slave communities, the conjurer was the most powerful, respected, and feared slave healer. Both male and female, conjurers wielded magic for their cures and curses that many former slaves called "hoodoo." By and large, whites tended to dismiss conjuring as evidence of "primitive" superstitions. Conjurers claimed the ability to communicate with the spirit world and the "haunts" (ghosts) that inhabited it; to read the meaningful signs evident in everyday life (an owl's hoot or a woodpecker's peck, for example); and, through their **charms** and potions, to control an individual's fate. At the Levi Jordan plantation in Brazoria County, Texas, archaeologists recovered what they identified as a conjuror's kit in a slave cabin. Made of two small kettle lids, it contained bones, chalk, bits of clay, and a **shell**. The same site included **doll** parts, **nails**, perhaps used for a **fetish** (nkisi), and other items arranged in what archaeologists interpret as a **cosmogram** shape.

Many former slaves reported to interviewers in the 1930s that they wore protective charms made from **coins** or other materials presumably fashioned by conjurers. A conjurer could both protect as well as impair an individual: slaves sometimes credited their unexplained or lingering illnesses to a conjurer's spell. An ex-slave from Texas who identified himself as a conjurer, William Adams, ascribed the magic's success to "faith" on the part of those who believed in conjuring. "If they has the true faith in such, it works. Otherwise, it won't." Although conjurers did take credit for the accidents, and even deaths, that sometimes befell cruel overseers or masters, their interventions were not always successful. On Josh Hadnot's Texas plantation, a woman who wore a small bag of sand as a conjuror's charm was said to "git too uppity and sass de marster, 'cause she feel safe." The slaveholder then whipped her "so hard he cut dat bag of san' plumb in two. Dat ruint de conjure man's business." Yet slaves' knowledge of healing sometimes worked to bring about their ultimate goal: freedom. In 1729, Virginia governor William Gooch (1681–1751) freed Papan, who revealed his secret cure for yaws and syphilis to the government, and in 1749, the South Carolina House of Assembly not only freed a slave named Caesar who revealed his cure for poisons and rattlesnake bites but also awarded him £100 per year for life.

*See also* Chamber Pots and Privies; Cast Iron Pots; Conjure Bags; Liquor; Pigs and Pork; Shrines and Spirit Caches.

FURTHER READING

Botkin, B. A., ed. *Lay My Burden Down: A Folk History of Slavery.* Athens: University of Georgia Press, 1989.

Brown, Kenneth L. "Material Culture and Community Structure: The Slave and Tenant Community at Levi Jordan's Plantation, 1848–1892." In *Working Toward Freedom: Slave Society and Domestic Economy in the American South,* edited by Larry E. Hudson, 95–118. Rochester, NY: University of Rochester Press, 1994.

Campbell, Edward D. C., Jr., with Kym S. Rice. *Before Freedom Came: African-American Life in the Antebellum South.* Charlottesville: University of Virginia Press for the Museum of the Confederacy, 1991.

Carter, Landon. *The Diary of Colonel Landon Carter of Sabine Hall, 1752–1778.* Edited by Jack P. Greene. Charlottesville: Published for the Virginia Historical Society by University Press of Virginia, 1965.

Dunaway, Wilma A. *The African American Family in Slavery and Emancipation.* New York: Cambridge University Press, 2003.

Fett, Sharla M. *Working Cures: Healing, Health and Power on Southern Slave Plantations.* Chapel Hill: University of North Carolina Press, 2002.

Mellon, James, ed. *Bullwhip Days: The Slaves Remember.* New York: Weidenfeld and Nicolson, 1988.

"Patients' Voices in Early Nineteenth-Century Virginia: Letters to Doct. James Carmichael and Son," Historical Collections at the Claude Moore Health Sciences Library, University of Virginia. At http://carmichael.lib.virginia.edu/story/slavecare.html.

Savitt, Todd L. "Medical Life in Antebellum Virginia: If You Got Sick and You Were Black," Department of History, Virginia Tech. At www.history.vt.edu/Jones/priv_hist3724/Slave Med/sickblack.html.

Savitt, Todd L. *Medicine and Slavery: The Diseases and Health Care of Blacks in Antebellum Virginia.* Urbana: University of Illinois Press, 1981.

"Slave Medicine," Lucy Meriwether Lewis Marks, Virginia Planter and Doctoress, 1752–1837, Monticello. At www.monticello.org/library/exhibits/lucymarks/medical/slavemedicine.html.

KYM S. RICE

**MILITARY EQUIPMENT.** From colonial times to the end of the Civil War, military equipment—the uniforms, **firearms**, ordnance, and accoutrements men used in wartime—changed considerably. Good matériel, however, often was denied to the African American population. Slaves and former slaves who served in the military faced the persistent problem of discrimination based on skin color and legal status. Enslaved African Americans, nevertheless, served ably in the major conflicts of the colonial era, early national period, and the Civil War.

Once in America, colonists had to fight a new kind of warfare. The first soldiers in America looked more medieval than modern, more European than American. In Virginia, colonists' body armor, similar to that worn in the Crusades, initially defended them against Native American arrows, and officers armed with single-shot

Black soldiers near Dutch Gap canal, Virginia, 1864. (Library of Congress.)

pistols might carry a shield into battle. In Europe, musketeers—protected in battle by pikemen armed with long spikes, called pikes—used heavy matchlock firearms that required a fork-rest for support. Native Americans, however, preferred unleashing short, intense raids rather than fighting European-style set battles and prolonged campaigns. European tactics and weapons, therefore, often failed colonists when fighting the Indian population.

Slaves eventually would adopt the English colonists' methods of fighting. Before the American Revolution, all the English colonies had legalized slavery, but not all African Americans were slaves. English settlers brought the first Africans to Virginia in 1619, but it took decades before chattel slavery became entrenched in the colonies. In the 1660s, Virginia instituted slave codes, which included a law that prevented African Americans from owning guns. In 1705, Virginia further barred slaves from possessing a "gun, sword, club, staff, or other weapon." Nevertheless, over the years, many Virginia masters allowed slaves to use guns on their farms or plantations to kill predators or hunt for food. Also, colonies other than Virginia were less strict about keeping weapons out of the hands of African Americans. In 1641 in New York, Dutch law allowed blacks armed with a tomahawk and half pike to defend colonists against Native Americans. The Southern colonies also were willing to arm slaves. In 1654, Maryland required that "every master of families provide Arms and Ammunition . . . for Every such Servant . . . Imploying [sic] them for the service of the Commonwealth."

In 1703, South Carolina passed a law that stated, "it shall and may be lawful for any master or owner of any slave, in actual invasion, to arm and equip any slave or slaves, with such arms and ammunition as any other person."

In the 17th century, white and black colonists could not rely on regular English troops for defense. They instead depended on militias, which were made up of local citizens and usually led by the colonial governor. Some slaves served in the militias, while others performed noncombat roles in the English army. In 1770, the 29th Regiment of Foot fired on a hostile mob in what patriots soon called the Boston Massacre. Among the 29th were slave drummers who had been purchased by the regiment's commander. The drummers dressed in tall hats, wore coats of "reversed colors" of yellow and red, and played drums painted yellow, the regiment's adopted color.

By the eve of the American Revolution, firearms became more available to the colonial population and were easier to use. The popular image of the patriot soldier carrying a hunting rifle, short knife under his belt, and powder horn slung over his shoulder illustrated several improvements in weaponry. A significant advance in firearms technology was the development of flintlock rifles and muskets. With its spiraled barrel, the rifle proved a more accurate and longer range weapon than the musket. Used by hunters and militiamen in the mostly rural North American colonies, the rifle had advantages over the smoothbore musket, which professional troops used in massed formations. But despite the fact that muskets were less accurate than rifles, they were more numerous and easier to load, and only muskets could be outfitted with a bayonet, which was invented in the late 1600s. Most of the men who fought in the American Revolution (1775–1783) did so with muskets rather than rifles.

When the Revolution began, it was uncertain what role, if any, slaves would play in the conflict. In November 1775, George Washington prohibited African Americans, free or slave, from joining the patriot armies. Because of manpower shortages, however, Washington eventually reversed his decision, and some former slaves distinguished themselves in battle. Among the most famous black patriot forces was the First Rhode Island Regiment that consisted of free blacks and former slaves. An observer described the men at the Battle of Rhode Island, "with their cocked hats and black plumes tipped with white, moving with charged bayonets as a single man."

Slaves also served in the Loyalist armies. Historians estimate that 100,000 slaves fled their masters to seek refuge behind English lines. Some enlisted in Virginia Lieutenant Governor Lord Dunmore's "Ethiopian Regiment," whose men bore sashes reading "Liberty to Slaves." Others worked as spies and guides for the English. More often, however, slaves were used to haul supplies, tend horses, and cook meals for the British armies.

Patriots and Loyalists, blacks or white, suffered from shortages of proper military equipment. Infantry uniforms often differed depending on state, unit, or availability of supplies, but eventually the U.S. Congress adopted blue uniforms—complete with black felt hat, waistcoat with white **buttons** and lining, and breeches—for the Continental Army. On the march, a well-outfitted soldier's gear consisted of a musket with detachable bayonet, a knapsack or haversack containing his mess kit and rations, a **blanket** and canteen, and a cartridge box that held 20 to 30 rounds. Very often, however, the reality of soldiering failed to live up to the ideal.

Although it had fought the American Revolution in defense of "life, liberty, and the pursuit of happiness," the United States, once independent, barred African Americans from joining the army. Many blacks continued to serve in the more integrated navy, while others aided Native Americans in their ongoing struggle against the U.S. government. At times, it was the absence of military equipment, rather than the presence of it, that made black resistance exceptional. Gen. Rufus Saxton (1824–1908) said of the Native American's slave allies he fought in Florida, "The Negroes would stand and fight back, even with bare hands." Many slaves were prepared to do anything to win their freedom.

African Americans played a small role in the relatively brief War of 1812 and Mexican War. During the Civil War (1861–1865), however, they served both the Union and Confederacy in great numbers. An estimated 180,000 African Americans, most of them former slaves, joined the Northern army, while another 10,000 enlisted in the navy. Most served in the infantry, but others became cavalrymen and artillerists. Many Northern whites did not believe former slaves would fight well—some black troops initially were given pikes rather than rifles, an action that angered abolitionists. Even after they proved their worth in battle, black soldiers did not receive the same wages as white troops, and nearly all their commissioned officers were white.

Former slaves, nevertheless, persisted, and they quickly learned the ways of modern warfare. The Civil War featured the first machines guns, rifled cannon, breech-loading carbines, ironclad ships, and telescopic sites. But the most important innovation of the era was the 0.58-caliber Springfield Model rifle, a muzzle-loading weapon. With its minié ball (or bullet), Civil War rifles had far greater range and accuracy than smooth-bore weapons. In the 1860s, close-formation combat proved far deadlier than it was in George Washington's time. The process of loading and discharging a musket, however, had not changed dramatically since the Revolution: an accomplished soldier could still fire only two or three rounds per minute under fire. A former slave using a Civil War–era rifle first had to tear open a cartridge containing the ball and powder; put the powder, wadding (a bit of crumpled paper or cloth), and ball down the muzzle; push the bullet to the end of the barrel with a ramrod; load a percussion cap on the "nipple" underneath the hammer of the rifle; and then fire. Yet, as complicated as muskets were in comparison to present-day firearms, former slaves mastered soldiering quickly and served bravely in some of the war's most important campaigns.

In the Confederacy, which consisted entirely of slave states, soldiers mostly used the same types of military equipment as their better-armed and supplied Northern enemy. The South was not as industrialized as the North, but it had millions of slaves who served as common and industrial laborers. Many were impressed by their masters into Confederate service. Slaves built entrenchments and fortifications, toiled in dangerous ordnance factories, unloaded railroad cars and wagons, drove animals, and were body servants in camps. Not until March 1865, however—a few weeks before the South surrendered—did the Confederate Congress allow African Americans to serve as soldiers. Some slaves used guns against Northern forces during the war, and in many cases when they accompanied their Confederate masters onto the battlefield, but for most of the conflict, white Southerners were too fearful of revolt to arm their black workers.

The Civil War ended with a Union victory and the abolition of slavery. Military equipment would change, but prejudice against black soldiers continued. African Americans repeatedly proved themselves to a white public that seemingly had forgotten the sacrifices they had made on the battlefield.

## FURTHER READING

Chartrand, René. *Colonial American Troops 1610–1774*. Oxford: Osprey, 2002.

Coates, Earl J., and James L. Kochan. *Don Troiani's Soldiers in America, 1754–1865.* Mechanicsburg, PA: Stackpole Books, 1998.

Edgerton, Robert B. *Hidden Heroism: Black Soldiers in America's Wars.* Boulder, CO: Westview, 2001.

Egerton, Douglas R. *Death or Liberty: African Americans and Revolutionary America.* New York: Oxford University Press, 2009.

Elting, John R. *Military Uniforms in America: The Era of the American Revolution,1755–1795.* San Rafael, CA: Presidio Press, 1974.

Johnson, Jesse J., ed. *The Black Soldier Documented 1619–1865.* Hampton, VA: Hampton Institute, 1970.

Jordan, Winthrop D. *White over Black: American Attitudes toward the Negro 1550–1812.* Chapel Hill: University of North Carolina Press, 1968.

Peterson, Harold L. *The Book of the Continental Soldier.* Harrisburg, PA: Stackpole Books, 1968.

Schneider, Dorothy, and Carl J. Schneider. *An Eyewitness History of Slavery in America: From Colonial Times to the Civil War.* New York: Checkmark Books, 2001.

Smith, John David, ed. *Black Soldiers in Blue: African American Troops in the Civil War Era.* Chapel Hill: University of North Carolina Press, 2002.

Tisdale, D. A. *Soldiers of the Virginia Colony 1607–1699.* Richmond, VA: Dietz, 2000.

Todd, Frederick P. *American Military Equipage 1851–1872,* Vol. 1. Providence, RI: Company of Military Historians, 1974.

Wakin, Edward. *Black Fighting Men in U.S. History.* New York: Lothrop, Lee and Shepard, 1971.

COLIN WOODWARD

**MINES AND MINING.** The early engineering of mines reflected the same vernacular architectural traditions that slaveholders used to construct their houses, barns, and bridges and the building knowledge brought to the task by the slaves that were used in the mines' construction. But the sturdiness of any mine was determined solely by the laborers who worked there. In mines where slaves worked, not only were specialized mining tools used but also tools that would be familiar to anyone employed in the building trades. Slaves swung picks and hammered the ore from the mountains, driving their chisels in deep. They packed black powder, lit fuses, and ran through the dark to escape the iron and coal torn out of the ground by the explosives. They shoveled ore into wooden wheeled carts and drove them along wooden tracks toward the surface on their hands and knees, pushing with their heads, often traveling great distances before reaching a place to stand. Enslaved workers in coal mines used hand picks with four-inch steel bits set into the iron to tear the coal from the veins. Slaves did all the same hard dangerous work that freemen did, but they did it with fewer timbers to protect them, fewer expensive tools, and often little or no light to guide them through a dark world in which men and boys sometimes were lost forever.

The slave hire agreement and the insurance policy were the pieces of material culture that mattered most to a mine owner who employed slaves. Early mining was extremely dangerous, and this offered an opportunity for a mine owner to benefit from the insurance policy he most likely held to protect himself from an enslaved worker's death. A slave who died in the mines could bring a good profit to an owner; so safety, which was expensive, could be an even lower priority. A well-insured, hired-out slave digging ore might therefore be at a much higher risk of losing his life when his employer and owner had little incentive to keep him alive.

Slaves were involved in every aspect of the mining industry, although not in every mine. Some mine operators reasoned that the upper levels of production could be made more stable by training slaves for jobs as skilled craftsman, engineers, "machine drivers," and even superintendents. The tools of a slave in the mining industry ranged from the cooks' pots, pans, and ladles, through the carpenters' bow saws, squares, and hammers, right up to the supervisors' desks, ink blotters, and quills.

The extraction and processing of iron in 17th-century Virginia began at Jamestown as early as 1608, although there was never any large-scale production on the island. More promising was a site near Richmond that had the water power necessary to power the blast furnace and mills necessary for iron ore production. Falling Creek, as it was named, began operation in 1619–1620 and by 1622 was able to produce enough cast iron pigs to ship back to England.

The manufacture of iron, both in pigs and in finished products like firebacks and cast iron pots, was undertaken by ironmasters from Saugus, Massachusetts, (established in 1646) to the Berks County, Pennsylvania, Colebrookdale Furnace in 1720, to the Principio Furnace alongside Maryland's Patapsco River in 1715. All of them (except Saugus) eventually used both purchased and hired slaves to mine the ore, process it, and in some cases, supervise many aspects of the ironwork's operation. For those who dug the ore and ran the furnaces and mills, an ironworks was a dangerous and dirty place, and the risk of injury or death was great. And though highly skilled slaves may have had more freedom to move about the countryside, they, too, were subject to the discipline imposed by their owners.

Slaves in California's mid-19th-century Gold Rush were in a far more enviable position. First, the mining was safer. It was hard work but performed on the surface in the light of day. Second, the men in the gold fields may not have cared about slavery back home, but they were decidedly opposed to one man, the slave owner, getting what two men had dug. This anti-slavery attitude was found everywhere: among miners, masons, dentists, doctors, lawyers, judges, and others.

## FURTHER READING

Bezís-Selfa, John. "Planter Industrialists and Iron Oligarchs: A Comparative Prosopography of Early Anglo-American Ironmasters." *Business and Economic History* 22, no. 1 (Fall 1993): 62–70.

Bezís-Selfa, John. "A Tale of Two Ironworks: Slavery, Free Labor, Work, and Resistance in the Early Republic." *The William and Mary Quarterly*, Third Series, 56, no. 4 (October 1999): 677–700.

Dew, Charles B. *Bond of Iron: Master and Slave at Buffalo Forge*. New York: W. W. Norton, 1994.

Dew, Charles B. "David Ross and the Oxford Iron Works: A Study of Industrial Slavery in the Early Nineteenth-Century South." *The William and Mary Quarterly*, Third Series, 31, no. 2 (April 1974): 189–224.

Lapp, Rudolph M. "Negro Rights Activities in Gold Rush California." *California Historical Society Quarterly* 45, no. 1 (March 1966): 3–20.

Lewis, Ronald L. *Black Coal Miners in America: Race, Class, and Community Conflict, 1780–1980*. Lexington: University of Kentucky Press, 1987.

WELLS TWOMBLY II

**MIRRORS.** Mirrors are in many ways the most magical of consumer goods. Before the 19th century, they most often were called looking glasses, and they were to look into and look beyond at one's face into other worlds. Mirrors have been important parts of myths and folk cultures. Mirrors were owned or used by enslaved men and women. "Negro Jack" purchased a mirror from Virginia merchant William Allason in 1761; the slave woman Sukey bartered for one from Virginia merchant John Hook in 1774. The small mirror of Casy Minnott (1732–1822), who lived in Concord, Massachusetts, is now in the Concord Museum as an example of a mirror owned by a slave. Her mirror is 6.5 by 5.5 inches and framed in simple pine ogee moldings painted black and nailed together. The foil backing of the glass is mostly gone. A folded piece of paper, taken from a penmanship practice book and inserted in the back, tells the story of its ownership. A label on the back written in 1861, the first year of the Civil War, by a relative, Cumming Davis, records some of Minnott's prayer, asking for blessing and long life.

Archaeologists have recovered mirror glass from numerous **slave quarters** throughout the South, including Carter's Grove near Williamsburg. Three pieces of mirror glass were uncovered there from **subfloor pits**, a feature thought by many to be the best place to recover personal slave items. Indeed, these pits also contained knives and forks, pins, and rum bottle glass, all items that could be purchased in the 18th-century cornucopia of consumer goods and all potentially playing part in the spiritual world of African Americans.

Probably known from the Egyptians, round mirrors spread through the ancient worlds of Greece, Asia, and China. By the Middle Ages, they could take multiple forms: flat, curved (to distort shapes), burning (to create fire), and "magic" (to serve in sorcerer's kits). Exotic items, they were small, made of metal or crystalline or blown glass and framed and backed with precious materials. Nonetheless, the image they might produce was crude.

The discovery in Venice of crystalline glass and the technique of glass blowing into cylinders revolutionized the manufacturing of mirrors. Twelfth-century northern Europeans developed the method of putting a lead backing on the greenish glass of the cylinders. Although the results were still quite imperfect, prices began to drop. Larger plates made mirrors possible for wall decoration, and their expense was soon measured in their size, not precious materials.

Although they became more common, mirrors still carried deep symbolism. When artists of the Renaissance began to master the powers of light and its depiction, mirrors were a favorite artistic trick as iconographic devices with deep moral play. Artists often used mirrors as symbolic icons for vanity, and in Europe women were naturally to blame for such weakness. If, on the one hand, mirrors denoted self-admiration and perhaps false images, by the 18th-century Enlightenment, mirrors were depicted as proof of the ability to see with clarity, and hence were signs of science and rationality. With these technological improvements, mirrors became inexpensive and were available as hand-held or wall-hanging mirrors or as large wall mirrors for interior decoration. In one late-18th-century Virginia store operated by John Hook, even the poor could buy a small, perhaps imperfect reflection of a face for a mere two and a half shillings, whereas the wealthiest planter could enjoy the largest looking glass at a cost of more than three pounds.

Reflective surfaces such as mirrors signified a number of ideas in African religion and divination. The physical properties of mirrors led to doubled possibilities: to view one's self (to critically examine, to preen, to decorate) and to reflect (to heighten available light and to flash or flicker when turned). Western commodities like mirrors functioned in a BaKongo ritual tradition, which valued light and transparency, enabling sight into another world. The transparency and reflective quality of particular beetle wings began to be extended and intensified with manufactured goods; the beetle's wings fused the glitter of the spirit with the ability to see to another world through flight. As mirrors became important trade items to West Africa, glittering objects such as mirrors soon became a fundamental component of African American spiritualism. Mirrors could, in essence, capture, attract, or repel a spirit, and these qualities played out in numerous superstitions and customs.

European mirrors were important trade goods, recorded, for example, in the areas occupied by multiple subgroups of the Igbo people in West Africa. Red cloth, velvet, and mock and coral **beads** were essential trade items, followed in importance by looking glasses and ornamental glass snuffboxes. A European trader recorded that the Ebo manifested a great desire for rum, small looking glasses, and cowries. One trader presented at least a dozen looking glasses as gifts to dignitaries on his route to the continent's interior. When visiting King Obie of the Igbo, the traders prepared a long list of gifts, including an armchair and a large looking glass. Upon being seated in the chair, the king called for a looking glass, examined himself in it, then burst out laughing—repeatedly looking and laughing.

Few such examples of mirrors in use are recorded in these early trade narratives. But other evidence indicates how mirrors were integrated into ritual practices at least by the 19th century. Titled African women carried mirrors in finely carved wooden frames as display items in their ceremonial installation, although use was not restricted to them. European missionaries penetrated the interior at Onitsha, where an Igbo trading group had been active for a century. A phrase "the glass is very dazzling" is recorded in the ex-slave Samuel Crowther's (1809–1891) translations of Douda in 1854. When he returned a few years later, Crowther recorded a telling story. The traders had earlier given a mirror to an African. The man sadly related how he was a great doctor, pretending to drive out *moa* (spirits) for which the people showed him much respect. One day, wanting to exhibit wonders to them, he told his people that he had been to see Beke or Oibo, his moa (spirit) companions, and they had given him a wonderful reflector. He placed it among his Ofos (markers of divinity) and smashed it to pieces. He wanted another mirror to continue his power.

Other African groups developed special uses for reflective glass. Very small pieces of glass used to produce glittering light effects probably spread from the East. Moorish conquests took mirrors throughout the Mediterranean. Persians, Indians, and Africans all used tiny fragments of silvered glass. As a result of this blending of cultures, northern Africans used the powers of the reflection of light to protect people and places from the "evil eye." Mirrors would flow into Western Africa as European trade goods and they ultimately would take on multiple layered meanings.

These patterns continued in America. In the 19th- and 20th-century South, mirrors functioned in several distinctive ways. Mirrors and black cats were both necessary to create some particular **charms** or nkisi. Gaining special powers with mirrors required a set of special conditions for activation, such as sacred materials (**grave** soil) and time (midnight). For example, one early 20th-century oral history informant suggested burying a mirror at a crossroad, then digging it up in three days. He cautioned not to look at it without having a cat or dog look first. Seeing a vision and having supernatural powers would then be possible. Another informant suggested going into the graveyard with a mirror and a new pair of scissors. At exactly midnight, if one called out the name of the deceased and dropped the scissors, the reflection of the dead man would appear, and through the reflection of the dead, one could ask him questions. The scissors meanwhile would cut away at one's fear.

Mirrors were strongly linked with black cats. With some variation, the custom required catching a black cat and boiling him. When the flesh is off the bones, each bone is put in the mouth. When the "lucky bone" is in one's mouth, one's image will disappear in the mirror. What is most compelling—although too tentative to be more than speculative—is that similar beliefs about lucky bones (from unlucky cats) are recorded in both black and white North Carolinian stories. But only mirrors are recorded for black informants.

Buried outside or standing next to the front door, mirrors take on protective powers and can flash back evil spirits from portals or boundaries. That flash of spirit has been documented extensively in modern African American **yard** art. Broken dishes, lamps, glassware, mirrors, and tin foil all have been recorded on African and African American graves. Known as early as the 19th century in North Carolina, the ragman in traditional jonkannu (musical street masquerade) ritual play wore small bits of mirror, as well as beads and bells, on the streaming rags of his costume.

The power to link the dead to the living also could be dangerous. If a mirror sees a corpse, it will capture that spirit. Hence, mirrors must be covered in the presence of a corpse. In a late-18th-century Connecticut needlework picture by Prudence Punderson, a covered mirror hangs over a coffin. Covering mirrors in the presence of death is a custom found a century later in North Carolina folklore, practiced by black and white mourners. The next person reflected in the mirror after the corpse will die. This illustrates a case in which the custom before burial is probably European in origin, although the treatment of the grave after death is probably African. Mirrors again express that duality.

Mirrors have a deep resonance in African and African diasporic culture, even as traditions evolve and take different specific forms. For example, the Mami Wati worship tradition is alive and flourishing in Africa and creolized Caribbean and Central American cultures. Mami Wata is a water spirit that can bring good luck and monetary gain; the mirror is considered by some to be the female goddess's most prized possession. The reflective surface covers the boundaries of water and land and allows special seeing of the future. But Mami Wata's mirror also is a reminder of critical preening and false pride of humans, a morality much like the earlier Renaissance European ideas about female vanity and false earthly pride.

Enslaved African diasporic peoples likely used mirrors for sight: to clean dirt from a face, admire a **ribbon**, or style **hair**. Perhaps they also were heirs and makers of spiritual practices that used mirrors to protect and harm others. Archaeologists and architectural historians have found shrines and "witchery kits" hidden in houses and cellars. Evidence points to shrines devoted to water spirits like Mama Wati. Some objects, like knife handles, have been carved and cut in ways similar to Kongo **cosmograms** and other forms of African expression.

All this evidence builds a remarkably strong case for spiritual practices in which material objects like mirrors were activated long after slaves were imported from Africa or generations after setting foot on African soil. Mirrors likely played an important role in the lives of the enslaved whenever they could manage to own and use them.

*See also* Cemeteries; Fetishes.

FURTHER READING

Drewal, Henry John. *Mami Wata: Arts for Water Spirits in Africa and its Diasporas*. Los Angeles: Fowler Museum at UCLA, 2008.

Gundaker, Grey, and Judith McWillie. *The Spirit of African American Yard Work*. Knoxville: University of Tennessee Press, 2005.

Hyatt, Harry Middleton. *Hoodoo–Conjuration–Witchcraft–Rootwork: Beliefs Accepted by Many Negroes and White Persons These Being Orally Recorded Among Blacks and Whites*. Hannibal, MO: Western, 1970.

Martin, Ann Smart. *Buying into the World of Goods: Early Consumers in Backcountry Virginia*. Baltimore, MD: Johns Hopkins University Press, 2008.

Puckett, Newbell Miles. *Folk Beliefs of the Southern Negro*. Chapel Hill: University of North Carolina Press, 1926.

Samford, Patricia. *Subfloor Pits and the Archaeology of Slavery in Colonial Virginia*. Tuscaloosa: University of Alabama Press, 2007.

Thompson, Robert Farris. *Flash of the Spirit: African and Afro-American Art and Philosophy*. New York: Vintage, 1984.

ANN SMART MARTIN

**MULES.** Mules are the draft animals most closely associated with the rural antebellum South and with **cotton** cultivation in particular. They are hybrids, the result of the union of a male ass (a "jack") and a female horse ("mare"), and can be either male or female. The mating of a female ass and a male horse is much less common. Mules were common animals in the ancient world, used as riding animals by kings and commoners alike, pulling carts and wagons, and used as pack animals. Breeding of the American mule began in the 18th century when plantation owners like George Washington imported different breeds of male asses from Europe to incorporate their most desirable traits in the mules bred here.

As a result of this breeding, some mules were particularly suited for specific uses and locations: **rice** farming, cotton cultivation, **sugar** plantations, mining, hauling, and farming. A breed that was suitable for one use was seldom suitable for another because of differences in size, weight, and temperament, so it was important to acquire the right mule for the task at hand. Over a period of about 20 to 30 years, mules gradually replaced **horses** and oxen as the draft animal of choice on Southern plantations. They were considered a more "modern" animal as compared with horses and oxen and were particularly suited to the agricultural reforms adopted by many Southern farmers and plantation owners, which included new types of plows and other agricultural implements and improved methods of plowing and land use. Even though horses and oxen continued to outnumber mules well into the 19th century, by the beginning of the Civil War, mules were found in all Southern states and many Northern ones as well.

An analysis of the information collected by the federal government in the years before the Civil War indicates that most of the plantation owners who owned mules were also slave owners. For these men and women, owning mules represented a major step in embracing progressive farming methods, and they had the enslaved manpower necessary to implement them. Therefore, it is not surprising that, at the war's conclusion, mules continued to grow in importance as the primary draft animal on Southern farms and former plantations, now worked by the black sharecroppers who were the formerly enslaved. The formerly enslaved men and women knew the animals, knew how to take care of them, and were familiar with the best ways to use them.

Mules figure prominently in one of the most persistent myths of the Civil War: the promise of "forty acres and a mule" for each freed slave family. This belief stems from a misunderstanding of Gen. William T. Sherman's Special Field Orders No. 15, issued January 16, 1865, which directed that land on the Sea Islands of Georgia and Florida be set aside for the use of the freed slaves who were following Sherman's army. Sherman ordered that the head of each black household receive no more than 40 acres and be lent—not given—a farm animal to work the land, but the terms of the distribution of the land, as well as how each household head was to receive a deed to it were left unspecified. The legislation creating the Freedman's Bureau also included language allowing freed slaves to lease no more than 40 acres from the Bureau, with an option to purchase the land at some unspecified date in the future. But the restoration of land to former Confederates pardoned by President Andrew Johnson put an end, for the most part, to this land redistribution. Even the Southern Homestead Act, passed in 1865 and repealed in 1876, only succeeded in getting a relative handful of former slaves settled on their own land, most of which was in Florida. But the symbol of "forty acres and a mule" endures as a reminder of the importance of land and the animal power necessary to work it that freed slaves so greatly desired.

## FURTHER READING

Ellenberg, George. *Mule South to Tractor South: Mules, Machines, and the Transformation of the Cotton South*. Tuscaloosa: University of Alabama Press, 2007.

"Forty Acres and a Mule," Henry George School of Social Science. At www.landandfree dom.org/ushistory/us15.htm.

Sherman, William Tecumseh. "Forty Acres and a Mule: Special Field Order No. 15," Teaching American History. At http://teachingamericanhistory.org/library/index.asp?document=545.

Smith, John David. "The Enduring Myth of 'Forty Acres and a Mule.'" *The Chronicle Review* 49, no. 24, February 21, 2003, B11. At http://h-net.msu.edu/cgi-bin/logbrowse.pl?trx=vx &list=H-Slavery&month=0302&week=c&msg=8PoiSd/kHvfYFICVKwWP9A&user=&pw=

MARTHA B. KATZ-HYMAN

# N

**NAILS.** Nails, which have been in use in various cultures for the past several thousand years, are the most commonly used fasteners employed in building construction and are widely used as fasteners in applications such as the manufacture of furniture, **shoes**, ships, wagons, and musical instruments. Nails are made in different forms for different uses, but they all have a point, a shank, and a head. The point allows the nail to pierce materials being fastened together, the shank provides surface area for friction to hold parts together, and the head provides a broader surface for driving with a hammer and securing the parts together.

Historically, nails most often were made of iron, or more recently, steel, copper, aluminum, and other materials. Blacksmiths periodically made nails, although commercial production of nails was carried out by specialists called nailsmiths or nailers. The smith softened bars of iron with heat, and then formed the point under a hammer by turning the bar back and forth between hammer blows. The hammer reduced the width and thickness, increasing the length and forming a point. Hammering the material on the corner of the anvil developed a distinct transition that formed the shank of the nail and determined the nail's length. The material was cut where the bar was still full size and held in a small heading tool, with the small lump of original-size iron used to form the head. The work was quite repetitive, but with repetition came efficiency. Although a newcomer to the trade might make only one nail every few minutes, a skilled worker could make two to three nails in a single minute.

Nails were produced in large quantity by employing many thousands of nailers in industrial settings and distributing the nails widely over multiple markets. Many of the nails used in colonial America were the products of nail makers working in two or three industrial cities in England, whose products were shipped to North America and sold by merchants in coastal cities. As settlement moved farther west in mainland North America, overland shipping of cargo added considerably to cost, prompting local manufacture.

Enslaved men and boys were employed in nailmaking throughout the 18th century and well into the 19th. In 1759, Allan Macrae, a Virginia merchant, advertised in the Annapolis *Maryland Gazette* for his runaway slave, Dick, whom he described as "by Trade a compleat Wheelwright, and so much of a Smith, as to make the Nails, and shoe those he makes." Almost 20 years later, in 1777, the executors of the estate of John Dalton of Alexandria, Virginia, advertised in the *Virginia Gazette* that, as part of dissolving the mercantile and shipping business of Carlyle & Dalton, which had its own blacksmith shop on the Alexandria waterfront, they were going to sell "8 NEGRO MEN, six of which are good smiths. They have served regular times to the trade, and do all kinds of ship and planters work, shoe horses &c. One of them has been used to gun work, and is a good nailor."

Another factor promoting local production was the onset of the Revolutionary War. The war interrupted trade with England, creating shortages of manufactured goods and creating opportunities for local workmen to fill the void. James Anderson, a Williamsburg blacksmith and armorer advertised in the *Virginia Gazette* for "a good blacksmith and nailer that is capable of acting as a foreman in my shops."

In later correspondence with the State of Virginia, he stated, "I have nine lads that's nailers, which the state may have for one year at 2/3 specia per day, the lads must be fed clothed washing and lodging fitting for apprentices. Eight of those lads shall make twenty five thousand nails per week." In the first decade of the 19th century in Baltimore, Maryland, Bernard Coskery, Enoch Betts, and Richardson Stewart, major manufacturers of nails, all employed enslaved men and boys.

In 1794, Thomas Jefferson decided to add nailmaking to his blacksmithing operation to supplement his income so that he could improve his agricultural lands. The workers were almost exclusively enslaved boys, whom he started off at the work when they were 10 years old. As he noted in his *Farm Book*, "Children till 10. years old to serve as nurses. From 10. to 16. the boys make nails, the girls spin. At 16. go into the ground or learn trades." He expected that, after six months of training, a 10-year-old boy could make 500 nails a day, and that, after a year, that same boy could make 800 nails a day. By the time these enslaved boys were 13 or 14 years old, they could make 1,000 nails a day, and at various times, the nailery's production averaged 10,000 nails per day. Jefferson kept track of every aspect of his nailmaking operation, measuring out each nail rod in the morning and then weighing the amount of nails made by each worker at the end of the day. Isaac Jefferson, who was born and grew up at Monticello, was among the most prolific and efficient of the nailmakers; from January through June 1796, he produced about 1,000 pounds of nails in six sizes. Isaac was taught to be a blacksmith, for like most of Jefferson's enslaved boys who worked in the nailery, Jefferson used those months and years of nailmaking to decide which trade would be suitable for each boy. Isaac became free by at least 1847 and remained a practicing blacksmith throughout his life.

Following the Revolutionary War, new methods of manufacture were introduced to nailmaking to make American production competitive with England. In 1796, Thomas Jefferson purchased a nailmaking machine, hoping to streamline nail manufacturing and increase his production. Cut nails were made using shears to cut wedge-shaped pieces off of the end of a flat, rectangular bar, with the width of the bar becoming the length of the nail. A separate hammering operation produced a head at the broad end of the wedge. Later machines were designed to produce the nail and form the head in a single operation. Between the handmade and the cut nails made by his enslaved nailmakers, Jefferson was able to make a profit at the business for several years. Decreased demand caused by labor and management problems at the nailery and competition from cheaper imported nails forced the end of his efforts by 1823. Wire nails began to be manufactured in the mid-19th century and are the most common in use in the 21st century.

Nails were used for nonutilitarian purposes as well. For enslaved men and women, nails could be used in a variety of African-derived rituals that could provide protection or healing. Perhaps the best-known example of this type of usage was found at the Levi Jordan plantation in Brazoria County, Texas. Among the materials found at several of the cabins excavated on the plantation were objects associated with BaKongo healing rituals and other spiritual practices, and among these objects were cut nails. The iron in the nails gave spiritual power to the user and in combination with other objects could impart healing or strength.

*See also* Charms; Conjure Bags; Fetishes.

FURTHER READING

Brown, Kenneth L. "Interwoven Traditions: Archaeology of the Conjurer's Cabins and the African American Cemetery at the Jordan and Frogmore Manor Plantations." In *Places of Cultural Memory: African Reflections on the American Landscape*, 99–114. Conference Proceedings, May 9–12, 2001, Atlanta, Georgia. Washington, DC: National Park Service, 2001. At www.nps.gov/history/crdi/conferences/AFR_99-114_KBrown.pdf.

Jefferson, Thomas, and Robert C. Baron. *The Garden and Farm Books of Thomas Jefferson*. Golden, CO: Fulcrum, 1987.

"Nailmaking," Thomas Jefferson Encyclopedia, Monticello. At http://wiki.monticello.org/mediawiki/index.php/Nailmaking#_ref-17.

"Rural Blacksmith: Adventures in traditional blacksmithing from Field's Blacksmith Shop," Farmers' Museum, Cooperstown, New York. At http://ruralblacksmith.blogspot.com/2009/05/tough-as-nails.html.

Singleton, Theresa A. "The Archaeology of Slave Life." In *Images of the Recent Past: Readings in Historical Archaeology*, edited by Charles E. Orser, 141–165. Walnut Creek, CA: AltaMira Press, 1996.

Stanton, Lucia. *Free Some Day: The African-American Families of Monticello*. Charlottesville, VA: Thomas Jefferson Foundation, 2000.

Whitman, T. Stephen. *The Price of Freedom: Slavery and Manumission in Baltimore and Early National Maryland*. Lexington: University of Kentucky Press, 1997.

KENNETH SCHWARZ

**NEGRO CLOTH.** Negro **cloth** was the generic name given to the coarse woolen fabric used for clothes for slaves. The cloth came in various forms, such as "plains," so-called to reflect the unadorned weave of the material, or the misleadingly named "cottons," which actually were woolens whose nap had been raised or "cottened" to give a more even finish to the cloth.

Slave **clothing** had two basic elements. **Linen** was worn next to the skin; outerwear was made from Negro cloth. Cheapness and durability were essential. Negro cloth was also drab. Much of it was "white," that is, uncolored, and those pieces that had been dyed came in a limited number of shades. This was deliberate. Masters were hostile to the expression of individuality by slaves through the use of vivid colors,

## Lowell Clothes

In Texas, Mariah Snyder and her family always wore "Lowell" cloth (also known as "negro cloth") named after the Massachusetts town where it was manufactured:

Massa Sam live in a great big, ceiled house, and had plenty land and niggers. The quarters was logs and any kind beds we could git. We wore lowell clothes and I never seed no other kind of dress till after surrender. We et meat and collards and cornbread and rough grub, and they biled all the victuals in a big, black pot what hung on a rack in the kitchen fireplace. We had red russet, flat shoes and no stockin's, but in winter we made wool panties to wear on our legs.

*Source:* George P. Rawick, ed. *The American Slave: Texas Narratives*, Vol. 5, Parts 3 & 4. Westport, CT: Greenwood Press, 1972.

sometimes prohibiting the wearing of fancy fabrics in colonial slave codes. It was something that the enslaved constantly sought to subvert, often using a Negro cloth garment as a blank canvas to which vegetable dyes could be applied or by adding scraps of illicitly obtained material to their costume. An Angolan-born slave in 18th-century South Carolina was described as embellishing his "white negro cloth" suit with "some blue between every seam."

Negro cloth invariably was imported from Britain before the American Revolution. It was manufactured in the wet, cold, and impoverished uplands whose inhabitants eked out additional income by **spinning** and weaving **wool** in domestic workshops. Mountainous mid-Wales was an important center, hence "Welsh plains," as was the Lake District in the northwest of England, which was the source of "Kendall **cotton**." In the 18th century, tremendous quantities were shipped across the Atlantic. Fitting out the entire captive population of British North America required several million yards of fabric. One Georgia planter told his London supplier in 1764 "that 5 yds of Plains usually makes a mans jacket & Breeches or a womans gown." It was taken for granted that a year's wear and tear would reduce slave clothing to tatters, so fresh imports were needed every autumn to see slaves through the winter.

In the post-Revolutionary decades, American textile production progressed. Many colonial planters had had their female slaves trained to sew Negro cloth into the jackets, breeches, and skirts needed for plantation use. After the war, slave owners bought spinning equipment and looms to allow them to substitute slave-made homespun for British imports. More important, the emergence of a mechanized woolen textiles sector in New England in the early 19th century allowed U.S. industrialists to oust their British rivals. By the 1820s, Yankee firms, such as the Peace Dale Manufacturing Company of South Kingstown, Rhode Island, were marketing their goods aggressively across the South and doing so with great success. Antebellum slaves were clothed by the North.

FURTHER READING

Baumgarten, Linda. *What Clothes Reveal: The Language of Clothing in Colonial America.* New Haven, CT: Yale University Press, 2002.

Stachiw, Myron O. *Negro Cloth: Northern Industry and Southern Slavery.* Boston: Boston National Historical Park, 1981.

CHRIS EVANS

**NETS AND SEINES.** Net and seines were used by slaves for fishing, both for commercial purposes for their owners and, on a smaller scale, to supplement their own diets. Nets allowed people to catch much larger quantities of **fish** than they could using **fishing poles**. A seine is a specialized type of fishing net, with floats on its upper edge and weights on the lower one, which cause it to hang vertically in the water. The seine would be dragged through the water, either pulled by fishermen on foot or in **boats**. Typically, the leading lines on one end of a seine were tied to a tree or wooden piling on the shore, while the net was taken by boat out into the water. As the boat followed a semicircular path paralleling the shore, the seine gradually was placed in the water. The other leading line was rowed to people on the shore, who would begin pulling in the seine, while others held the top of the net to keep it from collapsing and allowing the fish to escape. The catch was removed by hand, before being placed in **baskets**, in readiness for processing.

Made of twine and sometimes covered with liquid coal or wood tar for protection, nets and seines often could be quite large. The earliest seines known to have been purchased from England for use at George Washington's (1732–1799) home, Mount Vernon, in the early 1760s, were a pair, each measuring 210 feet long and 20 feet deep, made of small, one-inch mesh. After determining that this size was too deep for use in the Potomac River, Washington next ordered a longer seine, to allow the slaves to go farther out into the river, but one that was much less deep so that the net would not get torn up from debris on the bottom of the river. By 1771, he ordered the largest seine of all: it was 450 feet long, 10 feet deep in the middle, and tapered to 8 feet at the ends. The corks along the top were placed 2.5 feet apart, and the lead weights along the bottom had five feet between each. The hauling lines were 2,400 feet long. For Washington, as for many planters in the 18th century, the fisheries attached to their plantations were a major source of income and provided food to feed the slaves and generate extra income.

Slaves are known to have used seines for their own purposes. In 1760, the slaves at Mount Vernon asked for permission to borrow Washington's seine, which he allowed them to do. Years later, Elias Thomas, who grew up as a slave in antebellum North Carolina, recalled fishing in local rivers, sometimes using hooks and lines, but also making use of seines, at times when those bodies of water were low. Sylvia King, another former slave who was interviewed during the Great Depression, remembered that the older men and boys on the plantation spent their nights whittling a wide variety of useful objects, including needles for making nets for the seines.

FURTHER READING

Howell, Donna Wyant, comp. *I Was a Slave: True Life Stories Dictated by Former American Slaves in the 1930's.* Book 2: *The Lives of Slave Men.* Washington, DC: American Legacy Books, 2004.

Hurmence, Belinda, ed. *My Folks Don't Want Me to Talk about Slavery: Twenty-one Oral Histories of Former North Carolina Slaves*. Winston-Salem, NC: John F. Blair, Publisher, 1984.

Leach, Donald B. "George Washington: Waterman-Fisherman, 1760–1799. *Yearbook: The Historical Society of Fairfax County, Virginia* 28 (2001–2002): 1–28.

MARY V. THOMPSON

**NURSERIES AND NURSEMAIDS.** Increasingly over the antebellum era, enslaved infants were taken away from their mothers for much of the day and placed under the care of nursemaids, most of whom were children themselves. In turn, the caretakers were supervised by one or more adults, sometimes an older woman who had given birth to a large number of children but often someone—usually a woman—whose frailty or disability prevented her from engaging in more productive work. Adults whose tasks left them time to check periodically on the youngsters also were placed in the position of supervisor, and at times, the mistress or another member of the owning family looked in on them. The cook, in particular, was singled out as someone who could keep an eye on youngsters while doing double-duty in the kitchen, but many gardeners, seamstresses, and other workers kept watch over youngsters while going about their chores. More than one person might offer supervision. While the cook prepared meals, the dairy maid or mistress might check on the children, for example.

Although most nursemaids watched other slaves, some were recruited to care for an owner's children, an act that exposed them to very different material conditions of living, expectations of childrearing, and greater levels of training. Many of these nursemaids were young and subject to close scrutiny by household slaves and members of the slave-owning family who watched to ensure they met the exacting standards set for them.

In earlier times, enslaved mothers kept their infants and young children close, stopping work now and then to tend them as the need arose, with the help of older siblings and anyone else at hand. Slaveholders had long selected enslaved children as companions for their sons and daughters and expected maids to wash their children's bodies and **clothing**, prepare and feed them their meals, and keep an eye on them indoors and out, night and day. As **cotton** planting expanded across the South and plantations increased in size in the early years of the new nation, slaveholders pushed workers to greater efficiencies, and an increasing number of them established day nurseries for enslaved children in the belief they could keep them safe and well while sending all able-bodied adults, including mothers, to the field or other work sites to labor without the distraction of having youngsters nearby. At the same time, greater attention was paid to training children at young ages to work as nursemaids in the owner's home.

Slave parents watched the developments with trepidation. For parents, a child represented a chance to love and be loved, as well as a potential set of extra hands to help families carry out tasks of daily living. Raising children gave parents respite from the dehumanization of servitude and a cultural space in which they could resist the psychological dominion of slaveholders. Children signified hope that their people

---

**Nursemaid's Story**

William McWhorter's mother was a nursemaid in Georgia:

Dere warn't never no let-up when it come to wuk. When slaves come in from de fields atter sundown and tended de stock and et supper, de mens still had to shuck corn, mend hoss collars, cut wood, and sich lak; de 'omans mended clothes, spun thread, wove cloth, and some of 'em had to go up to de big house and nuss de white folks' babies. One night my ma had been nussin' one of dem white babies, and atter it dozed off to sleep she went to lay it in its little bed. De child's foot cotch itself in Marse Joe's galluses dat he had done hung on de foot of de bed, and when he heared his baby cry Marse Joe woke up and grabbed up a stick of wood and beat ma over de head 'til he 'most kilt her. Ma never did seem right atter dat and when she died she still had a big old knot on her head.

*Source:* George P. Rawick, ed. *The American Slave: Georgia Narratives,* Vol. 13. Westport, CT: Greenwood Press, 1972.

---

would survive physically and maintain connections of culture and kinship through ascending and descending generations. Enslaved parents wanted to raise their children according to their notions of proper procedures.

Slaveholders were determined to wrest control of infants from enslaved parents for a variety of reasons. After the U.S. Congress acted in 1807 to end the international slave trade the following year, slaveholders understood that slavery could continue only if children born in bondage survived to adulthood. Without new generations of workers to take the place of older ones who died, the slave system that had been evolving on the North American mainland since the 17th century would die out. Some Americans thought it should. By the mid-19th century, slaveholders found themselves on the defensive. They said that they acted as the stewards of slaves, for whom the slaveholders only had their best interests at heart. Ill, injured, and dying children hardly fit the paternalistic image slaveholders hoped to put forward, which encouraged them to take an interest in childcare arrangements. In the days before the discovery of antibiotics and modern knowledge of germs and bacteria, children fell ill and died in large numbers. Accidents too took their toll. Infant and child mortality rates were particularly egregious among the enslaved population.

Changing attitudes about why children became ill or were injured in accidents encouraged a shift in the way children were cared for throughout the nation. Whereas once people had attributed death and disease to fate or providence, now they attributed such outcomes to neglect or ignorance. The new way of thinking indicted adults who did not supervise children closely enough. Slaveholders—ever willing to blame parents, particularly mothers, for the poor outcomes associated with enslaved children's health—concluded that they should make other arrangements for ensuring their welfare.

The human impulse that encourages concern for other people, particularly children too young to fend for themselves, also played a role in slaveholder decision making, as did fear of what their parents might do if the children were neglected. Mistreatment of children might roil relations with adult slaves who could protest by slowing the pace of work, damaging property, threatening owners with physical harm, or withdrawing from the workforce. By law and custom, slaveholders could use violence or the threat of violence to make slaves do the owner's bidding, but pushed too hard, enslaved people sometimes engaged in actions detrimental to their owner's welfare. The constant use of violence interfered with the smooth operation of plantations, farms, and households and called into question the slaveholders' claim that enslaved people fared well under their paternalistic rule. Slaveholders thus favored a system of childcare that would keep youngsters safe, satisfy parents that their children were not being neglected, and consume few human or material resources. Earlier practices prevailed after 1807 on small farms and in households that did not employ many slaves, but the use of nurseries and nursemaids increased on large slaveholdings.

Some planters set aside a cabin or part of a larger building for infants and young children. Cabins and other structures tended to be cramped, dark, and smoke-filled. Some of the buildings set aside for childcare also housed sick slaves, a situation that exposed both infants and young caretakers to disease. In cooler weather, keeping infants warm and dry posed a challenge because owners rarely allocated them more than two sets of clothing or more than one blanket. In good weather, everyone might venture outside where unclad or lightly clad infants could be kept clean and dry more easily.

Even before the importance of sterilizing bottles for infants was recognized, everyone knew that a mother's milk was the best means of ensuring an infant's survival. Consequently, a new mother stayed with or near her baby for about a month following the birth. After this period of lying-in, mothers returned to productive or domestic labor in the owner's field, house, or yard, returning to breastfeed at intervals that grew further apart as the infant became capable of consuming supplemental foods and of being weaned. Mothers who visited the nursery checked on the nursemaids as well as the babies.

Attention given to infants in a communal nursery was more regimented than the care provided by individual mothers. Mothers preferred that a child receive attention as the need arose, but groups of children took their meals and baths and received preventative health care when supervising adults found time for them. Former slaves who had been cared for in day nurseries tended to especially remember feedings that resembled those of barn animals. Slops, perhaps cornbread mixed with buttermilk or **pot likker**, which was a broth made from cooking greens, were set out in troughs at which small children fed either with hands or **shells** used for spoons.

Nurseries were established to serve the needs of infants under the age of two or three. Any older children present helped care for children younger than themselves. The only requirement for the job of nursemaid was that a boy or girl be strong enough to lift a baby. A big part of a nursemaid's job was keeping an infant quiet and out of the way of the adult in charge, who could be engaged with other work or who might be too infirm to carry out many of the physical tasks of childcare. Boys and girls used time-honored ways of accomplishing this task: confining the infant to lap or arms, rocking the infant where hand-hewn cradles were available, or stuffing a milk-soaked rag or a piece of animal skin in the baby's mouth to encourage sucking. All posed dangers to the infant, and many an older child was blamed when a younger one wandered too near a fire, fell out of a cradle, or choked on a homemade pacifier. Infants tend to sleep much of the day, which provided some respite from constant watchfulness on the part of youthful nursemaids, but sleeping arrangements also posed a hazard. Most youngsters slept on **pallets** made of coarse cloth stuffed with straw, which had the advantage of being easy to clean and dry but which failed to keep an infant from rolling around on the floor and coming near the fireplace and other dangers. Enslaved children who cared for an owner's children did so in the owner's home, where they were trained and closely watched by house slaves, the mistress, and other members of the slaveowner's family. Unlike nursemaids in the slave quarters, they had access to a great array of material goods to keep the children safe and entertained, including walkers, buggies, swings, and cradles. Children who minded infants in an owner's family tended to be older than nursemaids who tended enslaved babies. They were tried and tested with a particular infant and assigned the job of nursemaid only after they proved themselves capable of taking direction and carrying out the necessary chores. Corrections for dereliction of duty could be swift and harsh. Offenses for which young caretakers were punished included rocking an infant too hard, failing to keep a bonnet on a child's head when out of doors, falling asleep while on duty, and refusing to obey a command. As this list of faults suggests, nursemaids not only kept an eye on their charges but also received instruction on how to act the part of a house slave. Knowledge about how a particular task was to be performed was deemed important by owners, but so was the nursemaid's demeanor. All nursemaids had to please members of the slaveholding family, including the child being attended. An ideal nursemaid was competent in performing tasks, ranging from comforting a child who awoke during the night to bathing a youngster's feet before bedtime; demonstrated loyalty; and carried out orders with the proper subservience.

Nursemaids who did not please owners were corrected or—if errors were too frequent or egregious—dismissed and set to other tasks. Before it got to that point, however, slaveholders encouraged the development of a close relationship between their children and their nursemaid. Girls were paired up with girls and boys were paired with boys more often than not, although an older girl or woman might supervise the care of both. Punishments occurred, but privileges and treats also were used to promote behavior that masters sought in a nursemaid.

Because they interacted regularly with members of the white family, black nursemaids of white children had access to clothing, food, and toys unavailable to other young slaves. They were expected to bathe more frequently and wear a better quality of clothing than other enslaved children, whose clothing often took the form of a one-piece garment made of coarse fabric and likened to a shirt or shift depending on the gender of the child who wore it. In an owner's home, nursemaids wore garments resembling the clothing of their charges. They ate food that was similar to or the same as that consumed by the owner's children, and they joined in play involving **dolls**, rocking horses, balls, wagons, and other popular toys of the day. No one mistook the similarities for equality, however. The clothes of nursemaids often were hand-me-downs. The nursemaids ate leftovers from the slaveholding family's meals, and the rocking horse was put away after the owner's child tired of playing with it.

Nursemaids who worked in their owner's home were keenly aware of the differences between their access to material goods and that of the children they minded. As one former nursemaid put it, "they had dainties and we had crusts." Although former slaves sometimes recalled dramatic instances in which they learned that they held a different status from that of free children, nursemaids who lived in close contact with their owners recognized these distinctions from an early age. They learned on a daily basis to bathe in a separate tub from the one used by the owner's children, to drink from a separate glass, and to sleep on the floor rather than in bed with the child they minded. In games of pretend, they deferred to the wishes of the owner's child in deciding who played which part.

Service to the white family could mean separation from a black family. Slaveholders often chose nursemaids for their children from the sons and daughters of household servants, an arrangement that was convenient for everyone involved. Mothers and sometimes fathers would be around to help correct a child learning the exacting nature of servitude. Such arrangements were not always possible, however, and some youngsters were taken from their families in the quarter to wait on an owner's child. The physical distance might be close enough that nursemaids could return to the **slave quarter** at night or at least occasionally, but the cultural distance could prove difficult to bridge. Children, then and now notorious as tattletales, sometimes told things to one set of adults that the other did not want revealed. One child told her owner of an enslaved man's plan to run away; another informed her parents of a slaveholder's intention to sell a woman.

Young nursemaids, like the children they tended, grew up. For nursemaids in the owner's family, games gave way to adult chores, and training for the performance of domestic tasks intensified. Many of these nursemaids lived a lifetime serving their childhood companions, moving with them to new homes when they married and began families of their own. Slaveholders preferred that household help be knowledgeable about family preferences in everything from preparing favorite foods to washing garments and greeting guests. Grown-up nursemaids carried this knowledge with them as they moved into new households where domestic routines learned in childhood were replicated. Theories of childrearing suggested that slaves trained from young ages would be more loyal and become more skilled than others, and many young nursemaids grew up to become waiting women and valets. They sometimes took over the care of children in succeeding generations of slaveholding families as well. In fact, adult nursemaids frequently were discouraged from establishing their own families. When pregnancies occurred, as they sometimes did before an owner authorized the nursemaid to marry, owners reacted as though their authority to control slaves had been undermined.

*See also* Cooking and Cooks.

FURTHER READING

Schwartz, Marie Jenkins. *Born in Bondage: Growing Up Enslaved in the Antebellum South*. Cambridge, MA: Harvard University Press, 2001.

White, Deborah G. *Ar'n't I a Woman? Female Slaves in the Plantation South*. Rev. ed. New York: W. W. Norton and Company, 1999.

MARIE JENKINS SCHWARTZ

# O

**OKRA.** Okra (*Abelmoschus esculentus*) is a member of the mallow family, relished for its mucilaginous pods that thicken soups and **stews**. When picked young, it also serves as a crispy vegetable. Okra was brought to the Western Hemisphere by means of the slave trade and probably arrived in British North America through its cultural and trade relations with the Caribbean. It was a common garden crop in many of the societies along the West and Central African coast and known as *kanja* among the Wolof, *nkru* among the Twi speakers in what is now Ghana, *okwuru* (the etymological root for "okra") among the Igbo, and *quingumbo* (from which "**gumbo**" is derived) among the Mbundu of Angola. The English captain Hugh Crow (1765–1829) noted in 1792 that at the port of Bonny and throughout West Africa, there was no want of "ocra" and that it was "well known throughout the West Indies as an ingredient in making soup." The zoologist, Joachim Monteiro (1833–1878), writing about 19th-century Angola, described okra under cultivation and reported it being sold at **markets**. Okra was not only valued for its pods but also for its edible leaves and seeds. It was used as a medicinal plant, especially to ease the birthing process. Okra was documented by Sir Hans Sloane (1660–1753) in Jamaica in the late 17th century and was noted by Peter Kalm (1716–1779) in Philadelphia in the 1740s where he found it growing in city **gardens**, writing that it was "reckoned a dainty . . . especially by the Negroes." References to okra are scant in the mid-18th century, but by 1781, Thomas Jefferson (1743–1826) noted in his *Notes on the State of Virginia* that "ochra" was one of Virginia's garden crops. In the same decade, Luigi Castiglioni (1756–1832) noted that in Carolina Low Country blacks cultivated a plant "brought by Negroes from the west coast of Africa and is called okra by them." The okra that Kalm, Jefferson, and Castiglioni described being eaten was probably a variety resembling the heirlooms known as "Cowhorn" and "Stubby" as well as white and red varieties of the plant.

Okra made its debut in a cookbook with the 1824 publication of *The Virginia Housewife* by Mary Randolph (1762–1828). Given her instruction to make "ochra soup" in an earthenware pipkin, the dish appears to originate in some of the earliest black communities in the colonial Chesapeake and Low Country. Randolph included okra in several recipes—as a soup, stewed with butter, and stewed with tomatoes. Other period recipes suggest that enslaved African Americans and other blacks introduced whites of all classes to okra mixed with **rice**, later known as Limpin' Susan, which is the cousin dish of **Hoppin' John**, fried okra, and a variety of okra stews made with **fish** and crab, akin to recipes found along the Rice and Gold Coasts of West Africa. Cookbooks from Maryland to Louisiana provide dozens of recipes calling for the vegetable.

Enslaved blacks also sold roasted and ground okra seed as a coffee substitute as late as the Civil War. Perhaps the most important dish made with okra was gumbo, a rich stew made with a flour thickener called a *roux* in the French tradition in Louisiana and along the Tidewater and Low Country coasts. Okra gumbos typically omit filé powder, made from pulverized sassafras leaves, which are a contribution of the Choctaw Indians.

## FURTHER READING

Crow, Hugh. *Memoirs of the late Captain Hugh Crow of Liverpool, Comprising a Narrative of his life, together with descriptive sketches of Africa, particularly of Bonny, the manners and customs of the inhabitants, the production of the soil, and the trade of the country, to which are added anecdotes and observations of the Negro character.* London: F. Cass, 1970.

Grime, William E. *Ethno-Botany of the Black Americans.* Algonac, MI: Reference Publications, 1979.

Harris, Jessica B. *The Welcome Table: African American Heritage Cooking.* New York: Fireside, 1995.

Hatch, Peter J. "Thomas Jefferson's Favorite Vegetables." In *Dining at Monticello: In Good Taste and Abundance,* edited by Damon Fowler, 55–64. Chapel Hill: University of North Carolina Press, 2005.

Randolph, Mary. *The Virginia Housewife: With Historical Notes and Commentaries by Karen Hess.* Columbia: University of South Carolina Press, 1984.

Weaver, William Woys. *Heirloom Vegetable Gardening.* New York: Henry Holt and Company, 1997.

MICHAEL W. TWITTY

# P

**PALLETS.** Pallets were only one of many types of bedding used the by the enslaved. In 18th- and early 19th-century Tidewater Virginia and Maryland, they usually were made of a length of coarse **linen** sewed into a rectangle that was then stuffed with any one of a number of fillings—feathers, straw, or **corn** husks, for example—and then laid either on the floor of the building where an individual lived or on some kind of **bed** frame. As bedding, pallets were considered better than just **blankets** laid over straw and much better than blankets laid on a dirt or wood floor, but they were not as good as a mattress laid on a bed frame.

Pallets were the kind of bedding that Thomas Jefferson (1743–1826) directed his overseer, Richard Richardson, to give to Edward Gillette, an enslaved man who lost all of his possessions in a fire in February 1800. Jefferson mentioned a "hempen roll bed," which was probably a pallet made of coarse linen fabric. Jefferson's female slaves who married men owned by Jefferson could expect to be given "a pot and a bed." Again, this meant some kind of pallet made of linen. In 1798, Julian Niemcewicz (1758–1841), a Polish visitor to George Washington's (1732–1799) Mount Vernon, noted in the description of one of Washington's **slave quarters** and its residents that "[t]he husband and wife sleep on a mean [poor quality] pallet, the children on the ground."

Very often those individuals who worked in the master's house slept on pallets kept there so they could be available whenever they were needed. Delicia Patterson, born in Boonville, Missouri, in 1845, was 92 when she was interviewed for the Federal Writers' Project in the 1930s. Patterson remembered that she "did not even have to sleep in the cabins. I slept on a pallet in the bedrooms with old marse's children. I was a pet anywhere I worked, because I was always very neat and clean, and a good worker." D. Davis, about 85 years old when he was interviewed near Marvell, Arkansas, said, "En de last two or three years of de trubble I wuz big enuf ter be doin sum wuk, so dey tuk me in de big house fer ter be er waitin boy round de house, en I slept en dar too on er pallit on de floor."

FURTHER READING

"Born in Slavery: Slave Narratives from the Federal Writers' Project, 1936–1938," American Memory, Library of Congress. At http://memory.loc.gov/ammem/snhtml/.

Niemcewicz, Julian Ursyn. *Under Their Vine and Fig Tree; Travels Through America in 1797–1799, 1805, With Some Further Account of Life in New Jersey.* Translated and edited by Metchie J. E. Budka. Elizabeth, NJ: Grassmann, 1965.

Stanton, Lucia. *Free Some Day: The African-American Families of Monticello.* Charlottesville, VA: Thomas Jefferson Foundation, 2000.

MARTHA B. KATZ-HYMAN

**PASSES.** For most of the 18th and 19th centuries, the power of a single piece of paper determined whether enslaved African Americans traveling outside their home plantations would be arrested as runaway slaves, jailed, or returned to their owners. A pass represented not only the temporary liberties sometimes granted slaves by owners, but also characterized the "give and take" negotiations that occurred between enslaved blacks and whites that ultimately helped to maintain slavery's status quo.

A slave might receive a pass for short-term travel on behalf of the master to pick up goods for market or to attend a religious service. A slave might receive a pass for several days to visit a wife or child held by a slaveholding family on another area plantation, city, or town: away "marriages" between enslaved couples were fairly common. Or a literate slave might forge a travel pass to create an opportunity for freedom or sell that possibility to another slave. The pass granted a temporary moment of "liberty" for a slave who seldom experienced great freedom. Time off from daily chores and duties was a commodity highly prized by enslaved African Americans.

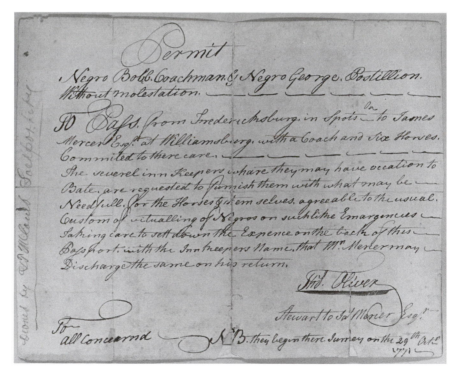

Travel permit for "Negro Bobb Coachman and Negro George Postillion" from Fredericksburg, Virginia, to James Mercer at Williamsburg, October 29–30, 1771. (Special Collections, John D. Rockefeller, Jr. Library, The Colonial Williamsburg Foundation.)

## Patrollers

John Van Hook told a story about Adam Angel who ventured off his Georgia plantation without a pass and was caught by the neighborhood patrols, called paterollers:

> When darkies wanted to get news to their girls or wives on other plantations
> and didn't want Marse George to know about it, they would wait for a dark
> night and would tie rags on their feet to keep from making any noise that the
> paterollers might hear, for if they were caught out without a pass, that was
> something else. Paterollers would go out in squads at night and whip any dar-
> kies they caught out that could not show passes. Adam Angel was a great big
> man, weighing about 200 pounds, and he slipped out one night without a
> pass. When the paterollers found him, he was at his girl's place where they
> were out in the front yard stewing lard for the white folks. They knew he
> didn't belong on that plantation, so they asked him to show his pass. Adam
> didn't have one with him, and he told them so. They made a dive for him,
> and then, quick as a flash, he turned over that pot of boiling lard, and while
> they were getting the hot grease off of them he got away and came back to
> his cabin. If they had caught Adam, he would have needed some of that spilt
> grease on him after the beating they would have give him. Darkies used to
> stretch ropes and grapevines scross the road where they knew paterollers
> would be riding; then they would run down the road in front of them, and
> when they got to the rope or vine they would jump over it and watch the
> horses stumble and throw the paterollers to the ground.

Many former slaves, including Ferebe Rogers from Georgia, recollected this
same song about patrollers:

> You had to have passes to go from one plantation to 'nother. Some de nig-
> gers would slip off sometime and go widout a pass, or maybe marster was
> busy and dey didn't want to bother him for a pass, so dey go widout one. In
> eve'y dee-strick dey had 'bout twelve men dey call patterollers. Dey ride up
> and down and aroun' looking for niggers widout passes. If dey ever caught
> you off yo' plantation wid no pass, dey beat you all over.
> Yes'm, I 'member a song 'bout –
>     "Run, nigger, run, de patteroller git you,
>     Slip over de fence slick as a eel,
>     White man ketch you by de heel,
>     Run, nigger run!"

*Source:* George P. Rawick, ed. *The American Slave: Georgia Narratives,* Vol. 13. Westport,
CT: Greenwood Press, 1972.

Slaves in rural Monmouth County, New Jersey, were granted passes to travel on holidays, to go to religious gatherings, and to do shopping chores for owners. Sometimes
owners in this Northern state did not issue travel passes but allowed their slaves to move
widely in the region. Southern slaveholders more carefully controlled their slaves' travel.

Slave patrols, widely called patrollers or pattyrollers by slaves, were on the regular prowl for slaves who were in the process of running away from a life of slavery or those who then posed as free men or women. The physical written document—whether called a travel pass or slave pass—had to be carried at all times and surrendered when demanded by whites. Failure to produce the pass could result in great danger for the slave. A slave who traveled without a pass signed by his or her master could expect punishment, incarceration, and the probable elimination of future freedoms. These punishments and restrictions existed throughout much of the emerging American nation, but the chaos of the Revolutionary War combined with the lingering effect of Lord Dunmore's 1775 Proclamation, stating that slaves who served the British side would be free, enabled many enslaved men and women to escape to the British lines, even if they did not have passes.

The pass was the tool that enabled many African Americans in the Upper South to escape slavery. The annual Christmas holiday included several days off for slaves and might feature an "away" visit with spouses, children, or other family members who lived on other plantations. In the case of Jermain Loguen (1813–1872), enslaved in Tennessee, the holiday also presented an opportunity to seek freedom because holiday celebrations delayed the searches of slave patrols and bounty hunters who were paid to recover runaway slaves. Traveling with a counterfeit pass that he purchased from another slave for $10, Loguen and a fellow fugitive narrowly avoided capture by several patrols and a wrong turn toward Louisville, Kentucky. They were able to cross over the Ohio River to eventual freedom in Canada. The antebellum author, runaway slave, and abolitionist Henry Bibb (1815–1854) also learned to write to forge a pass to use in his escape from slavery in Kentucky. When Bibb initially ran away, he was recaptured and threatened with resale in New Orleans. After he learned to write his own travel document, Bibb successfully escaped and made his way to Canada. Noted abolitionist Frederick Douglass (ca. 1818–1895), too, fled slavery in Maryland with the aid of a forged document that identified him as a free sailor, which he presented to a train conductor.

Although the pass system enabled some semblance of "free" movement for enslaved people that allowed them to maintain some contact with relatives or negotiate directly with owners for time off, the use of the documents symbolized the larger system of control and authority that slaveholders attempted to exert over enslaved African Americans. When in the hands of a literate slave, however, passes became a powerful tool for subversion.

FURTHER READING

Hodges, Graham R. *Slavery and Freedom in the Rural North: African Americans in Monmouth County, New Jersey, 1665–1865*. Madison, WI: Madison House Publishers, 1997.

"North American Slave Narratives," Documenting the American South Collection, University Library of the University of North Carolina at Chapel Hill. At http://docsouth.unc.edu/neh/texts/texts.html.

*The Rev. J.W. Loguen as a Slave and as a Freeman: A Narrative of Real Life*. Syracuse, NY: JGK Truair and Company, 1859. Documenting the American South Collection, University Library of the University of North Carolina at Chapel Hill. At http://docsouth.unc.edu/neh/loguen/loguen.html.

SUSAN KOZEL

**PEANUTS.** The peanut (*Arachis hypogaea*) is a tropical plant native to South America that was introduced to Virginia and the Carolinas during the slave trade from West and Central Africa, where it became a staple **food** after its introduction by the Spanish and Portuguese. In Senegambia, Ghana, and Central Africa, peanuts have been made into a number of quickly cooked street foods and serve as the base for savory and spicy **stews**, soups, and sauces. After their introduction in the Americas, peanuts slowly became a substitute for a similar indigenous plant widely cultivated in Sub-Saharan Africa, the Bamana or Bambara groundnut. Although the Bamana groundnut was brought to various locations in the Americas from Africa, including the Southern United States, it was cultivated locally by enslaved blacks in their **garden** patches and never became a commercial crop. This may be the plant that the English botanist Philip Miller (1691–1771) referred to in 1754: "the Negroes kept this a secret among themselves, therefore they could supply themselves with these nuts unknown to their masters." The peanut may have grown alongside the groundnut, and Miller found that "in South Carolina there is great plenty of these nuts, which the inhabitants roast, and make use of as chocolate." The peanut was known as the "goober pea" and the "pinder nut," both names coming from Central Africa, specifically the Kimbundu (nguba) and BaKongo (mpinda) languages. By the mid-18th century, the peanut was widely grown from Senegal to Angola in West and Central Africa, and from Virginia to the Lower Mississippi Valley and the Afro-Caribbean. The archaeological record suggests that peanuts probably were being cultivated by the 1760s at Rich Neck plantation, near Williamsburg, Virginia. By 1781, Thomas Jefferson (1743–1826) referred to the "groundnut" as one of the common crops in Virginia gardens, and by 1794, he was planting them at his experimental garden at Monticello. Several enslaved Virginians referred to cultivating their "goober patches." In the 1790s, formerly enslaved Haitians, who were part of the migration that followed the Haitian Revolution, wearing the tignon headwrap, were selling peanuts and peanut cake confections on the streets of Philadelphia. In the enslaved community, peanuts were roasted, made into sweet cakes, and cooked into stews and soups—all of which mirrored similar dishes from Africa. During molasses pulls, cured, roasted peanuts might be added to the cooking taffy to make a quick confection. In *The Carolina Housewife* (1847), Sarah Rutledge records several recipes for the groundnut, including a spicy groundnut soup reminiscent of stews based on peanuts from West and Central Africa. Up to and especially after the Civil War, peanuts began to be commercially cultivated using African American labor, starting near Wakefield, Virginia, in 1842, and outside Wilmington, North Carolina, in the 1850s. At Poplar Grove plantation in Wilmington, peanuts, rather than **cotton** or **rice**, were the main cash crop cultivated by an enslaved workforce. In addition to their meat, peanuts have been valued for their oil, a critical ingredient in deep frying and other cooking methods associated with the culinary influence of West and Central Africa.

*See also* Headwraps, Tignons, and Kerchiefs.

FURTHER READING

Edwards-Ingram, Ywone. "Medicating Slavery: Motherhood, Health Care, and Cultural Practices in the African Diaspora." PhD diss., College of William and Mary, 2005.

Grime, William E. *Ethno-Botany of the Black Americans*. Algonac, MI: Reference Publications, 1979.

Rutledge, Sarah. *The Carolina Housewife*. 1847. Reprint, Columbia: University of South Carolina Press, 1979.

Smith, Andrew F. *Peanuts: The Illustrious History of the Goober Pea*. Urbana: University of Illinois Press, 2002.

Weaver, William Woys. *Heirloom Vegetable Gardening*. New York: Henry Holt and Company, 1997.

MICHAEL W. TWITTY

**PERSONAL OBJECTS.** Enslaved men, women and children lived with a range of personal items that they acquired in a variety of ways. In general, most slave owners considered that these items, once acquired by their bondmen and bondwomen, became the property of those individuals, in spite of the fact that the men and women themselves were the property of their owners. These goods included **clothing**, tools, cooking equipment, and household goods of many kinds. They were used in a variety of ways, ways that were recognizable to slave owners and ways that had meaning to the enslaved but went unnoticed by their owners.

Masters provided for the most elementary material needs of their slaves: a roof over their heads, basic clothing, and simple food and cooking utensils. These were given to slaves on a more-or-less regular schedule. Food—usually **corn** or **wheat**, plus occasionally some meat—was distributed weekly. In 1732, William Hugh Grove, an Englishman, visited Virginia and noted that "[the slaves] are allowed a peck of Indian Corn per Week." In 1767, Landon Carter (1710–1778), a Virginia plantation owner, wrote in his diary that "we took out this day 16 Bushels of eared Corn from the M[angorike] Corn house to make the peoples' allowance." This schedule continued to be the practice into the 19th century. Martha Ogle Forman (1785–1864), who lived in Cecil County, Maryland, noted in 1842 in her diary that "Mr. Nowland gave out the people's meat, he gave each a hog's head and made out the rest of the allowance with beef." Ben Horry, a former slave interviewed around 1937 in South Carolina about his life as a slave, told his interviewer that "Sat'd'y time come to ration off. Every head on the Plantation to Brookgreen line up at smoke-house to draw he share of meat and rice and grits and meal." Annie Stanton, interviewed in 1937 in Alabama, told her interviewer that "[d]e rations for a week wuz 3 lbs of meat a week, 1 peck ob meal, potatoes an' syrup. . . . De overseer also gib tuh us flour and sugar fo' Christmas."

Clothing usually was issued twice a year, before the winter and before the summer. Johann David Schoepf (1752–1800), a German traveler through the Upper South in the years right after the Revolution, noted in North Carolina that "[w]ell-disposed masters clothe their negroes once a year, and give them a suit of coarse woollen cloth, two rough shirts, and a pair of shoes." Former slave George Womble, interviewed in 1937 in Georgia, stated that

> clothes were given to all the slaves once a year. An issue for the men usually consisted of one or two pairs of pants and some shirts, underwear, woolen socks, and a pair of heavy brogans. . . . The women were given one or two dresses that had been made of the same material as that of the men's pants.

Enslaved men and women sometimes received outmoded or worn clothing and other goods as gifts from their owners. Joseph Ball (1689–1760), who lived in London but owned property in Virginia, sent clothing back to the colony in 1749 and instructed his overseer to distribute it as follows:

> The old Cloths must be disposed of, as follows: The Grey Coat Wastecoat & breeches, with brass buttons, and the hat to poor Will: The stuff shirt to Mingo: and the Dimmity Coat & breeches and the knife in the pocket to Harrison: and Aron's Old Livery with one pair of the Leather breeches and one of the Linen frocks to Moses: and the other frock and rags & [illeg.] as you think fit.

Archie Booker, held as a slave in a plantation near Richmond, Virginia, and interviewed in Hampton, Virginia, in 1937, told his interviewer that, because his owner was the only man in the house, "Slaves had to wear his suits, no matter what size dey was. Dem suits of marsa's look right funny when de get pieced out wid all sorts of extra pieces."

**Wool blankets** were distributed to each slave every year or every other year, and many slave owners also gave their enslaved workers **pallets** or bedding of some kind. In 1809, Thomas Jefferson (1743–1826) wrote in his Farm Book that when two of his bondpeople married, he always gave them "a pot, and a bed, which I always promise them when they take husbands at home" and on May 28, 1811, he wrote in that same book that he "gave a sifter & a pot to Bedford John and his wife Virginia. also a bed."

In addition to essentials, slave owners supplied their bondpeople with tools, implements, and even special clothing required to do their jobs: plows, **hoes**, rakes, shovels, hammers, anvils, axes, saws, planes, chisels, pots, andirons, pot hooks, spinning wheels, looms, **livery**, and special footwear. These tools and special equipment were the property of the master and were expected to remain at the **slave quarters**, even if their users were sold to another owner.

Enslaved people also made goods for themselves. Nearly all slaves had some skill, whether it was as a field hand, a basketmaker, a carpenter, a blacksmith, a cook, or a spinner. With these skills, many were able to make the things that they needed or desired for daily life, ranging from the simple, such as mended clothing or **gourds** for drinking vessels and bowls, to the complex, such as sleeping platforms, stools, or even musical instruments for their entertainment.

Other slaves relied on their skills as farmers and foragers to increase the amount of food available to them both for their own tables and as a marketable commodity. Much of this food was grown by slaves at their quarters. Edward Kimber (1719–1769), an English novelist who traveled through Maryland in 1745 and 1746, described slave quarters as "a Number of Huts or Hovels, built some Distance from the Mansion-House; where the Negroes reside with their wives and Families and cultivate at vacant times the little Spots allow'd." Francis Taylor (1747–1799), a plantation owner in Orange County, Virginia, wrote in his diary, in May 1795, that his "Negroes [were] planting for themselves." Other observers noted that slaves raised poultry and caught fish. Traveler Thomas Anburey (1759–1840) described a planter near Charlottesville, Virginia, who, instead of providing his slaves with the usual **rations**, "grant[ed] his negroes an acre of ground, and all Saturday afternoon to raise grain and poultry for themselves." Using their **chickens**, eggs, produce, and foraged foodstuffs, slaves bartered to obtain goods. This bartering usually took place between slave and master. Not all enslaved people were able to raise their own food, however. William McWhorter, interviewed in Athens, Georgia, in 1938, reported that, although his owner gave his bondmen and bondwomen adequate food from his garden, they did not have a garden of their own because, he said, "dey never had no time of deir own to wuk no garden."

Another way in which slaves obtained goods was by theft. In 1737, Jacob, a slave held by William Fantleroy in Richmond County, Virginia, stole "two Cloth Jackets . . . One pair of Britches . . . one Felt Hatt . . . Two Woolen Caps . . . two new Oznabrig Shirts . . . one New Linen Shirt . . . One linen Sheet . . . One Frying pan [and] one Rug." In 1747, two of Landon Carter's (1710–1778) slaves, Manuell and Ralph, were indicted for breaking into Carter's mansion and stealing "two hundred and thirty three Ells of Dreheda Canvas. . . . Four Torinton Rugs . . . Four suits of Cotton Cloath . . . Ten yards of Half Thicks . . . Four Sides of Leather . . . Five files . . . [and] Two Dozen Hose." Goods stolen in such quantities were undoubtedly intended for resale. George Washington (1732–1799), in 1793, acknowledged such trade when he tried to prevent his former carpenter's daughter from going into business as he feared "her shop wd. be no more than a receptacle for stolen produce by the Negroes." He knew that without this source of cheap goods, poor whites "would be unable to live upon the miserable land they occupy." The goods taken by these slaves in Richmond County may have been stolen to **barter** or to sell, but other goods were stolen to assist in escaping, as reported by the owner of Sam, "a bright Mulatto Man Slave," who took with him "his Bedding, a new spotted Rug which he had stolen, and several Yards of mixed coloured Broadcloth, cut from a whole Piece that he had stolen, the remainder of which he distributed amongst the Sloop's Crew to bribe them to Secrecy."

Enslaved men and women also bought and sold goods on the open **market**. Food products were the most common items that slaves sold. James Mercer, writing in 1779 to a friend in Loudoun County, Virginia, wrote, "I know allready that Chickens or other fresh meat cant be had but in exchange & Bacon to spare will allow me a preference with the Country people or rather Negroes who are the general Chicken merchants." Besides bartering with his slaves, Francis Taylor also purchased such items as carp, oysters, cabbages, and potatoes for his own table, paying his slaves in cash.

Slaves earned money through selling products of their skilled labor. Robert "King" Carter (1663–1732) observed in 1731 that his slaves "surely must depend on a great deal of their Time in making Pails & Piggins & Churns for Merchandizing. Manuel tells me the smith does a great many jobs for neighbours." Jack, the slave who belonged to the estate of a Mr. Linton near Colchester, Virginia, earned credit of more than £100 from Glassford & Co. from 1760 to 1769 for mending bridges, building furniture, and selling poultry and other work. In 1768, William Allason (ca. 1720–1800) paid John Fitzhugh's "Negro Harry" for "puting up Shelves in Kitchen & making Stairs &c." In 1796, Francis Taylor paid his half-brother's slave, Tom, for "2 days work hooping nest ware & repairs of Porch etc." Willis Bennefield, interviewed in Hephzibah, Georgia, about 1936, told his interviewer that "[d]ey made dey own money. In slavery time, if you wanted four or five acres of land to plant anything on, marster give it to you, and whatever dat land make, it belong to you. You could take dat money and spend it any way you wanted to."

Some slaves also earned money through tips. In 1768, John Frere (1740–1807) of London wrote his cousin, John Hatley Norton (1745–1797) in Yorktown, Virginia, and asked him to send any plant or animal fossils that might be found in the area. Frere wrote, "if such Things are to be found, the Negroes I suppose for a small Gratuity wou'd bring them to you." And in 1794 George Washington instructed one of his overseers, William Pearce, to "[r]emember to give John the Gardener a dollar, the last day of every month, provided he behaves well; letting him know that it is on that express condition he is to receive it." James Wiggins, born in Anne Arundel County, Maryland, remembered being taken to Annapolis as a boy and how he would "dance in the stores for men and women, they would give me pennies and three cent pieces, all of which were given to me by the Revells [his owners]. They bought me shoes and clothes with the money collected."

With the money that slaves earned, they were able to buy goods of their own choosing, and the goods they bought were as varied as the goods available. In 1737, "Negro Jack" bought fabric, scissors, thread, hose, and penknives from Thomas Partridge. "Negro Jack," who had made furniture and other wooden articles for Glassford & Co. bought a wide range of goods, from rum and fabric to a wine glass and a plane iron between 1760 and 1769. Robert Carter III (1728–1804) noted in his diary in 1785 that he "paid old Nat a dollar he wanted, he wanted to buy Brandy to bury his Granddaughter Lucy, but I refused to sell; telling him he might lay out his Annuity as he pleased." Enslaved men and women in Thomaston, Georgia, purchased a wide variety of goods from local merchants, including cloth, plates, teaspoons, and even alcohol, although the latter was nominally forbidden by law to be purchased by slaves.

All of these goods generally were available on the open market to any person, white or black, who had the money to pay for them. Virtually all of the items used by slaves, whether given by their owners, used while doing a specific task, or acquired for personal use, were products of either English or American manufacture, and they generally were used in ways that were familiar to everyone, both black and white. Enslaved men and women, however, also used these items in ways both unknown and unnoticed by their white owners. **Cast iron pots** were used for cooking, but, overturned, as many formerly enslaved people related to the interviewers who worked for the Works Progress Administration's Federal Writers' Project, they were thought to muffle the sounds that the enslaved wanted to hide from their masters. Clay Bobbit, who was enslaved in Warren County, North Carolina, related that his owner, Richard Bobbit, was a harsh master, saying "We ain't gone swimmin' ner huntin' ner nothin' an' we ain't had no pleasures 'less we runs away ter habe 'em. Eben when we sings we had ter turn down a pot in front of de do'[door] to ketch de noise." Pewter spoons were used for eating and cooking, but, with the handle broken off, drilled with a hole and hung by a cord, a spoon could be worn as an amulet under regular clothing and, with its highly reflective surface, turn back evil spirits. Libations offered to gods known from Africa could be poured on the ground from ordinary stoneware or slip-ware bowls. And pins, crystals, and ceramic sherds (fragments) could be arranged under the floor of a slave quarter, in the northeast corner of a room, to provide a measure of protection for the building's residents.

*See also* Furnishings; Subfloor Pits.

FURTHER READING

"Born in Slavery: Slave Narratives from the Federal Writers' Project, 1936–1938," American Memory, Library of Congress. At http://memory.loc.gov/ammem/snhtml/.

"Digital Archaeological Archive of Comparative Slavery," Thomas Jefferson Foundation. At www.daacs.org/.

Katz-Hyman, Martha B. "'In the Middle of This Poverty Some Cups and a Teapot': The Furnishing of Slave Quarters at Colonial Williamsburg." In *The American Home: Material Culture, Domestic Space, and Family Life*, edited by Eleanor McD. Thompson, 197–216. Winterthur, DE: Henry Francis du Pont Winterthur Museum, 1998.

Paterson, David E. "Slaves, Slavery and Cash in a Georgia Village, 1825–1865." *The Journal of Southern History* 75, no. 4 (November 2009): 879–930.

MARTHA B. KATZ-HYMAN

**PIGS AND PORK.** The domesticated swine (*Sus scrofa*) is perhaps the animal most associated with the diet of enslaved people on Southern plantations. Pigs and pork, not common in much of historic West and Central Africa, were far more essential to the Northern and Western European diet. Pigs were first brought to the South by the earliest Spanish explorers and English settlers. They were running wild by the time most enslaved Africans first encountered them in the 17th century. The "hog and **hominy**" diet associated with African Americans did not truly begin until the 19th century, when salt pork and other preserved pork products became standard issue **rations** in the enslaved community. In the 17th century, enslaved blacks would have surely tasted pork, but the much cheaper salt **fish** formed a larger part of their diet. Through the mid-18th century, enslaved people enjoyed a greater diversity of preserved or less common, fresh meats that included beef and mutton as well as pork. With the eradication of wild predators, better breeding methods and better livestock care, pigs became the most important source of meat in the antebellum enslaved South.

In West and Central Africa, except in areas influenced by Islam, which forbids the consumption of pork, the few pigs available were traditionally considered a delicacy to be fried or roasted whole and well seasoned. For the most part, smoked or salted pork, an innovation from the colder regions of Northern Europe, were not familiar to tropical Africans, and they had to adapt. Their palettes had a taste for smoked proteins, salty foods, and foods that provided ample grease and fat for stocks and sauces—all of which was possible with pork. Because some planters believed that fresh meat contributed to disease, they considered preserved meat to be better suited to the enslaved diet. Slaves received one to three pounds of salted or pickled pork rations per week, based on their gender, age, and labor. Fresh pork was only enjoyed at summer barbecues, where a young "shote" might be killed, butchered, and roasted over hardwood coals for several hours, or at hog-killing time, held when temperatures were low enough that the freshly slaughtered meat would not spoil.

Preserved pork was not cut into strips and eaten like bacon in the morning. Rather, salt pork and fatback supplied an important way to keep the iron pots, pans, and skillets seasoned with a layer of grease so that **food** did not stick to the surface. A piece of pork might be boiled over and over again over the course of a week in pots of greens, cowpeas, or any other available vegetables or tubers from the garden or gathered from the wild. Pokeweed, a semitoxic leafy green valued for its purgative qualities, became known as "pork salad," because it was so often paired with salt pork. In Virginia, a pigpen often was seeded with turnip greens to take advantage of the heavy compost and muck, with the result being that when the pigs were slaughtered or preserved the greens would be enjoyed with the meat. Slaves often referred to the "rusty piece of bacon" that flavored many of their dishes. The liquid in which this "rusty piece" was boiled became the basis for **pot likker**, a rich stock produced from the boiling of salt pork and cabbage or leafy greens. The savory meat, seasoned with the salt and pepper used to preserve it, was a welcome addition to an otherwise-bland diet. According to Louis Hughes, a Virginia man sold into slavery in Mississippi,

> Cabbage and meat, boiled, alternated with meat and peas, were the staple for summer. Bread was furnished with the meals and **corn** meal dumplings, that is, little balls made of meal and grease from the boiled bacon and dropped into boiling water, were also provided and considered quite palatable, especially if cooked in the water in which the bacon was boiled.

Former slave and noted abolitionist Frederick Douglass (ca. 1818–1895) observed, "As a general rule the slaves did not come to their quarters to take their meals, but took their ash-cake (called thus because baked in the ashes) and piece of pork, or their salt herrings, where they were at work."

Barbecues were a rare opportunity to enjoy fresh meat. A large hog or a young shoat would be slaughtered and roasted over the course of a night and a morning, brushed with salted water often flavored with red peppers, vinegar, butter, **herbs**, and other seasonings. Barbecues were held most often during the summer "laying by" period when the enslaved community could afford to take off, or, after the American Revolution, for the Fourth of July.

The most salient part of the pig in the enslaved diet was offal, known as "pluck," which the enslaved community enjoyed fresh at hog-killing time. In West and Central Africa, the tender innards of large domesticated animals were considered a delicacy as well as spiritually potent. Heads, feet, intestines, livers, and kidneys were divided among individuals according to social rank, age, grades, and gender. Among some groups, the intestines and livers might be used in forms of divination. In the West African port of Bonny, English Capt. Hugh Crow (1765–1829) reported that the chiefs there would sell European traders livestock to eat, but requested that the head, feet, tails, and innards be returned for the Africans to eat. Coming from a tradition that valued thrift and did not waste any part of an animal that was edible, and living in a social caste where farm laborers were expected to take the "lesser" parts of an animal, enslaved African Americans simply "made do" and regarded the rare bits

## Barbecue

Former slave Louis Hughes elaborated on barbecues in Virginia:

Barbecue originally meant to dress and roast a hog whole, but has come to mean the cooking of a food animal in this manner for the feeding of a great company. A feast of this kind was always given to us, by Boss, on the 4th of July. The anticipation of it acted as a stimulant through the entire year. Each one looked forward to this great day of recreation with pleasure. Even the older slaves would join in the discussion of the coming event. It mattered not what trouble or hardship the year had brought, this feast and its attendant pleasure would dissipate all gloom. . . . The day before the 4th was a busy one. The slaves worked with all their might. The children who were large enough were engaged in bringing wood and bark to the spot where the barbecue was to take place. They worked eagerly, all day long; and, by the time the sun was setting, a huge pile of fuel was beside the trench, ready for use in the morning. At an early hour of the great day, the servants were up, and the men whom Boss had appointed to look after the killing of the hogs and sheep were quickly at their work, and, by the time they had the meat dressed and ready, most of the slaves had arrived at the center of attraction. They gathered in groups, talking, laughing, telling tales that they had from their grandfather, or relating practical jokes that they had played or seen played by others. These tales were received with peals of laughter. But however much they seemed to enjoy these stories and social interchanges, they never lost sight of the trench or the spot where the sweetmeats were to be cooked.

The method of cooking the meat was to dig a trench in the ground about six feet long and eighteen inches deep. This trench was filled with wood and bark which was set on fire, and, when it was burned to a great bed of coals, the hog was split through the back bone, and laid on poles which had been placed across the trench. The sheep were treated in the same way, and both were turned from side to side as they cooked. During the process of roasting the cooks basted the carcasses with a preparation furnished from the great house, consisting of butter pepper, salt and vinegar, and this was continued until the meat was ready to serve.

*Source:* Louis Hughes. *Thirty Years a Slave: From Bondage to Freedom: The Institution of Slavery as Seen on the Plantation and in the Home of the Planter.* Milwaukee, WI: South Side Printing Co, 1897. At http://docsouth.unc.edu/fpn/hughes/hughes.html.

of fresh, nutritious organ meat as delicacies. Heads, feet, brains, tails, intestines (chitlins or chitterlings), sweetbreads, kidneys, lights, heart, tripe, and the chine bone (the spine scraped of chops and chunks of meat) were placed in bubbling pots with onions and peppers and other seasonings that masked the strong gamy taste of those parts of the hog. Alice Hutcheson of Athens, Georgia, interviewed as part of the

Work Progress Administration's Federal Writers' Project remembered, "De bestes' time was hog killin' times. Us chillun wukked den. Dey hung up de hogs all night and nex' day us out 'em put 'em down in salt and cooked up de lard. Us chillun got some of dem good old skin cracklin's when dey got brown." The cracklings in turn would be mixed with cornmeal to make cracklin' bread, another delicacy only seasonally enjoyed as fall turned to winter. These traditions eventually came to be known as "soul food."

The best parts of the preserved pork—bacon, hams, middlings, side meat, and so on—were rarely distributed to enslaved workers. An enslaved person might never taste a quality country ham that was smoked over hickory, oak, apple, or sassafras. Hams and bacon sometimes would drip fat and salt onto the floorboards of smokehouses, and then these boards would be randomly pulled and cooked into pots of beans. Stealing hogs—an offense punishable by whipping, branding, or being sold away—was one of the most serious crimes in plantation life. To protect slave owners' status and interests, enslaved workers were rarely, if ever, allowed to raise their own hogs or other large livestock. **Chickens** were acceptable stock for enslaved people, but hogs represented a different sort of power in the hierarchy of the plantation. It is perhaps no accident that the legends associated with revolutionaries such as Gabriel Prosser (1776–1800) and Nat Turner (1800–1831) portray them as devising their plots to overthrow the inequities of slavery while eating a meal of stolen roast hog. The Haitian Revolution (1791–1803) was said to have begun with the slaughter and consumption of a black hog by the legendary houngan or Vodoun priest, Makandal.

Enslaved blacks felt the intense inequality when they were given cast-off parts of the pig. Some enslaved people recalled having to eat rotting hog guts thrown into the dirt because the foods given to them as part of the ration system led to an unbalanced diet and malnourishment. This association led to the shame that some African Americans began to feel for not only the eating of offal, but also for the consumption of pork, which was seen as a cultural indignity. In the 21st century, despite the negative cultural associations passed down from slavery, and concerns for dietary health, there has been resurgence in the pork barbecue, the celebration of chitlins, and the use of lard and quality heritage salt pork in Southern black foodways.

*See also* Hoecakes.

FURTHER READING

Crow, Hugh. *Memoirs of the late Captain Hugh Crow of Liverpool, Comprising a narrative of his life, together with descriptive sketches of Africa, particularly of Bonny, the manners and customs of the inhabitants, the production of the soil, and the trade of the country, to which are added anecdotes and observations of the Negro character.* London: F. Cass, 1970.

Douglass, Frederick. *Life and Times of Frederick Douglass: His Early Life as a Slave, His Escape from Bondage, and His Complete History to the Present Time.* 2nd ed. New York: Bedford/St. Martin's, 2002.

Harris, Jessica B. *The Welcome Table: African American Heritage Cooking.* New York: Fireside, 1995.

Hilliard, Sam Bowers. *Hog Meat and Hoecake: Food Supply in the Old South, 1840–1860.* Carbondale: Southern Illinois Press, 1971.

Hughes, Louis. *Thirty Years a Slave: From Bondage to Freedom: The Institution of Slavery as Seen on the Plantation and in the Home of the Planter.* Milwaukee, WI: South Side Printing Company, 1897.

Morgan, Philip D. *Slave Counterpoint: Black Culture in the Eighteenth-Century Chesapeake and Lowcountry*. Chapel Hill: University of North Carolina Press, 1998.

Rawick, George P., ed. *The American Slave: Kansas, Kentucky, Maryland, Ohio, Virginia, and Tennessee Narratives*, Vol. 16. Westport, CT: Greenwood Press, 1972.

MICHAEL W. TWITTY

**POT LIKKER.** Pot likker (or liquor) is the by-product of boiling greens with salted meat and sometimes onions, peppers, and spices. This liquid is then used as a stock, the basis for sauce or sopping gravy in traditional Southern cuisine. It was popular in the enslaved community to add flavor to bland-tasting **hoecakes** or ashcakes and other forms of cornmeal dishes including mush. Pot likker was emblematic of the culinary tradition of enslaved people being thrifty. The rich stock was one of the first **foods** fed to enslaved children as a supplement to mother's milk because of its rich taste. For formerly enslaved people reflecting on their days under the whip, pot likker brought up mixed feelings of nurturance, comfort, near-starvation, and even the indignities of being sold at auction.

In the days when whole hams were boiled in large **cast iron pots**, only the skin and rind of the ham and the water it was boiled in was offered to enslaved people. The indignity of only being allowed the leftovers after many hours of work made pot likker a symbol of slavery's power imbalance. Enslaved children were weaned on pot likker from their swaddling days and later consumed it mixed with **corn** mush and other leftovers thrown into collective troughs to be eaten out with a spoon, **shell**, or bit of broken shingle.

Lunsford Lane of North Carolina, a former domestic slave, reported that the pot likker eaten by enslaved children was largely soaked up by cornmeal dumplings boiled with the meat of the Great House. Sarah Wooden Johnson, a former enslaved woman from Prince George County, Virginia, noted that pot likker was "good and

---

### Pot Likker in Song

Noted abolitionist Frederick Douglass' autobiography included what was called a juba-patting (thigh- or knee-patting, to accompany a dance) song that mentioned pot likker:

> We peel de meat,
> Dey gib us de skin;
> And dat's de way
> Dey take us in;
> We skim de pot,
> Dey give us de liquor,
> And say dat's good enough for nigger.

Songs like this were used to derisively condemn the way slaveholders would force enslaved cooks to prepare food for the whites and then only give the slaves the bare leavings of the pot.

*Source:* Frederick Douglass. *Life and Times of Frederick Douglass: His Early Life as a Slave, His Escape from Bondage, and His Complete History to the Present Time.* 2nd ed. New York: Bedford/St. Martin's, 2002.

greasy," and was particularly valued for kush, a scramble of old cornbread, red pepper, and onions that was a savory treat beloved by children. A good pot likker was said to be greasy enough to "wink back" at the cook. Leonard Black from Anne Arundel County, Maryland, recalled that he had "a pint of pot liquor and the skin off the pork" for his breakfast and dinner while having only a linsey slip to wear and no **shoes**. Many enslaved blacks remembered pot likker as a bare-bones source of nourishment. For others, pot likker was another tool of slavery that turned human beings into a commodity. William J. Anderson, sold at auction in Natchez, said that "slaves are made to shave and wash in greasy pot liquor, to make them look sleek and nice." Sometimes enslaved people's mouths would be smeared with pot likker before going on the **auction blocks** to make them appear well fed.

FURTHER READING

Anderson, William J. *The Narrative of William J. Anderson.* Chicago: Daily Tribune Book and Job Printing Office, 1857.

Lane, Lunsford. *Narrative of the Life of Lunsford Lane.* Boston: Hewes and Watson's Print, 1845.

Perdue, Charles L. *Weevils in the Wheat: Interviews with Virginia Ex-Slaves.* Charlottesville: University Press of Virginia, 1992.

Rawick, George P. *The American Slave: Kansas, Kentucky, Maryland, Ohio, Virginia, and Tennessee Narratives*, Vol. 16. Westport, CT: Greenwood Press, 1972.

MICHAEL W. TWITTY

**POTTERY.** Pottery refers to objects made out of clay that generally are fired in some manner, either in a pit or kiln. Types of pottery include earthenware, stoneware, and porcelain, determined by the chemical properties of the clay body. Earthenware is created when clay is fired or burned at low temperatures up to 2150°F; stoneware is achieved between 2190°F and 2370°F, and porcelain between 2340°F and 2460°F.

During the colonial period, earthenware was the predominate type of pottery made in North America. Clay was found throughout the eastern seaboard, particularly along the Fall Line. Native Americans used this local clay to produce bowls, jars, pipes, burial, urns and more. The colonists brought their pottery and ceramic traditions from Europe; the wealthiest would bring small quantities of exported Chinese porcelain. Africans brought with them their own ceramic traditions, which were manifested in different ways.

Slaves used the pottery made by Native Americans along with the salt-glazed stoneware and creamware made in England. In the South, African slaves also made their own pottery—bowls and jars for cooking, serving, and eating **food**—along with pipes for smoking. The term "**colonoware**" is used to describe low-fired, unglazed pottery made by slaves and Indians during the colonial period. Within many African cultures, women were the potters. They passed along their methods for making pots to their daughters and other women in their community, much like the Native Americans did. African forms and incised decoration survived the trip across the

375

Storage jar made by David Drake in Edgefield, North Carolina, in 1858. The jar is inscribed on two sides. One side is inscribed "L.m. nover 3, 1858/ Dave." The other is marked "I saw a leopard & a lions face/ then I felt the need—of grace," an adaptation from the Book of Revelation. (Collection of the Museum of Early Southern Decorative Arts, Old Salem Museums and Gardens. © MESDA. Used by permission.)

Atlantic, along with certain ways of using the bowls for cooking, preparing, serving, and eating food. The slave-made pottery was found primarily at plantation sites in Virginia, North Carolina, South Carolina, Georgia, and Florida, where the African/ slave population was greater than the white population. Slaves might have used colonoware for ritual purposes, marking the interior or exterior base with an "X," which was often encircled. Archaeologists have found most of these marked pots in rivers and other water features. The incised "X" also was made on alkaline-glazed stoneware vessels produced with slave labor in the Edgefield District of South Carolina during the 19th century. It is not clear, however, whether the meaning was the same when the stoneware pots were found intact in **kitchens** and farmhouses.

### Production Pottery

In the late 18th and early 19th century, the production of ceramics in America began to change. The colonists sought to establish "factories" to produce pottery for their own needs instead of importing wares from England or purchasing and trading vessels from the Native Americans. Potters were experimenting and trying to make porcelain. Many potters in the South relied on slaves to perform the labor-intensive tasks. Such was the case in Virginia, South Carolina, and Georgia. In 18th-century Georgia, blacks were hired by potters, such as Andrew Duche and a Mr. Radiguey, as workmen or apprentices at their pottery and tile "manufacture." The men who were hired out by their owners, or in some instances, free blacks did most of the labor-intensive jobs of digging, hauling, and refining the clay; loading, firing, and unloading the kiln; and then loading the wagons to deliver the bricks, tiles, or pots.

By 1817, slaves were working at Pottersville and the Rev. John Landrum pottery in Edgefield, South Carolina. These potteries were, in essence, small factories producing stoneware jugs, jars, pitchers, and churns along with small tablewares. These durable utilitarian wares met the day-to-day needs of local people—from cobblers and farmers to plantation owners. The alkaline-glaze stoneware tradition that developed in South Carolina was not a European ceramic tradition, but one with its origins in China and the Far East. It was a low-cost alternative to saltglaze and more durable than lead-glazed earthenware.

## Plantation Pottery

It was not unusual for large plantations to have brick kilns if sources of local clay were available. Slaves performed the backbreaking work of digging and hauling clay from the sides of the riverbanks. It also would have been difficult to dig clay from areas where it was already half-baked from the sun and heat. Many of the bricks bear the fingerprints of the slaves who filled the molds and fired the kilns.

Bricks made on a Georgetown plantation were found on a submerged vessel in the Black River near Brown's Ferry in South Carolina. Middleton plantation on the Ashley River in the Charleston area had brick kilns. Slaves owned by Henry and John Horlbeck most likely operated the brick kilns at Boone Hall plantation along the Cooper River outside Charleston, South Carolina, in the early 19th century. When not growing **cotton**, the slaves would fire the kilns during the winter months.

## Dave the Potter

Pottersville was the first pottery in South Carolina and the United States to produce alkaline-glazed stoneware. Various members of the Landrum family owned and operated Pottersville until 1839 when it was sold. The slaves named Daniel, Sam, George, Abram, Old Harry, Young Harry, and Old Tom worked at Pottersville. The most significant and well-known slave to work at Pottersville was named Dave. Mortgaged at age 17 and sold numerous times before he was 40, Dave spent his life turning pots and later writing poetry on the sides of the stoneware vessels he turned. Dave learned to read and write before the laws were written making it illegal to do so. Restrictions placed on the movements and activities of slaves increased following the 1822 purported slave revolt led by Denmark Vesey (1767–1822) in Charleston, South Carolina. Dave wrote numerous poems, including "A better thing I never saw, when I shot the lions jaw" on November 9, 1836. He became a master potter, eventually working primarily for Lewis Miles from 1840 until Miles died in 1868. Dave, who took the last name Drake after Emancipation, provided a record of his work habits and his personality when he signed and dated these stoneware jars. The dates range from every day of the week and every month of the year. The earliest jar attributed to Dave is dated 1821 and the last signed piece is dated 1864. During his life, Dave was held by and worked for three brothers, John, Amos, and Abner Landrum, along with their nephews Harvey and Reuben Drake in their potteries. In 1840, Dave wrote about his status as a slave and about his job, "Dave belongs to Mr. Miles,/ where the oven bakes & the pots bile." Mr. Miles was Lewis Miles, the son-in-law of John Landrum and brother-in-law of B. F. Landrum. Based on family records and legal documents, Dave also was held by B. F. Landrum, who operated a pottery not far from his father's property in the Edgefield District. Slaves who worked in the **kitchens** would have used the stoneware jugs, jar, pitchers, and churns made by Dave and the other potters. These heavy utilitarian vessels were not for fine dining room table settings of the plantation house, but were kept in the kitchen. A few of the slip-decorated cups, bowls, and pitchers may have been used for breakfast and midday meals, or they would have been used on the table of the middle and lower classes, but not the planter class. The storage jars also may have been used by the slaves in their households, as meat was portioned out to the different families on the plantations. Dave wrote rhyming couplets about how much and what the jars would hold, "Put every bit all between/surely this jar will hold 14" and "A noble jar for pork or beef—then carry it around to the Indian chief."

### Face Jugs

Slaves were depicted on the sides of the jars made in Edgefield, as is the case with a large water cooler made at the Phoenix Factory by Thomas Chandler (1810–1854). Iron and kaolin slip were used to depict a slave wedding on one side. Other jugs from the Phoenix Factory bear pictorial images of African Americans. These "painted" images contrast with the face vessels made by Thomas Chandler and those made by the slaves. Many of the slave-made face jugs have been attributed to slaves who either worked at the Thomas Davies factoryi, also in the Edgefield area, or to those who brought them to the brickworks to be fired, around the time of the Civil War. Thomas Davies' account books from the Palmetto Fire Brick Works (1862–1865) in Aiken, South Carolina, provide the names of the 18 slaves who were hired out to work for him. The account book outlines their monthly wages along with the names of their owners. Jim, Dennis, Bob, Silas, Romeo, and Ike were the slaves of R. O. Starke who hired them out to Davies for $90 a month. The wages were $15 a month, and the "boys" were paid for overtime work. This rate was $2.50 higher than what was charged for many of the other slaves who worked for Davies.

These face jugs were generally small, with applied eyes, nose, mouth, and ears. The eyes were often rolled pieces of kaolin, so they were white in appearance with an incised dot for the pupil. The teeth were also very white; a few had rock teeth, whereas others have been attributed to the unknown potter called the "Master of diagonal teeth," so-called because of the potter's consistent use of diagonal teeth in surviving face jugs. The rest of the vessel was glazed and fired to a dark brown but most often to the soft olive-green of the alkaline glaze. Jim Lee created a figural vessel between 1860 and 1870 that represents the local preacher Reverend Pickett in his Civil War uniform, complete with applied clay epaulets and **buttons**. The vessel is atypical of the Edgefield face vessels, and the primary function of these pieces is still an enigma. A few of the vessels have a red waxy or paint-like residue around the mouth and nostrils.

Several of the Edgefield potteries annually produced vessels holding more than 40,000 gallons, as indicated in the Census of Industry records for the 1850s. Lewis Miles's factory employed seven men and two women and produced vessels that could hold more than 40,000 gallons and were valued at $4,000. Thomas Chandler employed 11 men and women, and his output was valued at $2,500. Collin Rhodes employed three men and three women, and his stoneware was valued at $2,000. At a price of $0.10 per gallon, these factories turned a profit. The wares were sold throughout the state and into the neighboring states of Georgia and North Carolina.

In the 1830s and into 1850s, spurred by economic depression and increased opportunities for more land and a fresh start, families moved westward and settled into Georgia, Alabama, Mississippi, and eventually as far away as Texas. The alkaline-glazed stoneware tradition moved westward as well. Those who operated potteries assisted by their slaves include the Cribbs, Presley, William, and Rushton families in Alabama and the Cogburn, Chandler, Frazier, and Wilson families in Texas.

An examination of the Wilson Pottery in Guadalupe, Texas, shows the role of African Americans as slaves and as freedmen in the production of pottery. John Wilson, of North Carolina, settled in Texas and soon opened a pottery that operated from 1857 to 1869. Hyrum and John, two of his slaves, were trained in the production of pottery in the Edgefield tradition using a groundhog kiln and the alkaline glaze. John Chandler, a former slave of Edgefield potter Thomas Chandler, and his associate Marion J. Durham, made their way to Guadalupe, Texas, in 1864, where they worked at the John M. Wilson Pottery. In 1869, Durham purchased the pottery from Wilson. The same year, Hyrum, James, Wallace, Andrew, and George Wilson established their own pottery, producing stoneware of a slightly different style from that of the Guadalupe and John Wilson potteries. The business, H. Wilson & Company, operated until 1884.

After the Civil War, African American potters continued to work in those areas; some like the Wilsons in Texas and Wash Miles in South Carolina established their own potteries and were successful. Others continued to work for their former masters. In the late 19th and early 20th centuries, traditional potteries faced a sharp decline as the economic landscape changed and the need for large stoneware vessels decreased with the advent of glass jars and metal cans.

*See also* Tobacco Pipes.

FURTHER READING

Baldwin, Cinda K. *Great and Noble Jar: Traditional Stoneware of South Carolina.* Athens: University of Georgia Press, 1993.

Brackner, Joey. *Alabama Folk Pottery.* Tuscaloosa: University of Alabama Press, 2006.

Brown, Michael. *The Wilson Potters: An African-American Enterprise in 19th-Century Texas.* Houston, TX: Bayou Bend Museum and Gardens, Museum of Fine Arts Houston, 2002.

Burrison, John A. *Brothers in Clay: The Story of Georgia Folk Pottery.* Athens: University of Georgia Press, 1983.

Ferguson, Leland. *Uncommon Ground: Archaeology and Early African America, 1650–1800.* Washington, DC: Smithsonian Institution Press, 1992.

Koverman, Jill Beute, ed. *"I Made This Jar . . ." The Life and Works of the Enslaved African-American Potter, Dave.* Columbia, SC: McKissick Museum, 1998.

Vlach, John Michael. *The Afro-American Tradition in the Decorative Arts.* Cleveland, OH: Cleveland Museum of Art, 1979.

JILL BEUTE KOVERMAN

**POUNDERS.** A pounder, also called a pestle, is a tool shaped out of stone or wood that is used in many cultures for food production. Pounded **yams**, for instance, are a central ingredient in fufu, a West African **stew** that has several African American adaptations.

In the Carolina Low Country's **rice**-growing areas, pounders were an essential tool in rice production, much of which was done by hand. Through "pounding," striking repetitively in a downward motion, workers milled rice grain by removing its rough hull. Rice pounders, long wooden cylinders pointed at either end, could weigh as much as 10 pounds. It took skill and experience not to crush the rice grains during pounding as well as strength to bring the heavy pounder down over and over again on the rice. By one estimate, male and female slaves who harvested rice were required to pound some 44 pounds of rice daily, to produce between four to six pecks (32 to 48 quarts) at harvest. Even highly skilled individuals who could work at the fastest speeds still needed to pound the rice for at least five hours per day to make their quotas.

Although 21st-century historians debate whether rice's successful establishment as a cash crop in the 18th-century Carolinas is directly attributable to African slaves, it is true that many individuals enslaved there hailed from West African regions, such as Senegambia, where rice was grown for **food**. In Africa, women pounded rice, but in the American South's rice plantations, work usually was not segregated by gender.

Some larger antebellum rice plantations established mechanized pounding mills, but for two centuries much of rice cultivation generally consisted of backbreaking manual labor performed by enslaved men and women.

FURTHER READING

Carney, Judith A. *Black Rice: The African Origins of Rice Cultivation in the Americas.* Cambridge, MA: Harvard University Press, 2002.

Edelson, S. Max. "Beyond 'Black Rice': Reconstructing Material and Cultural Contexts for Early Plantation Agriculture." *The American Historical Review* 115 (February 2010): 125–135.

---

### Pounding Rice

William Henry Davis pounded rice in South Carolina:

Oh, I beat rice many a day. Yes'um, beat rice many a day for my grandmother en my mamma too. Had a mortar en a pestle dat beat rice wid. Dey take big tree en saw log off en set it up just like a tub. Den dey hollow it out in de middle en take pestle dat have block on both it end en beat rice in dat mortar. Beat it long time en take it out en fan it en den put it back. De last time it put back, tear off some shucks en put in dere to get de red part of de rice out en make it white. Ain' nobody never been born can tell you more bout dem pestles en mortars den William Henry Davis know.

*Source:* George P. Rawick, ed. *The American Slave: South Carolina*, Vol. 2. Westport, CT: Greenwood Press, 1972.

---

Eltis, David, Philip Morgan, and David Richardson. "Agency and Diaspora in Atlantic History: Reassessing the African Contribution to Rice Cultivation in the Americas." *The American Historical Review* 112 (December 2007): 1329–1358.

Eltis, David, Philip Morgan, and David Richardson. "Black, Brown, or White? Color-Coding American Commercial Rice Cultivation with Slave Labor." *The American Historical Review* 115 (February 2010): 164–171.

Fox-Genovese, Elizabeth. *Within the Plantation Household: Black and White Women of the Old South.* Chapel Hill: University of North Carolina Press, 1988.

Hall, Gwendolyn Midlo. "Africa and Africans in the African Diaspora: The Uses of Relational Databases." *The American Historical Review* 115 (February 2010): 136–150.

Hawthorne, Walter. "From 'Black Rice' to 'Brown': Rethinking the History of Risiculture in the Seventeenth- and Eighteenth-Century Atlantic." *The American Historical Review* 115 (February 2010): 151–163.

Krauthamer, Barbara. "Black Women, Slavery, Kinship and Freedom in the American Southeast." In *Women and Slavery.* Vol. 2, *The Modern Atlantic,* edited by Gwyn Campbell, Suzanne Miers, and Joseph Calder Miller, 100–127. Athens: Ohio University Press, 2007.

KYM S. RICE

**PUNKAHS AND FLY BRUSHES.** The punkah, a ceiling-mounted fan often hung in Southern antebellum dining rooms, is inextricably tied to the institution of chattel slavery. The punkah is a crucial part of early American material life and attests to the complex social interactions between black slaves and white masters. Punkahs were exclusively used by slaves for the benefit of whites. The most popular version was a shaped wooden board attached to a cord, allowing it to be swung back and forth. The punkah was manipulated by young slaves who stood in a corner and pulled the cord to move the fan. The moving element created a breeze adequate enough to cool diners, but more important, the airflow kept flies and other insects from settling on diners and food during the meal. Nearly 40 examples survive throughout the South, with most clustered in Virginia, Mississippi, and Louisiana. The construction of these fans varied widely: some were improvised from local materials like pine, cypress, or walnut, while others were carefully crafted on a grand scale, making use of more exotic materials like highly figured mahogany. In the American context, the punkah also was referred to as "fan," "shoo fly," or "great fan." Although the origins of the U.S. form are unclear, the word punkah is of Southeast Asian origin, derived from the Hindi word *pankha*, meaning "hand fan made of palmyra leaves." It is documented as appearing in the English lexicon in the mid-17th century. British émigrés to India had difficulty with the heat, and, as a result, the punkah became omnipresent in British households and British-controlled public buildings in 18th-century India. The British version of the ever-present punkah was a large swinging fan made of **cotton**, stretched across a rectangular wooden frame and suspended from the ceiling. The fan was especially popular in dining rooms, parlors, and bedrooms. The punkah operator or punkah-wallah, as he commonly was called, worked the fan by pulling on a cord to agitate and refresh the air in hot weather. The punkah-wallah occupied the lowest caste in British India. The menial tasks performed by servants, particularly the ever-present punkah-wallah, often produced the charge of delinquency from ill-humored masters. The sight of the laboring punkah-wallah might have been so distasteful to the British that the wallah frequently resorted to operating the punkah by way of a

Punkah in dining room of the main house of Melrose plantation, Natchez, Mississippi. (Library of Congress.)

long cord out of sight of the person being cooled. It is this feature, the removal of the punkah-wallah's labor from view, that best characterizes the Indian form of the punkah and enables more careful consideration of the popularity of the American form.

Evidence suggests that an Indian punkah was imported into the United States during the first quarter of the 19th century. According to family history, Fulwar Skipwith (1765–1839), an American diplomat who frequently traveled overseas, procured the punkah from India for his aunt, Helen Skipwith Coles, the mistress of Tallwood, an Albemarle County, Virginia, plantation. Now lost, this punkah was constructed of a triangular wood panel festooned with classically ornamented wallpaper. It retained, however, a crucial element of the Indian-style punkah: slaves could labor out of sight. The Tallwood punkah is the only known American fan to have enabled the slaves to labor out of sight. Thomas Jefferson's (1743–1826) never-realized 1808 design for an automated fan at Monticello, Albemarle County, Virginia, had the punkah attached to a clock works to ensure continuous movement of the fan without the need for a slave to operate it. The removal of the slave to a different space from the person being fanned or the outright elimination of the need for a fanner at all is of particular note when considering the material culture of slavery. The absence of slaves guaranteed a modicum of privacy for diners, and they did not have to restrict conversation or behavior.

For slaveholders, the slave-operated punkah offered them physical comfort and an opportunity to display their wealth. The sight of a slave with both hands fully engaged in powering the fan for the comfort of the diners undoubtedly would have been regarded as an extravagant use of labor. This visual display was a part of a system of dining room labor that often included other liveried servants. An amply spread table laid with matching sets of fine china and sterling silver also contributed to the aura of plenty.

For the enslaved workers serving time at the punkah, dining room conversation could be illuminating. Booker T. Washington (1856–1915), the famed African American educator and orator, was born into slavery on a **tobacco** farm in Hale's Ford, Franklin County, Virginia. In his autobiography, *Up from Slavery*, Washington recalled that, as a young boy, he was required to go to the main house at meal times to fan flies, using a large set of papers fans operated by a pulley. Washington noted that because of his access to dining table conversation, he was able to learn a great deal about the progress of the Civil War and his impending freedom. Although these fans were not constructed or acquired by slaves, the enslaved were able to use their time working at the fan to their own benefit. Young slaves tending the diners were also freed from outdoor work and more likely to eventually take up service within the household upon coming of age. Laboring at the fan enabled slaves to limit and subvert the constraints of the slave system.

Washington's memories also show that survival in slave regimes provided a motive for acquisition of what might be considered to be performance skills. Apart from the work involved in enacting their servitude and inferiority while guarding their

Virginia dining room with a punkah on the ceiling, operated by an enslaved woman, from *Sketchbook of Landscapes in the State of Virginia* by Lewis Miller, Virginia, 1853–1867, watercolor and ink on paper. (Abby Aldrich Rockefeller Folk Art Museum, The Colonial Williamsburg Foundation. Gift of Dr. and Mrs. Richard M. Kain in memory of George Hay Kain.)

---

**Keeping the Flies Away**

Neal Upson kept the flies off the table in the master's house in Georgia:

Marse Frank said he wanted 'em to larn me how to wait on de white folkses' table up at de big 'ouse, and dey started me off wid de job of fannin' de flies away. Mist'ess Serena, Marse Frank's wife, made me a white coat to wear in de dinin' room. Missy, dat little old white coat made me git de onliest whuppin' Marse Frank ever did give me." Here old Neal paused for a hearty laugh. "Us had comp'ny for dinner dat day and I felt so big showin' off 'fore 'em in dat white coat dat I jus' couldn't make dat turkey wing fan do right. Dem turkey wings was fastened on long handles and atter Marster had done warned me a time or two to mind what I was 'bout, the old turkey wing went down in de gravy bowl and when I jerked it out it splattered all over de preacher's best Sunday suit. Marse Frank got up and tuk me right out to de kitchen and when he got through brushin' me off I never did have no more trouble wid dem turkey wings.

*Source:* George P. Rawick, ed. The *American Slave: Georgia Narratives*, Vol. 13. Westport, CT: Greenwood Press, 1972.

---

autonomy, enslaved people found significant everyday triumphs by mimicking and in a sense mastering, through imitation, their masters and mistresses. Frequent contact with whites, especially the sort facilitated by wielding the fans, allowed slaves to attune themselves to manners and mannerisms of the ruling class. In turn, slaves were able to engage in mimicry with an eye toward becoming masters of their own circumstances. An historical example of this is Ellen and William Craft's (1826–1891; 1824–1900) courageous escape from slavery in Georgia. The daughter of an African American slave mother and a white slave owner, Ellen Craft was able to use skills gleaned from exposure to whites to impersonate a Southern slave owner by cutting her hair short and dressing in trousers and top hat. With her husband, William, who joined in the charade by masquerading as her enslaved valet, the Crafts made a daring escape by train and steamship.

Besides the punkah, other objects such as the fly brush, a handle with feathers, were deployed to offer diners relief. Henry Coleman, who was enslaved on Fairfield plantation, Charleston County, South Carolina, recounted to a Federal Writers' Project interviewer in the 1930s the process of creating and using a fly brush. Coleman noted that young children were required to climb up to the peafowl roosts to catch and extract feathers from them. The long, colorful feathers were then used to construct a fly brush. Coleman described being directed to place himself in a swing above the dining room table to fan the flies and gnats off of the food. He acknowledged that seating a young slave in a swing above the dining room table was a widespread practice and that slaveholders even installed a set of stairs to ease access to the swing. Coleman had to manipulate the fly brush with a fair amount of skill to avoid getting the feathers into the gravy and splattering the table. Whipping was a frequent punishment for such an offense. Coleman also noted that young enslaved children were punished for falling asleep at their task. But this unusual job afforded Coleman the opportunity to observe his owners and their guests and gain knowledge of white customs and practices that would serve him well as an adult.

*See also* Livery.

FURTHER READING

"Born in Slavery: Slave Narratives from the Federal Writers' Project, 1936–1938," American Memory, Library of Congress. At http://memory.loc.gov/ammem/snhtml/.

Garrett, Elisabeth Donaghy. *At Home: The American Family, 1750–1870*. New York: Harry N. Abrams, 1989.

Washington, Booker T. *Up from Slavery*. Edited by William T. Andrews. New York: Oxford University Press, 1995.

DANA E. BYRD

# Q

**QUILTS.** Quilts and slavery often are linked in the modern imagination, but while enslaved women certainly were involved in quiltmaking, it is less clear how often they were able to make quilts for their own use or how or whether these quilts differed from those made by quilters of European ancestry. Of the thousands of pre-Emancipation quilts in private and museum collections, only about a dozen are plausibly identified as slave-made quilts, and all were made for the slaveholding family in the materials, techniques, and designs fashionable at the time. Surviving antebellum examples made by free African American women for their own use follow the same stylistic trends as their white counterparts; this is also true of most quilts known to have been made by former slaves in between the Civil War and World War II.

Contemporary accounts show that many slaves, almost exclusively female, were active in home **textile** production, as were most American women before the Civil War regardless of race or status. Slave owner diaries and Federal Writers' Project interviews of former slaves in the 1930s frequently describe them carding **wool** and **cotton**, spinning and dyeing yarn, knitting, weaving, and **sewing** for the entire household. But the enjoyable pastime of "patchwork" or "piecing," which is assembling a quilt's patterned top, is almost never mentioned. Far more common are references to "quilting," which is joining the completed top, insulating filling, and **cloth** back with rows of stitching, a tedious job made more bearable by its collective, social nature.

The scarcity of antebellum slave-made quilts and the absence of authenticated examples made for their own use is understandable in context. Quilts often are associated with poverty, but they originated in prosperity, and before the mid-1830s, few but the most affluent households owned more than one. It seems unlikely that quilts would be more widespread in the **slave quarters**, where materials and free time were scarce. In isolated rural areas, which relied almost entirely on home-woven cloth, **blankets** and woven coverlets remained far more common; blankets sometimes appear in lists of items distributed to slaves every one or two years.

As both mass-produced cloth and the cash to buy it grew more available after 1870, quilts became commonplace in African American households. By the early 20th century, however, quiltmaking was widely regarded as old fashioned, and after a brief if enthusiastic revival in the 1930s and 1940s, the craft was nearly abandoned in much of the United States. In little more than a century, it had evolved from decorative needlework to an anachronistic means of "making do" preserved in rural areas, especially in the impoverished Deep South. As African Americans migrated north and west during World War II, this comparatively recent tradition traveled with them.

Quilts rarely were treated as historic artifacts until the 1970s when the bicentennial revived interest in American crafts. This missing history was notable in the first observations made about the work of quilters outside the American mainstream, including African Americans. Similarities between modern African textiles and a select group of mostly 20th-century quilts led to hasty conclusions that black quilters had inherited a unique aesthetic from their African ancestors, consisting of improvisation, asymmetry, repetitive design, and bold colors and patterns arranged in vertical strips. But it does not seem possible that the African fabrics usually cited could have been the source of these qualities. Multicolored *kente*, boldly patterned *bogolanfini*, "Kuba cloth," painted-resist *adire eleko* (cloth on which designs are painted with cassava starch paste that is removed after the cloth is dyed, leaving white patterns on a blue background), Fon and Fante appliquéd panels, and patchwork Madhi tunics first appeared generations after the last slave arrived on North American shores. These fabrics were made by people rarely taken into bondage or were so closely linked to ritual use that translation into everyday, utilitarian objects is hard to imagine.

The textiles American slaves' African ancestors did make and use were subtler and more complex than their modern counterparts suggest. Surviving examples and contemporary descriptions indicate that while large cloths were made by joining several narrow strips along their lengthwise edge, this construction typically was obscured by overdyeing or painting in delicate patterns. "Women's cloth" was made of only one or two checked or striped panels between two and three feet wide. Symmetry was common and, in some cultures, such as among the Kongo, amounted to an obsession. Because most textiles were made from dye-resistant vegetable fiber such as cotton, the colors worn by most people were limited to natural white, blue, black, and shades of brown, ranging from gold to chocolate. Bright hues such as crimson, purple, and green were limited to accent colors in prestige garments, obtained from yarn unraveled from European cloth. Thus, most African-born slaves, especially the women employed in textile production on American plantations, would have remembered making and using hand-woven cotton left natural white or in solid, striped, checked, or tie-dyed blue and brown. This was a sophisticated, often monochromatic palette quite different from the bold mixture of colors in the ostensibly "traditional" African American quilt.

Quilt historians also pointed out that, contrary to logic, the older the quilt, the less likely it was to fit the stereotype. It soon became apparent that the compositional qualities assumed to be Africanisms were also the norm in the earliest British and American quilts; they remain so in regions with no discernible African presence, such as among the Midwestern Amish and Canadian Mennonites and in rural New Mexico, Australia, and Wales. The common thread among these quilters is conservatism, either philosophical or economic. Long after frugal "improvisational" styles were abandoned in more prosperous, urban areas in favor of complicated decorative patchwork, they were retained by communities that rejected changing fashion or could not afford to follow it. A quilt's appearance was determined less by race than by economic factors, such as materials, tools, available time, and purpose as a decorative item or functional bedcover.

Assembling a quilt top was often a solitary occupation, but quilting usually was done by many hands at once, often those of elderly women unable to be otherwise employed or in the off-season when laborers were not needed in the fields. Depending on the quilt's intended user, this work might be done in the slave owner's house, the building where cloth was woven, outdoors, or in a sufficiently large and well-lit slave cabin. A slave owner's quilt might take as much as a week to finish, while several slave quilts might be completed hurriedly in a single night. Whether for slave owner or slave, this work might take place at a "bee" or "frolic" permitted or even sponsored by the slave owner. As at similar events for **corn**-husking and cotton-picking, once the work was over, participants and their families would enjoy **food**, music, games, and dancing. Most descriptions of bees are vague recollections of early childhood by elderly former slaves or nostalgic reminiscences by former slaveholders, so it is hard to tell whether their mention means they were commonplace events or so rare as to be memorable.

The wide variety of living conditions experienced by enslaved African Americans in urban and rural areas as house servants, craftsmen, laborers, and farmers makes conclusive statements about the prevalence and appearance of slave-owned quilts impossible, except to say that they reflected the circumstances of the maker rather than a universal aesthetic. However, a few references in **slave narratives** and the materials known to have been used for slave clothing do provide some clues.

In summer, fieldworkers and laborers commonly were dressed in a heavy homespun or factory-made cotton in natural white, **indigo** blue, and brown checks and stripes referred to by the catchall term "**Negro cloth**." Winter garments were made of a homespun wool and cotton blend called linsey, worn by both races in rural areas where it was sometimes the only cloth available. Unlike cotton, wool takes color easily, so linsey often was woven in stripes and plaids as well as solids, sometimes in surprisingly bright colors. However, these fabrics' bulk and loose weave make complex, precise patchwork and quilting extremely difficult. The few surviving 19th-century linsey quilts, made by white settlers in frontier areas such as the Ohio Valley, are in simple medallion and strip formats or patchwork designs with comparatively large pieces and are rustic interpretations of earlier British forms. Some incorporate old blankets for the top, back, or filling. Appearance was important but secondary to function, resulting in what modern eyes can interpret as spontaneity or intentional asymmetry. It is possible that the quilts made by enslaved laborers and field workers were similar to these examples. The question remains whether many such people had access to any fabric they did not desperately need for **clothing**. Until puberty, most children wore nothing but a simple tunic; adults typically received only one or two outfits each year. These were worn and repaired until they disintegrated, then used to patch other garments.

House servants, seamstresses, craftsmen, and slaves in urban areas often wore somewhat better clothing; seamstresses in particular might be able to accumulate scraps of the lightweight, tightly woven, printed fabric that permitted small pieces and more elaborate, finer quilting. Their post–Civil War quilts, like those made by free black women before Emancipation, reflect both the time they were able to devote to design and construction and their interest in prevailing trends in quilt style. It seems doubtful these quilts are much different from those they might have made in the antebellum period.

Beginning in the 1990s, a popular belief spread that, in the South before the Civil War, quilts with geometric patterns were used to help fugitive slaves escape north to freedom, either as signal flags, maps, teaching devices, or awards to those arriving in Canada. Although often presented as legitimate oral history or at least a plausible theory, the "**Underground Railroad** Quilt Code" is one of several late 20th-century quilt-related myths.

For most of the story's brief history, few African Americans regarded it as credible or had even heard of it. Specific claims that it is part of family oral tradition are recent and rare, incorporating familiar Biblical themes, romantic or racial stereotypes, and ancestors who either used the Quilt Code only to help others flee or who heard about it secondhand or thirdhand. No authentic "Code" quilt or artifact supporting these stories has ever been produced.

Like other urban legends, as the myth spread through popular culture, variations appeared involving groups as disparate as Long Island Native Americans and European Jews under Hitler. Sometimes the story refers to famous abolitionists such as Harriet Tubman (1822–1913) and Frederick Douglass (ca. 1818–1895), although neither of these former slaves mentions anything resembling it. Nor do quilts appear among the codes, signals, and escape methods described in the accounts left by hundreds of successful escaped slaves and Underground Railroad participants.

In reality, many fugitive slaves, particularly in the Deep South, headed south toward Mexico and the Caribbean, not north; most traveled alone, not in groups; most escapes were spontaneous, not planned; and most were unaided by the Underground Railroad, a loosely knit organization operating mostly in the North and mid-Atlantic. Even families claiming the story as authentic oral history do not agree on how quilts were used or displayed, or what their patterns meant. The messages attributed to many of the patterns have nothing to do with escape, are condescendingly obvious, or direct fugitives to take unnecessary risks. Several of the Quilt Code's most important patterns are known to have originated generations after the last American slave fled bondage.

The 20th-century design known as Double Wedding Ring illustrates the Quilt Code's historical and logical incongruities. Initially it was said that this instructed fugitives heading for Canada to stop in Cleveland, dress in their best clothes, and marry in a cathedral. When this seemed implausible, the story was revised: it might have told them to get their "slave rings" cut off in a church with stained-glass windows, or might refer to a sound. Another version says that to advertise it was a safe place for slaves to hide, at midday a church would ring its bells and hang a Double Wedding Ring quilt from its steeple.

The Quilt Code evolved gradually beginning in the late 1980s, after a series of popular but poorly researched exhibits and books about African American quilts included vague suggestions that quilts somehow could have been used as escape signals. By 1993, Ozella McDaniel Williams, a black vendor in a Charleston, South Carolina, tourist mall, was using the story to sell quilts, culminating after her death in 1998 with the publication of Raymond Dobard and Jacqueline Tobin's *Hidden in Plain View: A Secret Story of Quilts and the Underground Railroad*.

Promoted through popular media such as Oprah Winfrey's talk show, the book was embraced unquestioningly by the general public even as historians criticized it as unscholarly and ahistorical. Authors Dobard and Tobin acknowledged in the introduction that they ignored generally accepted research methods by "present[ing] a theory before finding a wealth of tangible evidence," but they have refused to address skeptics' questions. In 2007, Tobin complained to *Time* magazine that "people have tried to push the book in directions it was not meant for."

Among *Hidden in Plain View*'s critics were Williams's own relatives, who denied Tobin's assertion she had confirmed the story with them. Shortly after the book's discussion on *Oprah*, a Williams niece began giving presentations on her own version of the Quilt Code. Another Williams briefly operated a Quilt Code museum and gift shop in an Atlanta storefront, claiming to possess "written firsthand evidence" but refusing to reveal it. Both maintain the Quilt Code was brought from Africa by Williams's grandmother Eliza, a free itinerant seamstress who taught it to slaves as she traveled with her husband and children. Records later revealed Eliza was born in Georgia and would have been only a child when the Civil War began.

## FURTHER READING

Allen, Gloria Seamon. "Quiltmaking on Chesapeake Plantations." In *On the Cutting Edge: Textile Collectors, Collections, and Traditions*, edited by Jeannette Lasansky, 56–69. Lewisburg, PA: Oral Traditions Project, 1994.

Benberry, Cuesta. *Always There: The African-American Presence in American Quilts*. Louisville: Kentucky Quilt Project, 1992.

Brackman, Barbara. *Facts & Fabrications: Unraveling the History of Quilts and Slavery: 8 Projects—20 Blocks—First-Person Accounts*. Lafayette, CA: C & T Publishing, 2006.

Durand, Sally Graham. "The Dress of the Ante-bellum Field Slave in Louisiana and Mississippi from 1830 to 1860." MA thesis, Louisiana State University, 1977.

Fellner, Leigh. "Betsy Ross Redux: The Underground Railroad 'Quilt Code'," Hart Cottage Quilts. At www.ugrrquilt.hartcottagequilts.com.

Fellner, Leigh. "What We Think We Remember: Diaspora-era African Textiles and African-American Quilts," Hart Cottage Quilts. At www.hartcottagequilts.com/africantextiles.

German, Sandra K. "Surfacing: The Inevitable Rise of the Women of Color Quilters' Network." *Uncoverings* 14 (1993):137–168.

Holstein, Jonathan. *Abstract Design in American Quilts: A Biography of an Exhibition*. Louisville: Kentucky Quilt Project, 1991.

Huff, Mary Elizabeth Johnson, and J. D. Schwalm. *Mississippi Quilts*. Jackson: University Press of Mississippi, 2001.

Jonson, Geraldine. "More for Warmth Than for Looks: Quilts of the Blue Ridge Mountain." In *Pieced by Mother: Symposium Papers*, 47–60. Lewisburg, PA: Oral Traditions Project of the Union County Historical Society, 1988.

Kriger, Colleen E. *Cloth in West African History*. Lanham, MD: AltaMira Press, 2006.

Stachiw, Myron O. "'For the Sake of Commerce': Rhode Island, Slavery, and the Textile Industry." An Essay by Myron O. Stachiw to Accompany the Exhibit "The Loom and the Lash: Northern Industry and Southern Slavery." Providence: Rhode Island Historical Society, 1982.

Wright, Giles R. "Critique: Hidden in Plain View: The Secret Story of Quilts and the Underground Railroad, June 4, 2001," Historic Camden County. At www.historiccamdencounty.com/ccnews11_doc_01a.shtml.

Zegart, Shelly. "Myth and Methodology." *Selvedge* 21 (January/February 2008).

Zegart, Shelly. "Passionate about Quilts." At www.shellyquilts.com/go/resources/read.php?article=myth-and-methodology.

LEIGH FELLNER

# R

**RATIONS.** Rations were the **food** allowances provided by slaveholders to enslaved individuals or families. Regional custom, the kind of labor performed, and state slave codes frequently established the types and amounts of food that a planter was expected to provide to his enslaved workforce. The study of food rations on farms and plantations offers a glimpse into the ways that slaveholders sought to control and manipulate the lives of their enslaved workforce and its community life. Because enslaved life varied from time to time and place to place, "typical" rations for an enslaved person are not easily encapsulated by any one account.

As early as 1732, William Hugh Grove recorded that enslaved workers in Virginia were allotted a peck, equal to the dry measure of two gallons, of **corn** per week. Later in the 18th century, Johann Bolzius (1703–1765) observed South Carolina African Americans living on sweet potatoes, broken **rice**, corn, and beans as their predominate rations, depending on the season. These rations seem to have been partly based on allotments doled out on **slave ships**, where corn, rice, **yams**, or other edible tubers and cowpeas and beans were supplied to meet the dietary tastes of the enslaved Africans being transported. The early ration system also paralleled similar eating habits among poor laboring whites and their dietary expectations as indentured servants, as the system grew out of the need to supply the physical needs of fieldworkers who labored between 12 and 16 hours per day. The *Maryland Journal and Baltimore Advertiser* reported in 1788 that "[a] single peck of corn a week, or the like measure of rice, is the ordinary quantity of provision for a hard-working slave; to which a small quantity of meat is occasionally, though rarely, added."

By the 19th century, rations were described as being disbursed to slaves on a weekly basis. Saturdays, Sundays, or Mondays are most often mentioned as the days when enslaved people were given their provisions. Formerly enslaved people remembered laborers coming piecemeal or lined up as a group to collect a certain amount of corn, preserved pork or **fish**, and sometimes salt, molasses, and other foods seasonally provided at the plantation storehouse. A heavily guarded building, the plantation storehouse was essentially the food bank of the property, and rations were carefully tracked to ensure that theft did not occur and that each worker received what the planter thought each ought rightfully to receive. Age, gender, labor, and status all determined

---

## Food for the Week

Former Texas slave William Stone sang a song about food rations on his Texas plantation:

> Dat ration day come once a week,
> Old massa rich as Gundy.
> But he give 'lasses all de week,
> And buttermilk for Sunday.
> Old massa give a pound of meat,
> I et it all on Monday;
> Den I at 'lasses all de week,
> And buttermilk for Sunday.

Emma Taylor from Texas remembered stealing potatoes to get enough to eat:

> All de victuals was issued out by de overseer and he give 'nough for one week, den iffen us eat it all up too soon, it am jist go without. Lots of times, I went down to de 'tato patch a long time after everybody am in bed, and stole 'tatoes, so we wouldn't be hungry next day. I allus covered de hole up good and never did git cotched. De dogs got after me one time, but I put pepper in dey eyes and dey stopped. I allus carried pepper with me.

*Source:* George P. Rawick, ed. *The American Slave: Texas Narratives*, Vol. 5, Parts 3 & 4. Westport, CT: Greenwood Press, 1972.

Cicely Cawthorn described the rations that were kept in the smoke house in Georgia: "They 'lowanced slaves their rations once a week. Great big smoke-house! It was something to see all the vittals that come from the smokehouse once a week, syrup, meal, flour, bacon, a big hunk if there was a family."

*Source:* George P. Rawick, ed. *The American Slave: Georgia Narratives*, Supp. Ser. 1, Vol. 3, Part 1. Westport, CT: Greenwood Press, 1978.

---

how much or how little food a person was allotted. Autobiographer and former slave Harriet Jacobs (1813–1897) remembered that in eastern North Carolina, "[t]hree pounds of meat, a peck of corn, and perhaps a dozen herrings were allowed each man. Women received a pound and a half of meat, a peck of corn, and the same number of herring." The most prized field laborers, craftsmen, and house servants had an advantage in the ration system; women, children, and the elderly did not always fare so well. Many enslaved women did not receive extra rations during pregnancy, elderly men too old to work might be denied an allowance completely, as they were on Harriet Jacob's plantation, and children largely were fed on mush and only tasted a diversity of foods as they became food producers and procurers within their family circle.

The number and types of rations differed greatly according to each planter's policy. In the 19th-century Chesapeake, a peck of corn, half a pound of salted pork, and three or four salted herrings might serve as a week's rations. In Texas, five or six pounds of dried beef might be given out. According to Charles Ball, a Maryland slave who was hired out to the Washington Navy Yard in the 1820s, a meat allowance might only be given out once a month on other farms. Molasses was dispensed by the quart or gallon depending on the size of the family, and other types of rations similarly were given out on the basis of need. Extra food sometimes could be obtained through extra work or **barter**, trade, or theft. Some enslaved people did not collect rations at all but had their meals prepared at a common **kitchen**, where a group of older or elderly women cooked and disbursed corn mush, ashcakes or **hoecakes**, preserved pork, and broths or soups by order of the planter, his wife, or an overseer. According to ex-slave Eleazar Powell who was hired out to work in Mississippi, "The slaves received two meals during the day. Those who have their food cooked for them get their breakfast about eleven o'clock, and their other meal after night."

Attitudes toward the rations system varied. For some 19th-century observers, it justified their notion that slavery was preferable to being a poor, free white, without support. Noted landscape architect Frederick Law Olmsted (1822–1903) on visiting the South stated, "I think the slaves generally (no one denies there are exceptions) have plenty to eat; probably are fed better than the proletarian class of any other part of the world." To the contrary, Mississippi river captain Tobias Boudinot reported, "The slaves down the Mississippi, are half-starved, the boats, when they stop at night, are constantly boarded by slaves, begging for something to eat." Rev. Horace Moulton, a Methodist minister who spent five years in Georgia, observed, "As a general thing on the plantations, the slaves suffer extremely for the want of food." Former slave Lillian Clarke of Virginia noted that her Aunt Lucinda received "one salt herrin' fish up on a shelf fer her to eat. Mind you, dats all po' Cinda got fer all day long. No ain't giveno bread with hit. She had to eate dat or nothing." Abolitionist Frederick Douglass (ca. 1818–1895) and other former enslaved persons sang songs of derision and complaint that noted the lack of food and inadequate rations they received each week.

## Regional Variations

Perhaps the only truly common ration across the South's various regions was corn. Alewife and blueback herring, anadromous fish that live in saltwater but return to freshwater to spawn, were central to the diet of enslaved workers from the southern Mid-Atlantic through the greater Chesapeake and Tidewater North Carolina. In these same areas, especially during the colonial period, terrapin and shad also occasionally served a similar role, while in the Low Country salted mackerel or mullet might be the fish allotted. In those parts of the South where large quantities of **pigs** were raised for the production of preserved pork, a standard meat ration was more likely than in other areas. Sweet potatoes formed an especially important part of the slave diet, from the sandier soils of southern and eastern Maryland sweeping south and west along the coastal plains to Texas. Broken rice was most endemic to the southeastern rice coast in the counties around Wilmington, North Carolina, to northeastern Florida, as well as southern Louisiana. Temporary seasonal gluts of buttermilk as well as fruit grown on the plantation or farm occasionally were disbursed at the discretion of the slaveholder. In the **cotton** kingdom's heyday where the cultivation of the crop might require the labor of an entire enslaved community for 10 months each year, certain types of produce commonly were raised for the enslaved community's consumption and were factored into a ration system, including cabbages or **collards**, sweet potatoes, and field peas. As domestically produced molasses and cheaper molasses from the Caribbean became more affordable, syrup became a ration used to restore energy with the hidden benefit of providing necessary iron in the diet.

### Rations as a Matter of Power

In the antebellum period some planters published their formulas on how to best supply food, **clothing**, and other essentials to enslaved people to maintain their health while remaining financially beneficial for the slaveholder. Periodicals such as *Debows Review* and the *Southern Planter* offer insight into discussion among planters on how best to use rations to guarantee compliance and "domestic tranquility" on the plantation. And yet, all plantations had serious deficiencies in their rationing system. As standardized as the ration system became, it was not a guaranteed source of food for slaves. Many slaveholders used rations, as any other necessity or reward associated with slavery, as a means of control. Rations did not always include meat or fish, especially in the Low Country where, according to one witness, "meat, when given, is only by way of indulgence or favor." Certain foods were dangled before enslaved workers as treats rather than the allowances that they had a right to by law or custom. In other cases, inadequate provisioning led to substandard food supplies that either were preserved poorly or ran out before new provisions could be acquired. Salt, coffee, wheat flour, **sugar**, or other "luxuries" might be provided only at special times such as Christmas. Many enslaved communities never encountered these goods. Such was the custom that cornmeal became known as "common," and wheat flour as "seldom" in enslaved communities.

FURTHER READING

Covey, Herbert C., and Dwight Eisnach. *What the Slaves Ate: Recollections of African American Foods and Foodways from the Slave Narratives*. Santa Barbara, CA: Greenwood Press, 2009.

Joyner, Charles. *Down by the Riverside: A South Carolina Slave Community*. Urbana: University of Illinois Press, 1984.

McKee, Larry. "Food Supply and Plantation Order: An Archaeological Perspective." In *I, Too, Am America: Archaeological Studies of African-American Life*, edited by Theresa A. Singleton, 218–239. Charlottesville: University of Virginia Press, 1999.

Morgan, Philip D. *Slave Counterpoint: Black Culture in the Eighteenth-Century Chesapeake and Lowcountry*. Chapel Hill: University of North Carolina Press, 1998.

Weld, Theodore. *American Slavery as It Is*. New York: American Anti-Slavery Society, 1839.

MICHAEL W. TWITTY

**RAZORS.** Instruments for the removal of **hair** from the bodies of both men and women are of prehistoric origin. These razors were made of shaped flint, sharpened **shells** or even sharks' teeth, and similar instruments were used until improvements in metalworking technology ca. 3,000 BCE led to the adoption of copper and solid gold razors with blades that could be resharpened. Examples of these types of razors have been found in Egyptian tombs. Shaving as a customary grooming habit is of relatively recent origin and considered to have started with the Romans in the fifth century BCE, although it was difficult and painful because the tools available were not the most efficient or safe.

With the invention of the straight razor in the 18th century, following the invention of hardened steel in Sheffield, England, shaving became less difficult although no less dangerous, because the straight razor, used incorrectly or by someone with little experience, easily cut the skin, sometimes with serious consequences. Straight razors are made of one piece of shaped, hardened steel with one ground edge that, with proper care, can be resharpened many times. The handle, usually formed of two scales (protective pieces of bone, horn, ivory, or wood), is attached to the razor with a pin so that the razor can rotate to be stored between the scales. From the mid-18th century forward, most of these razors were manufactured in Sheffield, the center of English cutlery and edge tool making.

Razors were the principal implements used by barbers. From the 18th through the mid-19th centuries, free and enslaved African American men dominated the barbering trade in both the North and the South. Individuals received their training as barbers either by apprenticeship or through previous service as a valet or waiting man to a slaveholder—a job that often garnered preferential treatment from owners and deference from other slaves. Sometimes, as in the relationship of Virginia plantation owner, Landon Carter (1710–1778), and his enslaved waiting man, Nassau, this bond was fraught with tension caused by the closeness of master and slave, specifically, Carter's constant struggle to make Nassau adhere to the conventional boundaries of the master-slave relationship, and Nassau's refusal to do so.

Particularly in cities, barbering was a lucrative trade that catered to a white clientele. In fact, antebellum African American barbers were criticized for refusing to serve their fellow blacks and for deferring to whites too much on the job. Studies of wealth in the antebellum period rank barbers among the most affluent entrepreneurs in the African American community. Their financial success translated into property owning including, in some cases, slaves.

Many barbers also dressed hair and some performed bloodletting treatments such as leeching and cupping. In addition to razors, the tools necessary for the barbering trade included shears for cutting hair, towels, bibs, and basins for rinsing. Barbers used hair tonic and scent or cologne on their customers and also sold them by the bottle. They routinely provided cigars and newspapers for their best clients. As the 19th century progressed, barbershop interiors became more elaborate and included upholstered chairs for clients to sit in that sometimes reclined, towel racks, spittoons, and wall-mounted **mirrors** for viewing.

William Johnson, who became a successful barber in antebellum Natchez, Mississippi, was born a slave. His diary (1835–1851), which is published, gives a detailed account of his life and work in his business. At his death in 1851, Johnson owned 16 slaves, several barber shops, a bathing house as well as other property. The National Park Service restored his residence and opened it as a museum in 2005. Undoubtedly aided by his close association with whites, William Meekins, a Richmond, Virginia, barber, became active in the **Underground Railroad**, helping individuals escape slavery and also contacting their families with news about their whereabouts.

## FURTHER READING

Bristol, Douglas Walter. *Knights of the Razor: Black Barbers in Slavery and Freedom*. Baltimore, MD: Johns Hopkins University Press, 2009.

Carter, Landon. *The Diary of Colonel Landon Carter of Sabine Hall, 1752–1778*. Edited by Jack P. Greene. Richmond: Virginia Historical Society, 1987.

Durbin, Gail. *Wig, Hairdressing and Shaving Bygones.* Aylesbury, Bucks: Shire, 1984.

Isaac, Rhys. *Landon Carter's Uneasy Kingdom: Revolution and Rebellion on a Virginia Plantation.* New York: Oxford University Press, 2004.

Johnson, William. *William Johnson's Natchez: The Ante-Bellum Diary of a Free Negro.* Edited by William Ransom Hogan and Edwin Adams Davis. 1951. Reprint, Baton Rouge: Louisiana State University Press, 1993.

Smith, Joseph. *Explanation or Key, to the Various Manufactories of Sheffield, with Engravings of Each Article.* Edited by John S. Kebabian. South Burlington, VT: Early American Industries Association, (1816) 1975.

Tonkin, Ellen. *History of Shaving.* Nottingham: Arts Department, Castle Museum, ca. 1980s.

Unwin, Joan. *Sheffield Industries: Cutlery, Silver and Edge Tools.* Stroud, England: Tempus, 1999.

KYM S. RICE

**RIBBONS.** Ribbons are relatively narrow widths of woven fabrics with selvage edges used in multiple ways: to bind, tie, decorate, and signify. Some of the most common and complicated little special commodities available in the world of the slave, ribbons drew meanings from multiple cultures and times and functioned in myriad ways.

Ribbons gave great sensuous pleasure and imparted deep symbolic meaning for many early modern cultures. Wrapping a maypole in Europe, or flapping from a tambourine's pounding, ribbons represented the rays of the sun. Brightly colored ribbons that fluttered and flew appealed in West African spiritual practices using particular bright colors and in bodily movement of dance that swayed and turned as seen, for example, in current Yoruba practices. In the 21st century, wearing a ribbon expresses allegiance to a particular cause or denotes honor at competitive events. But in these places and times, the most common use for ribbons has been in proximity to bodies: to ornament (wrapping necks or hatbands), connect (tying together aprons or **shoes**), and contain (tying back **hair**). Ribbons are part of fashion, seen or unseen.

Enslaved African Americans used ribbons in all these ways. Most of their **clothing** was supplied in a drab, often undyed state, so many wished to differentiate their garb from others or make it more colorful. Especially when dressing up in their best apparel, they used ribbons to ornament and embellish their clothing. Texas slave Larnce Holt remembered going to social events like dances where "all da guls wear ribbon around their waists. And one around de head." His own black pants had red ribbons up the legs. Others used ribbons to dress up and personalize hand-me-down clothing from mistress or friend. Even holiday rituals like the performance of John Canoe (Jonkanu), documented for slaves in North Carolina, used dress up and role play, and particular characters had special costumes bedecked with trailing ribbons.

Something as mundane as a colored snippet is also romantic and sensual in its position on the body and its place as a transmitter of emotions. Giving a ribbon as a token of courtship was a common English custom and signified both gift and promise. Tempie Herndon, a Piedmont North Carolina slave, remembered with great pride how her new husband formalized their wedding by carving a big red **button** into a ring. He had carved and finished it with such care that it looked like a red satin ribbon, and she wore it for fifty years.

Ribbons were actively traded as **barter goods** and slaves purchased them at local stores. One country store in Virginia placed an order for 20 dozen assorted fashionable ribbons priced by the dozen at six to eight shillings a dozen. A few specifically named colors were priced at six to eight pence apiece. "Negroe Jack" bought one yard of ribbon for ten pence at another Virginia store in 1764. "Love ribbons" were sold in 18th-century Virginia stores; women tucked these inexpensive tokens in the bosom or around the neck, both places of bodily eroticism.

By the time of the American Revolution, it had become quite fashionable to wear a ribbon wrapped around one's neck. One of the most famous portraits of an 18th-century African American woman was of poet Phillis Wheatley (1753–1784), and she is displayed as a proper civilized woman—her hair in a demure cap and a black ribbon winding her neck. Enslaved women may have used ribbons in wrapping their hair. Only shreds of evidence form a picture of ribbon usage in slavery. If a garment was preserved, the ribbons may have been removed and reused. If the ribbons were saved in some form, they were sometimes of poor quality and hence decayed. Ribbons held together the sides of shoes with a metal buckle; on several archaeological sites of enslaved people the ribbon has decayed, but the buckle remains.

Ribbons have another important connection to slavery. The five pages of the **Emancipation Proclamation** from January 1, 1863, are preserved the National Archives in Washington, D.C., and were bound with narrow blue and red ribbons, attached to a wax impression of the seal of the United States. The ribbons remain even as the seal has worn away.

*See also* Negro Cloth.

FURTHER READING

Baumgarten, Linda. "Clothes for the People: Slave Clothing in Early Virginia." *Journal of Early Southern Decorative Arts* 14 (1988): 44–45.

"Born in Slavery: Slave Narratives from the Federal Writers' Project, 1936–1938," American Memory, Library of Congress. At http://memory.loc.gov/ammem/snhtml/.

Fraser, Rebecca J. *Courtship and Love among the Enslaved in North Carolina.* Jackson: University Press of Mississippi, 2007.

Martin, Ann Smart. *Buying into the World of Goods: Early Consumers in the Virginia Backcountry.* Baltimore: Johns Hopkins University Press, 2008.

Martin, Ann Smart. "Ribbons of Desire: Gendered Stories in the World of Goods." In *Gender, Taste, and Material Culture in Britain and North America in the Long Eighteenth Century,* edited by Amanda Vickery and John Styles, 179–200. New Haven. CT: Yale University Press, 2006.

Morgan, Phillip. *Slave Counterpoint: Black Culture in the Eighteenth-Century Chesapeake and Low Country.* Chapel Hill: University of North Carolina Press, 1998.

ANN SMART MARTIN

**RICE AND RICE FIELDS.** Before **cotton** was king in the South, there was rice. Rice plantations were the first successful large agricultural plantations to develop in the southeastern United States. Beginning in colonial South Carolina, rice became an important crop as colonists looked for profit. Other successful products from the Caribbean such as **indigo** and **sugar** never were grown as successfully and because of environmental conditions never achieved the potential that rice production attained in the southeast.

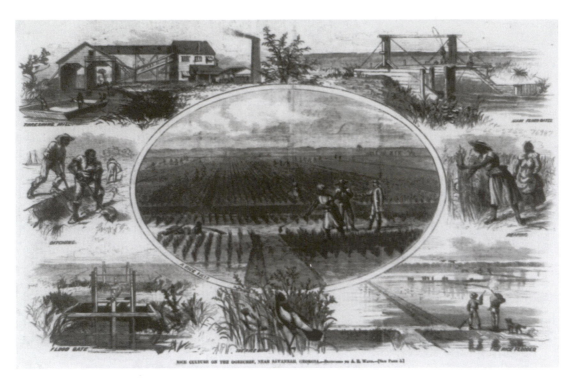

Rice culture on the Ogeechee, near Savannah, Georgia. Engraving of sketch by A. R. Waud, 1867. (Library of Congress.)

Before the development of tidewater rice in the mid-18th century, the plant had been cultivated successfully in limited amounts in upland areas. When rice was first introduced, few people in the South owned slaves and even fewer owned large numbers of slaves. Most slaves at the time were field hands associated with subsistence farms that grew varieties of produce for local consumption. Slaves and indentured servants still commonly worked together with the owners of the land to produce products for local markets. But it was the introduction of rice from Madagascar that grew in tidal freshwater areas that opened the region to the first successful agricultural business in the southeastern United States. Unlike upland farming, tidal rice was extremely labor intensive, requiring large amounts of work throughout the year. This created the need for substantial numbers of slave laborers for the first time in the colonial Southeast. Thus, as the need for labor for growing rice plantations steadily grew in the region, the tide of slavery spread from Caribbean sugar plantations to rice plantations in South Carolina and Georgia.

### Field System
Rice is a labor-intensive crop. To produce large harvests, rice plantations had well-engineered water control systems. Plantations and fields had to be carved out of the low-lying marsh areas adjacent to freshwater river systems. These areas were full of wild animals and infested with pests that often brought harm to the fields and laborers. Initially fields had to be laid out in units of production. Fields were designed to be incorporated into an intricate system of canals and earthworks that allowed water to flow into the system during high tides and for water to exit the system during

low tides. River banks were designed to be at sufficient height so that spring runoffs could not overflow the earthworks. In addition, the fields were enclosed by additional earthworks to form large field sections. These, too, were built sufficiently high to prevent water escaping from the system once the field was flooded. Some of the interior banks were designed to be lower and allow water to over-top them so that entire field sections could be flooded. Controlling this system were numerous trunks, gates, and weirs. During parts of the year, water would be let into the system to flood and water the fields. Control of this system was vital because too much or too little water at any time could destroy the crop or allow an infestation of pests. The maintenance of this system was a part of the regular farming activities associated with planting of the rice. Workers would be required to maintain and clean out the canal system to ensure its proper functioning. In addition, any breaches in the system constantly had to be guarded against to prevent the flooding of the fields at inappropriate times. In the event of a breach in one of the main earthworks, all workers would be required to repair the breach as quickly as possible and to assist in controlling internal gates to prevent the spreading of the water to other sections of the plantation.

## Labor

Rice cultivation used the task labor system, with each task divided so that it would take the average laborer 8 to 10 hours to complete. Unlike the sunup to sundown systems associated with cotton planting, the rice plantation system provided a system whereby hard work was rewarded with free time. Although physically more demanding than plantation systems like cotton, rice plantation labor provided more free time for the slaves once work was completed. Once the task was finished for the day, slaves were allowed to hunt, **fish**, tend their own fields, or even engage in paid labor projects. Typical tasks assigned might include hoeing or planting a certain portion of a field. For such a task as hoeing, typically about a quarter-acre of a field was assigned per person to work per day. However, planting and threshing often involved larger acreage than the field hand could cover in a single day.

The plantation system was one of divided labor. The plantation owner sat at the top of the system, although frequently not directly involved in day-to-day operations. The owner typically would hire an overseer or appoint one of his own children to oversee the daily operations of the plantation. Although a white overseer was required, he often did not directly control the plantation workforce. He generally served as a token head and was responsible for the overall welfare and conditions of the slaves. Controlling most daily activities were **slave drivers**. The driver was the highest-ranking slave on plantations and often was as close to the owners as their household slaves were. Drivers oversaw the regular tasks associated with the planting cycle. They assigned work and supervised its completion in a timely manner. Drivers often carried **whips** as symbols of their power and could use them to issue punishments for deviations from the task at hand. The driver would be the first to wake in the morning and was responsible for getting all the hands out into the fields. On large plantations, multiple drivers would be overseen by a head driver. Under the driver were all the slaves that belonged to the plantation owner except those who worked directly in the house or at other tasks for the owner. For example, valuable carpenters would ply their trade in shops on the plantation. The driver would divide the laborers up into groups and assign the tasks to be completed that day. A full task was assigned to the hands who were capable of completing it, while injured or sick slaves who still were capable of work would be assigned a fraction of the task to match their ability. Thus, if a field required 10 hands to **hoe** it, a driver might assign any given number of people to the task so that the resulting work was done by the equivalent of 10 fully capable people. In addition to the field hands, the driver also supervised the care of the sick and children. Slaves too young to work would be placed in a type of daycare while their parents worked the fields. Slaves too elderly to work generally would be placed in charge of the children or in the **kitchens** to cook communal meals. Meals were brought out into the fields so that the work would not be greatly interrupted. Generally, once the tasks were completed, slaves were allowed to spend free time as they wished. During periods of harvest, times of intense pest infestation, or other emergencies, additional work was required.

It was not unusual for white plantation owners and overseers to avoid the rice fields entirely. Many owners preferred to live in nearby cities where social activities were more available and thus they visited their plantations infrequently. In addition, fear of yellow fever brought on by the mosquitoes so prevalent in the marshes kept many whites away and sustained the driver in a more powerful position than he held on other types of Southern plantations.

### Yearly Cycle

Rice planting often started in March. Fields were prepared by plowing down the old growth and preparing long trenches for the new plantings. The new plantings used the rice seed obtained from the previous year's harvest, using about two to three bushels of seed per acre of land. Once planted, the first controlled flooding occurred. The water was allowed to stay upon the land for up to a week to thoroughly saturate the soil, and then it was drained off. During each flooding event, water levels were precisely controlled. In the first flooding, water was kept on long enough to start the seeds growing but not long enough for the seeds to rot. Once the rice started to grow in the beds, the water was taken off and the fields were permitted to dry. The rice was then allowed to grow to a seedling, when again water was placed on the field for up to another week. Again, it was important to allow the water to remain on the field long enough to hydrate the plants and beds but not so long as to damage the plants. After the water was again drained off, the first hoeing began. This hoeing was intended to gently break up the soil and prevent the start of any weeds. After the hoeing was completed, another water cycle began in the fields. This time the field was completely covered by water. The object was to remove any debris or weeds that existed in the fields and, more important, to remove any of the pests. Once all of the debris was removed, water could be drawn down to uncover the plants. It was important that plants in low areas were not drowned and plants in higher areas of the field were covered with sufficient water. No field ever would be completely level, but yearly work tried to bring the lows and highs together. The water then was gradually removed from the fields and another period of hoeing took place. The final phase of flooding took place in the fields and was controlled as the plants grew to their final height. This period of controlled flooding would last until the rice was ready for harvest in the late summer, when the water would be drained off for the final time that season. The rice then was harvested by hand and tied in bundles or sheaves, which were stacked at the edge of the field to dry further. The bundles would be

## Rice Production

Maggie Black grew up on a South Carolina rice plantation and described rice production there:

Dey grow dey own rice right dere on de plantation in dem days. Hadder plant it on some uv de land wha' wuz weter den de udder land wuz. Dey hadder le' de rice ge' good en ripe en den dey'ud out it en hab one uv dem big rice whipping days. Heap uv people come from plantation aw 'bout en help whip dat rice. Dey jes take de rice en beat it 'cross some hoss dat dey hab fix up somewhey dere on de plantation. Honey, dey hab hoss jes lak dese hoss yuh see carpenter use 'bout heah dese days. Dey'ud hab hundreds uv bushels uv dat rice dere. Den when dey ge' t'rough, dey hab big supper dere fa aw dem wha' whip rice. Gi'e em aw de rice en hog head dey is e'er wan'. Man, dey'ud hab de nicest kind uv music dere. Knock dem bones togedder en slap en pat dey hands to aw kind uv pretty tune.

Dem dey hab rice mortars right dere on de plantation wha' dey fix de rice in jes uz nice. Now dey hab to take it to de mill. Yuh see dey hab uh big block outer in de yard wid uh big hole in it dat dey put de rice in en take dese t'ing call pestles en beat down on it en dat wha' knock de shaft offen it. Coase dey ne'er hab no nice pretty rice lak yuh see dese days cause it wuzn't uz white uz de rice dat dey hab 'bout heah dis day en time, but it wuz mighty sweet rice, honey, mighty sweet rice.

*Source:* George P. Rawick, ed. *The American Slave: South Carolina Narratives*, Vol. 2. Westport, CT: Greenwood Press, 1972.

collected and either taken to a local rice mill to be processed or processed in a winnowing shed. Rice for next year's planting would be threshed by hand, instead of at the mill, because the mills often would damage the seed.

Initially, all rice was hand-threshed and winnowed on site. This required the field hand to first beat the stalks to remove the rice. The stalks were placed over a clean floor or fabric and beat with a pole with a stick tied to it. These flailing sticks would separate the rice from the stalk. The rice then was collected and placed into large mortars to be pounded. The outer husk would be cracked, and when the rice was thrown into the wind, it would separate the husk from the rice kernel.

The milling of the rice would last until the end of fall or early winter depending on the quantities to be prepared. Also, depending on the market, rice could be sold as rough rice (unhusked), white rice, or further milled into rice flour. Once the rice was milled, it was placed in barrels and shipped to market. During the next few months, the fields would lay fallow and await the next year's spring, when plowing would start the season over again. During this resting period, equipment was mended and the gates and earthworks repaired. If new fields were to be prepared, land-clearing activities were assigned, trees cut, and intricate water systems put in place. No part of the year was ever wasted on a rice plantation.

### Daily Life

In general, the daily life of the enslaved on rice plantations was governed by two factors. The first was the fact that many plantations were managed by absentee owners. Because they feared yellow fever and preferred life in the nearby cities, most elite planters spent little time on their lands. Unlike cotton plantation owners who lived near their fields, these absent planters did not oversee and enforce such intense labor standards. This lack of supervision over large numbers of slaves promoted greater freedom that permitted elements of traditional African music, dance, and language to survive. The second factor that determined life on rice plantations was the task system. Because of the laborious work associated with rice cultivation, drivers and overseers were careful not to assign too much work. Working in wet mud or water for days at a time stressed many workers' physical well-being. For those capable of the work, the task system offered workers the opportunity to pursue additional activities of their choosing.

Although work needed to be done on the plantation year-round, time was provided for observing certain holidays as was a weekly time for religious instruction. The daily life for most slaves on these rice plantations did not differ significantly from day to day. Awakened in the morning by the driver, the slaves were assigned a daily task that was to be completed in an efficient and timely manner. Slaves who were found loafing or working at a slow pace could face punishment from the driver. Generally, the drivers would attempt to rectify any situation through verbal reprimands, but for the most part, they were allowed to whip anyone who did not follow their commands.

Once the task work was completed for the day, individuals were free to use the time as they saw fit as long as they followed the general rules. Slaves were not allowed to leave the plantation without a note from the overseer or owner. Slaves were not to cause "mischief" or attempt to escape to freedom. Slaves from time to time, however, were known to damage the canals or open the gates, causing damage to the fields. In addition, mills or winnowing sheds were burnt to the ground by slaves on some South Carolina plantations in retaliation for being kept in bondage. Slaves caught in such acts were punished. Slaves who were caught trying to escape were whipped, placed in leg irons, and then sent back into the fields. Slaves found guilty of more serious crimes often were considered too much trouble to keep and usually proved resistant to most punishments, and they were sold and separated from family members.

Most slaves on rice plantations used their time in other pursuits. Some slaves supplemented their diets by hunting and fishing, while others tended **gardens**. Those with skills in demand were able to find employment or create goods for **markets** that allowed them to earn money toward purchasing their freedom.

Enslaved African Americans who worked on rice plantations suffered from hazardous environmental conditions and the hard work. The rice plantation system, however, offered enslaved individuals more freedom than found on other types of plantations elsewhere in the South. Living in large groups with limited supervision, slaves on rice plantations were better able to preserve African cultural traditions and to establish strong communities.

*See also* Baskets; Nurseries and Nursemaids; Passes; Pounders; Slave Pens, Slave Jails, and Slave Markets.

FURTHER READING

Carney, Judith A. *Black Rice: The African Origins of Rice Cultivation in the Americas.* Cambridge, MA: Harvard University Press, 2002.

Doar, David. *Rice and Rice Planting in the South Carolina Low Country.* Charleston, SC: Charleston Museum, 1970.

Edelson, S. Max. "Beyond 'Black Rice': Reconstructing Material and Cultural Contexts for Early Plantation Agriculture." *The American Historical Review* 115 (February 2010): 125–135.

Eltis, David, Philip Morgan, and David Richardson. "Agency and Diaspora in Atlantic History: Reassessing the African Contribution to Rice Cultivation in the Americas." *The American Historical Review* 112 (December 2007): 1329–1358.

Eltis, David, Philip Morgan, and David Richardson. "Black, Brown, or White?: Color-Coding American Commercial Rice Cultivation with Slave Labor." *The American Historical Review* 115 (February 2010): 164–171.

Fox-Genovese, Elizabeth. *Within the Plantation Household: Black and White Women of the Old South.* Chapel Hill: University of North Carolina Press, 1988.

Hall, Gwendolyn Midlo. "Africa and Africans in the African Diaspora: The Uses of Relational Databases." *The American Historical Review* 115 (February 2010): 136–150.

Hawthorne, Walter. "From 'Black Rice' to 'Brown': Rethinking the History of Risiculture in the Seventeenth- and Eighteenth-Century Atlantic." *The American Historical Review* 115 (February 2010): 151–163.

Krauthamer, Barbara. "Black Women, Slavery, Kinship and Freedom in the American Southeast." In *Women and Slavery.* Vol. 2, *The Modern Atlantic,* edited by Gwyn Campbell, Suzanne Miers, and Joseph Calder Miller, 100–127. Athens: Ohio University Press, 2007.

Smith, Julia Floyd. *Slavery and Rice Culture in Low Country Georgia, 1750–1860.* Knoxville: University of Tennessee Press, 1985.

DANIEL HUGHES

**RUNAWAY SLAVE ADVERTISEMENTS.** From the 17th century until the 1865 passage of the Thirteenth Amendment, masters wanted to regain possession of their runaway slaves as quickly as possible. Some owners placed advertisements in newspapers to alert people about escaped slaves, provide information to identify the individuals who had run away, and offer a reward to encourage whites to capture runaways and return them to the advertisers. Details in the advertisements help 21st-century scholars learn about the attitudes of masters toward their slaves, the **clothing** worn by slaves, the material objects that enslaved laborers used, the skills that slaves possessed, the ties that enslaved laborers formed to family and friends, the reasons why some slaves escaped, and the ways in which slavery varied in the United States.

Slave owners wanted to regain possession of escaped laborers for several reasons. First, the act of running away was a direct challenge to the institution of slavery and the laws that whites used to control slaves. Second, masters depended on the work of the enslaved men, women, and children who tended plantation crops, practiced trades, and took care of domestic work. In addition, owners wanted to have possession of the people whom they saw as their personal property and the equivalent of cash.

Having learned of a slave's escape, an owner usually waited several weeks or even months before writing an advertisement. Masters put off the expense of placing an announcement in a newspaper because they believed that they knew where the escapees had gone and that many of these individuals would return on their own. Owners expected some runaways—described as "absentees"—to head back after they spent a

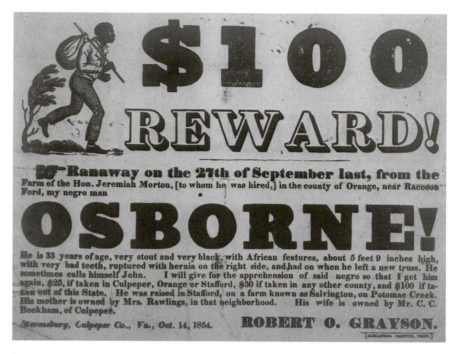

Runaway slave announcement concerning an enslaved man named Osborne, from Culpepper County, Virginia. (Library of Congress.)

few days with family members. Slave owners used the term "lying out" in reference to runaways who remained in the area of their home plantation. Some lying-out slaves left to protest harsh treatment from an overseer. While away, they demanded better treatment in the form of time off, additional food, new clothes, and amnesty for leaving the plantation. If the absentee and lying-out slaves did not return after a short time, masters began to search for them on plantations where their family members lived.

After waiting in vain for some escapees to return and failing to locate these individuals in the local area, a number of slave owners might decide to place an advertisement in their newspaper. Masters classified this group of runaways as "fugitives." Some fugitives ran short distances from their master's home; others tried to get as far away as possible from their owner's property.

Many of the advertisements began with "Ran," "Run," "Ran away," or "Run away." Often the printer set the opening in bold, capital letters to catch the eyes of the reader. Other openings included the date a slave ran away and the place from which the escape was made. Also, some advertisers used a reward to attract whites and interest them in helping to capture a runaway.

Having gained the reader's attention, the advertiser turned to pertinent details about the appearance of the escaped slave. When possible, owners included the name of the escapee, often in capital letters, the fugitive's gender, and a physical description of the individual. In some cases, the master also knew the approximate age, height, and hairstyle of the runaway. If the escapee had scars—either from ritual **scarification** in Africa or work-related injuries—or body piercings, the advertiser noted this information in the announcement.

In addition to details about a fugitive's appearance, owners often described the clothing that the individual wore when last seen. A runaway who wore ill-fitting clothes made of coarse osnaburg was a field slave. An escapee attired in finer, tailored clothing was a domestic slave. Some masters knew that the runaway took additional garments, sometimes pilfered from the slaveholder, when leaving and included information about these items.

After describing a runaway's appearance and attire, the advertiser turned to additional details that a white person could use to identify a fugitive. Announcements might include the master's subjective assessment of a slave's personality. Owners used a wide range of adjectives to describe escapees. Some were shy, surly, or bold. Others were self-confident, determined, resourceful, and articulate. An owner might comment on the skills of the escapee if he was a proficient agricultural worker or a trained artisan or if she was an accomplished domestic slave. If a master thought that a skilled slave carried the tools of his trade—including carpentry, joining, blacksmithing, and shoemaking—enabling him to earn money and try to pass as a free black in an urban area, it was noted in the advertisement.

Some slave owners commented on the possible destination of the fugitive. The advertisers who included these details did so because they had knowledge about the escapee's family and friends. Masters noted the location of a spouse's plantation or a runaway's previous owner if they believed that the runaway left to see relatives and others whom they knew. These destinations ranged from a few miles from the owner's residence to hundreds of miles away. The distances that a fugitive traveled increased in the 19th century. The domestic slave trade divided families and tore apart the communities slaves had created. This forced migration led to an increased number of slaves running off to visit spouses, children, and other kin. Many runaways traveled along rivers—including the Ohio, Mississippi, and Tennessee—to their previous homes. Others moved north along the Natchez Trace and then across the Appalachian Mountains to find family members.

Advertisers knew that slaves escaped for reasons other than to visit relatives and friends. Some slaves departed from their master's property because they were preachers and wanted to teach enslaved men, women, and children about their faith. Masters were aware that some escapees struck out from plantations, cities, and towns because they believed that they had a right to their freedom. During the American Revolution, thousands of slaves ran to the British to fight against their "rebel" masters and to seize their independence. In the 19th century, abolitionists helped slaves to escape and find freedom in Northern states and in Canada.

After noting a wide range of details that would help a white person to identify an escapee, some owners reminded readers that they should not assist a runaway. Many advertisers concluded their notice with information about the amount of the reward and where the captured fugitive should be taken. A few noted that a particular slave had been outlawed and could be returned dead or alive.

The odds of escaping slavery were small, and runaway slave advertisements helped many masters regain possession of enslaved laborers. In some instances, whites captured fugitives who refused to state either their name or that of their master. Local officials placed the escapee in jail until the master could be notified. Jail keepers placed advertisements in newspapers to let readers know about the slaves held in prisons. Often the notices written by jailers were shorter and had fewer details because the runaway refused to provide information. The jailer noted the gender and physical description of the escapee. The announcement concluded with an appeal to the owner to claim the slave and to pay the costs of keeping the fugitive in prison as well as a reward to the white person who found the escapee.

Details in the runaway slave advertisements and notices placed by jail keepers indicate that whites were aware of the humanity of enslaved laborers even though they considered these men, women, and children to be personal property. Taken as a whole, the particulars about 17th-, 18th- and 19th-century fugitive slaves reveal the variety of experiences that enslaved men, women, and children had during the time that slavery was legal in Britain's North American colonies and the United States. Rural slavery differed from urban slavery; bondage in the 17th century differed from that of the 19th century. Runaway slave advertisements and notices of captured runaways indicate that people in bondage sought freedom no matter when or where they lived and labored.

***See also*** Abolition Imagery; Slave Pens, Slave Jails, and Slave Markets.

FURTHER READING

Costa, Tom. "The Geography of Slavery in Virginia." At www2.vcdh.virginia.edu/gos/.

"Enslavement: Runaways," Toolbox Library: Primary Resources in U.S. History and Literature, National Humanities Center. At http://nationalhumanitiescenter.org/pds/maai/enslavement/text8/text8read.htm.

Franklin, John Hope, and Loren Schweninger. *Runaway Slaves: Rebels on the Plantation.* New York: Oxford University Press, 1999.

Greene, Lorenzo J. "The New England Negro as Seen in Advertisements for Runaway Slaves." *Journal of Negro History* 29, no. 2 (April 1944): 125–146.

Smith, Billy G., and Richard Wojtowicz. *Blacks Who Stole Themselves: Advertisements for Runaways in the* Pennsylvania Gazette, *1728–1790.* Philadelphia: University of Pennsylvania Press, 1989.

JULIE RICHTER

# S

**SALE NOTICES.** Ship captains, slave traders, and slave owners used both hand-written and printed notices to announce their intention to sell recently enslaved African men, women, and children and slaves who were transferred from one owner to another. These notices contained details about when and where slaves were sold and suggest the ways in which these sales spread the institution of slavery in America.

During the trans-Atlantic slave trade, ship captains and slave traders notified prospective purchasers of the arrival of a cargo of bound Africans. These notices contained information designed to attract purchasers to the sales. Ship captains and slave traders often began the announcement with the vessel's name, the African port from which it departed, and the captain who guided the ship across the Atlantic Ocean. Often, these details were in bold, italicized, or large text to catch the reader's eye. Next, the authors turned to the particulars of the sale. They noted the number of slaves to be sold as well as the date, time, and place of the sale. Each enslaved man, woman, and child would be sold to the highest bidder who promised to make payment within the time specified in the announcement. Many notices concluded with the name of the person or company in charge of the sale. On occasion, a ship captain or slave trader added a postscript in which he noted the amount of space that a vessel had to carry crops that a planter wanted to ship to England.

The authors of the sale notices made sure that as many people knew about the auctions as possible. Some whites read hand-written announcements posted on **courthouse** doors and on the walls of their local tavern. Other potential purchasers found details about sales in newspapers. Prospective buyers often examined the bodies of the Africans before the sale because they wanted to buy laborers who were strong and in good health after the long voyage across the Atlantic Ocean.

At the appointed time on the specified day, whites led African men, women, boys, and girls from the ships that carried them from their homes to the western shore of the Atlantic Ocean. They frequently forced these individuals to stand on wooden **auction blocks** as potential owners bid on them. It was difficult for the Africans to walk to the auction blocks if chains bound their hands and or feet together. During the sales, males and females may have had a piece of coarse **cloth** to drape over their bodies. Some Africans retained possession of jewelry—made of **beads** or cowrie

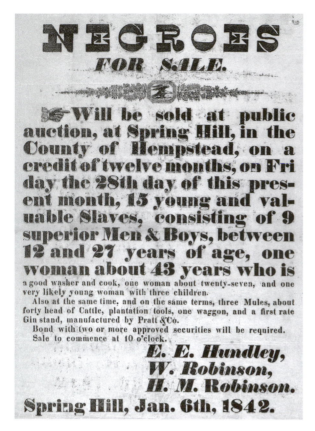

NEGROES
FOR SALE.

☞ Will be sold at public auction, at Spring Hill, in the County of Hempstead, on a credit of twelve months, on Friday the 28th day of this present month, 15 young and valuable Slaves, consisting of 9 superior Men & Boys, between 12 and 27 years of age, one woman about 43 years who is a good washer and cook, one woman about twenty-seven, and one very likely young woman with three children.

Also at the same time, and on the same terms, three Mules, about forty head of Cattle, plantation tools, one waggon, and a first rate Gin stand, manufactured by Pratt &Co.

Bond with two or more approved securities will be required. Sale to commence at 10 o'clock.

E. E. Hundley,
W. Robinson,
H. M. Robinson.
Spring Hill, Jan. 6th, 1842.

Negroes for sale notice, Spring Hill, Arkansas, 1842. (Library of Congress.)

shells—that served as a reminder of their life in Africa. After the sale, the African became, in the eyes of the purchaser, a possession. Slave owners provided their slaves with the minimum allotment of items each year in terms of **clothing**, **blankets**, **food**, and shelter.

During the 17th, 18th, and 19th centuries, African slaves and their descendants always had a measure of uncertainty in their lives because an owner could sell family members, friends, and kin at any point in time. Some owners sold slaves as a form of punishment for those who disobeyed and as an example to other enslaved men, women, and children of what could happen to them if they challenged their master's authority. Other masters transferred slaves to other whites to gain money to pay their debts. Whatever the motivation behind the sales, masters used notices to inform purchasers about the place and time of sales as well as any skills possessed by the available slaves.

By the third quarter of the 18th century, as **tobacco** production declined, an increasing number of masters in Virginia and Maryland sold portions of their labor force to other planters in the western part of their colonies because they did not have enough work to keep all of their slaves busy. These sales began to shift the center of the slave population westward from the Atlantic Coast. The gradual relocation of slaves within the United States changed after 1793 when the **cotton** gin helped to make cotton a highly profitable crop. Cotton producers wanted more slaves to work on their plantations. After 1800, the domestic or intrastate slave trade grew in response to the increased demand for enslaved laborers to produce cotton in states in the Lower South and **sugar** in Louisiana. This forced migration disrupted slave families and communities throughout the Upper South and shifted the majority of the country's slaves to the Lower South.

During the 19th century, slave traders—both individuals and companies—moved hundreds of thousands of slaves within the country. Slave traders and their agents actively looked for enslaved men, women, and children whom they could purchase and then resell in the Lower South. They read notices of slave sales, purchased enslaved workers at auctions and estate sales, and then transported these men, women, and children to slave markets in Southern cities. Some traders chained slaves together in groups called **coffles** and forced them to walk hundreds of miles to places in Alabama, Mississippi, or Louisiana where they would be sold. Other traders made slaves walk part of the way before they loaded the enslaved people on flatboats that carried them down the rivers that flowed into the Mississippi River and then down to New Orleans. Slave traders also shackled men, women, and children before putting them on **boats** in Baltimore, Maryland; Richmond and Norfolk, Virginia; or Charleston, South Carolina, to cities in the Lower South where planters gathered to purchase more enslaved laborers.

Once a slave trader arrived at the appointed destination with a group of enslaved laborers, this individual placed a notice of the upcoming sale in the newspaper and posted announcements near the city's slave market. The authors of 19th-century sale notices included many of the same details that appeared in announcements from the colonial and early national periods. Slave traders began their notices with the date, time, and location of the sale. Often this information was in bold or italicized text to catch the reader's attention. Next, they listed information about the enslaved laborers to attract prospective purchasers. The traders included information about the number of available laborers as well as the number of men, women, and children to be sold. Additional details included the ages of the enslaved workers, the state where the slaves had lived and worked, and the skills possessed by the laborers.

On the day of the sale, the traders led men, women, boys, and girls from the pens in which they had been held and led them to the auction blocks. Whites gathered in the slave markets in New Orleans, Natchez, Charleston, Savannah, and other cities in the Lower South to purchase enslaved laborers. For a master, the sale was an opportunity to increase production on a plantation and increase the family's wealth. For the slaves, the transfer to a new owner was an indication that their old life was gone and they would be forced to learn how to use different agricultural implements to tend a different crop and create a new life as family members had done since the first sale notice.

*See also* Auction Advertisements; Ships; Slave Pens, Slave Jails, and Slave Markets.

FURTHER READING

Berlin, Ira. *Generations of Captivity: A History of African-American Slaves.* Cambridge, MA: Belknap Press of Harvard University Press, 2003.

"Enslavement: Sale," Toolbox Library: Primary Resources in U.S. History and Literature, National Humanities Center. At http://nationalhumanitiescenter.org/pds/maai/enslavement/text2/text2read.htm.

Franklin, John Hope, and Alfred A. Moss, Jr. *From Slavery to Freedom: A History of African Americans.* 8th ed. New York: Alfred A. Knopf, 2003.

Handler, Jerome S., and Michael L. Tuite, Jr., eds. "Slave Sales and Auctions: African Coast and the Americas." The Atlantic Slave Trade and Slave Life in the Americas: A Visual Record, Virginia Foundation for the Humanities and University of Virginia. At http://hitchcock.itc.virginia.edu/Slavery/index.php.

Rothman, Adam. *Slave Country: American Expansion and the Origins of the Deep South.* Cambridge, MA: Harvard University Press, 2005.

JULIE RICHTER

**SCARIFICATION.** Many West African tribes marked their members through ritual scarification, which involved cutting the **skin** with a sharp instrument in patterns, oftentimes during the ceremonies that initiated males and females into adulthood. The scars that resulted conveyed complex meanings to Africans that ranged from ethnic identity to social status. Many first-generation African slaves possessed these "country marks," which whites described in 18th- and 19th-century newspaper advertisements for slave sales and runaway descriptions or recorded on slave registers and related documents, but whites seldom understood their significance.

These marks typically consisted of a series of small slashes, rings, or dots that could appear on the face, the chest, the back, the arms, or the stomach. Sometimes, slave-holders also used the term "country marks" to refer to filed teeth. In November 1767, the New Bern, North Carolina, sheriff reported in the *Virginia Gazette* that he had several male slaves in custody including, "Jack about 23 year old, about 5 feet 4 inches high, of a thin visage, clear eyed, his teeth and mouth stand very much out, his six rings of his country marks round his neck, his ears full of holes, and cannot tell his master's name." Another man named Sampson "is much marked on his body and arms with his country marks." Will, imprisoned there, too, was "marked on the chin with his country marks." A daguerreotype portrait of Renty, an elderly slave born in the Congo and photographed by Joseph T. Zealy on B. F. Taylor's South Carolina planta-tion in 1850, illustrates a series of small slashes that comprise these markings.

By the early 19th century, as fewer slaves arrived directly from Africa and the native-born enslaved population increased in North America, slaveholders' references to "country marks" gradually declined.

*See also* Runaway Slave Advertisements; Sale Notices.

FURTHER READING

Gomez, Michael A. *Exchanging Our Country Marks: The Transformation of African Identities in the Colonial and Antebellum South*. Chapel Hill: University of North Carolina Press, 1998.

Rose, Willie Lee. *A Documentary History of Slavery in North America*. Athens: University of Georgia Press, 1999.

Wallis, Brian. "Black Bodies, White Science: Louis Agassiz's Slave Daguerreotypes." *American Art* 9 (Summer 1995): 39–61.

Walvin, James. *Black Ivory: Slavery in the British Empire*. New York: Wiley-Blackwell, 2001.

KYM S. RICE

**SCULLERIES.** Sculleries were designated locations in which dishes were washed and other tasks related to the preparation, cleaning, and storage of **food** service materials were completed. Domestic slaves who were responsible for food preparation and service used the scullery to clean pots and pans, cooking utensils, and serving pieces. Some foodstuffs may have been prepped in the scullery, such as vegetables for the cook to use. Sculleries served as a place to store serving pieces until needed at the table.

The tasks carried out by scullery maids or scullions were key elements of food serv-ice in any household—the **kitchen** and dining rooms depended on clean dishes. These tasks were tedious and strenuous, especially if they fell to a young enslaved girl, which appears to have been a relatively common practice. To wash dishes, the scul-lery maid transported water in buckets to the scullery and then heated the water in a large boiler over a fire. The scullery maid then combined the heated water with soap in a wooden tub or sink and scrubbed the dishes with a cloth or brush. In some house-holds, accommodations were made for built-in boiling pans, as well as devices to fun-nel water from a nearby source. Special tools, such as dish drainers, also are mentioned in period documents. These conveniences eased some of the physical burden of dishwashing, but the scullery maid needed to scrub the pots and pans and other kitchen and dining equipment just the same.

In the 17th century, designated sculleries were unknown and dishwashing tasks likely took place in the same areas used for cooking and laundry. As formal plantation landscapes and urban houses developed in the 18th century, specialized sculleries became more prevalent, although still uncommon except for a wealthy minority. By the mid-19th century, running water in houses revolutionized dishwashing, making the task more efficient than a century before. Large households had a designated scullery more often than those households with a smaller workforce, regardless of time period. In those houses that did boast a designated scullery, it usually was located next to the main kitchen or near food service areas such as the pantry. For example, at Blennerhasset, a 1798 house built on an island in the Ohio River, the kitchen and scullery together made up one **dependency**. In more modest settings, however, the cleaning of dishes and preparation of foodstuffs may have happened in a space within the kitchen or outside in a work **yard**. According to one 19th-century memoir, enslaved workers washed dishes in the pantry instead of a separate scullery.

Aside from its work function, the scullery space, like most service spaces, appears to have been appropriated by its enslaved workforce for unrelated activities at times. One 19th-century published account, for instance, recalls a slave wedding in a "wash-kitchen."

***See also*** Cast Iron Pots.

FURTHER READING

Evans, Nancy Goyne. "Everyday Things: From Rolling Pins to Trundle Bedsteads." In *American Furniture 2003*, edited by Luke Beckerdite, 27–94. Milwaukee, WI: Chipstone Foundation, 2003.

"First Person Narratives of the American South," Documenting the American South Collection, University Library of the University of North Carolina at Chapel Hill. At http://docsouth.unc.edu/fpn/.

GRETCHEN GOODELL

**SERVANTS HALLS.** Servants halls most simply were gathering places for people involved in the domestic service of a household. For enslaved workers, the servants hall provided a location for resting when not attending to their duties, dining, or participating in leisure activities. Servants halls allowed for fellowship among enslaved individuals and provided a place in which slaves could socialize away from the watchful eyes of masters or overseers. The servants hall did not follow one architectural format, but instead might constitute a small area within the **kitchen**, a room in the cellar of the house, or even its own building.

**Evolution**

In the 17th century, when a household was wealthy enough to include domestic workers, slaves usually shared accommodations with their masters. For the large majority of colonists, architecture at this time reflected an informal living arrangement, often in a two- or three-room structure. Separate accommodations for servants quarters did exist for a wealthy minority in 17th-century America. For instance, at the Clifts plantation in Westmoreland County, Virginia, a servants quarter was constructed in addition to the main house as early as 1665. Whether this quarter was used only for sleeping or also for recreation is unknown.

In the late 17th and early 18th century, the increased importation of an enslaved workforce and changing ideas of privacy and hierarchy transformed the slaveholding household. At this time, areas for indentured servant and slave living and working gradually began to be separated from family spaces in more and more households. As labor changed, so, too, did the architecture and room use. Eighteenth-century inventories and other period documents regularly reflect specialized servants halls or related spaces that were located in designated service areas of the house or plantation. Logically, these spaces appear to have been placed in locations that were convenient to the domestic workers (near the kitchens, smokehouses, and **dairies**) but removed from the sight and hearing of the family and their guests.

Regardless of its size or location, in the 18th and 19th centuries, the servants hall was the domain of the domestic workers, both free and enslaved. This shift in the location of servant relaxation and recreation from family spaces to removed locations was seen in both rural and urban locations. The Norfolk, Virginia, house of Moses and Elizabeth Myers, for instance, included a basement kitchen until renovations in the early 19th century relocated the kitchen and its related service areas to a building behind the main house. This shift not only relocated the smells and sounds of the kitchen, but also removed the domestic slaves from being directly under the eyes of their master.

## Function

The distinction of who regularly used the servants hall is unclear, as it appears that such spaces were used not just by domestic workers in the household, but also by stable hands, craftsmen, and even field slaves. In some large households, servants halls were designated for the dining and recreation of lower servants and slaves, while the more highly regarded servants dined at a table overseen by the housekeeper or steward. Divisions of the domestic labor forces appear to have been made along color lines as well. In George Washington's (1732–1799) presidential household in Philadelphia, Pennsylvania, for example, a servants hall was present off the rear of the house, in addition to separate quarters for white servants, a white coachman, and enslaved stable hands.

Servants halls appear to have been used not only as gathering places for domestic slaves and servants, but also as residences for both free and enslaved workers. In an inventory dated 1760, Gawen Corbin's Westmoreland County, Virginia, estate includes a servants hall furnished with two **beds** and one **spinning** wheel. The servants hall as residence is also seen at George Washington's Fairfax County, Virginia, estate, Mount Vernon, where the structure is designated as a place for housing visitors, who were likely lower-level strangers and the servants or slaves of the guests. Such flexible use of the servants hall appears to be in keeping with the common practice of changing the function of service spaces as deemed necessary for work and living needs. Plantations and other sites with enslaved labor were dynamic places, with some flexible service structures or areas that could change function as needed based on workforce, projects, and architecture. The physical servants hall, therefore, may not always have had one designated function, but instead appears to have shifted function as the need arose, or even served multiple functions at any one given time.

That same 1760 inventory, with its inclusion of a spinning wheel, serves as evidence that servants halls may not always have offered a respite from the slaves' daily tasks. With a location usually near the kitchen and its offices or work areas, the servants hall was in the perfect position to also act as a secondary work space—for **sewing** or polishing candlesticks or even spinning yarn. The identification of the servants hall with leisure, however, cannot be underestimated, as period accounts from those of the gentry or master's class almost universally attest. In such narratives, the servants hall is viewed as a place of revelry and celebration—it is in this spot that Christmas games are played, music and song are heard, and good food is found. Although these narratives likely are romanticized, the identification of the servants hall as a place of leisure, not work, cannot be ignored.

Domestic slaves still were expected to be on call even when dining or relaxing in the servants hall. In the 17th and early 18th century, servants were more readily available, often living and working in spaces shared by the family or at least near enough for easy communication. The removal of domestic workers from the family realm into designated service areas meant that other means were needed to summon the servants and slaves. Elaborate bell systems were installed in houses beginning in the late 18th century, enabling the master's family to call for assistance from various removed parts of the house. The bell-pulls led to a series of **bells**, often in a servants hall, that were identified either by labels or by their distinct sound tone. The servants hall in the White House during President Andrew Jackson's (1767–1845) administration, for instance, featured a bell system. Thus, free and enslaved domestics could be summoned by their masters without seeing them or interacting directly.

The servants hall also was used for special occasions in the enslaved community. According to 19th-century narratives, weddings between slaves and births of slave children occasionally occurred in the servants hall. The Christmas holidays also provided a time for merriment, and such revelry regularly would take place in the servants hall, complete with music, song, dance, games, and other festive activities.

English and American prescriptive literature, such as cookbooks and household manuals, provide illustrations of the expected function of servants halls as well as the performance of those who used and cleaned them. Landscape designers and architects delineated plans that formalized the layout of servants halls, keeping in mind their locations, access, and lighting. The health and welfare of one's servants began to be an issue discussed in such literature by the mid-19th century, and new accommodations for heating and hygiene started to appear in building plans and domestic literature.

The layout of the servants hall was not universal, but a fireplace for heat was a necessity. In some servants halls, storage was accommodated, such as in Sir John Colleton's (d. 1777) house in Charleston, South Carolina, where a closet was noted in the servants hall in a 1777 inventory. The **furnishings** of a servants hall were dependent on size of the household, hierarchy of the service workers using the space, placement in the house or on the plantation, as well as other factors. When inventories of such spaces exist, their furnishings reflect a relatively bare, utilitarian space, usually consisting of tables, seats, fireplace equipment, and sometimes an item such as a press or cupboard used for storage.

FURTHER READING

Andrzejewski, Anna Vemer. *Building Power: Architecture and Surveillance in Victorian America.* Knoxville: University of Tennessee Press, 2008.

"First Person Narratives of the American South," Documenting the American South Collection, University Library of the University of North Carolina at Chapel Hill. At http://docsouth.unc.edu/fpn/.

Herman, Bernard L. *Townhouse: Architecture and Material Life in the Early American City, 1780–1830.* Chapel Hill: University of North Carolina Press, 2005.

Joyner, Charles. "The World of the Plantation Slaves." In *Before Freedom Came: African-American Life in the Antebellum South,* edited by Edward D. C. Campbell, Jr., with Kym Rice, 50–99. Richmond: Museum of the Confederacy and University Press of Virginia, 1991.

Lawler, Edward, Jr. "The Slave Quarters," The President's House in Philadelphia, Independence Hall Association. At www.ushistory.org/presidentshouse/slaves/slavequarters.htm.

Lounsbury, Carl, ed. *An Illustrated Glossary of Early Southern Architecture and Landscape.* New York: Oxford University Press, 1994.

Neiman, Fraser D. "Domestic Architecture at the Clifts Plantation: The Social Context of Early Virginia Building." In *Common Places: Readings in American Vernacular Architecture,* edited by Dell Upton and John Michael Vlach, 292–314. Athens: University of Georgia Press, 1986.

Seale, William. *The President's House.* Washington, DC: White House Historical Association, 1986.

GRETCHEN GOODELL

**SESAME.** The sesame (*Sesamum indicum*) plant is indigenous to Sub-Saharan Africa and is valued for its oily white seeds. At some point during the late 17th or early 18th century, sesame was brought from Senegambia to South Carolina bearing its Wolof and Bamana name, *benne*. Although it was known by a different name in Central Africa, where a substantial number of enslaved Africans in South Carolina also originated, sesame was cultivated and transported by the Portuguese from Angola to Brazil in the 17th and 18th centuries. By the height of the trans-Atlantic slave trade, the plant was raised in almost every slave society from the Lower South through the Caribbean to South America. By the late 18th century, enslaved South Carolinians harvested great quantities of sesame with other crops such as **gourds, collard** greens, and **watermelon.** This mirrored West African traditions where benne seed was companion planted with other crops and used by some groups to give spiritual warning not to steal produce when planted on the borders and edges of the garden. Among some African ethnic groups such as the Yoruba, sesame was one of the symbols of the deity of smallpox for whom the spotty nature of the seeds recalled the pock-marked skin of the deity. To steal from a garden surrounded by his sacred plant was an invitation to bring on his wrath.

Thomas Jefferson (1743–1826) was so impressed by the cultivation of benne by the enslaved Africans and blacks of the Low Country that he decided to plant "benni" at Monticello, hoping that it might become a substitute for more expensive olive oil, which had to be imported. Jefferson noted in 1808, "It was brought to S. Carolina from Africa by the Negroes, who alone have hitherto cultivated it in the Carolinas and Georgia. They bake it in their bread, boil it with greens, enrich their broth." The sesame that was used to "enrich their broth" probably added something of a thickening and emulsifying quality to **pot likker** and other stocks. Enslaved blacks made soup and puddings from the seed. In early Florida, "Negroes use it as food either raw, toasted or boiled in their soups and are very fond of it. . . ." An 1847 cookbook, *The Carolina Housewife*, by Sarah Rutledge (1782–1855), contained a recipe for Bennie Soup. The recipe called for sesame seed, oysters, flour, and hot pepper. Slaves also parched the seeds and used its oil, and, as in West Africa, used benne to make cakes, confections, and candies. Charleston's black cooks created innovative confections such as benne wafers, benne candy, and quick breads seasoned with sesame. Some benne creations may have been introduced or reinforced in the South when formerly enslaved Haitians skilled in confectionary arts came with their owners in the 1790s to places such as Charleston and Savannah.

## FURTHER READING

Gamble, David. *The Wolof of Senegambia*. London: International African Institute, 1957.

Grime, William Ed. *Ethno-Botany of the Black Americans*. Algonac, MI: Reference Publications, 1979.

Harris, Jessica B. *The Welcome Table: African American Heritage Cooking*. New York: Fireside, 1995.

Hatch, Peter J. "Thomas Jefferson's Favorite Vegetables." In *Dining at Monticello: In Good Taste and Abundance,* edited by Damon Fowler, 55–64. Chapel Hill: University of North Carolina Press, 2005.

Rutledge, Sarah. *The Carolina Housewife*. Facsimile of the Original 1847 Edition with introduction by Anna Wells Rutledge. Columbia: University of South Carolina Press, 1979.

Wilson, Mary Tolford. "Peaceful Integration: The Owner's Adoption of His Slaves' Food." *Journal of Negro History* 49, no. 2 (April 1964): 116–127.

MICHAEL W. TWITTY

**SEWING ITEMS AND NEEDLEWORK.** Sewing items such as needles, scissors, straight pins, and thimbles were essential tools in the domestic production of **textiles**. On Southern plantations, these tools were used by skilled enslaved seamstresses to produce everyday clothes, linens, and, on some plantations, fine needlework and lace. These seamstresses provided essential labor that was valued by all members of the plantation household. Enslaved seamstresses were hired out and often produced goods for sale to neighboring plantations.

### Sewing

Plantation-based textile production often began with raising sheep, or growing flax or **cotton**. Plantations produced their own cloth through the 1840s when inexpensive, factory-produced cloth became more widely available. Some plantation owners, however, either could not or preferred not to purchase mass-produced **cloth** and continued to control every step of textile production, particularly when producing textiles for use by their slaves.

Female slaves produced clothing, linens, and other household textiles for the entire plantation household. Learning either from their mistress or their mother, slave girls learned to sew at a young age. Enslaved seamstresses managed clothing production for the plantation household, performing a variety of tasks from preparation of raw materials to production of finished goods. Sewing, especially fine needlework, was time and

Sampler attributed to black pastor William Levington, Baltimore, Maryland, 1832. Silk and crinkled silk embellishment threads on a linen ground of 28 by 28 threads per inch. (The Colonial Williamsburg Foundation.)

labor intensive. White mistresses could not produce enough finished goods to keep their families fashionably dressed. The value of skilled enslaved seamstresses to the household is reflected in the increasing number of advertisements and rising prices for such slaves in the 19th century, often rivaling the prices for young male slaves.

The nature of textile production varied by region and by size of plantation. While most textile production focused on the coarse clothing worn by slaves, or everyday **clothing** or undergarments worn by the white members of the household, slaves who were particularly adept at fine needlework might tat lace, embroider fabrics, or complete other highly specialized forms of needlework. On smaller plantations, seamstresses often performed a variety of sewing-related tasks. On larger plantations, slaves might specialize in one or two areas of textile production, such as **spinning**, weaving, dyeing, cutting cloth, producing finished garments, knitting, or embroidery. The enslaved seamstress might specialize in making only clothing for men or women. Despite these divisions of labor, rarely were a slave's sewing-related chores her sole occupation. Often such work was organized around a slave's primary work in the field as revealed by archaeological evidence from plantation sites, which suggests that sewing tasks were performed in the evening hours after fieldwork had been completed. Sewing chores also might be completed during periods of inclement weather, illness or old age, pregnancy, or while caring for young children.

Despite the added burden such work placed on enslaved women, slaves who were skilled at sewing-related tasks often enjoyed greater material benefits. For example, former Oklahoma slave Sarah Wilson remembered that by the age of eight she was skilled enough at sewing to be hired out by her mistress. Although she ate in the **kitchen** during these sewing circles, Wilson often ate the same lunch as the white women. A Virginia slave, Elizabeth Keckley (1818–1907), who learned to sew from her mother, used her skills as a seamstress to save enough money to buy freedom for herself and her son in the 1850s. A skilled seamstress had access to sewing notions, fabrics, and other cast-offs that could be used to embellish her own clothing and that of other slaves and to supplement the master's meager allotment. Proximity to the master and the mistress, as well as her value to the household, also placed the enslaved seamstress in a position to bargain for nonprovisioned items either for herself or on behalf of other slaves.

### Sewing Items

Mass production of sewing items developed in the second quarter of the 19th century, which allowed masters to more cheaply provision enslaved women with sewing tools.

While plantation seamstresses used a variety of tools, their sewing items may be divided into four broad categories: pins, needles, thimbles, and shears or scissors. All of these items were used by enslaved seamstresses in the course of their work. Peggy Sloan, who had been a slave in Arkansas, related that "My grandma could cut a man's frock-tail coat . . . Grandma was a milliner. She could make anything you used a needle to make."

### Pins

Depending on their purpose, pins varied widely in length and diameter. The most commonly used pins were called short-whites by their manufacturers. Meant for common sewing, short-whites usually are about one inch long and about one-sixteenth of an inch in diameter. Long-whites, or middlings, are general purpose pins used for a variety of sewing tasks. On some plantations, where enslaved seamstresses engaged in decorative sewing, lills or minnekins might have been used. Measuring less than half an inch in length and less than four-hundredths of an inch in diameter, lills are the smallest and finest of the straight pins and are used primarily for pinning fine fabrics.

### Needles

A basic sewing item, needles have been fashioned from a variety of materials such as wood, bone, ivory, **shell**, and various metals. The 18th-century invention of crucible steel and the 19th-century invention of needle-making machines aided the mass production of smooth, uniform needles. Eyed needles, including sewing needles, darning and embroidery needles, tapestry needles, and specialty needles, were the most common types used by female slaves. Knitting needles, crochet hooks, and bodkins also were used by enslaved seamstresses.

Eyed needles are distinguished from one another by differences in the shape, size, and placement of the needle's eye; the cross section of the shank; the shape and form of the point; and the overall size, length, form, and quality of the needle. Sewing needles have a bevel eye and are divided into four categories: sharps, betweens, blunts, and milliner's or straw needles. Sharps are ordinary sewing needles and are manufactured in sizes 1–12. Some sharps are made with a small, round eye with a long groove beneath, also known as a guttered eye. Shorter and often stronger than sharps, betweens are used for delicate sewing (sizes 8–12) and quilting (sizes 5–7). Like sharps, betweens are made with either a bevel or a guttered eye. Blunts are shorter and thicker than betweens and are manufactured in larger sizes (1–9). Betweens and blunts primarily are used by tailors and experienced seamstresses. Milliner's or straw needles (available in sizes 1–10) are used for hat-making and other tasks requiring a longer needle and also come with a bevel or guttered eye. Darning needles come in sizes 12–14 and have a longer eye allowing for easier threading of **wool** or heavy cotton. Embroidery needles come in sizes 1–12 and were used, as the name implies, for various kinds of embroidery, including crewel work. Tapestry needles have blunt points and a large eye and are used to work wool thread on a net base. Specialty needles were used in sewing gloves or making lace.

Knitting needles are straight, slender rods with points at either end. Made from a variety of materials, including wood, bone, and steel, knitting needles were used to make socks, suspenders, collars, and gloves. Bodkins are similar to sewing needles but generally larger. They were used for running drawstrings and threading and rethreading the ribbons, cording, and laces used to fasten garments. Crochet hooks were introduced into the United States in the early 19th century and may well have served the same purpose as bodkins in sewing as well as producing crocheted textiles.

### Thimbles

Thimbles originally were made to be worn on the thumb during sewing. Thimbles protected the finger and helped pushed the needle through the fabric. The introduction of stamped brass thimbles in the late 1820s provided a cheaper alternative to materials such as silver, gold, and mother-of-pearl. Although thimbles were made of a variety of materials, only those made of brass and steel were strong enough for everyday use. American production of thimbles did not take off until the second quarter of the 19th century when factories in Massachusetts, New Jersey, Pennsylvania, and Rhode Island began producing millions of thimbles in brass, gold, silver, and steel.

### Scissors

Scissors and shears work on the same principle: two opposite cutting edges work against each other to cut fabric, thread, leather, and other materials. Shears work by spring action, while scissors work by pivoting in the center. Generally made of steel, scissors are more common in sewing than shears. Scissors come in a variety of sizes, which can be used for cutting cloth, snipping threads, or making delicate lace.

FURTHER READING

Beaudry, Mary C. *Findings: The Material Culture of Needlework and Sewing.* New Haven, CT: Yale University Press, 2006.

Dunaway, Wilma A. *The African-American Family in Slavery and Emancipation.* New York: Cambridge University Press, 2003.

Groves, Sylvia. *The History of Needlework Tools and Accessories.* New York: Arco Publishing Company, 1973.

Heath, Barbara J. "Engendering Choice: Slavery and Consumerism in Central Virginia." In *Engendering African American Archaeology,* edited by Jillian E. Galle and Amy L. Young, 19–38. Knoxville: University of Tennessee Press, 2004.

Wares, Lydia Jean. "Dress of the African American Woman in Slavery and Freedom: 1500–1935." PhD diss., Purdue University, 1981.

Weiner, Marli F. *Mistresses and Slaves: Plantation Women in South Carolina, 1830–80.* Urbana: University of Illinois Press, 1998.

Williams, William H. *Slavery and Freedom in Delaware, 1639–1865.* Wilmington, DE: SR Books, 1996.

Yetman, Norman R. *Voices from Slavery.* New York: Holt, Rinehart, and Wilson, 1970.

JULIE HOLCOMB

**SHELLS.** Enslaved African Americans used various types of shells for multiple ends. Cowries, conch shells, clams shells, and oyster shells served both mundane and spiritual purposes. *Cypraea moneta,* "money cowries," are small sea snails that live in the

Pacific and Indian Oceans. Their shells have been used by Asian and African cultures for thousands of years as objects of personal adornment, elements of spiritual practices, and currency. In the 16th through 19th centuries, Europeans traded cowries, and other goods, for African slaves. Within Africa, cowries served as currency, as items of personal adornment, and as divination tools.

Not many African artifacts survived the trans-Atlantic voyage. Cowries, because they were worn on the body, are an exception. Archaeologists have recovered cowry shells in Louisiana, Maryland, New York, North Carolina, Tennessee, and Virginia, and in Barbados, in places where enslaved Africans and African Americans lived, worked, or were laid to rest. Andrew Jackson's Hermitage in Tennessee; Utopia Quarter in James City County, Virginia; Fairfield plantation in Gloucester County, Virginia; Monticello, Virginia; and Ashland plantation in Louisiana are some of the locations where cowries were found. Some of these cowries have been modified, with the top surface cut away, so that they could be worn in the **hair**, strung as pendants, or used for divination.

Several of the excavated cowry shells come from **subfloor pits**, which were storage pits dug into the ground inside some slave dwellings in Kentucky, Maryland, Mississippi, Missouri, North Carolina, Tennessee, and Virginia. Four of these subfloor pits that were used as ancestral **shrines** in the 18th century were located within the remains of slave cabins at Utopia Quarter in Virginia. One of these shrines contained two modified cowries in association with other artifacts; the other contained seven whole fossil scallop seashells and other objects.

Enslaved African Americans and free blacks carved shells into **buttons** for practical use as clothing fasteners. Several tools for manufacturing and carving shell and bone objects were excavated in a slave and tenant cabin at Levi Jordan plantation in Texas. These tools were found in association with a series of freshwater shells and marine shells, as were several locally produced bone and shell buttons. Additionally, a mass-produced, store-purchased button was modified by inscribing it with a six-pointed star. This symbol is found on other African and African American ceremonial objects, which suggests that this button may have been used as a **charm**. An elaborately carved shell cameo with an image of a woman standing near a cabin also was found at Levi Jordan. This cameo likely was produced by the craftsperson who manufactured the buttons. Self-produced objects, such as the cameo, likely were important to those who made and owned them.

Enslaved African Americans used shells of various types as grave markers, grave decorations, grave offerings, and grave goods. Shells typically were placed on top of **graves** with other objects, such as broken ceramics, glass, **mirrors**, lamps, and water pitchers. In some regions of the Caribbean, such as the Danish West Indies, conch shells were placed on top of the graves of enslaved laborers, alongside other objects such as iron **hoe** blades. Shells also were found within some burials as items of personal adornment, which also may have served as charms. An enslaved African man was buried at Newton plantation in Barbados with a necklace consisting of 5 cowry shells, 1 agate, 14 glass **beads**, 21 dog canines, and 5 **fish** vertebrae. Given the spiritual associations of these various objects, this man was probably a spiritual practitioner.

The African Burial Ground in New York City (ca. 1650–1783) contains four graves with associated clam shell and oyster shell markers or offerings on top of the burials. Three graves exhibit the pattern seen in the Caribbean of placing a shell on top of a grave with an iron object. A clamshell fragment and iron **nail** were placed on top of the coffin of a young child; a man had an complete oyster valve associated with an iron nail placed on top of his coffin; and a woman had an oyster shell encircled by an incomplete iron object, possibly a horseshoe or the hafting end of an iron tool, placed on the lid of her coffin. Another man had at least one whole oyster shell placed on top of his coffin.

At least two burials at the African Burial Ground contained shells within the coffin. A young child was buried with a fragment of local hard clamshell near the left clavicle bone. This may indicate that the shell was worn as a pendant. An African woman, between 39 and 64 years old, was interred with a strand of 70 European glass beads, 1 African ground glass bead, and 7 cowries around her waist. She was also wearing a bracelet of 40 European seed beads around her wrist.

Shells placed on graves may have been selected because of their association with water. In BaKongo religion, the spirit world is believed to be located under rivers, lakes, and streams. Shells placed on graves served as symbols of the deceased's passage through water to the spirit world of the ancestors. Iron also had powerful symbolism within many West and Central African cultural traditions, particularly the Yoruba. The iron objects found with shells on top of burials probably were selected for these symbolic associations.

Conchs may have been selected for grave markers because of their association with spiritual protection. In the Caribbean, conch shells also were used by the enslaved as musical instruments and as a means of communication. On St. Croix in the Danish West Indies, the enslaved were roused for work each morning and released at the end of the day by the sound of the **slave driver** blowing the conch. It is symbolic that when the enslaved revolted on St. Croix in 1848, resulting in their freedom, they initiated the revolt by blowing conch shells across the island.

*See also* Bells and Horns.

FURTHER READING

Brown, Kenneth, and Doreen Cooper. "Structural Continuity in an African-American Slave and Tenant Community." *Historical Archaeology* 24, no. 4 (1990): 7–19.

Creel, Margaret Washington. *A Peculiar People: Slave Religion and Community-Culture among the Gullahs*. New York: New York University Press, 1988.

Perry, William, Jean Howson, and Barbara Bianca, eds. *The African Burial Ground Archaeology Final Report*, Vol. 1. Washington, DC: Howard University, 2006.

Samford, Patricia. *Subfloor Pits and the Archaeology of Slavery in Colonial Virginia*. Tuscaloosa: University of Alabama Press, 2007.

Thompson, Robert Farris. *Flash of the Spirit*. New York: Vintage Books, 1983.

Vlach, John Michael. *The Afro-American Tradition in Decorative Arts*. 1978. Reprint, Athens: University of Georgia Press, 1990.

LORI LEE

**SHIPYARDS.** Slaves worked in American shipyards up and down the Atlantic and Gulf coasts, from the inception of American shipbuilding in the mid-1600s to slavery's end in 1865. They played a part in all the maritime trades, including ship carpentry, sail making, pump and block making, ship rigging, anchor making, and caulking. Enslaved shipwrights sawed, hammered, and planed the keels and decks of

New England–built brigs, Baltimore clippers, and both U.S. and Confederate Navy ships, such as the first USS *Constellation* and the CSS *Virginia*.

As early as the 1650s, Richard Cutts's Piscataqua River shipyard in New Hampshire had eight enslaved workers. In the early 1700s, slaves built ships in Boston, Charleston, New York, and Philadelphia. Many of these men were hired from their owners by the shipyard proprietors, who paid rates that suggest that the slaves were skilled artisans. By the mid-18th century, white shipbuilders in South Carolina and Georgia were seeking statutory protection from slave competition by petitioning colonial legislatures to ban slaves from shipyard work.

Colonial newspaper advertisements suggest that slaveholders arranged to have talented young black boys trained for shipyard work: Charleston's newspaper carried ads in the 1740s for the sale of slaves "brought up" as ship carpenters or caulkers. Apprenticeship indentures were often the vehicle for recording contracts by which a slave owner secured the craft training of a young African American in return for the ability to sell that young man as a skilled worker upon his completion of the apprenticeship.

Investing in slave artisans could bring profit. Slave ship carpenters could be sold for 50 to 80 percent more than prices for field hands. But if slave artisans were costly to buy, those who could afford them obtained labor at a price well below that demanded by free white artisans. As a result, the number and proportion of slaves found in colonial American shipyards was low in New England and the Mid-Atlantic, where relatively cheap white labor was comparatively abundant. From Virginia to the Deep South, however, enslaved shipbuilders were much more prominent. In both Northern and Southern colonies, shipyard owners with the largest operations were most likely to own or hire enslaved workers.

In the early Republic, the use of slaves in shipyards would, like slavery in general, take on a more regional character and become a fact of life only from Maryland southward. In Baltimore, the nation's great boomtown in the years from 1770 to 1815, buying and hiring slaves allowed shipyard owners to expand their operations rapidly. In 1800, federal census data showed more than 40 slave owners whose occupation was ship carpenter, sail maker, or the like. Four of the city's top 10 slave owners, in terms of the numbers of slaves, were shipbuilders or rope makers.

David Stodder (d. 1806), who enslaved 22 blacks, launched the USS *Constellation* in 1797, from his Fell's Point shipyard. The *Constellation* served the nation for more than 50 years. In its first major mission, it took part in the war against the "Barbary Pirates" of Tripoli in North Africa to punish North African states that raided American shipping in the Mediterranean and enslaved captured sailors. By the 1820s, the *Constellation* sailed the West Indies in search of Americans who were participating in the by-then illegal slave trade.

Slave owning and slave hiring made good economic sense as long as a shipbuilder could ensure that slaves would be fully employed year-round. In practice, this meant large operators, with high and inelastic demand for their product, wanted to use slave labor as a cheaper alternative to waged white labor. Subcontractors to the shipping construction business, such as sail makers and riggers, were less likely to own slaves. But even the very highly specialized business of making flags and colors for ships found an occasional slave owner: Baltimore's Mary Pickersgill (1776–1857), the city's best-known manufacturer of flags and ship's colors, owned female slaves who helped her in her business.

One or more of these enslaved women, in all likelihood, helped make the Star Spangled Banner that flew over Fort McHenry during the British bombardment in 1814.

Throughout the first half of the 19th century, enslaved shipyard workers dominated the industry in the Deep South, even as their presence faded in Northern ports in the aftermath of gradual emancipation, or in the Upper South, as manumission of skilled slaves generated free black people who continued to build ships. By the 1830s, a teenage Frederick Douglass (ca. 1818–1895), working as a ship caulker in a Baltimore shipyard, noted that most of the black ship carpenters in his yard were free. But in Washington (DC) Navy Yard; in Gosport Yard in Norfolk, Virginia; and in Pensacola, Florida, the Navy hired hundreds of enslaved workers from their owners. As maritime culture spread to the Gulf coast, shipyards in Biloxi, Mobile, and New Orleans also employed black shipbuilders.

By the 1830s and 1840s, these maritime workers, especially in Chesapeake or North Carolina ports, had more day-to-day autonomy and far more uncontrolled contact with white and black people from outside their region than did plantation workers. Slave sailors, watermen, ferrymen, and shipyard workers could and did become involved in efforts to free themselves and others. Several narratives of enslaved people who escaped to freedom attest to the anti-slavery potential of work in shipyards or on the docks. Examples include the narrative of Moses Grandy (b. 1786?) or some of William Still's (1821–1902) accounts of escapes by water from Norfolk or the Eastern Shore of the Chesapeake.

Slave shipwrights continued to do their work into the age of ironclad warships. When Virginia Confederates captured the U.S. Navy Yard at Gosport, they found that departing personnel had burned and scuttled the USS *Merrimack*, which was in the yard for a refit. In an attempt to break the U.S. Navy blockade of the Chesapeake's mouth, Confederates raised the *Merrimack*, converted it into an ironclad ship, and relaunched it as the CSS *Virginia*. The *Virginia*, famous for its fight with the USS ironclad the *Monitor*, was largely built by slave labor, in the final chapter of 200-plus years of slavery in American shipyards.

*See also* Boats; Ferries; Woodworking Tools.

FURTHER READING

Cecelski, David S. *The Waterman's Song: Slavery and Freedom in Maritime North Carolina.* Chapel Hill: University of North Carolina Press, 2001.

Goldenberg, Joseph A. *Shipbuilding in Colonial America.* Charlottesville: University of Virginia Press, 1976.

Starobin, Robert S. *Industrial Slavery in the Old South.* New York: Oxford University Press, 1970.

Whitman, T. Stephen. *The Price of Freedom: Slavery and Manumission in Baltimore and Early National Maryland.* Lexington: University Press of Kentucky, 1997.

T. STEPHEN WHITMAN

**SHOES.** No other item of dress more vividly captures and retains the physical imprint of its wearer than footwear does; and few garments have been as universally worn by both males and females at all ages and all ranks throughout history. No generalizations, however, can reflect the variety of footwear worn by enslaved individuals in America between the early 17th century and the end of slavery.

---

### Making Shoes

Addie Vinson recalled the footwear made by itinerant female shoemakers on her Georgia plantation:

> All de Niggers went barfoots in summer, but in winter us all wore brogans. Old Miss had a shoe shop in de celler under de big house, and when dem two white 'omans dat she hired to make our shoes come, us knowed wintertime was nigh. Dem 'omans would stay 'til dey had made up shoes enough to last us all winter long, den dey would go on to de next place what dey s'pected to make shoes.

*Source:* George P. Rawick, ed. *The American Slave: Georgia Narratives,* Vol. 13. Westport, CT: Greenwood Press, 1972.

Shadrach Cyrus talked about shoes made on his Mississippi plantation:

> We all wore shoes made on de plantation. Marse John had a tan vat for preparing de cattle hides to make shoe leather. The vat wuz ten feet wide and fifteen feet long—on Dillon's creek where there wuz plenty of water. Bark from red oak trees wuz put in de vat wid de hides to get off de hair—den de hides would be put on a pole and de side de meat wuz on, wuz scraped clean wid a knife somethin' like a curry knife—this wuz called dressin' de hide. Dey could take deer hides and carry them through the same process as de cow hides—alum wuz beat up wid eggs to make de buckskin limber—we see no buckskin shoe strings dese days! Deer skins wuz used to make whips, too. Big Gus and old man Dick wuz the shoemakers, also big Ike. Maple and sumac wuz de kind uv trees they made de tacks out uv. Missus Lizzie would give de shoemakers de beeswax to rub de thread wid, and dat would make de thread stick together, usin' 'bout three strands.

*Source:* George P. Rawick, ed. *The American Slave: Mississippi Narratives,* Supp. Ser. 1, Vol. 7, Part 2. Westport, CT: Greenwood Press, 1978.

---

Evidence from the 17th and 18th centuries suggests little unique about slaves' shoes, most commonly termed "Negro shoes" in documents and **runaway slave advertisements**. With few exceptions, runaway slaves' footwear as described in newspaper advertisements uses the same descriptors, styles, and varieties worn by runaway white servants from the same locales. By 1758, more anatomically suitable shoe lasts, which are the wooden forms on which shoes are made, were adopted for male slaves' shoes with "broad flat toes," through size 12, to account for proportions and foot shapes more commonly associated with non-shoe-wearing or sandal-wearing peoples, versus the narrower proportions made for European shoe-wearers' feet, accustomed to compression and distortion, especially at the toes. Barefootedness among slaves seemed

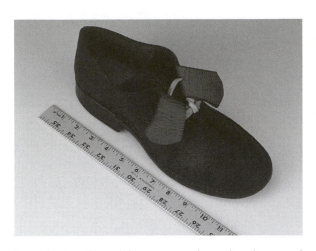

Reproduction shoe of the type worn by enslaved men and women in 18th-century Virginia. (The Colonial Williamsburg Foundation.)

rare, with the possible exception of the Low Country Carolinas and Georgia and among children. Prices for slaves' shoes in 18th-century Virginia were only six pence to one shilling lower than median shoe prices overall. When recorded, the annual issuance of adult slaves' shoes was two pair per year from the 18th century well into the 19th century in most locales—the same number allowed orphans, apprentices, and soldiers.

Throughout the 18th and 19th centuries, slave footwear was imported as well as commercially made in America. Shoes also were made domestically onsite, at first by indentured shoemakers and later by enslaved shoemakers, for intra- and interplantation distribution. Makeshift shoes also were homemade. Surviving account books detail 18th-century domestic shoemaking operations at Thomas Jefferson's (1743–1826) Monticello, George Mason's (1725–1792) Gunston Hall, and Robert Carter III's (1728–1804) Nomini Hall plantations, all in Virginia.

From at least 1784 on, New England shoemakers supplied mass-produced shoes for the "Southern Trade" (slavery). Manufacturers, especially in Worcester and Lynn, Massachusetts, were leaders in this trade. From 1810, New England merchants described "Nigger shoes," "Jackson ties," and "Red Russets," and shoes that were "extra wide, sevens to elevens . . . just the thing for the Southern market." The russet color that resulted from using less expensive and possibly more durable undyed leather for the shoe uppers created a de facto distinction in dress. Some slaves disliked this prominent color and made their own shoe-blacking from soot and fats to turn them the more conventional black. Some cheap black dyes could shorten the service-life of the leather.

Durability for rough use characterized the 19th-century shoes worn by field slaves in the Deep South. One Mobile, Alabama, factory in 1851 produced slave "brogans" (ankle boots) that surpassed the quality of all other boots, with triple rows of steel hobnails reinforcing the soles, and the seams in the uppers reinforced with copper rivets. In 1860, a novel idea was advertised in Atlanta, Georgia, to make slave shoes with russet uppers nailed to thick wooden soles. These wooden-soled shoes became an expedient that spread beyond the slave community during the war years.

*See also* Clothing and Footwear.

FURTHER READING

Garsault, François A. M. de *Garsault's 1767 Art of the Shoemaker: An Annotated Translation*. Edited and translated by D. A. Saguto. Williamsburg, VA: Colonial Williamsburg Foundation, 2009.

D. Al Saguto

**SHOTGUN HOUSES.** The shotgun house remains a living tradition, a form that resulted from the amalgamation of several features common in African, Caribbean Indian, and European housing traditions. The building shape derived from Caribbean, the framing techniques from European, and the spatial associations from African, particularly Yoruban, influences. The form emerged in the Creole culture of the West Indies and traveled with free people of color from Haiti to New Orleans by the early 1800s. It spread across the South from the Atlantic to Pacific oceans and eventually into cities such as Austin, Texas; Chicago, Illinois; and St. Louis, Missouri.

The shotgun house sits perpendicular to the street with the gable end and principal entrance covered by a porch facing the street. The structure is one room wide and one story tall and at least one to three or more rooms deep so it extends deep into a narrow town lot. The historic shotgun home deviated from much residential architecture in the South because the façades of standard Anglo-American homes ran parallel to the street and the entrance was on this long edge.

Slaves and free people of color in towns and cities might construct such small homes. The porches extending onto the streets afforded them a covered overhang to sit and work and interact with neighbors and passersby.

From the late 19th into the early 20th century, the structure moved from urban settings into mining towns, oil fields, railway yards, and **cotton** fields as industrialists and planters built temporary housing for wage laborers, cotton pickers, and migrants. These structures usually were made of precut dimensional lumber and box construction, also known as stud-less vertical plank construction.

*See also* Slave Housing.

FURTHER READING

Kniffen, Fred B. "Louisiana House Types." *Annals of the Association of American Geographers* 26, no. 4 (1936): 179–193.

Kniffen, Fred B. "The Physiognomy of Rural Louisiana." *Louisiana History* 4, no. 4 (1963): 291–299.

Vlach, John Michael. "Afro-Americans." In *America's Architectural Roots: Ethnic Groups That Built America*, edited by Dell Upton, 42–47. Washington, DC: Preservation Press, 1986.

Vlach, John Michael. "The Shotgun House: An African Architectural Legacy." In *Common Places: Readings in American Vernacular Architecture*, edited by Dell Upton and John Michael Vlach, 58–78. Athens: University of Georgia Press, 1986.

Williams, Michael Ann. "Pride and Prejudice: The Appalachian Boxed House in Southwestern North Carolina." *Winterthur Portfolio* 25, no. 4 (1990): 217–230.

DEBRA A. REID

**SHRINES AND SPIRIT CACHES.** Archaeological investigations conducted across the southeastern United States at sites where enslaved African Americans resided often yield artifacts and features that cannot be assigned an obvious function. Typically, these types of objects are European or Native American in origin and sometimes show modifications from their original form. Generally speaking, these modifications may include reshaping an object or adding geometric designs to an object. Some examples of objects of this nature that have been recovered from slave cabins include pierced **coins**, broken glass, blue **beads**, white **buttons**, **shells**, pins,

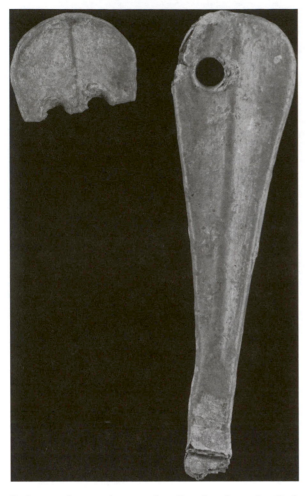

Broken and pierced spoon handles found at the Rich Neck plantation site, Williamsburg, Virginia. (The Colonial Williamsburg Foundation.)

amulets, horseshoes, **cast iron pots**, and ground ceramic sherds (fragments), as well as spoons, bricks, **marbles**, and other objects with an "x" or **cross** scratched onto the surface. In some instances, these objects are found together in clusters or caches and often placed in **subfloor pits** or holes that were dug beneath the floors of slave cabins, placed between interior and exterior walls, or beneath outdoor stairs leading into a slave cabin. The precise locations of these pits and caches were often hidden and out of the direct view of the plantation overseer and other slaves, a somewhat privately maintained space. The locations themselves may be symbolic and suggest that objects placed in such caches possessed different meanings to enslaved African Americans who placed them in these contexts.

Shrines are tangible places that can be used to facilitate communication with the spirits of ancestors and deities. They represent sacred spaces and are created out of objects that serve as a link between the physical world and the cosmological world. Shrines also create a dialogue between the living and the dead. The objects used in association with shrines are often believed to embody spirits or serve as symbolic representations of cosmological beings. These objects are often referred to as **charms**, or when placed together, spirit caches. Charms may also serve as individual shrines.

It has been recognized that enslaved Africans who were transported to the Americas brought with them cosmological beliefs and ideas about protection. Therefore, understanding the ideologies of enslaved African Americans is necessary to understand how objects functioned within the context of the day-to-day lives of slaves. In many African communities, deceased ancestors are revered and play a vital role in daily routines and protection of the community. By remaining in contact with ancestors, individuals or community members may be able to influence certain aspects of their lives such as health, agricultural pursuits, individual achievements, and other community issues. Contact with ancestors often is maintained through shrines that are created in public and private spaces.

Enslaved African Americans living on plantations were integrated forcibly into the plantation system and were obligated to conduct themselves in a manner dictated by the plantation master or overseer. The **work routines** performed by slaves were determined by the daily tasks and routines required by the plantation. European American plantation owners often provided many of the objects and materials used by slaves; however, it is apparent that these objects were not always viewed or used by slaves in the same manner that slaveholders intended.

Subfloor pits found beneath slave cabins in Virginia could represent personal shrines or shrines to honor ancestors. Although the pits likely were dug initially as storage pits or root cellars, a function approved by the plantation overseer, the nature of the objects placed within the pits indicate the pits also were used as shrines. The contents of several subfloor pits in Virginia were compared with those of 10th-century and 21st-century shrines of the Igbo, a cultural group in West Africa from which many slaves in Virginia originated, and similarities in the items were noticed. Caches of items including shells, animal bones, wine bottles, copper and metal objects, cast iron pans, white clay **tobacco pipes**, white objects, and pollen remains of grapes were found on the surface of the pits. White is considered a sacred color in many areas of West Africa, and white stones commonly are found in ancestor shrines. The evidence of the white tobacco pipes, shells, and other white objects also may be symbolic. Tobacco and wine commonly are used as offerings to the ancestors, and the presence of the pollen remains of grapes and wine bottles may suggest the offering of libations. In addition, shells are associated with water, and in many regions of West and Central Africa, rivers or other bodies of water are believed to possess spirits.

A series of cabins occupied by slaves and emancipated slaves at the Levi Jordan plantation in Texas were analyzed. Analysis suggested that one cabin was occupied by a curer or magician because several caches of items such as chalk, iron kettles, small **doll** parts, **nails, medicine** bottles, coins, and water-worn pebbles were found in four small pits located in the four corners of a cabin. Generally, each pit contained different items. The alignment of the pits and caches was north to south and east to west, and if a line were extrapolated between the pits it would intercept in the center of the cabin, which was void of a pit or cache of artifacts. The location of the four artifact caches was interpreted to represent the BaKongo symbol for the cosmos, a cross or **cosmogram**. The BaKongo are a cultural group from West Africa from which many slaves originated. The cosmogram symbolically represents the idea that the living are in a continuous cycle of birth, life, death, and rebirth. The vertical line connects the living world above with the dead below, and the horizontal line serves as a boundary between the living and the dead and the higher God and lesser spirits. Physically these are represented by the land, sky, and water.

**Graves** also functioned as shrines. In many areas of South Carolina, grave goods such as shells, plates, **mirrors**, bottles, lamps, and bedposts were placed on graves. Sometimes the last object that individuals used or medicines they used before their death were taken to the grave and dispersed or buried with them. Frequently, such objects were thought to keep away unwanted spirits and to protect or guide the spirit of the deceased. In some instances, objects such as bedposts were believed to help the dead rest. These graveyard practices were carried out by surviving family or community members and were a reflection of how the community viewed death and honored the lives of the individual after death. Such graves were located in public spaces and could be visited and seen by most anyone.

*See also* Conjure Bags.

FURTHER READING

Brown, Kenneth, and Doreen C. Cooper. "Structural Continuity in an African-American Slave and Tenant Community." *Historical Archaeology* 24, no. 4 (1990): 7–19.

Orser, Charles E., Jr. "The Archaeology of African-American Slave Religion in the Antebellum South." *Cambridge Archaeological Journal* 4, no. 1 (1994): 33–45.

Raboteau, Albert J. *Slave Religion: The "Invisible Institution" in the Antebellum South.* Oxford: Oxford University Press, 1978.

Russell, Aaron E. "Material Culture and African American Spirituality at the Hermitage." *Historical Archaeology* 31, no. 2 (1997): 63–80.

Samford, Patricia M. *Subfloor Pits and Archaeology of Slavery in Colonial Virginia.* Birmingham: University of Alabama Press, 2007.

Wilkie, Laurie A. "Magic and Empowerment on the Plantation: An Archaeological Consideration of African-American Worldview." *Southeastern Archaeology* 14, no. 2 (1995): 136–148.

Young, Amy L. "Archaeological Evidence of African-Style Ritual and Healing Practices in the Upland South Plantation." *Mid-continental Journal of Archaeology* 22, no. 1 (1996): 95–115.

STACEY L. YOUNG

**SKIN.** By the time of the American Revolution, the blackness of a slave's skin signified the forced commodification of their labor. At the outset of North American slavery in the early 17th century, however, skin color often provided only a visible physical difference between Europeans, Native Americans, and Africans. Although the overwhelming majority of North American slaves descended from Africa and thus possessed dark skin pigmentation, they often worked alongside English and Irish indentured servants. In some cases, African slaves worked alongside their masters. For example, Anthony Johnson (d. 1670) was sold as "Antonio a Negro" to the Bennett family at Jamestown in 1621. Johnson worked as a slave in the Bennetts' **tobacco** fields, during which time he married, raised four children, and engaged in small-scale farming on the side. Within the Chesapeake plantation economy, slaves frequently possessed the time and unspoken permission to grow their own **food** or manufacture and sell small goods. After securing freedom for himself and his family, Johnson amassed wealth in the form of land and slaves, and he even took his neighbor to court for luring a slave away from his plantation. At this early juncture in the history of North American slavery, skin color did not necessarily translate into permanent servitude or racial discrimination.

The ability of the Johnson family to enjoy social and economic upward mobility in a society with slaves reflected contemporary theories about race and skin color that developed first in Europe and later in the United States. Many early racial thinkers attempted to classify humanity according to skin complexion and other physical characteristics but did not always create racial hierarchies with whites at the top and blacks at the bottom. Instead, skin color remained fluid, flexible, and mutable. According to some 17th- and early 18th-century racial theorists, climate and other natural influences could alter skin color. For example, the French naturalist George Buffon (1707–1788) argued that it was possible for a person's skin to lighten or darken according to temperature and climatic exposure. Buffon contended that excessive heat explained the dark skin color of Africans, and he believed that, over generations, the skin of African descendants living in the more temperate climates of Europe or

"An Affecting Scene in Kentucky." A racist attack on Democratic vice presidential candidate Richard M. Johnson. The Kentucky congress member's nomination, in May 1835, as Van Buren's running mate for the 1836 election, raised eyebrows even among party faithful, because of Johnson's common-law marriage to a mulatto woman, Julia Chinn, with whom he fathered two daughters. The artist ridicules Johnson's domestic situation and the Democrats' constituency as well. Seated in a chair with his hand over his face, a visibly distraught Johnson lets a copy of James Watson Webb's *New York Courier and Enquirer* fall to the floor and moans, "When I read the scurrilous attacks in the Newspapers on the Mother of my Children, pardon me, my friends if I give way to feelings!!! My dear Girls, bring me your Mother's picture, that I may show it to my friends here." On the right are his two daughters, Adaline and Imogene, wearing elegant evening dresses. One presents a painting of a black woman wearing a turban, and says, "Here it is Pa, but don't take on so." The second daughter says, "Poor dear Pa, how much he is affected." A man behind them exclaims, "Pickle! Pop!! and Ginger!!! Can the slayer of Tecumseh be thus overcome like a summer cloud! fire and furies. oh!" Johnson is reported to have slain the Indian chief Tecumseh. Flanking Johnson are a gaunt abolitionist (right) and a black man. The abolitionist holds a copy of the *Emancipator*, a Hartford, Connecticut, newspaper, and says, "Be comforted Richard; all of us abolitionists will support thee." The black man pledges, "de honor of a Gentlemen dat all de Gentlemen of Colour will support you." On the far left is a stout postmaster who says, "Your Excellency, I am sure all of us Postmasters and deputies will stick to you; if you promise to keep us in office." The print seems to date from early in the campaign of 1836. (Library of Congress.)

North America could become as light as the skin of Europeans. Johann Blumenbach (1752–1840), the father of craniology, or the study and classification of skulls, agreed with Buffon that climate could affect skin color and further cautioned against creating racial hierarchies based on beauty and aesthetics. In 1787, Rev. Samuel Stanhope Smith (1751–1819), professor of moral philosophy at the College of New Jersey (now Princeton University), also argued that blacks and whites possessed equal innate characteristics that were only mitigated by environmental factors. Smith observed that white Pennsylvanians were considerably lighter in skin color than whites in the South Carolina Low Country. Likewise, Benjamin Rush (1746–1813), physician and close friend of Thomas Jefferson (1743–1826), equated blackness with a mild and noncontagious disease that, over time and with proper treatment, could be restored to its "natural" white state. Thus, slavery based strictly on a person's skin color remained unfixed in some parts of North America. As in Latin America, where race and skin color were quite fluid and complex ideas, 17th-century North American slavery allowed at least the possibility for freedom, wealth, and social mobility without regard to skin color.

Despite the relative fluidity of race, whiteness and blackness did connote real and drastic differences in some parts of North America. Theory and practice often clashed as the plantation revolution transformed societies with slaves into slave societies in which blackness and whiteness shaped identity. Planters dramatically increased their purchase of slaves directly from Africa. The linguistic barriers and the forced physical separation of slaves from white laborers created a new social climate increasingly marked by an emerging black-white binary. As whites rose in social status, blacks sank deeper into harsher and increasingly racialized forms of slavery. To sustain this new social order, slave owners used brutal force and coercion. Violence against slaves increased dramatically. Owners used the lash, the branding iron, and the gallows much more frequently both as punishment and as regular reminders of slaves' subordinate positions. Thus, the black skin of slaves became the tangible surface on which masters represented and asserted their power and authority.

Violence against black slaves often translated into new social hierarchies based on race. At the time the United States won independence from England, North American slavery was becoming synonymous with blackness. While nominally free, blacks living in the northern United States immediately after the Revolution experienced new and increased racism. Seventeenth-century social hierarchies based on one's socioeconomic function as slave, servant, free laborer, or slave owner, for example, gave way to much more rigid and permanent social identities based on one's skin color. For these racial theorists, skin color became the outward manifestation of a person's immutable inner character. Many whites developed and supported biological theories of origin and adaptation that justified the continued enslavement of African Americans. Thomas Jefferson disagreed with Rush, arguing that blacks were inferior, not only in physical appearance but also in mental capacity and disposition as well. Although he noticed kindness as an admirable and naturally endowed attribute among his own black slaves, Jefferson believed Negroes to be incapable of controlling their emotions and unable to use logic and reason. Jefferson conjectured that, at some point, whether at original creation or through time and circumstance, Negroes represented a separate species from whites. In doing so, Jefferson radically departed from the widely accepted notion that all humans belonged to a single species.

Jefferson was but one of dozens of racial thinkers who, by the early 19th century, attempted to link blackness with innate inferiority and even separateness of species. In 1810, Samuel Morton (1799–1851), a physician from Philadelphia, proposed that whites and Negroes indeed were separate species because of the generationally declining fertility of mulattoes, the offspring of white and black parents. Thus, Morton's conclusions supported the polygenist theory of human origins that suggested a series of separate creations represented by the different races of mankind. Both polygenists and many monogenists, who argued that racial variation had followed a single human creation, attributed the degraded condition of blacks under slavery to racial inferiority.

Despite the emergence of a black-white binary in 19th-century racial thought, detailed racial categories pervaded biological and cultural debates about racial mixing. In particular, racial theorists responded to what many whites considered the dangerous practice of miscegenation, or sexual intercourse between a white person and a person of color. In 1847, German-born naturalist Johann von Tschudi (1818–1889) identified 23 racial hybrid categories that had resulted from European colonization of the Americas and the trans-Atlantic slave trade. These categories rested on the presence or absence of nonwhite blood. For example, Tschudi used the terms "mulatto," "quadroon," and "octoroon" to describe persons possessing one-half, one-quarter, or one-eighth of black blood. The presence of sizable mixed-race populations in the free North, the slaveholding South, and throughout Latin America and the Caribbean alarmed many whites, who felt threatened by the possibility that a person of black ancestry might pass as white. As a result, slave codes grew more rigid, and no matter how light a free person's skin color may have been to the naked eye, courts of law defined persons of any mixed ancestry as black.

Scholars have debated which came first: black slavery or the racial ideas of black inferiority and white superiority. Many agree that the institution of slavery and theories of racial difference were mutually sustaining projects. While slavery increasingly subsumed much of the North American economy in the 18th and early 19th centuries, skin color and physical appearance became the visual medium through which racial thinkers and pro-slavery advocates developed fixed categories. These hierarchies in turn provided whites with convenient and "scientific" justification for the continued subjugation of blacks. Blackness also was attributed to many immigrant groups that did not fit into the black-white binary created by slavery. In 1790, Congress reserved naturalized citizenship for "free white persons." In 1854, the California Supreme Court ruled that Chinese immigrants were black and therefore could not testify against whites. Even after emancipation and the Voting Rights Act of 1867, Southern state governments successfully disenfranchised and discriminated against African Americans and other nonwhites on the grounds that the whiteness of one's skin and thus one's cultural superiority was something that needed to remain uncontaminated and safe from blackness.

## FURTHER READING

Berlin, Ira. *Many Thousands Gone: The First Two Centuries of Slavery in North America.* Cambridge, MA: Belknap Press of Harvard University, 1998.

Campbell, James T., Matthew Pratt Guterl, and Robert G. Lee, eds. *Race, Nation, and Empire in American History.* Chapel Hill: University of North Carolina Press, 2007.

Gossett, Thomas. *Race: The History of an Idea in America.* New York: Schocken Books, 1965.

Haney-Lopez, Ian. *White by Law: The Legal Construction of Race.* New York: New York University Press, 1996.

Horsman, Reginald. *Race and Manifest Destiny: The Origins of American Racial Anglo-Saxonism.* Cambridge, MA: Harvard University Press, 1981.

Young, Robert J. C. *Colonial Desire: Hybridity in Theory, Culture, and Race.* New York: Routledge, 1995.

CLIF STRATTON

**SLAVE BADGES.** Slave badges were the legally mandated visible proof of an urban slave's hired-out status. Enslaved men and women not under direct control of their masters, but working in another's employ, or following a particular trade on their own, they were required by law to wear these badges or have them on their person. Only a fixture of urban, and not rural, slave life, badge laws existed in several Southern cities, but the artifact, for reasons not understood, survives only in Charleston, South Carolina.

In Charleston, the evolution toward the wearing of slave badges began quite early. Founded in 1670, Charleston, a city heavily dependent on slave labor, was the capital of the colony that had a black majority by 1708, and the city remained primarily black well through the era of slavery. By 1690, slaves leaving their plantation needed a "ticket" as proof of permission to travel; by 1712, slaves were not allowed to hire out their services for their own enrichment. In 1721, those hiring the services of enslaved persons belonging to someone else needed a certificate, note, or memorandum, and by 1764, those slaves were required to wear "a ticket or badge." Newspaper advertisements suggest that such early badges may have been made out of pewter; no examples of them are known to exist.

When Charleston was officially incorporated in August 1783, one of the earliest statutes passed focused on slave badges. Different badge categories cost different prices, depending on what profession or activity the slave pursued; badges had to be procured annually. At this same, free people of color also were required to wear a different type of metal badge to reflect their status. Some of those latter badges, featuring a liberty cap on a staff, have survived, but no badges meant for enslaved persons are known from this era.

Many of the laws were not followed, and harsh penalties were instituted. In 1789, the city of Charleston revoked all the badge laws for hired-out enslaved men and women and for free people of color. For 11 years no one wore badges in the city and no laws requiring badges for free people of color were ever passed after 1789. But this changed in 1800, when a new series of laws came into effect. Hundreds of these slave badges, sometimes called "slave tags," have survived, and the information on these collectible items fills in the historical record regarding the objects and the laws that called them into being.

The 1800 Charleston law on slave badges brought back the annual nature of the badge, stating they could be "renewed" at the end of the year. Early on in the process, some badges with the year stamped at the bottom of the badge were renewed by having that bottom edge snapped off and the new year stamped in the blank area. Categories were emblazoned on the badges, and the prices varied depending on the profession the slave followed. The city eventually advertised annually for badge makers. The first known badge maker was Ralph Atmar, Jr. (1767–1809), a goldsmith and engraver. He made his badges out of copper in an octagonal shape with a hole at the top from which to suspend the badge or sew it to a hat or garment. All badges for all subsequent years also were made of copper, and all had holes for suspension or sewing. There is no known image of any slave wearing a badge. Many badges have been found with rough edges bent over, a sign that a slave probably bent the corners back to keep from being pricked or having threads catch on them. The badge shapes would vary: some years featured round badges; others were fairly square, with or without cropped corners; on other years, the square badges, instead of having a hole centered along the top side, had it placed in a corner so that the badge would hang in the shape of diamond. All badges for all subsequent years, except for those produced in 1800, would identify Charleston in an arc at the top; the other data varied in position on the metal artifact, but a number always appeared on the slave badge, along with a year and a category. In 1848, 1849, and 1850, when unincorporated parts of the city were annexed into Charleston proper, badges now were marked "Charleston," "Charleston Neck," or "C. N." for Charleston Neck to denote hired-out slaves whose masters lived in these annexed areas. Some makers would stamp their name on their badges. The information was engraved, punched, and stamped, with each maker varying it every year. According to information found on two slave badges from the same year, by 1806, the number on a badge was the sequential

Copper slave badge, Charleston, South Carolina, 1823. (The Colonial Williamsburg Foundation.)

number of the badge sold within a particular category. This may have been the practice from 1800 on, or possibly the first badge sold was number 1, and the second number 2, regardless of category.

After some variation in the early years, these categories were standardized by about 1813. The categories included "mechanic" (meaning a skilled worker or artisan), "porter," "fisher," servant," or "fruiterer." The last category, earlier called "huckster," was applied mostly to women who sold fruit and vegetables and other consumables primarily in the city market and generally was the most expensive badge, selling for $6.00 in 1800, $15.00 in 1806, $5.00 in 1813, and $25.00 in the inflationary period of 1865. The "mechanic" badge was next in expense, with the annual price ranging from $3.00 in 1800, $5.00 in 1837, $7.00 in 1838, and finally $35.00 in 1865. "Fisher" badges were generally the least expensive, starting at $1.00, rising to $2.00 in 1837, and to $4.00 in 1840 for a male "fisher." No "fisher" badges were allowed to be sold in 1865, perhaps in fear of allowing enslaved men and women to escape in **boats** to the federal troops besieging the city. "Porters" started at $2.00, increasing to $4.00 in 1837, and topping out at $20.00 in 1865. "Servant" or the occasional "house servant" badges were the most common, starting at $1.00 and rising to $2.00 in 1826. The exception was for a servant younger than 14, whose badge went for $1.00, until that category was abolished in 1837. After 1830, house servants no longer had to wear their badges, but still they had to have been purchased and shown when necessary. The final price in 1865 for a mechanic's badge was $35.00.

The badges went on sale in January of each year, but the income and expenses were counted in fiscal years that ran from September to August. By 1806, masters buying badges for slaves had to take an oath swearing that the particular slaves were their property or that of someone living in the city of Charleston. These badges were intended to keep those outside of the city from hiring their slaves out in town and overpopulating the city with unhoused and unsupervised slaves. At first, limits were placed on the numbers of slaves who could be hired out and for whom badges could be procured, but these limits were relaxed in 1837. By 1806, the city treasurer was enjoined to keep a register of slaves who had been granted badges, with their owners' names, their ages, and employments, along with the badge number. If any of these badge books survived, their contents would be invaluable in linking badges found with the bondsperson who wore it. Not one page of one volume of a badge book is now known to exist. But should any surface, a new era in badge history and identification will occur.

These badge books served a function at the time, that is, proving whether a person had paid for a badge, and whether a badge was claimed to have been lost. The penalties for working without a badge were quite severe. Slaves could be whipped at the workhouse for not having a badge, or for wearing someone else's badge, with the number of lashes or "stripes" noted in the statutes. Owners could be fined. If hired out, it was against the law for slaves to keep any of the money their hired labors produced. All had to be turned over to their masters—or the slave could face punishment.

Contemporary evidence, letters to the editor of local papers, correspondence, and other financial accounts show that these laws often were ignored. Many slaves grew wealthy on their labor and some even managed to buy their freedom from their masters before new South Carolina laws made the emancipation process much more difficult—and virtually impossible—in 1820. Lower-middle-class white laborers sent petition after petition to the South Carolina legislature and to Charleston City Hall to try to prevent this hiring out practice of slaves, because the slaves could produce goods and provide services less expensively than free whites could. But the city and state often replied that because society was based on slavery, the slave-hire practice could not be abolished. As a consequence, Charleston in antebellum times never developed a strong white working class.

To appease the feelings of those petitioners, government authorities attempted to ensure that slave badge laws and hiring out procedures were followed. So laws were written and badges were made in such a way to solicit help from the general populace and enroll them in enforcement issues. Those citizens spotting and turning in a slave breaking the badge and hiring laws were rewarded with half the fine the owner would have to pay; the other half would go to the policeman. For those who were illiterate, the varying shapes and sizes of badge each year would telegraph what was current and what was not. In fact, Sheriff John J. Lafar (1781–1849), who also made badges for the decade of the 1820s, varied his badges each year. One year they would be square, hanging parallel to the ground, the next year, the square badge, with its pin hole in a corner, would dangle diagonally, diamond shaped. One would be able to "read" the current year of a badge with a quick glimpse from across the street. Because the original wearer of an individual badge could be beaten if another slave was found wearing it, slaves appear to have damaged or destroyed their badges at the end of calendar years. This would account for the few number of badges known to have survived, compared with the tens of thousands that were made between 1800 and 1865; it also would account for the fact that many that are found have been deliberately folded, broken and bent, and why some are found tossed in bodies of water, privies, and trash pits.

Badges and hiring out laws were an integral part of the city and its finances. For those years that the total number of badges produced can be deduced and the total number of slaves in the city is known, as many as 25 to 30 percent of slaves in any given year were hired out, varying with economic times and conditions. Estimates, for instance, suggest that as few as 300 to 400 slave badges were sold and worn ca. 1808 and 1809 during a time of economic depression, whereas more than 5,000 slave badges bearing the date 1860 were worn in that year.

This was the time when hire badges became a crucial, if ironic, emblem of hope for many African Americans in the city. For years, since the passage of an 1820 law that allowed emancipation only for individual slaves through a successful petition to the state legislature, many slaves had been acting as though they were free. Some had been purchased by free relatives; others had been transferred to white owners who acted as owners in name only. Such trusteeships were made illegal in 1840, but for decades, lax enforcement of the law gave many men and women in this condition a sense of security. They often paid capitation taxes required for free people of color of certain ages and used that receipt as "proof" of their free status.

But in 1859 and 1860, city government, in response to yet another plea from the white apprentices and mechanics, began to crack down on these people who had been acting as though they were free. Many were caught and sold to new masters; others fled Charleston. To help bolster their chances of staying free, many of those in this legal limbo bought slave badges and wore them in an attempt to have white citizens believe they were accounted for legally. A newspaper in Charleston noted the rush on the badge office and another paper in Philadelphia described African Americans arriving there from Charleston still with their slave badges on as they escaped to freedom.

Slavery, the hiring out of slaves, and the wearing and enforcing of badge laws continued unabated in Charleston during the Civil War years. As copper for the badges grew scarce, it was not uncommon for a badge maker to stamp new information on the reverse of a badge from the previous year. Sales of badges continued into 1865, even as the city was besieged and federal troops took control after Confederates left on February 17. In 1866, all slave-related laws, including those on badges, were abolished.

The first mention of slave badges as a curiosity and relic of lost times came about a generation later. Some badges possibly were sold as souvenirs by the early 20th century. Some counterfeits were known to exist by the 1930s. As collectors began to realize the unique history of these items, demand for them grew, prices shot up, and unethical "diggers" often began trespassing on private property and sites under development in the city of Charleston in search of these relics. Counterfeiting has grown quite rampant, and many people buy these badges in hopes of being able to trace the original wearers and return them to their descendants. But the slave badges are mute; only the name of one slave has been found engraved on one badge. The stories they suggest are nonetheless compelling and the badges are links to those who wore them day in and day out as they navigated a way of life different from many others bound in slavery.

*See also* Whips.

FURTHER READING

Greene, Harlan, Harry, S. Hutchins, Jr., and Brian E. Hutchins. *Slave Badges and the Slave-Hire System in Charleston, South Carolina, 1783–1865*. Jefferson, NC: McFarland and Company, 2004.

Singleton, Theresa. "The Slave Tag: An Artifact of Negro Slavery." *South Carolina Antiquities* 16 (1984): 41–65.

HARLAN GREENE

**SLAVE COLLARS.** The slave collar was a sign and symbol of slavery. It simultaneously signified ownership and servitude. The collar placed around the necks of slaves profoundly dehumanized them. Beyond its symbolic value, the slave collar was among the cruelest kinds of physical torture and punishment slaves had to endure on plantations in the Caribbean and the Americas throughout the Atlantic slave trade. Slave collars were most often used to punish slaves who tried to escape or as a punishment exacted on their family members or on those who resisted in other ways that were judged to be especially dangerous to the owners' maintenance of control and domination.

Iron slave collars were not an invention of the Atlantic slave trade. In ancient Rome, early Christian slave owners placed collars on slaves who tried to escape. Ulpian, a third-century Roman jurist, recorded that Archdeacon Felix ordered a bronze collar placed around the neck of one of his slaves, which was inscribed: "I am the slave of the Archdeacon Felix. Hold me so that I do not flee." For the Europeans and Americans involved in the Atlantic slave trade, however, more brutal rather than declamatory styles of slave collars were required. Owners felt threatened by the active level of resistance shown by many slaves. The owners knew that Maroon communities of escaped slaves were viable and growing, particularly in South America and the West Indies, and that known escape routes in many locations beckoned the slaves and their hopes for freedom. Because the value of the slaves was in their labor, executing them for trying to escape was not a viable financial option, nor was trading them to other plantations, so flogging and collaring became the standard mode of punishment on most plantations. Slave collars were used on both male and female slaves, young and old alike, for either a set period of time or never to be removed at all. Slave collars generally were not used on slaving vessels, where male slaves were routinely manacled two-by-two with ankle chains.

There were several styles of slave collars. All were iron and locked or riveted around the neck of the slave. Some were designed purely to shackle, while others were made to discourage escape attempts; these often had long hooks and **bells** attached to the collar, which made it difficult for a slave to swim or run away without drowning or detection. Robert Smalls (1839–1916), an escaped South Carolina slave who delivered a Confederate ship into Union hands in 1862 and went on to serve in the Union Navy and then in the U.S. House of Representatives, remembered a collar with long outward reaching horizontal bars that resembled cows' horns. These arms would catch in bushes or on trees, making it impossible for a slave to run away or even to sleep on the side, back, or belly. Another style of collar had iron vertical levels extending

## Punishment

John Crawford remembered how his Mississippi owner, Grandpappy Jake Crawford, put collars on disobedient slaves:

When I think of what the 'calcitrant niggers did and what Grandpappy did, I feel like laughin' all over agan. There were some niggers wouldn't work, and they went off in the swamplands, down in the bottoms on the place, and they would sleep in the bresh all day, and at night slip up to the potato kiln, where they baked the potatoes in ashes, and take out potatoes and go to the smokehouse and get the meat, and they cook and eat in the swamps. Grandpappy finally koch them with the dogs and brought them up to the house, and then he sent for a smithy. He had thought up a way to keep them where they b'longed. He had a iron band put round they leg and one round they waist, and a iron pole that went straight up in the air fastened on the side of they leg through the iron bands. And five feet over they heads he hung a brass bell on the top where they can't reach it. Then he turned them loose and told them, "Don't you let me hear that bell leavin' the place, or God have mercy on your black hides."

*Source:* George P. Rawick, ed. *The American Slave: Texas Narratives,* Supp. Ser. 2, Vol. 4. Westport, CT: Greenwood Press.

The son of a Texas slaveholder and his female slave, J. W. Terrill was forced to wear a slave collar:

My father took me away from my mother when at age of six weeks old and gave me to my grandmother, who was real old at the time. Jus' befo' she died she gave me back to my father, who was my mammy's master. He was a old batchelor and run saloon and he was white, but my mammy was a Negro. He was mean to me.

Finally my father let his sister take me and raise me with her chillen. She was good to me, but befo' he let her have me he willed I must wear a bell till I was 21 year old, strapped 'round my shoulders with the bell 'bout three feet from my head in steel frame. That was for punishment for bein' born into the world a son of a white man and my mammy, a Negro slave. I wears this frame with the bell where I could't reach the clapper, day and night. I never knowed what it was to lay down in bed and get a good night's sleep till I was 'bout 17 year old, when my father died and my missy took the bell offen me.

Befo' my father gave me to his sister, I was tied and strapped to a tree and whipped like a beast by my father, till I was unconscious, and then left strapped to a tree all night in cold and rainy weather. My father was very mean. He and he sister brung me to Texas, to North Zulch, when I 'bout 12 year old. He brung my mammy, too, and made her come and be his mistress one night every week, He would have kilt every one of his slaves rather than see us go free, 'specially me and my mammy.

My missy was purty good to me, when my father wasn't right 'round. But he wouldn't let her give me anything to eat but cornbread and water and little sweet 'taters, and jus' 'nough of that to keep me alive. I was allus hongry. My mammy had a boy called Frank Adds and a girl called Marie Adds, what she give birth to by her cullud husban', but I never got to play with them. Missy worked me on the farm and there was 'bout 100 acres and fifteen slaves to work 'em. The overseer waked us 'bout three in the mornin' and then he worked us jus' long as we could see. If we didn't git 'round fast 'nough, he chain us to a tree at night with nothin' to eat, and nex' day, if we didn't go on the run he hit us 39 licks with a belt what was 'bout three foot long and four inches wide.

I wore the bell night and day, and my father would chain me to a tree till I nearly died from the cold and bein' so hongry. My father didn't lieve in church and my missy 'lieved there a Lord, but I wouldn't have 'lieved her if she try larn me 'bout 'ligion, 'cause my father tell me I wasn't any more than a damn mule. I slep' on a chair and tried to res' till my father died, and then I sang all day, 'cause I knowed I wouldn't be treated so mean. When missy took that bell offen me I thinks I in Heaven 'cause I could lie down and go to sleep. When I did I couldn't wake up for a long time and when I did wake up I'd be scairt to death I'd see my father with his whip and that old bell. I'd jump out of bed and run till I give out, for fear he'd come back and git me.

I was 'bout 17 year old then and I so happy not to have that bell on me.

*Source:* George P. Rawick, ed. *"The American Slave: Texas Narratives,* Vol. 5, Parts 3 & 4. Westport, CT: Greenwood Press, 1972.

three or four feet high, from which bells were hung to make incessant noise and detection easy. Also, many slave collars were designed so that additional chains could link the collars to leg or arm manacles and thereby further restrict movement.

In testimony given before the British and Foreign Anti-Slavery Society in England in 1841, Madison Jefferson, a slave born in what is now West Virginia, related how he was collared after his third unsuccessful escape attempt at age 20. After receiving 150 lashes and having brine poured on his wounds, he was locked in a dungeon for two days. Subsequently, for several days, he was forced to parade in front of the house in chains and a collar from which extended a tall vertical crossbar with a bell hanging from it; each and every step caused the bell to ring. He escaped the following year (ca. 1838–1839) and made it safely to Canada, where he worked for two years as a farm hand. At one farm, he met a 12-year-old English boy who taught him to read and brought him to England, where he gave his testimony before the Anti-Slavery Society.

Incredibly, some slaves managed to escape while wearing slave collars. In 1862, during the Civil War, the Fourth Wisconsin Volunteer Infantry provided refuge to two male slaves named Old Steve and Charley. The soldiers were able to file off the rivets to remove the slave collar worn by Old Steve. It later was sent to the Wisconsin Historical Society, where it remains. Steve joined the Union Army.

Slave collars frequently were observed and described in travel narratives written by visitors to plantations and port towns throughout the Caribbean and the Americas in the 18th and 19th centuries. Whatever the views of the authors about slavery itself, generally the slave collar was recognized as a serious and awful punishment. One of the late 18th century's most cited texts concerning slavery, *Narrative of a Five Years' Expedition against the Revolted Negroes of Surinam in Guiana on the Wild Coast of South-America,* based on a manuscript written in 1790 by John Gabriel Stedman (1744–1797) and published in 1796, famously records the case of a 14-year-old slave named Cadety, who was flogged and collared into madness. Stedman's narrative states that an iron triangular collar, called a pot hook, was put around Cadety's neck, which for a month prevented him from escaping or sleeping, and it also provided the means to chain him exposed on a pier, from which he was forced to bark at every boat that passed by. Narratives like Stedman's, as well as geography books and encyclopedias, often included engraved plates and illustrations that depicted slave collars. Even if readers of these texts lived in non-slaving locations, certainly they could identify the cruel intention and purpose of the slave collar.

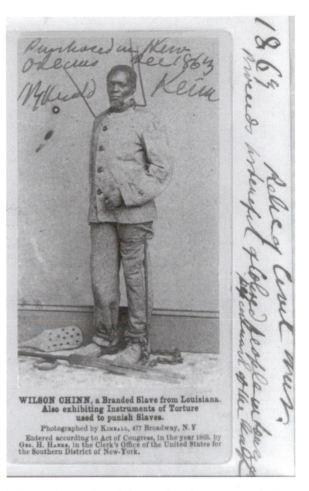

Wilson Chinn, a branded slave from Louisiana, with slave collar, 1863. (Library of Congress.)

Remarkably, decorative and symbolic representations of collars in 17th- and 18th-century English portraiture glorify the wealth and social standing of a particular individual or family. African servants sometimes were included in these portraits; the Africans were not legally slaves in England, but the collars they wore symbolically marked them as slaves. For example, a young servant owned by Lord James Cavendish (d. 1751) is included in a portrait by an unknown artist that featured Cavendish, his father, the Duke of Devonshire, and his father-in-law, Elihu Yale. The boy servant, serving wine, is wearing fancy English dress and a slave collar, which signifies his status as Cavendish's property. A collared male African youth is present in an individual portrait of Elihu Yale (1649–1721), painted by James Worsdale (ca. 1692–1767). Yale, who as the second governor of the English East India Company settlement in Madras, India, from

1687–1692, witnessed the emergence of a lively slave trade for young children. There is an interesting American connection to this portrait. In 1718, upon receiving an appeal from Massachusetts Bay Colony leader Cotton Mather (1663–1728), Elihu Yale donated a box of goods to the Collegiate School of Connecticut, which then sold it for cash. To thank him for his gift, the school was renamed Yale University.

The slave collar also became an iconographic image for the abolitionist movement in England, which had active publishing and marketing campaigns. Anti-slavery poetry in **books**, handbills, and newspapers often included images depicting the suffering or the piety of slaves. One such handbill, printed to celebrate the August 1834 law that declared slavery illegal in the British Empire, presented James Montgomery's (1771–1854) poem, "The Negroes' Vigil," accompanied with an illustration of a pious black male, who is seen praying on one knee, but wearing a slave collar and ankle and wrist chains. Similarly sympathetic visual representations of slaves wearing collars and chains can been seen on other products produced by the abolitionist movement; these included wall hangings, plates, mugs, trays, glasses, medallions, and medals, and all were available in a wide range of styles and prices.

During the centuries of the Atlantic slave trade, whether used as a method of punishment or used symbolically by those who abhorred slavery, the slave collar, perhaps more than any other object, came to represent the profound cruelty of slavery.

*See also* Abolition Imagery.

FURTHER READING

Amussen, Susan Dwyer. *Caribbean Exchanges: Slavery and the Transformation of English Society, 1640–1700.* Chapel Hill: University of North Carolina Press, 2007.

Blassingame, John W., ed. *Slave Testimony: Two Centuries of Letters, Speeches, Interviews, and Autobiographies.* Baton Rouge: Louisiana State University Press, 1977.

"Curators' Favorites: Fugitive Slave Collar," Wisconsin Historical Society. At www.wisconsinhistory.org/museum/artifacts/archives/001446.asp.

Glancy, Jennifer A. *Slavery in Early Christianity.* New York: Oxford University Press, 2002.

Taylor, Eric Robert. *If We Must Die: Shipboard Insurrections in the Era of the Atlantic Slave Trade.* Baton Rouge: Louisiana State University Press, 2006.

Thompson, Alvin O. *Flight to Freedom: African Runaways and Maroons in the Americas.* Kingston, Jamaica: University of the West Indies Press, 2006.

Wood, Marcus. *Blind Memory: Visual Representations of Slavery in England and America, 1780–1865.* Manchester: Manchester University Press, 2000.

LINDA E. MERIANS

**SLAVE DRIVERS.** Slave drivers were agricultural bondsmen with diverse responsibilities in field production and labor supervision on large plantations or small farms. In the management structure of large plantations, the slave driver ranked below the overseer, steward, and planter. In the slave hierarchy, the driver's status was comparable to that of the slave artisans and household slaves. The position of driver originated in 17th-century South Carolina, where seasoned slaves supervised the field labor of new slaves by standing behind and "driving," or coercing, them to perform their new duties. By the 19th century, the position and responsibilities of the slave driver had expanded. Depending on the size of the agricultural unit, several occupational levels could exist, including the head driver, also known as the overdriver; the underdriver; and the foreman, who directed field task gangs.

Most drivers were men, although some slave women worked in the capacity of drivers when supervising "trash gangs" of young children, superannuated slaves, and women in an advanced stage of pregnancy. The male slave driver was usually in his 30s or 40s. In some instances, drivers were younger, and some managed to retain their positions into their 60s. Most slave drivers were intelligent individuals with forceful personalities and physical power or presence who also possessed leadership and management skills. Their major responsibility was to maintain a highly disciplined, efficient, and well-coordinated productive agricultural slave labor force.

The commercial agricultural South was dominated by a single-crop economy. High productivity required an extremely regimented workforce, specialization in field labor, and a high degree of labor interdependence and cooperation. Rigid discipline was required to maintain assembly-line fieldwork to meet production goals. In fulfilling these responsibilities of his position, the slave driver often has been compared to a shop foreman. His major purpose was to "drive" the slaves to maintain efficiency and discipline. Given authority to punish field hands, the driver historically was often called "whipping man" or "whipping boss."

But the slave driver was more than a "straw boss," whipping man, or foreman who supervised field hands from sunup to sundown. Drivers collected information on field production, which they analyzed, interpreted, and passed on to the overseer, steward, or planter. In the absence of an overseer and often the owners, the driver had to schedule production and plan how to deploy limited resources. In fulfilling these diverse responsibilities, the slave driver in this management capacity thus provides an example of slave "intrapreneurship." Possessed of both practical and specialized knowledge of crop production, the slave driver could dominate field operations in the production of **cotton**, **sugar**, **tobacco**, and **rice** that brought in the plantation dollars. The slave driver James Pemberton, who managed Jefferson Davis's Brierfield, Mississippi, plantation, was representative of the slave driver as intrapreneur. In October 1846, Pemberton reported to Davis that his enslaved workforce at Brierfield had picked 170,000 pounds of cotton, more than 300 bales.

Slave drivers were both generalists and specialists in the performance of their management duties, but more than anything else perhaps they had to be "people managers" who knew how to set goals and motivate the field laborers. Their expertise was invaluable in contributing to the agricultural productivity of the antebellum South. Given the high rate of periodic absentee ownership, and that only 30 percent of plantations and farms had white overseers, perhaps two-thirds of slaves worked directly under a black man. Planter compensation for the success of slave drivers varied. High-top leather boots, greatcoats, and top hats in addition to the whip often were symbols of the driver's status and position. Because drivers seldom were "bred," opportunities existed for the slave driver to groom a promising son for this "privileged" position. Often the driver was rewarded with better housing and more abundant **food**. The position also could be used to mitigate punishment of family members and friends; it also could be abused, to mete out punishment to enemies as well as to obtain sexual favors. Sometimes, planters provided drivers with extra land for their personal use with permission to use other slaves to cultivate the plot. Produce raised could be taken to town by the driver and sold for cash. Some drivers received money incentives in wages and bonuses, amounting in some instances to hundreds of dollars, for their efficiency in labor management and field production.

The management styles developed by drivers to maintain their position have become the source of great historical controversy. Historians, however, have been reluctant to accept the neoabolitionist description of the cruel, sadistic, and brutal slave driver portrayed by Sambo and Quimbo in Harriet Beecher Stowe's (1811–1896) 1852 novel *Uncle Tom's Cabin*. Rather, most historians tend to agree that although some slave drivers were crueler than whites, most protected and helped other slaves.

The management operations of a capital-extensive, labor-intensive, single-crop agricultural unit encouraged development of a performance-oriented business culture as opposed to that of a paternalistic profit-sharing business culture. Even privileged slaves with specialized skills were compensated inadequately, despite the perquisites that could be derived from their positions. Yet most slave drivers attempted to retain their often-unenviable positions as field managers. The duration of their tenure required that they push for optimum labor productivity and efficiency to meet the production goals and profit expectations of their masters. In so doing, drivers often found it difficult to act in the best interests of the slave community.

After freedom, some drivers were able to use their knowledge of field production and farm management, and their personal ties to former masters, to become successful owners of small farms. A few continued working for their former owners as sharecroppers or tenant farmers; others took whatever job they could find. White hostility, racism, and discrimination prevented most former slave drivers from using their management skills developed during slavery to their own advantage after the Civil War.

*See also* Whips; Work Routines.

FURTHER READING

Blassingame, John W. *The Slave Community: Plantation Life in the Antebellum South*. Rev. ed. New York: Oxford University Press, 1979.

Genovese, Eugene D. *Roll, Jordan, Roll: The World the Slaves Made*. New York: Pantheon Books, 1974.

Miller, Randall M., ed. *"Dear Master": Letters of a Slave Family*. Ithaca, NY: Cornell University Press, 1978.

Miller, Randall M. "The Man in the Middle: The Black Slave Driver." *American Heritage* 30 (1979): 40–49.

Owens, Leslie Howard. *This Species of Property: Slave Life and Culture in the Old South*. New York: Oxford University Press, 1976.

Starobin, Robert S., ed. *Blacks in Bondage: Letters of American Slaves*. New York: New Viewpoints, 1974.

Van DeBurg, William L. *The Slave Drivers: Black Agricultural Labor Supervisors in the Antebellum South*. Westport, CT: Greenwood Press, 1979.

JULIET E. K. WALKER

**SLAVE GALLERIES.** Slave galleries provided tangible evidence of the degree of autonomy white church congregants held over Christian slaves and freedmen alike. The galleries were small rooms built behind balconies, usually in the back of affluent

> ## Separate Worshipping
>
> Cicely Cawthorn noted the separate upstairs gallery for slave congregants at a Georgia church she attended: "We belonged to the white folks' church, but we didn't go in at the door of the church, though. They had a stairway on the outside where we could go up, and then after we got up the stairs we'd be in the church, in the gallery."
>
> *Source:* George P. Rawick, ed. *The American Slave: Georgia Narratives*, Supp. Ser. 1, Vol. 3, Part 1. Westport, CT: Greenwood Press, 1978.

**churches**. Some galleries included bleacher-type seating. The rooms afforded a cramped space for slaves to worship at the same time as their masters, but they also visually and spatially separated slaves from other congregants.

The precedent for having separate galleries for slaves could have begun as early as 1667 when a Virginia statute ruled that slaveholders could baptize their slaves without altering the slave's legal status as bound for life. Pious and charitable members of the colony's state church, the Church of England, opened the worship service to Christian slaves but devised ways to maintain the racial status quo. Separate galleries allowed joint worship without the appearance of equality in the church.

Galleries became significant after South Carolina slaves from the heavily Catholic Kongo organized on September 8 and rebelled on Sunday, September 9, 1739, which according to the Protestant Julian calendar is the nativity of Mary. The Stono Rebellion motivated Protestants to keep closer watch on their slaves on Sundays and to be more aggressive about Protestant baptism and public worship regardless of the slaves' faiths. As evangelical Protestantism influenced church formation across the nation, some whites authorized black Protestant ministers to preach to black congregations in branch churches. Renewed concern about slave rebellions led some states such as Mississippi in 1830 to outlaw all-black churches, and biracial worship and separate galleries for slaves became more common. Religion became another tool of white manipulation over slave culture, and galleries facilitated the segregation.

Galleries appeared in the antebellum North as well. They separated free congregants of color from white church members, much as "negro pews" functioned during the post–Civil War era of segregation. The galleries built into St. Augustine's Episcopal Church on Manhattan's Lower East Side in 1828 separated free blacks from white congregants. In these spaces, skilled black artisans rubbed elbows with servants bound to pious masters.

FURTHER READING

Boles, John B., ed. *Masters and Slaves in the House of the Lord: Race and Religion in the American South, 1740–1870.* Lexington: University Press of Kentucky, 1988.

Raboteau, Albert J. *Slave Religion: The "Invisible Institution" in the Antebellum South.* 1980. Revised, New York: Oxford University Press, 2004.

Sevcenko, Liz, Reverend Deacon Edgar W. Hopper, and Lisa Chice. "St. Augustine's Episcopal Church and the Lower East Side Tenement Museum: The Slave Galleries Restoration Project." In *History as Catalyst for Civic Dialogue: Case Studies from Animating Democracy,* edited by Pam Korza and Barbara, 1–25. Schaffer Bacon. Washington, DC: Americans for the Arts, 2005.

Smith, Mark M. "Remembering Mary, Shaping Revolt: Reconsidering the Stono Rebellion." *Journal of Southern History* 67, no. 3 (2001): 513–534.

DEBRA A. REID

**SLAVE HOSPITALS.** Many slaves endured serious health problems, undoubtedly due to their working and living situations. Because of their long hours at work, inadequate nutrition, poor and unsanitary living conditions, and in some cases, having to endure the various effects of cold, hot, and wet weather with little protection, enslaved African Americans were more susceptible than all but the poorest whites to many diseases and conditions. These included cholera, typhoid, influenza, hepatitis, diarrhea, parasitic infections, and a variety of sexually transmitted diseases. In addition, it has been suggested that potentially fatal respiratory infections like pneumonia and tuberculosis were widespread in enslaved populations, due, in part, to chronic poor nutrition as well as substandard **slave housing** that often admitted the winter cold and excessive summer heat. All these conditions undermined the slave's immunological system. Other health misfortunes that befell enslaved individuals included injuries from fights, brutal punishments, sustained work-related accidents, and dental and pregnancy complications. All serious health-related issues required some degree of medical attention in an era before antibiotics and sterile techniques were discovered.

Medical scholars characterize 18th- and early 19th-century **medicine** in general as harsh, ineffective, and experimental. Reputable public health institutions were rare; most Americans avoided hospitals at any cost. For almost all early Americans, regardless of race or economic circumstances, any attempt at surgery usually was fatal. Medicine in the United States during this period reflected medical practitioners' superficial training as well as their sparse and limited understanding of diseases, including the connection between bacteria and disease.

By the 19th century, many Americans grew more concerned with sanitary living conditions. In the case of slaveholders, their attitudes toward medical care and other living conditions for their slaves gradually became more paternalistic during the antebellum period, in large part because the institution of slavery increasingly came under threat. Some slave owners published articles in *Southern Agriculture* and other similar journals that detailed the careful attention that they claimed to provide to the enslaved individuals under their charge in areas like housing and health.

In the event of sickness, most slave masters routinely treated their slaves themselves first before they called a physician. In addition to attributing enslaved ill health to what they characterized as a fundamental weakness in character, many slave owners believed that slaves feigned illness to get out of work and "tested" individuals to see whether they were really sick even before ministering to them themselves. Whatever the circumstances, their primary concern was to keep their workers fit for their work. If the "home" treatment did not help to improve the slave's condition, the slave owner would then send the slave to a physician or, more commonly, ask the physician to come to the plantation to conduct an examination. Obtaining a physician for a sick slave usually was a last resort because it was expensive.

Especially on antebellum plantations with large workforces, the accumulation of medical problems among the enslaved workforce led to the establishment of a separate

Former slave hospital, one of the earliest built by enslaved African Americans, at Melrose plantation, Melrose, Louisiana. (Library of Congress.)

structure on the property known as the "slave hospital" or the "sick house." These treatment facilities were similar to those established in the West Indies, where the medical care was decidedly different from in the American South. In both regions, however, slaveholders saw the establishment of slave hospitals as a cost-effective way to nurse slaves back to health and, thus, to keep them working. These facilities also allowed for the separation of workers with contagious diseases from the general enslaved population.

Although some owners contracted with local physicians to make the rounds periodically among their slaves and provide medical treatment to the sickest individuals, the supervision, organization, and operation of the plantation hospital fell to the master, mistresses, overseer, or the overseer's wife and children. Elderly female slaves who could no longer do strenuous work frequently were assigned jobs as nurses or midwives. Many slave hospitals included maternity wards for slave births. For slaveholders, this was yet another way to safeguard their investment.

The size of these facilities varied. On Butler's Island, Pierce Butler's (1806–1867) Sea Island plantation outside Darien, Georgia, the two-and-a-half-story slave hospital consisted of four rooms plus a **loft** and was located at one end of the **slave quarter**. Butler's wife, the actress Fanny Kemble (1809–1893), described the building as dirty and dark. In contrast, the Georgia plantation of James Hamilton Couper (1794–1866) boasted a large slave hospital that included heating. A slave hospital survives on Magnolia plantation, Natchitoches, Louisiana, and a reconstructed example exists at Somerset plantation, Creswell, North Carolina.

Enslaved African Americans regularly engaged, usually in secret, in their own healing practices within their community that were distinct from the treatments given by whites.

FURTHER READING

Breeden, James O., ed. *Advice among Masters: The Ideal in Slave Management in the Old South.* Westport, CT: Greenwood Press, 1980.

Byrd, W. Michael, and Linda A. Clayton. *An American Health Dilemma: A Medical History of African Americans and the Problem of Race: Beginnings to 1900.* New York: Routledge, 2000.

Kenny, Steven C. "A Dictate of Both Interest and Mercy, Slave Hospitals in the Antebellum South." *Journal of the History of Medicine and Allied Sciences* 65, no. 1 (January 2010): 1–47.

Randall, Vernellia R. *Dying While Black.* Dayton, OH: Seven Principles Press, 2006.

Vlach, John Michael. *Back of the Big House: The Architecture of Plantation Slavery.* Chapel Hill: University of North Carolina Press, 1993.

Wilson, Harriet A. *Medical Apartheid: The Dark History of Medical Experimentation on Black Americans from Colonial Times to the Present.* New York: Doubleday, 2006.

FRED LINDSEY

**SLAVE HOUSING.** Housing arrangements were a critical aspect of slaves' everyday material world. The observed diversity of housing reflected a complex interaction between slave and master that varied by different geographic, temporal, economic, and demographic circumstances. Understanding this architectural realm demonstrates individual slaveholders' ideologies for slave management, the ways that slaves supported their own communities, and how slave housing defined important aspects of African American families and cultures. Studies of the buildings typically called "slave quarters" help one to understand the modern cultural politics of slavery and its public interpretation at museums and historic sites. Remarkable for their variety, **slave quarters** materially represent the dynamic negotiation between slaves and masters as to the location and design of shelter, living and working conditions, household composition, and social life. Despite slave housing's variability on colonial and national American farms and plantations and within cities, key patterns exist as to construction format and materials and placement on the landscape that changed over time.

The fields of anthropology, archaeology, architectural history, and history have contributed to studies of slavery, slave housing, and the African Diaspora. Because few slave habitations survive, primary sources for interpreting slave housing include architectural evidence from surviving buildings, archaeological sites, and documentary accounts, such as census and tax records and period fire insurance policies. For example, in the Chesapeake region, no standing 17th-century slave quarters remain and only a few, better built 18th-century structures remain. More 19th-century examples exist, but these tend to be larger quarters near the mansion houses of upscale plantation estates. Constructed of more durable materials, these quarters received more architectural investment and reflected the residential core's stylistic orientation. The same structures typically were modified in later periods by other architectural uses, repairs, and cultural sensibilities. In contrast, archaeologists have uncovered the ephemeral remains of log cabins and earthfast (post-in-ground) construction from various periods throughout the South.

Another bias stems from scholarly tendencies to examine relatively few contexts of slavery. From studies of slave population and ownership, it is clear that 90 percent of African Americans lived in rural settings, mostly on farms and small plantations with five or fewer other slaves. Larger slave groupings, ranging from 15 or 20 to more than

Sotterly slave cabin, Hollywood, Maryland. (Library of Congress.)

100 and 200 slaves, resided on large plantations encompassing a thousand or more acres. Owners of these plantations, while a small minority, together held a third or more of a county's slave population. Architectural and archaeological studies have focused on large plantations, such as George Washington's (1732–1799) Mount Vernon and Thomas Jefferson's (1743–1826) Monticello in Virginia. These estates have survived

Interior of Sotterly slave cabin, Hollywood, Maryland. (Library of Congress.)

better, are associated with detailed documentary collections, and have received more funding and attention by the historic preservation organizations charged with their maintenance and public interpretation. At the same time, these locations do represent an important context for addressing slavery and slave housing, as large plantations formed nodes of broader African American communities. Nonetheless, this scholarly trend has excluded more in-depth research into slave housing on farms and urban lots.

Within mainland America, slave housing and associated work buildings built and occupied by slaves span more than 375 years of European and American systems of bonded labor, different environmental regions, agricultural and industrial regimes, town and urban contexts, and varying enslaved African American and free black populations. It is no wonder that differing architectural arrangements existed under which slaves lived together, prepared **food**, and developed strategies for improving their material and social conditions. Slave housing ranged from available spaces like attics, cellars, and closets of masters' dwelling houses, to unspecified parts of outbuildings and "mixed-use" structures like **kitchens**, stables, or workshops outfitted with a room or two for slaves. The larger category of buildings involved independent structures purposely constructed for house slaves, and these took on various forms. Moving from small to large, masters used single-cell cabins, double-cell quarters, or duplexes, often sharing a central chimney, and then multiple-room barracks and two-story **dormitories**.

### Terminology

The generic term "slave housing" encompasses a variety of living arrangements, but the period terms of "cabin" and "quarter(s)" require definition given their continued popular use. Within the 18th-century Chesapeake region, for example, the English terms "cabin" and "quarter" acquired new meanings that approximate the modern association with slave houses. Cabins implied smaller domestic buildings of lesser construction, most often of log, associated with the lower class and, increasingly, slaves. This sense of minimal construction contributed to the relative lack of period documentation and the reduced survival of cabins into the modern era.

The term "quarter" developed from the 17th-century "quartering house" (for indentured servants) and eventually was associated with slave housing. Quarters usually entailed a one-story structure with one or two rooms and unfinished interiors and dirt floors, shuttered windows, and end chimneys of wood and mud construction. "Quarter" could refer to an individual dwelling or a clustered group of slave houses separated from masters or overseers. Additionally, the term "quarter" sometimes constituted a legal division of a larger farm or plantation that encompassed crop fields, woods, housing for slaves and perhaps an overseer, and other agricultural or industrial support buildings.

Quarters were distinguished further by location and the tasks assigned to the buildings' residents. House servants and craftsmen usually lived in quarters near the owner's main dwelling and residential complex, collectively noted as the "home house quarter." Enslaved agricultural workers ("field hands") resided in smaller cabins near fields known as a "farm quarters." Quarters could be placed in single file along a road or plantation "street," in parallel rows, or as a "slave village" where African Americans found greater opportunities for privacy and self-expression. A number of these variations could occur on one plantation, depending on its physical expanse and the owner's wealth. More slaves and larger plantations usually meant more quarters of varying kinds and qualities in different locations.

---

## Stone Huts

When interviewed in Maryland, M. S. Fayman remembered the slave housing made from stone on the Kentucky plantation where she was enslaved:

> Let me describe the huts, these buildings were built of stone, each one about 20 feet wide, 50 feet long, 9 feet high in the rear, about 12 feet high in front, with a slanting roof of chestnut boards and with a sliding door, two windows between each door back and front about 2 x 4 feet, at each end a door and window similar to those on the side. There were ten such buildings, to each building there was another building 12 x 15 feet, this was where the cooking was done. At each end of each building there was a fire place built and used for heating purposes. In front of each building there were barrels filled with water supplied by pipes from a large spring, situated about 300 yards on the side of a hill which was very rocky, where the stones were quarried to build the buildings on the farm. On the outside near each window and door there were iron rings firmly attached to the walls, through which an iron rod was inserted and locked each and every night, making it impossible for those inside to escape.

*Source:* George P. Rawick, ed. "*The American Slave: Kansas, Kentucky, Maryland, Ohio, Virginia, and Tennessee Narratives*, Vol. 16. Westport, CT: Greenwood Press, 1972.

---

### Patterns of Construction and Change

Throughout time, wooden slave housing, whether of earthfast, log, or frame construction, dominated rural and urban scenes throughout the South. Brick and stone construction, which also was used and obviously survives better, was seen more often on upscale plantations and came to replace wooden quarters because of fire hazards. Roofing materials predominantly consisted of wood, either split shingles, slabs, or rough boards. This pattern existed in urban areas, although fire insurance policies in Virginia indicate that higher incidences of terra cotta tile, metal, and gravel roofs occurred during the antebellum period. Earthfast slave quarters relied on vertical timbers set in postholes to which other framing members were joined or nailed. This construction method prevailed throughout the 17th century, reflecting the Chesapeake region's broader building practices. Based on archaeological evidence, earthfast slave quarters continued well into the 18th century and usually had wood and mud chimneys, earthen floors, clapboard siding, and wood shingle roofs.

Log construction proved to be an increasingly popular option during the 18th and 19th centuries. Log buildings were cheaper and faster to erect and required fewer carpentry skills and specialized tools. Such construction relied on local materials, trees for logs, which were left in the round or hewn on two or four sides, and clay for chinking between logs, including those of the wooden chimney. Besides clay chinking, stones, brick, saplings, and short boards could fill the gaps between logs. One-room log cabins with a sleeping **loft** and a dirt floor constituted the primary housing format that slaves in many regions and time periods experienced. Larger log buildings

451

emerged, whether as duplexes, two-story structures, or as two single-cell buildings joined by a covered passageway, known as a **double-pen houses** or **dogtrot houses**.

Two-room buildings, called a "duplex" or a "double quarter," were another common building format. Widely distributed geographically, the duplex often involved a one-story structure with a garret above, while the two groundfloor rooms had separate exterior doors and no interior communication. Each room had its own fireplace, with many duplexes having a central chimney. Although not confined solely to the antebellum period, surviving duplexes date from the 1820s to the 1850s. Generally of more substantial and weather-tight construction, duplexes had continuous foundations or masonry piers, raised wooden floors, glass windows, and brick or stone fireplaces. Some duplexes had interior wall plaster and trim boards, yet many reflected an economy of investment with only ladder access to garrets and plain sheathing or exposed framing with whitewash treatment.

Frame construction became more frequent in the 19th century, often reflecting a new attitude among masters for "improved" quartering arrangements that maintained the health of a now self-reproducing labor force. Glazed windows became a regular feature, whereas earlier quarters had few and small windows, covered only with wooden shutters or other materials. Still, archaeological research indicates the presence of window glass within slave building sites of different time periods and construction formats. This evidence is corroborated by the writings of antebellum masters whose use of windows in slave buildings fulfilled multiple functions. Windows symbolized to the other whites that masters possessed the wherewithal to invest in first-rate openings for slave quarters. The same windows provided proper light and ventilation that kept slaves healthy, and the gained lighting allowed for extra indoor work.

Over time, many masters abandoned larger barracks-style housing for mixed slave groupings and adopted a modular style of smaller, family-focused log quarters. This change underscored a new mind-set among wealthier and worldlier slave owners who accepted the late 18th- and early 19th-century advances in Southern agriculture that led to better built quarters. Mixing Christian duty and a new sense of paternalism, planters took on the practices of scientific management and agricultural reform and blended it with overt racism and a sharp business approach to slave management.

Like the change in construction formats, the size of slave quarters also changed. Larger quarters characterized Chesapeake slave housing of the 1760s and 1770s, often with two-room plans and containing between 200 and 260 square feet per room and 400 to 500 square feet per structure. By the late 18th and early 19th centuries, smaller quarters, often with a single room having 140 square feet of interior space, became the norm, while early to mid-19th-century quarters expanded to about 230 to 250 square feet. Perhaps for reasons of control, masters began to prefer smaller slave houses, such as a 12- by 14-foot (168 square feet) or a 16-by 18-foot (288 square feet) building. Overall, though, slave quarter sizes throughout the South encompassed a considerable range of variation, running from incredibly small quarters at 8 by 8 feet, to those 18 by 20 feet and larger, discounting larger arrangements. Although duplexes entailed more space, commonly measuring 16 by 32 feet (512 square feet), these buildings usually were designed for two households.

Smaller, more private slave buildings did not reflect only masters' intentions and their changing management practices. By the antebellum period, African American populations in the Upper South had attained greater demographic and family stability. They also gained greater negotiating power as the former **tobacco** plantation regime gave way to **wheat** and other grains, more craft activity, and the requirement for slaves to work on different tasks while contributing to their own subsistence through gardening, gathering, hunting, and the production of marketable goods. Masters' continued dependence on slave labor may have permitted slaves more autonomy and given them a greater ability to influence masters as to working and living conditions, including the establishment of more family-based households. From the master's perspective, slaves with more stable families were less likely to run away or rebel. Consequently, the rise of better built quarters and kin-based households suggest a negotiated outcome between slave and master.

### Urban Slave Housing

Except for a few well-known locations like Charleston, South Carolina, urban slave housing has received less architectural and archaeological study than rural housing. Parallels existed between urban and rural slave housing, particularly the use of small buildings, a minimal investment of construction, the confinement of quarters to the house lot's side or rear portions, and the accommodation of slaves within the spare and sparsely furnished spaces of the **master's house**. Still, clear differences can be delineated. Most urban masters had only one or two slaves, a pattern that contributed to the increased frequency of a single slave building on city properties. Data from pre–Civil War fire insurance policies demonstrate that urban slave masters relied on two main categories of structures. The first, designated "separate" buildings, had the primary function of housing slaves, frequently in a detached building. The second category, "mixed-use" buildings, involved structures having one or more work-related functions in addition to housing slaves, such as kitchens, smokehouses, or stables. Given the common practice of "hiring out" surplus slaves to employers and the practice of these slaves "living out" from owners or employers in antebellum cities, urban settings invariably contained more rental arrangements for housing slaves, with lodging tenements offering a more autonomous setting for slave domestic life. The higher frequency of brick slave housing in cities resulted from restrictions placed on construction practices in American cities after disastrous fires. Last, larger slave owners tended to build multiple-room buildings, often two-story structures that sometimes housed other support functions like kitchens, **laundries**, and privies.

Some masters used separate quarters on urban estates that followed the plantation pattern of a mansion and its **dependencies**. More typical settings were back buildings and various outbuildings located at the property's rear edge. When freestanding kitchens existed, they were typically either a two-room, single-story plan with a central chimney or a two-story building with a groundfloor single-room kitchen, while slaves resided upstairs in a loft space. Distinct residential districts for free and enslaved African Americans defined a notable feature of the urban landscape. Boarding houses, back alleys, and rude cabins made up the "shanty town" with which masters and white citizens had little familiarity and where African Americans had more opportunities to pursue their own social life and cultural values.

### Slave Housing as Creolized Architecture

Although certain architectural characteristics found in African American housing—particularly the **shotgun house** form, spatial units of 10- or 12-foot squares, and thatched roofs and wattle wall construction—have been postulated as African inspired, the vast majority of slave houses appear to fall within European American building traditions. While drawing on these long-standing cultural traditions for worker and lower class housing, slaveholders designed quarters to make statements that expressed their ideas about political economy, individual social status, and negotiations with workers. This housing offered enslaved workers the possibility of shelter that needed minimal maintenance. Masters regularly determined the number and variety of occupants within slave households based on family relationship, gender, age, and work skills. They often controlled the buildings' placement, the degree of material investment, and construction format, making it difficult to interpret the contributions of the enslaved. As a consequence, standing slave structures and their documentary references more clearly connote masters' intentions.

Still, slave quarters can be considered to be creolized and negotiated entities, reflecting the constant dynamic of power between masters and the slaves who built and maintained these structures and incorporated their own cultural sensibilities. Historic documents and archaeological investigations indicate that masters had relatively little influence on slave quarters' interiors. Slaves found ways both to supplement and subvert what masters provided to make quarters suit their needs and cultural preferences. Period accounts underscore that masters and overseers rarely entered slaves' houses and that some slaves had door **locks** for their residences.

Masters provided few interior **furnishings** and little furniture, most likely a crude boxed bed and a cast iron cooking vessel. Beyond periodic **food rations** and **clothing allotments**, slaves had to supply much of their own material world, whether through theft, trade, purchase, or self-production. Archaeology reveals how slaves modified and used quarters, providing evidence of African retentions, resistance to domination, and insights into slaves' personal possessions and their participation in broader consumer trends. Furniture hardware, spikes, hooks, and storage containers ranging from barrels to **subfloor pits** define critical contributions slaves made to create their own domestic spaces. Food-related objects, numerous types of glass and ceramics, metal containers, and utensils attest to a condition of resource access defined by slaves that improved their living standards and projected a sense of personal and group identity.

*See also* Beds; Cast Iron Pots; Chamber Pots and Privies; Two Rooms over Two Rooms Houses.

FURTHER READING

Breeden, James O. *Advice among Masters: The Ideal in Slave Management in the Old South.* Westport, CT: Greenwood Press, 1980.

Digital Archaeological Archive of Comparative Slavery, Thomas Jefferson Foundation. At www.daacs.org/.

Herman, Bernard L. "Slave and Servant Housing in Charleston, 1770–1820." *Historical Archaeology* 33, no. 3 (1999): 88–101.

Morgan, Philip D. *Slave Counterpoint: Black Culture in the Eighteenth-Century Chesapeake and Lowcountry.* Chapel Hill: University of North Carolina Press, 1998.

Pogue, Dennis J. "The Domestic Architecture of Slavery at George Washington's Mount Vernon." *Winterthur Portfolio* 37, no. 1 (2002): 3–22.

Samford, Patricia M. *Subfloor Pits and the Archaeology of Slavery in Colonial Virginia*. Tuscaloosa: University of Alabama Press, 2007.

Vlach, John Michael. *Back of the Big House: The Architecture of Plantation Slavery*. Chapel Hill: University of North Carolina Press, 1993.

DOUGLAS W. SANFORD

**SLAVE-MADE OBJECTS.** Enslaved artisans shaped silver, wood, clay, and other materials into coffee pots, tables, ceramics, and other decorative and utilitarian objects. They fashioned objects for their own communities—objects that often survive only through brief documentary references or in archaeological contexts.

An ongoing survey of surviving period documents from the southern part of the United States at the Museum of Early Southern Decorative Arts (MESDA) in Winston-Salem, North Carolina, has documented the identities of nearly 3,000 enslaved artisans. The earliest identified is a carpenter named Jack in Westmoreland County, Virginia, in 1674. Jack is typical of the enslaved artisans who have been identified in the survey. He surfaces in the documentary record only once: in an inventory of his owner's possessions. Often a single reference—in a **runaway slave advertisement**, a descriptive adjective in a deed, a brief note in an auction record, a line in a will, a reference in a probate inventory—is the only evidence of an enslaved artisan's life and work. Jack is typical in that he worked in a building-related trade. Most enslaved artisans identified in MESDA's survey labored in industrial or building trades. A smaller number were employed in skilled trades as varied as silversmithing and bookbinding.

### Industrial Slavery

Alexander Spotswood (ca. 1676–1740), who served as the Royal Governor of Virginia between 1710 and 1722, saw the potential for profit in the iron ore deposits of Virginia's backcountry. During his governorship and afterward, he amassed large tracts of iron-rich land for himself and encouraged its settlement by German ironworkers. Spotswood also saw the potential for slave labor in his mining and furnace operations. Ironworking was long, hard, and hot work that required skilled and unskilled labor to mine, transport, smelt, refine, and cast finished objects. When Spotswood died in 1740, his will made special mention of the enslaved craftsmen working at his Tubal Furnace in Spotsylvania County. It noted that "[w]hereas the said tract . . . called the mine tract is . . . appropriated for the carrying on an iron work . . . it is necessary that at least Eight able working Slaves with twenty Children belonging to them should be annexed to the said Land and employed in the said Work."

Other industrialists recognized the economic value of enslaved artisans. In York County, South Carolina, the Aera Furnace made extensive use of slave labor. In 1779, the Aera Furnace advertised its immediate need for such laborers in Charleston, South Carolina, newspapers. The furnace owners knew that Charleston slaveholders were worried about the safety of their slave property in the face of an impending attack on the city by the British. Earlier in the war, Lord Dunmore (John Murray, 1732–1809), the royal governor of Virginia, had promised freedom to any slave who successfully escaped to British lines. The

## Do It Yourself

As former Texas slave Abram Sells pointed out, on many plantations enslaved individuals made nearly everything needed by their masters and themselves:

Massa Rimes have a commissary or sto' house, whar he kep' whatnot things—them what make on the plantation and things the slaves couldn' make for themselfs. That wasn't much, 'cause we make us own clothes and shoes and plow and all farm tools and us even make our own plow line out'n cotton and iffen us run short of cotton sometime make them out'n bear grass and we make buttons for us clothes out'n li'l round pieces of gourds and kiver them with cloth.

*Source:* George P. Rawick, ed. *The American Slave: Texas Narratives*, Parts 3 & 4. Westport, CT: Greenwood Press, 1972.

Zack Herndon, formerly enslaved in South Carolina, made candles:

Us had tallow candles. Why ev'ybody know'd how to make taller candles in dem days, dat wudd'n nothing out de ordinary. All you had to do, was to kill a beef and take de taller from his tripe and kidneys. See, it de fat you gits and boil it out. Stew it down jes' as folks does hog lard dese days. De candle moulds was made out'n tin. Fer de wicks, all de wrapping string was saved up, and dar wasn't much wrapping string in dem times. Put de string right down de middle o' de mould and pour de hot taller all around it. De string will be de wick fer de candle. Den de moulds was laid in raal cold water so dat de taller shrink when it harden, and dis 'low de candle to drap easy from de mould and not break up. Why, it's jes' as easy to make taller candles as it is to fall off'n a log.

*Source:* George P. Rawick, ed. *The American Slave: South Carolina Narratives*, Vol. 2. Westport, CT: Greenwood Press, 1972.

Paul Smith from Georgia created hats and baskets:

When us warn't out in de fields, us done little jobs 'round de big house, de cabins, barns, and yards. Us used to holp de older slaves git out whiteoak splits, and dey larnt us to make cheer bottoms and baskets out of dem splits. De best cheer bottoms what lasted de longest was dem what us made wid red ellum withes. Dem old shuck bottoms was fine too; dey plaited dem shucks and wound 'em 'round for cheer bottoms and footsmats. De 'omans made nice hats out of shucks and wheat straw. Dey plaited de shucks and put 'em together wid plaits of wheat straw. Dey warn't counted much for Sunday wear, but dey made fine sun hats.

*Source:* George P. Rawick, ed. *The American Slave: Georgia Narratives*, Vol. 13. Westport, CT: Greenwood Press, 1972.

furnace owners advertised that "no situation in the State is more healthy and secure from an enemy." Ironically, the furnaces were at work producing munitions for the Continental Army, as well as domestic items such as firebacks emblazoned with the Revolutionary slogan "Liberty or Death." In the months following their capture of Charleston, British forces moved inland and captured and destroyed the ironworks.

Industrial slavery lasted until the Civil War. In Richmond, Virginia, the Tredegar Ironworks on the James River depended on both slave and free laborers. On the eve of the Civil War, the furnace relied on a labor force that was roughly half enslaved. The enslaved craftsmen at Tredegar helped to support the Confederate war effort by the production of munitions at the factory throughout much of the Civil War.

Enslaved laborers also worked in ceramics. Like ironworking, industrial **pottery** operations required large amounts of skilled and unskilled labor to mine and transport clay, shape it into pots, fire it in kilns, and pack and transport the finished product. The Edgefield District of South Carolina is the region most commonly associated with the production of pottery by enslaved craftspeople. Thousands of enslaved families worked in that region's pottery plantations producing large quantities of alkaline-glazed stoneware from local materials. Edgefield is where David Drake—often called "Dave the Slave" or "Dave the Potter"—worked. Dave was born around 1780 and died sometime around 1870. Of the thousands of enslaved craftspeople whose names are known from across the South, Dave is the only one who spoke through his work. During his lifetime, Dave signed and dated more than 100 examples of his work. Even more remarkable, Dave inscribed many of his pots with short poems that, when read in sequence, offer an autobiography of their maker in clay. Dave worked at a time when teaching a slave to read and write was of questionable legality in South Carolina. Moreover, he identified not only himself on his signed pots, but also his owner. Dave's marked pots were affidavits of his literacy—signed and dated—that often found themselves in front of slaves on plantations elsewhere where the vessels were used to store meat and other consumables.

Archaeological sites around Edgefield reveal a great deal about the daily life of the enslaved communities at the pottery plantations. Like on the South Carolina **rice** plantations, the slave communities were given some autonomy in where and how they lived. Evidence also indicates that the slave communities of Edgefield set up their own kiln sites where they produced ceramic objects for the use of their communities. Many of these objects were utilitarian, but the slaves also produced creative objects. Small face jugs, whose exact purpose remains unclear, were made at these sites for the use of the enslaved communities to which the potters belonged.

## Plantation Artisans

Slaves performed a variety of labor on plantations. Much of what is known in the 21st century about the range of labor performed by slaves on plantations comes from account books, the Works Progress Administration Federal Writers' Project **slave narratives**, and the relatively few contemporary observations that survive in the documentary record. Most plantation craftsmanship was focused on meeting the needs of the plantation. Masters whose slaves were skilled in carpentry, metalworking, and needlework found ready application for those skills. These plantation artisans also found ways to apply their skills to the enslaved communities of which they were part.

Much of this work survives only as archaeological fragments. In some cases, masters set their skilled slaves to work in an attempt to diversify their plantation beyond a single cash crop. The best, and most studied, example of this is Thomas Jefferson's (1743–1826) Mulberry Row at Monticello, outside of Charlottesville, Virginia. Jefferson's slaves produced furniture and hardware for the plantation and items for sale to other plantations nearby.

### Charleston, South Carolina

Antebellum Charleston, South Carolina, was powered by enslaved labor. Little evidence survives in much of the United States detailing how enslaved persons were taught a craft or to work a trade, but Charleston's slave codes reveal some of the role enslaved artisans played in the urban economy. Almost as soon as Charleston whites began to make use of enslaved labor, apprentices and journeymen in the city pushed for legislation against what they saw as unfair competition. They wondered why a master craftsman would pay a decent wage to them when he could purchase a lifetime of labor in a slave. Charleston's apprentices and journeymen lobbied for strict laws that set limits on masters' ability to teach their slaves a trade. In 1764, a South Carolina statute allowed white craftsmen to train only their own slaves, and only if they "have and constantly employ one white apprentice of journeymen for every two Negros or other slaves they shall so teach and thenceforth employ." In the same period, Charleston implemented a system of license tags for any slaves who worked outside of their master's house.

One of the many enslaved craftsmen at work in Charleston during the 18th century is known only as Abraham, a silversmith in the workshop of Alexander Petrie (ca. 1707–1768). Petrie, a Scottish trained silversmith, was one of Charleston's most prolific silversmiths in the 1750s and 1760s. Petrie was also one of the earliest silversmiths in America to use sheet silver made with mechanical rolling mills for the production of hollowware vessels like tea and coffeepots. This technology allowed Petrie's shop to produce hollowware much more quickly than other silversmiths who began an object by hammering out silver ingots by hand. It also allowed his shop to produce standardized forms that could be decorated to suit a client's taste and budget. Petrie advertised that he was closing his shop in July 1765. When he died three years later, his probate inventory revealed that he still owned a variety of silversmithing tools as well as Abraham, who was identified in the inventory as a silversmith. That Petrie retained tools and a skilled silversmith in his possession after closing his shop suggests that some work may have continued by Abraham.

Abraham's value as a silversmith becomes clear in Petrie's estate papers. When Petrie died, and an initial appraisement of the estate was made, Abraham was not the most valuable of Petrie's slaves. When the estate went to auction the following year, Charleston's silversmithing community turned out in force; an accounting of the estate sale reveals many of Charleston's other silversmiths in attendance. When the sale ended, Abraham was the most valuable of Petrie's possessions: his value was more than double the initial estimate. He was purchased for $810 by the silversmith Jonathan Sarrazin (active ca. 1754–ca. 1790), whose advertisements soon afterward reveal an expanded repertory of objects for sale.

## Training

In general, little direct evidence shows how any slave learned a craft or trade. Undoubtedly, some slaves began work as laborers in an industrial or shop setting, showed an aptitude, and over time learned or were taught skills that enhanced their value and productivity. A few slaves were taught a trade through the formal apprenticeship system. A 1743 indenture from King George County, Virginia, records both Spence Monroe (ca. 1727–1774) and his slave Muddy being apprenticed to the cabinetmaker Robert Walker. The indenture document is important because it records how two young men—one free, the other enslaved—were treated as they committed to a period of education in the "trade & mystery" of a craft.

Monroe, the father of future U.S. President James Monroe, was an orphan bound out to Walker to learn the useful trade of a cabinetmaker. Monroe also was considered a gentleman, whose inherited landholdings would ensure that he would not need to rely on his trade for survival. In recognition of his elevated status, the indenture between Monroe and Walker gave him the right to "Eat in Company with the said Rob. Walker or the Chief of his Journeymen." Muddy was singled out for special treatment based on his status as Monroe's slave. He was to be "Employed in no Other Business than in the way of the said trade and Shop Business. Only a day or two at Planting or gathering Corn or on Such Emergency Occasions." Despite the indenture's special provisions reflecting each man's social and legal status, what is remarkable is the document's expectation that both men receive the same education from Walker. And presumably that both men, after the prescribed period of time, leave with the same set of skills.

## Craft as a Path to Freedom

In a few cases, enslaved artisans were able to use their skills to gain freedom. Most used their trade to earn money on the side to purchase their freedom from their master.

In 1818, James Woodward (1769–1839), a Norfolk, Virginia, cabinetmaker, entered into an agreement with an enslaved cabinetmaker named James to lend him $120 with which to buy his freedom. In return for the $120, James promised "for 12 months next ensuing . . . he shall . . . work as a Journeyman Cabinetmaker . . . until the full value . . . shall be repaid him."

In Alexandria, Virginia, a potter named David Jarbour (active 1820–1841) used his skill as a potter to purchase his freedom from the merchant Zenas Kinsey in 1820 for $300. After becoming a free man, Jarbour continued to work as a potter alongside other free black artisans in Alexandria's Wilkes Street Pottery. In 1830, a decade after becoming a free man, Jarbour created a pot nearly three feet tall with exuberant cobalt-blue decoration that he signed on the bottom: "1830 / Alexa / Maid by / D. Jarbour." It is possible that Jarbour created his ambitious jar, the only pot he is ever known to have signed, in a bid for the top job at the pottery as an overseer.

*See also* Ironwork; Mines; Passes; Slave Badges.

FURTHER READING

Ackermann, Daniel. "'Black and White all Mix'd Together': The Hidden Legacy of Enslaved Craftsmen," Museum of Early Southern Decorative Arts. At http://mesda.org/onlineExhibits_sprite/mesda_Enslaved-Craftsmen.html.

Culp, Brandy S. "Mr. Petrie's 'Shop on the Bay.'" *Antiques and Fine Art* Anniversary Issue (2007): 250–255.

Digital Archeological Archive of Comparative Slavery, Thomas Jefferson Foundation. At www.daacs.org.

Gordon-Reed, Annette. *The Hemingses of Monticello: An American Family.* New York: W. W. Norton, 2008.

Todd, Leonard. *Carolina Clay: The Life and Legend of the Slave Potter Dave.* New York: W. W. Norton, 2008.

DANIEL K. ACKERMANN

**SLAVE NARRATIVES.** Slave narratives are accounts by former slaves about their experience in slavery. Such works provide a window into the world in which slaves lived and worked. The narratives, which reached their peak of popularity in the 1840s and 1850s, typically cover the master-slave relationship, the psychology of slaveholders, and the moral nature of slavery. The narratives challenge the once-popular notion that plantation slavery was a golden age in which the masters provided for the slaves and the slaves labored in relative contentment. As first-person accounts, the narratives are particularly powerful condemnations of a savage system.

Slave narratives had a clear purpose. All of these autobiographies were written to end slavery. Slave narratives incorporated literary conventions and rhetorical styles of the day to appeal to readers. They also touched on themes and ideals, such as religious faith, family, and individual independence and freedom, that would appeal to the American public. The slave narrative first emerged in the late 18th century. Some of these early accounts critiqued slavery in terms of natural rights and humanitarian principles. By the 1780s, evangelical Christian groups in Great Britain and the United States came to sponsor the publication of works critical of slavery. These religious groups, often Methodists or Baptists, helped to shape the language and themes of the slave narrative by focusing on the ex-slave's physical and spiritual journey. They aimed to use the works to disseminate religious ideas and convert souls. When more radical anti-slavery societies in the United States in the 1830s and 1840s demanded the immediate abolition of slavery, the narrative shifted focus to exposing the evils of the Southern plantation and attacking the false paternalistic myths supporting it.

The first American slave narrative, in 1760, was the *Narrative of the Uncommon Sufferings and Surprising Deliverance of Briton Hammon, a Negro Man.* Hammon, who survived a shipwreck and subsequent captivity in the Caribbean, contrasted his self-image as a free English subject with his barbaric Catholic captors. Hammon reconnected with his "good" master on a ship bound for New England and became a slave in America for an unknown period. In the narrative, he exploited anti-Catholic feeling at the time of the French and Indian War while emphasizing the rights of Englishmen. In essence, Hammon made the point that slavery was incompatible with English liberty. His publisher, however, sold the story as a colorful tale of captivity by the Spanish and Native Americans at a time when captivity tales were a popular genre.

*A Narrative of the Most Remarkable Particulars in the Life of James Albert Ukasaw Gronniosaw, an African Prince* is the first slave narrative that directly addresses the evils of slavery. First published in 1772 in England and then reprinted in serial form in America, the narrative emphasizes Gronniosaw's passage from African heathen to Protestant Christian. Gronniosaw's narrative went through numerous editions because it appealed to various readerships simultaneously. Gronniosaw provided spiritual autobiography, travel narrative, and political commentary. Like other early slave narratives, the book apparently reflects the commercial aims of its publishers more than the abolitionist thoughts of the former slave who wrote it.

*The Interesting Narrative of the Life of Olaudah Equiano, Written by Himself* is one of the most descriptive and moving autobiographies written by a slave as well as one of the earliest. Equiano is widely regarded as the father of the slave narrative and penned his 1789 narrative as a protest against slavery during a public campaign against the trans-Atlantic slave trade in both England and America. His strong religious faith and his belief that God had a purpose for him led him to take action by spreading abolitionist ideas. He also carefully catered to his evangelical audience by making sure to demonstrate his spiritual path to religious salvation. Although considerable discussion among scholars continues as to whether Equiano was born in Africa or in South Carolina,

Former slave Richard Amerson, who was interviewed by the Federal Writers' Project, ca. 1937. (Library of Congress.)

Equiano wrote about enduring slavery from capture in Africa through the horrifying Middle Passage with the detail of one who had gone through this experience, and then proceeded to tell the story of his life as a plantation laborer in Virginia. He emphasized that he was a decent, ordinary person who did not deserve to be enslaved, thereby making the point that no one should be enslaved. By writing, Equiano challenged the notion that slaves were unthinking, unfeeling pieces of property. The narrative was an example of black abilities, showing that people of African descent could do more than serve. Equiano effectively demonstrated his humanity. He went from being an object to be sold by others to being internationally famous.

The decades just before the Civil War were the heyday of the published slave narrative. The narratives of the 1830s, 1840s, and 1850s emphasized the depravity of Southern planters, the hypocrisy of Southern Christianity, scenes of brutal whipping and torture, rebellious slaves who were murdered, and the strategic mechanisms by which the planters maintained slavery. Most of the 19th-century slave narrators made their names as orators before they became writers, and these narratives reflect a more audience-grabbing style. Frederick Douglass (ca. 1818–1895), William Wells Brown (1818?–1884), William and Ellen Craft (1824–1900; 1826–1891), J. W. C. Pennington (1807–1870), and Samuel Ringgold Ward (1817–ca. 1866) all shaped the style and content of their narratives while on stage.

Arguably the best-written and certainly the most widely read of all American slave narratives is Douglass's 1848 account of his life. Douglass, who spent 20 years as a slave before escaping to freedom, viewed slavery as bondage of the mind as much as of the body. By putting pen to paper, he freed himself while also answering critics who claimed that such an articulate man never could have been a slave. Douglass wrote to issue an indictment of slavery by providing evidence of evil. His work inspired abolitionists and undoubtedly created new ones.

Harriet Jacobs (1813–1897), writing under the pen name of Linda Brent, was the first woman to write a slave narrative, which was published in 1861. *Incidents in the Life of a Slave Girl* emphasized domestic life. Jacobs wrote about her inability to live properly as a Christian and remain chaste in slavery because of the sexual demands of her master. This narrative showed that slavery for women entailed far more sexual exploitation than previously had been widely known or discussed.

Long after slavery had ended, a second group of slave narratives emerged. Under the New Deal of the 1930s, the Works Progress Administration (WPA) created the Federal Writers' Project. The WPA aimed to document the lives, experiences, and cultural traditions of ordinary Americans. Many of these Americans were people with memories of living under slavery. WPA employees conducted oral histories with about 2,000 former slaves living in Arkansas, Florida, Indiana, Mississippi, Missouri, North Carolina, Ohio, Virginia, and other states. The narratives, completed between 1936 and 1938, suffer from the faults typical of oral histories, such as having memories of the past influenced by events in the present and interviewer bias. Former slaves, starving during the Great Depression, often remembered the days of slavery as a time when **food** was plentiful. Some ex-slaves responded differently to the same question when asked by a white person than when asked by a black person. Nevertheless, these narratives are important for their tantalizing details of enslaved life. They capture the lives of ordinary people who otherwise probably would have taken their memories of slavery to the grave.

***See also*** Abolition Imagery.

FURTHER READING

Allison, Robert J., ed. *The Interesting Narrative of the Life of Olaudah Equiano: Written by Himself*. Boston: Bedford/St. Martin's, 2007.

Andrews, William L. *To Tell a Free Story: The First Century of Afro-American Autobiography, 1760–1865*. Urbana: University of Illinois Press, 1986.

"Born in Slavery: Slave Narratives from the Federal Writers' Project, 1936–1938," American Memory, Library of Congress. At http://memory.loc.gov/ammem/snhtml/.

Carey, Bryccan. "Where Was Equiano Born? (And Why Does It Matter?)," Olaudah Equiano, or, Gustavus Vassa, the African. At www.brycchancarey.com/equiano/nativity.htm.

Douglass, Frederick. *Narrative of the Life of Frederick Douglass: An American Slave, Written by Himself*. Boston: Bedford/St. Martin's, 1993.

Fisch, Audrey, ed. *The Cambridge Companion to the African American Slave Narrative*. New York: Cambridge University Press, 2007.

Jacobs, Harriet A. *Incidents in the Life of a Slave Girl: Contexts, Criticisms*. Edited by Nellie Y. McKay and Frances Smith Foster. New York: W. W. Norton, 2001.

Starling, Marion Wilson. *The Slave Narrative: Its Place in American History*. Boston: G. K. Hall, 1982.

CARYN E. NEUMANN

Price, Birch & Company slave pen exterior, Alexandria, Virginia, ca. 1861. (Library of Congress.)

**SLAVE PENS, SLAVE JAILS, AND SLAVE MARKETS.** After 1807, when the United States no longer participated in the trans-Atlantic slave trade, which brought millions of Africans to the Americas, a domestic slave trade arose. Historians estimate that from 1820 to 1860, 2 million enslaved African Americans were sold in what is often referred to as the "internal slave trade." That is, slaves were sold from one owner to another in the United States. Of those 2 million sold, about 660,000 were sold from states in the Upper South, especially Maryland, North Carolina, and Virginia, to states in the Lower South, especially Alabama, Louisiana, and Mississippi, where the boom in **cotton** production fueled a demand for slave labor. Those sold through the interregional slave trade typically were purchased by traders in the Upper South where they were held in "slave pens" or "slave jails" before being marched or transported South by railroad or by **boat** where they were sold once again, often at auction.

This forced migration of hundreds of thousands of enslaved people usually was accompanied by family separations. Pro-slavery propagandists asserted that family separations were rare and occurred only in unusual circumstances. Historians have determined, however, that more than half the slaves sold by a trader were forcibly separated from a spouse or one or both of their parents. Slaves were sold for a wide variety of reasons, including punishment, to pay debts or secure mortgages, or, at the death of an owner, to settle an estate. Pro-slavery platitudes notwithstanding, families usually were not sold intact because they did not bring the most profit. What maximized profits for slaveholders were individual slaves, ages 15 to 30. Young mothers were sold away from their husbands and children, young fathers from their wives and children, and children from their parents.

Slave traders were a diverse group, but there were two main types: the auctioneer, or crier, as he was often called, who stood on the platform coaxing the audience into bidding ever higher prices, and the itinerant trader who scoured the countryside looking for slaves to buy from a planter or at local courthouse sales to resell at another location. Although most records that survive deal with the urban traders, it was those traders working in the countryside who set the interregional slave trade in motion. Such traders sometimes worked for themselves, buying a small number of slaves in the countryside and then bringing them to the city for sale. Many of these traders were associated with larger traders and served largely as employees scouring the countryside for "stock," as traders often referred to the people whom they sold, to send to the urban salerooms. Such men tended to have an intimate knowledge of an area, where they visited regularly, talked with planters, visited courthouse sales, and remained constantly on the look-out for slaves they could buy for less than they would sell for in the city.

In a number of cities in the Upper South, a sizable infrastructure developed that was dedicated to the slave trade, among them Baltimore, Maryland; Washington, DC; and Alexandria and Richmond, Virginia. These cities became primarily slave-collecting and resale centers, and a large network of traders provided slaves to feed the demand in urban markets. One of the largest and most financially successful slave-trading firms was the partnership of Isaac Franklin (1789–1846) and John Armfield (1797–1871), who had an organized network of traders stationed in cities throughout the region, including Richmond and Warrenton, Virginia, and Fredericktown and Baltimore, Maryland, among others.

Price, Birch & Company slave pen interior, Alexandria, Virginia, ca. 1861. (Library of Congress.)

Once purchased by a trader, slaves usually were transported to the urban center by boat or railroad, or they were marched over ground. After being transported, they were placed in a slave jail. Franklin and Armfield's headquarters in Alexandria, Virginia, was similar to many in that it consisted of multiple buildings together on one property surrounded by a high wall. Ethan Allen Andrews (1787–1858), who visited Franklin and Armfield's in 1836, left a description of the property. The first building he entered, the three-story brick house that fronted the street and had the name emblazoned over the doorway, served as the dwelling house. It had a parlor into which prospective clients were received. The main building originally was built as a house and was used as such by Armfield. In preparing the property to be used as a slave jail, Franklin and Armfield had made important alterations to the property. The lot was surrounded by a "high, white-washed wall . . . giving to it the appearance of a penitentiary." Behind the dwelling house was a "spacious yard nearly surrounded with neatly white-washed two story buildings devoted to the use of slaves." The **yard** was divided by a "strong grated door of iron" into a men's section and a women's section. The yard where the women were confined had a **kitchen** building and a tailor's shop where slaves were given two sets of **clothing** before their journey to the markets in Natchez, Mississippi. At the rear of the yard was a "long building, two stories high, in which the slaves pass the night." At the time of Edwards's visit, about 100 slaves were in the yard, whom they were preparing to transport over land to Natchez where they would be confined in a series of makeshift frame buildings just outside of town in an area referred to as "Forks of the Road."

Richmond, probably the largest slave-trading center in the Upper South throughout most of the 1840s and 1850s, had multiple jails, most of which were within a few blocks of each other and only a few blocks from Thomas Jefferson's (1743–1826) Virginia State Capitol building. The most notorious was called Lumpkin's Jail, and its site has been recently excavated by the City of Richmond. Operated by Robert Lumpkin (d. ca. 1865), like the complex at Franklin and Armfield's, it also consisted of a series of buildings on about a half-acre of land. To outsiders, the most notable feature would have been the 10- to 12-foot fence that had iron spikes, which was clearly designed to ensure that the slaves held there not only could not escape but also could not easily communicate with people outside the enclosure. Inside the enclosure, there were several buildings: Lumpkin's house, a boarding house where those selling or buying slaves could board at rates considerably less than those at the Exchange or City Hotels, a kitchen and tavern building, and a jail for slaves awaiting sale. It was described soon after the Civil War as "a low, rough, brick building known as the 'slave jail.'" A visitor to Lumpkin's jail reported that

> On one side of the open court was a large tank for washing, or lavatory. Opposite was a long, two-story brick house, the lower part fitted up for men and the second story for women. The place, in fact, was a kind of hotel or boardinghouse for negro-traders and their slaves.

Not all slave traders operated jails. Many instead used those owned by others and paid daily rates for boarding and medical care if required.

After being held in jails, sometimes for weeks at a time, slaves eventually were sold, often to another trader. Sales sometimes occurred at the jails and sometimes in salesrooms. Richmond had quite a few salesrooms located in the vicinity of the jails. These rooms were generally small and low-ceilinged with little furniture or decoration. Englishman William Chambers (1800–1883), who visited Lumpkin's in 1853, described an interior thusly:

> [C]onceive the idea of a large shop with two windows, and a door between; no shelving or counters inside; the interior a spacious, dismal apartment, not well swept, the only furniture a desk at one of the windows, and a bench at one side of the shop, three feet high, with two steps to it from the floor.

What stood out about these buildings was that there was so little to distinguish them. They were, essentially, just like any other general commercial structure in the city. The one thing they all shared was that they consisted primarily of a large undivided interior that sometimes held crowds as large as a hundred.

Unlike retail stores selling dry goods or clothing, the auction rooms contained no shelves for holding merchandise, but they did contain a piece of furniture specifically built for the trade conducted there—the auction block. Different descriptions and illustrations document the presence of **auction blocks**, but generally they were platforms that allowed for the auctioneer and the slaves being sold to be raised above the standing audience so that all could get a clear view of the "stock." In addition to these dedicated slave auction rooms, slaves also were sold at auction in the basement of several of New Orleans' leading hotels, including the Exchange Hotel and the St. Charles Hotel. The number of these rooms and their presence in the city for decades speak to the how interwoven the slave trade was into the fabric of life in the urban cityscape.

In many towns throughout the South, auctions often occurred near the courthouse or on a designated street corner. In Charleston, another major slave-trading center, the sale of slaves occurred in the center of town, until a city ordinance stated that the sales had to move indoors in 1856. Just north of the Exchange Building on East Bay Street was a small open square. The Exchange Building was among the most important colonial public buildings in the city. Located at the terminus of Broad Street in the center of the wharves and the commercial part of town, it served as both the custom house and the post office building. There, every day of the week except Sunday, the auction of slaves regularly occurred. To this location, each trader brought the slaves he planned to auction, and the sales took place in turn. Most of the auction sales in the city took place from this location: slaves, lots of lands, houses, and shares of stock among other items. If newspaper advertisements are any indication, the sale of slaves formed the majority of the business.

After the city ordinance moved sales away from the Exchange Building, the most popular site for slave auction became the site referred to in advertising as "Ryan's Mart" and then later "The Mart, Chalmers Street." Operated first by slave trader Thomas Ryan and later by Ziba B. Oakes, it was essentially one large room constructed on a narrow lot that stretched from Chalmer's Street north to Queen Street. Behind the auction room was an open yard that also contained a four-story jail building and a kitchen building. The facade of this long narrow structure, about 20 by 60 feet, had octagonal piers that stylistically blended with the building to the right, the German Fire Engine House, and with numerous buildings throughout the city dedicated to slave management and reform: among them the Arsenal building (1825), which became the Citadel in 1849, and the Work House (1850). Journalist Charles Coffin (1823–1896), who wrote about the site when he visited it after Charleston came under the control of federal troops at the end of the Civil War in 1865, described a "large iron gate in front, above which, in large gilt letters, was the word MART." Inside, Coffin noted that on one side there was "a long table running the entire length of the hall, while on the other side were benches."

## Slave Market Experience

After he was marched from Virginia to Savannah, Georgia, George Carter was imprisoned in a slave pen before being sold:

W'en I wuz sixteen yeah ol', Massa sol' me an' some mo' Niggers down Sout'. 'Cose us ain't want tuh go, but us hab tuh. We wuz chained togedder all duh way frum Norfo'k tuh Savannah. An' w'en us got heah dey put us in a slabe pen right under whar B. H. Lebey's sto' use tuh be. Duh nex' mornin' wuz sale day. Dey brung us heah fuh duh Central Railroad. I wuz de only one not sol' tuh duh Central . . . Dere wuz a pen under duh Pulaski House whar dey lock up duh Niggers w'enebuh dey got heah in duh night, an' duh man what hab 'em in charge done stop at duh hotel. Duh rag'lar jail wa'nt fuh slabes but dere wuz a speck'lator jail at Hab'sham an' Bryon Street. Dey look up duh slabes in duh speck'lator jail when dey brought 'em heah tuh de auction. Mos' ob duh speck'lators come in duh night befo' duh sale an' stop at duh Pulaski House. Duh slabes wuz took tuh duh pen under duh hotel.

*Source:* George P. Rawick, ed. *The American Slave: Georgia Narratives*, Supp. Ser. 1, Vol. 3, Part 1. Westport, CT: Greenwood Press, 1978.

Jordan Smith described slave markets in Virginia and New Orleans:

They was a trader yard in Virginia and one in New Orleans and sometimes a thousand slaves was waitin' to be sold. When the traders knowed men was comin' to buy, they made the slaves all clean up and greased they mouths with meat skins to look like they's feedin' them plenty meat. They lined the women up on one side and the men on the other. A buyer would walk up and down 'tween the two rows and grab a woman and try to throw her down and feel of her to see how she's put up. If she's purty strong, he'd say, "Is she a good breeder?" If a gal was 18 or 19 and put up good she was worth 'bout $1,500. Then the buyer'd pick out a strong, young nigger boy 'bout the same age and buy him. When he got them home he'd say to them, "I want you two to stay together. I want young niggers."

*Source:* George P. Rawick, ed. *The American Slave: Texas Narratives*, Vol. 5, Parts 3 & 4. Westport, CT: Greenwood Press, 1972.

The largest slave-trading center was New Orleans. It was through this city's sales-rooms that so many of the slaves bound for the **cotton** and **sugar** fields of the Southwest passed. New Orleans had many places that were similar to those found in Richmond and other cities: multibuilding compounds where slaves were held and then later offered for sale. New Orleans had more traders than any other city in

America. In the 1856 directory, there were 17 individuals or businesses listed as slave traders and another 38 listed as auctioneers, many of whom probably sold slaves. Their jails and salesrooms were concentrated in the blocks around the St. Charles and the St. Louis hotels, especially on Barrone and Gravier streets. Like Charleston, where the sale of slaves was a public matter, in New Orleans, many visitors were surprised to see that slaves were sold in the grand rotundas of the St. Charles and the St. Louis hotels. Many were struck by the juxtaposition of the genteel and lofty interiors and the horrific sights they witnessed as slaves were sold to the highest bidder. Few places survive in the 21st century to attest to the material presence of the slave trade in cities across the American South. In Alexandria, Virginia, the main house that stood at the center of the Franklin and Armfield's establishment is now the home of the Freedom House Museum; in Charleston, South Carolina, the Mart on Chalmers Street is operated as the Old Slave Mart Museum. In Richmond, Virginia, recent archaeological excavations have revealed the location of Lumpkin's Jail, but most of the other traders' jails and the auction room are below Interstate 95. In most other Southern cities, no evidence remains of the place where 2 million enslaved men, women, and children were sold in the American slave trade.

*See also* Auction Advertisements; Courthouses; Sale Notices.

FURTHER READING

Andrews, Ethan Allen. *Slavery and the Domestic Slave-Trade in the United States: In a Series of Letters Addressed to the Executive Committee of the American Union for the Relief and Improvement of the Colored Race.* Boston: Light and Stearns, 1836.

Deyle, Steven. *Carry Me Back: The Domestic Slave Trade in American Life.* New York: Oxford University Press, 2005.

Johnson, Walter. *Soul by Soul: Life Inside the Antebellum Slave Market.* Cambridge, MA: Harvard University Press, 1999.

Obadele-Starks, Ernest. *Freebooters and Smugglers: The Foreign Slave Trade in the United States after 1808.* Fayetteville: University of Arkansas Press, 2007.

Tadman, Michael. *Speculators and Slaves: Masters, Traders, and Slaves in the Old South.* Madison: University of Wisconsin Press, 1989.

MAURIE D. MCINNIS

**SLAVE QUARTERS.** The buildings in which enslaved African Americans were routinely housed varied slightly in plan and construction details, but they were all generally small, cramped quarters that resembled prison cells rather than homes. John Finnely, who was enslaved in Alabama, reported "us have cabins of logs with one room and one door and one window hole." Similarly J. T. Tims from Mississippi recalled "Before the [Civil] War, we lived in an old log house. It had one window, one door, and one room." Ella Johnson remembered that her South Carolina quarters were "just little one-room log cabins." And she added, "Usually there were two windows. The floor was wood too, although I know on some plantations the poor old slaves had just the bare ground for a floor." Meager buildings also were described by former Georgia slave Robert Shepherd as dangerous structures because of their "chimblees [chimneys] made of sticks and red mud. Them chimblees was all the time catching fire." When compared with even the most modest of planters' residences, slave houses

Slave houses on the Hermitage plantation, Savannah, Georgia. Photo by Walker Evans, 1935. (Library of Congress.)

unquestionably bore signs of their occupants' social marginality. They were buildings that signaled clearly who was owned, while the planter's house by its location, form, and mode of decoration indicated who held the power of ownership.

In 1854, Frederick Law Olmsted (1822–1903), who would soon rise to prominence as one of America's great landscape architects, undertook a journey of discovery across the South during which he made many careful observations of the extant types of **slave housing**. At a plantation in South Carolina, he observed that the slaves' cabins were

> built of logs, with no windows—no opening at all, except the doorway, with a chimney of sticks and mud; no trees about them, no porches, or shades, of any kind. Except for the chimney, I should have conjectured that it had been built for a powder-house, or perhaps, an ice house—never for an animal to sleep in.

While the critical tone of his remarks is consistent with his abolitionist perspective, his observations of the shoddy cabins constructed for enslaved blacks match well with the statements of some plantation owners. In an article that appeared in the *Southern Cultivator* in 1856, a Mississippi planter writing under the pseudonym "Omo" offered a strong critique of slave housing almost equal to that written by Olmsted: "In general, negro houses are knocked up in a very careless, bungling manner—always too small and too low. . . . These old, dirty habitations, together with the other numerous deleterious influences inseparably connected therewith, are well-calculated to generate disease."

Slave quarters most often were built with logs, largely because the forested tracts encountered by colonial-era settlers had to be cleared of trees to create the open space required for fields and pastures. The creation of farmsteads not only provided planters with operational land, but also supplied them with more-than-adequate supplies of the raw materials needed to construct the necessary buildings and fences. Although log construction was the chief mode of building during the first phase of settlement, other materials and techniques were used as well. Planters looking to move beyond quarters that were rough emblems of the pioneer era would turn to wood-framed structures covered with board siding. Those planters looking to make an even bigger and perhaps a more sophisticated impression opted to build brick and stone masonry buildings. Along the Georgia coast and parts of northern Florida, a primitive form of concrete known as **tabby** was appropriated from examples left by 17th-century Spanish colonists.

Because most planters tended to overcrop their land, the profits that they so ardently hoped for could fall off rather steeply within a single decade. Their response to failing crop yields most often was to abandon their holdings and move farther west in the hope of finding better soil conditions. One result of the forced African American migration across the Black Belt of the Deep South (so named for a band of rich black topsoil that extended the whole expanse of the lower South and not for the dark **skin** of the planters' captive workforce), was the dispersion of certain log construction techniques from the Eastern Seaboard all the way to Texas. The simplest mode of log construction used round logs that were notched at their ends and stacked in alternating tiers to form an enclosed pen. Once the walls were raised to a sufficient height, openings would be cut for doors, windows, and a fireplace. But using timbers that were round in section required that a "saddle," which was a scooped-out depression in the top of the log, be cut about five inches back from the end of the log. This notch provided a place to set the next tier of logs as the walls of a log pen were raised to their desired height. Other modes of log construction were more complicated, requiring that trees be hewn or sawn down to a thickness of 6 to 10 inches, creating a log that was more plank-like in appearance. The ends of these logs were shaped into either an inverted "V" or a "dovetail" or flanged form that would connect a log to an adjacent timber by means of what might be called a "keying" process. Logs were thus interlocked in a manner that withstood movement in a horizontal direction and ultimately kept the components of a wall fixed in a reasonably vertical alignment. During the late antebellum period, log slave quarters were often clad with sawn board siding to make them look more like framed buildings, which were regarded as more prestigious structures.

Although most slave quarters were wood-based and shaped either as pens of stacked logs or carpentered frames sheathed with some manner of board siding, other less conspicuous modes were used as well. The houses reserved for slaves living close to a plantation owner's brick mansion might be made from brick. Such a gesture might have been aimed at demonstrating the owner's authority by populating the mansion's surroundings with diminutive, and therefore visually subordinate, structures. Given that the vast majority of domestic structures on plantations were built with wood, the presence of a slave quarter rendered in brick and graced with a neat but simple cornice was an effective way for plantation owners to declare their economic and social eminence. If planters were willing to "waste" their money by beautifying the appearance of their slave quarters, then they certainly would be understood to have considerable reserves of wealth. This clearly was the case at Ben Venue, a plantation in Rappahannock County, Virginia. Owner William Fletcher placed three small brick houses in front of his house, all of them decorated with raised parapets that echoed a similar feature on his mansion. Standing seemingly at attention while awaiting a command, it would appear that the enslaved persons who occupied these buildings must be ready to serve at a moment's notice.

The slaves on any plantation usually built their own quarters, typically under the supervision of the planter or his overseer. That house carpenters were among the most highly valued enslaved workers on an estate is exemplified by various reports of runaways that were printed in local newspapers. For example, a runaway notice published in the *Virginia Gazette* in 1767 advertised that a "Negro fellow" named Bob had run off and specified that "[h]e is an extraordinary sawyer, a tolerable carpenter and currier, pretends to make shoes, and is a very good sailor." That same year, a Charleston newspaper similarly extolled the virtues of several escaped slaves, noting that two of them were "good workmen at the cabinet maker's business"; another was a "good sawyer," who "handles his tools so well in the coarser branches of that trade, as to be capable of making a tolerable country carpenter." Perhaps one of the more spectacular accounts of abilities of an enslaved builder is found in the letters of Thomas Jefferson (1743–1826).

John Hemings, a Monticello slave, was hired out in 1825 to work on the repairs to a recently fire-damaged plantation house belonging to Jefferson's grandson, Francis Wayles Eppes (1801–1881). In a series of letters written to Jefferson, Hemings breezily describes his efforts at roof repair and the installation of a Chinese railing, folding doors, sash weights for windows, and parlor cornices. When Jefferson became impatient for his valuable carpenter's return to Monticello, Hemings wrote back: "I hope by the next [letter] to be able to let you know when I shall finish and when to send for me." Enslaved artisans with skills honed by constant requests for their best effort were certainly able to assert a certain level of independence even as they labored to complete the tasks assigned to them by their masters.

A longer view of early African American efforts to develop their own sense of place requires that more attention be paid to the way enslaved blacks lived within their own niche within a larger setting. The slave housing at George Washington's (1732–1799) Mount Vernon provides a clear example of how Washington used buildings as a way of demonstrating and enforcing the lowly status of his bondsmen. Julian Niemcewicz (1758–1841), a Polish visitor who traveled through the newly emergent American republic during the last decade of the 18th century, offers the following description of Washington's behavior as a slaveholder:

> We entered one of the huts of the Blacks, for one cannot call them by the name of houses. They are more miserable than the most miserable cottages of our peasants. The husband and wife sleep on a mean pallet, the children on the ground; a very bad fireplace, some utensils for cooking, but in the middle of this poverty some cups and a teapot.

Niemcewicz also observed that this family had planted a vegetable **garden** and was also raising a flock of **chickens** that they could sell to obtain other "amenities." But even when Washington's slaves acted on their own behalf, their efforts routinely were thwarted because their cabins often were moved annually to new locations and thus their gardens had to be abandoned. In a letter written in 1794 to one of his overseers, Washington reveals that some slave houses at Mount Vernon were small enough that they could easily be shifted from one location to another as he deemed necessary. He recommends the larger houses should be moved with the assistance of "rollers" (round logs), while smaller buildings, probably measuring less than 14 by 14 feet, were simply

## Accounts of Slave Quarters

Former Georgia slave Paul Smith described the slave quarters on the plantation where he lived:

> Slave quarters was jus' little one room log cabins what had chimblies made of sticks and red mud. Dem old chimblies was all de time a-ketchin' on fire. De mud was daubed 'twixt de logs to chink up de cracks, and sometimes dey chinked up cracks in de roof wid red mud. Dere warn't no glass windows in dem cabins, and dey didn't have but one window of no sort; it was jus' a plain wooden shutter. De cabins was a long ways off from de big house, close by de big old spring whar de wash-place was. Dey had long benches for de washtubs to set on, a big old oversize washpot, and you mustn't leave out 'bout dat big old battlin' block whar dey beat de dirt out of de clothes. Dem Niggers would sing, and deir battlin' sticks kept time to de music. You could hear de singin' and de sound of de battlin' sticks from a mighty long ways off.

*Source:* George P. Rawick, ed. *The American Slave: Georgia Narratives*, Vol. 13. Westport, CT: Greenwood Press, 1972.

Foster Weathersby remembered the close community that the slave quarter provided in his Mississippi experience:

> We had comfortable clo'se an' livin' qua'ters. De cottages was small, and built side by side in a long row by de side of de road. We liked livin' together lak dat ruther dan bein' scattered as many of 'em was. You see, we could collect up at times in de evenin', even effen we was tired, and have some enjoyment layin' around under de big trees, hummin' and singin' to de tune of some old guitar, and tellin' tales and talkin' of de hopes and fears of de comin' war to free us.

*Source:* George P. Rawick, ed. *The American Slave: Mississippi Narratives*, Supp. Ser. 1, Vol. 10, Part 5. Westport, CT: Greenwood Press, 1978.

to be loaded onto a cart and hauled off to their new locations near the fields selected for that season's crops.

The clearest understanding of the once-commonplace earthfast structures built directly on the ground can be gained from a close look at the Road View Farm **kitchen** that once stood in New Kent County, Virginia. Located about 20 miles east of Richmond, this building, now lost, was carefully recorded in 1936 by historians employed by the Historic American Buildings Survey. Measuring slightly more than 14 feet on each side, the kitchen was supported by 14 posts set deeply into the ground all around the perimeter of the building. Because these posts were round in section and marked by stubs where branches had been cut away, the building's carpenters clearly had gone into the woods to cut down the trees that they deemed suitable for this particular structure. The exterior of the building was covered with vertical siding, but it had no interior finish. The deep historical roots of the building—which extend to medieval times—were most spectacularly revealed by the absence of a fireplace. In this structure, the cooking fire was lighted on the dirt floor and the entire eastern end of the structure functioned as a chimney. The rising smoke escaped through a sort of smoke bay created by ending the **loft** floor about three feet from the eastern wall. The wall at that end of the loft was tilted toward the gable at a slight angle, leaving a gap of 20 inches at the apex of the roof. In this way, a large funnel-like opening was created above the level of the loft floor that directed the smoke out of the building through a square wooden flue. The throat of the chimney was, in fact, the roof itself. To protect the end wall from burning, the central portion of the wall was lathed and coated with plaster, although it has been suggested that a cast iron fireback may have been used as well to protect the section of the wall closest to the floor. This building could have been built as early as 1820, and it shows the continuing influence of 17th-century behavior. Although such structures generally were loathed by Jefferson and other members of the "plantocracy," the kitchen at Road View Farm, which survived into the 20th century, clearly outlasted the venerable sage of Monticello. The existence of this building demonstrates that the preference for earthfast structures was more deeply embedded in local construction practices than many scholars have imagined. These buildings not only filled a need for structures that were relatively easy to erect but also proved to be more durable than generally has been understood. When African Americans built spaces that they could claim for themselves, they shared a sense of pride in what they had been able to do even while held as captives.

## FURTHER READING

"Born in Slavery: Slave Narratives from the Federal Writers' Project, 1936–1938," American Memory, Library of Congress. At http://memory.loc.gov/ammem/snhtml/.

Breeden, James O. *Advice among Masters: The Ideal in Slave Management in the Old South.* Westport, CT: Greenwood Press, 1980.

Olmsted, Frederick Law. *The Cotton Kingdom: A Traveller's Observations on Cotton and Slavery in the American Slave States. Based upon Three Former Volumes of Journeys and Investigations.* 2 vols. New York: Mason Brothers, 1862.

Vlach, John Michael. *Back of the Big House: The Architecture of Plantation Slavery.* Chapel Hill: University of North Carolina Press, 1993.

JOHN MICHAEL VLACH

**SLAVE SHIPS.** During the course of nearly four centuries, ships from Europe and North America carried about 7.5 million Africans across the Atlantic, where the captives were then sold into slavery. The vessels used in the so-called Triangular Trade were generally typical of the sailing ships employed in the overseas trade of their time.

These ships often were away from their home ports for between 12 and 18 months in some of the most difficult waters in the world, subject on the one hand to storms

"The Abolition of the Slave Trade or the Inhumanity of Dealers in Human Flesh Exemplified in Captn. Kimber's Treatment of a Young Negro Girl of 15 for Her Virjen [sic] Modesty." Print shows sailor on a slave ship suspending an African girl by her ankle from a rope over a pulley. Capt. John Kimber stands on the left with a whip in his hand. Illustration attributed to Isaac Cruikshank; etching published by S. W. Fores, London, 1792. (Library of Congress.)

and on the other to being becalmed, often spending months in tropical waters that inflicted serious damage to wooden hulls by teredo worms and other hazards. Ships needed to be designed with hulls that were fast to cover the Middle Passage as quickly as possible and to keep the mortality of the enslaved to a minimum, yet have sufficient size and capacity to accommodate the bulky cargoes of tropical goods that were brought back to Europe. They also needed stability, however, to withstand the heavy

---

### Middle Passage

Philip Evans's grandfather, who was captured in Africa, survived the Middle Passage:

> My pappy often tell mammy and us chillun, dat his pappy was ketched in Africa and fetched to America on a big ship in a iron cage, 'long wid a whole heap of other black folks, and dat he was powerful sick at de stomach de time he was on de ship.

*Source:* George P. Rawick, ed. *The American Slave: South Carolina Narratives*, Vol. 2. Westport, CT: Greenwood Press, 1972.

storms of the Atlantic and to be able to carry sufficient armament to protect themselves from pirates and from enemy action.

Increasingly, ships used in slaving, like other cargo vessels, grew in size over the centuries, and the most successful slaving ships were among the largest of their day. Generally, traders seemed to have adapted existing vessels, and this was certainly true of Dutch and French merchants. By the second half of the 18th century, however, many British traders, particularly in Liverpool, were using ships specifically designed for the slave trade. Joseph Manesty, a Liverpool merchant probably best known because John Newton (1725–1807), who wrote the hymn "Amazing Grace," was one of his captains, ordered two ships "for the African trade" from a builder in Newport, Rhode Island, in 1745. He instructed that they were to be built of "the best White Oak" and he specified strong masts and heavy planks for the hulls. They were to be "sharp" enough for speed, but "full" enough for supporting the armaments and accommodating the cargo. The sides were to be flared for "more commodious stowing" of the enslaved. He also insisted, however, on plain features for such parts as the captain's cabin. A small number of wrecks have been found, but the only fully excavated slave ship is the *Henrietta Marie*, which sank off Key West, Florida, in 1700 on her way back to London after delivering a cargo of 190 slaves to Jamaica. Very little of the ship itself remains but what does confirms that she was a typical cargo ship. Only the poignant remnants of her cargo—iron shackles; a blunderbuss, which was a muzzle-loading gun; and cannon and some of her trade goods such as **beads** and iron bars—testify to her involvement in the slave trade.

The best-known slave ship is almost certainly the *Brooks* (also known as the *Brookes*), illustrations of which were featured in the literature of abolition campaigns in Britain, France, and the United States. The illustration of a slave deck with its silhouetted figures of Africans laid side to side evokes the horrors of the slave trade. The description in the accompanying text is equally graphic and shocking.

The *Brooks* had been built in Liverpool in 1781 and at 297 tons was one of the largest ships of its time. The abolitionist text provides precise details of its size, including the internal dimensions of the decks and platforms, which accommodated the enslaved, and the headroom, which at two feet six inches was too small to allow an adult to sit up. The layout of the 482 bodies in fact underestimates the capacity of the vessel, which on more than one voyage carried more than 600 Africans to the Caribbean.

The remainder of the text provides a vivid description of life aboard the ship, based on the experience of Alexander Falconbridge (ca. 1760–1792), a former surgeon in the trade. It describes the horrors of life below decks—the routines of daily life and the sufferings inflicted on "our fellow-creatures." In 11 voyages, the *Brooks* carried 5,482 Africans across the Atlantic. Some 4,980 individuals survived the journey.

Within two years of the beginning of the British abolition campaign, laws that regulated ships involved in the slave trade were introduced by the British Parliament. The Slave Carrying Act of 1788, often called the Dolben Act after the member of Parliament who introduced it, limited the number of slaves that could be carried to five for every three tons of capacity for the first 200 tons and one for every ton above that. Each slave ship was required to have a physician on board for the welfare of the crew and the enslaved who was charged to keep a log of the sickness and death of the enslaved. In reality, the act had little effect on the sufferings of those being transported.

Slaving was a complex and risky business, and considerable experience was required to organize a slaving voyage. The merchant usually worked in conjunction with others to finance the voyage to minimize the financial risks. When the cost of outfitting the vessel, purchasing the cargo, and paying the crew and other elements such as agents' fees and insurance are taken into account, the total cost of an average voyage from Europe in the late 18th century was £10,000 to £12,000 (almost US$1 million in the 21st century). The cargo to be bartered on the African coast had to be prepared carefully with a mixture of goods chosen specifically for the trading location. The instructions given to captains often to refer to "a choice cargo . . . very suitable for" or "specially chosen for" a specific location in Africa.

Many of the most successful merchants had developed a network of contacts with individual African traders and knew them and their requirements. They also had good contacts with agents in the Caribbean who handled the sale of the enslaved.

The other key player in organizing a successful voyage was the captain of the vessel. Although the captain would be given detailed instructions by the ship's owners about where he was to trade, what cargo he was to buy, what he was to pay, and where he was to sell the enslaved, once the vessel was at sea, he was virtually responsible for the outcome of the voyage. He not only had to undertake all the duties of running the ship, including plotting the course, making decisions about speed and weather, and maintaining discipline, but also had to undertake all the commercial decisions. His ability to establish relationships and negotiate with African traders and to know when to settle, when to move along the coast, and when to set off across the Atlantic were all crucial to the successful outcome of the voyage.

On board, the captain was supported by a first mate and usually a second and third mate, who, along with the surgeon and boatswain, formed the senior members of the crew. They were responsible for the operation of the ship, including the disciplining of the crew, who were often a hard, ill-bred, and violent lot. The other important members of the crew were the armorer in charge of weapons and the carpenter. This latter position was often paid as much as the first mate, not only because he built the accommodation for the enslaved during the outward passage but also because he was often responsible for the maintenance of the shackles and other restraints on board.

Life on board slave ships for the Africans during the Middle Passage was dreadful. John Newton, writing 30 years after he left the trade, wrote

> the slaves lie in two rows, one above the other, on each side of the ship, close to each other, like books on a shelf. I have known them so close, that the shelf would not easily contain one more . . . the poor creatures thus cramped for want of room, are likewise in irons, for the most part both hands and feet, two together, which makes it difficult for them to turn or move, or to attempt to rise or to lie down, without hurting themselves or each other.

Men were accommodated separately from the women and young children. The men were naked and were shackled together in pairs. Women were allowed a small piece of cloth for modesty, but this did not stop them being the subject of unwanted sexual attention from members of the crew. Although most captains tried to prevent this, it seems to have been a frequent occurrence. And sometimes, it was the captains themselves who were guilty. In the 1770s, French Capt. Philippe Liot "mistreated a very pretty Negress [and] broke two of her teeth" and raped an 8- or 10-year-old girl on three occasions "whose mouth he closed to prevent her from screaming."

The Africans spent most of their time in hot, stuffy, putrid holds, but they were allowed up on deck in small groups once a day when the weather was good so that they could exercise. They were strictly supervised, the crew being equipped with guns, and sometimes the captives had cannons trained on them. This did not prevent Africans from trying to escape. It is likely that the enslaved attempted revolts on at least 1 in every 10 voyages, which usually were put down with extreme violence and brutality. Leaders of revolts were punished severely and frequently killed. Torture was used to extract confessions. Newton recorded a potential uprising in his log and commented that he "punished them with the thumb screws and afterwards put them in neck yokes." It is not surprising that these uprisings were almost always unsuccessful. One of the few documented revolts that succeeded was on the French vessel *Diamant* off the coast of Gabon in 1774. Three men were able to get free and hid in the women's toilet, thus surprising the crew. They managed to take the helm, and the captain and crew took to the dinghy in fright. The crew members were seized by local Africans and ransomed to a Dutch captain who was later reimbursed.

The captives were rationed bread and received a bean- or **yam**-based stew two times daily. They might drink some water three times a day. The owners of one slave ship warned Liverpool Capt. Luke Mann about feeding the captives: "You must not give your slaves too much provisions; they are accustomed to low diet in their own country." On one occasion, when Newton was going overbudget toward the end of the voyage, he ordered his crew to "[g]ive the slaves bread now for their breakfast for cannot afford them 2 hot meals per day."

The cramped conditions and fetid atmosphere where the captives were held in the ships took its toll on them. In the early days of the trade, mortality rates may have been as high as 1 in 5, but this rate was gradually reduced to about 1 in 15 by taking more care in terms of sanitation and the overall treatment of the enslaved. Owners and captains came to realize it was in their financial interest to look after their cargo. Orders to the captain of the Dutch vessel *De Nieuwe Hoop* specifically mentioned the care of the enslaved and instructed that "the doctor and supercargo [the person responsible for the cargo—the enslaved Africans—until the ship reached its destination] check mouths and eyes of slaves every morning and try to discover if anything ails them." By the 18th century, most ships carried a surgeon, who was generally highly paid, usually second only to the captain. Few surgeons were specifically trained to deal with tropical diseases and had to adapt their general medical knowledge. Only the French India Company (*Compagnie des Indes*) appeared to show much interest in special training. Most of their surgeons had two or more assistants, who were to be given an hour's medical instruction daily. A training school for ships' surgeons was established in Rotterdam in 1769, but by then, the Dutch slave trade was almost at an end. In general, however, little evidence indicates that any of this instruction was effective.

The most common disease on board ship was dysentery. A sample of 3,563 deaths among 20,653 slaves on 42 Dutch West Indies Company vessels during the 17th and 18th centuries shows that one-third died of dysentery, and that smallpox, scurvy, and tuberculosis claimed a further one-third of lives. But mortality from "sudden death," "illness," and "fevers" was also high. The mental torment of mistreatment and incarceration also took its toll. Some 28 deaths were attributed to suicide and a further 20 to mental causes, such as "died of grief."

The enslaved faced other threats to life as well. Two incidents show the inhumane attitude that prevailed in the trade. In the first incident, the Dutch slaver *Leuden* was grounded in the Marowin River on the eastern coast of Surinam in stormy conditions in January 1738. When the ship tilted and was clearly going to founder, the crew locked the hatches of the slave holds because they feared that if the Africans got free they would rush for the lifeboats. The 73 crew and only 14 slaves, working on deck at the time, were able to escape. When they reached Paramaribo, however, the surviving slaves were sold. The remaining 702 Africans drowned.

In the second incident, in 1781, a number of captive Africans were ill on the Liverpool ship *Zong*, captained by the infamous Luke Collingwood (ca. 1733–before 1783). Collingwood thought they would die. He was concerned that if the Africans died from starvation, no insurance could be claimed. When water was running out, Collingwood gave orders for a total of 132 slaves to be tossed overboard. He thought that the owners could claim that the Africans had died from "perils of the sea" and thus be entitled to compensation. The ensuing court case became a cause celèbre and alerted the public to the horrors of the slave trade.

The horrific experiences of the Middle Passage brought Africans together. Slaves who had been transported in the same ship referred to each other as shipmates and, despite being frequently separated on arrival, maintained a bond for the rest of their lives. Physician Thomas Winterbotham, writing in the 1790s, remarked, "those unfortunate people who have gone to the West Indies in the same vessel, ever after retain for each other a strong and tender affection." But the voyage also strengthened ties in other ways. In such a hostile environment, cultural traditions became a vital means of survival, and Africans clung to such vestiges of their former lives as they could. They were occasionally allowed to bring **drums** and musical instruments on board, although these items often were confiscated because the crew recognized they could be used to communicate privately. Other items were sometimes smuggled aboard, including **charms** and herbal medicines. Singing and storytelling also helped Africans maintain their culture.

The abolition of the trans-Atlantic slave trade by Britain in 1807 and the United States in 1808 was a major turning point. By bullying and persuasion, the other main European powers followed suit over the next two to three decades. A huge trade continued in the Southern Atlantic, centered on Cuba and Brazil, until the 1860s, but in general, the former slave ships found new cargoes to trade.

*See also* Abolition Imagery; Herbs.

FURTHER READING

Burnside, Madeleine, and Rosamarie Robotham. *Spirits of the Passage: The Transatlantic Slave Trade in the Seventeenth Century*. New York: Simon and Schuster, 1997.

Postma, Johannes. *The Dutch in the Atlantic Slave Trade*. New York: Cambridge University Press, 1990.

Rediker, Marcus. *The Slave Ship*. New York: Viking, 2007.

"Voyages." The Trans-Atlantic Slave Trade Database. At www.slavevoyages.org/tast/index.faces.

Walvin, James. *Black Ivory: Slavery in the British Empire*. 2nd ed. Oxford: Blackwell Publishers, 2001.

TONY TIBBLES

**SPINNING HOUSES.** Spinning houses developed as a specialized craft shop on Southern plantations. Slave artisans worked in them, spinning **cotton**, **linen**, and **wool** into **cloth**. The spinning houses, in conjunction with other specialized craft shops on plantations, indicated the quest on the part of some planters to be self-sufficient, growing and processing as much within their plantation borders as possible to clothe their slaves. The slaves did much if not all the work that produced the raw products as well as the finished cloth that they sewed to make their own **clothing**.

The structures took many forms, including single- and double-story buildings, some log, some frame, and some finished masonry. Spinning as well as weaving and finishing often occurred in the one structure, and equipment included wool cards, a heckle for flax processing, flax and cotton spinning wheels, one or more looms, and even kettles for dyeing and finishing cloth. Spinning houses included machines that replaced hand labor as those machines became perfected, including the cotton gins, spinning jennies, and flying shuttle looms, and slaves performed all skilled or manual labor, whether done by hand or machine.

The wood-frame spinning house at Mount Vernon was built in 1775. Perhaps it constituted a statement on the part of the Revolutionary commander George Washington (1732–1799) that indicated the increasingly independent nature of Virginia. Southern slave colonies had depended on English products since their inception, but building a spinning house in the Revolutionary era provided tangible evidence of the ability for planters to declare themselves independent of the English **textile** trade as well as British governance. During the 1810s, in keeping with the industrialization of textile production in the United States, Thomas Jefferson (1743–1826) indicated that some slaves in his spinning house used spinning jennies and flying shuttles, and he advised his correspondent to construct a spinning house with a door wide enough to accommodate 24 spindles.

Labor in spinning houses followed gendered patterns, with women predominantly performing all tasks associated with carding, spinning, and weaving. Young girls learned the tasks from older women skilled in production. Girls who showed little aptitude for spinning or weaving quickly shifted to other less skilled tasks. Once the cloth was woven and finished, women sewed the cloth into garments or bedding. The production did not meet demand, however, and Northern factories also exported "slave cloth" to Southern buyers.

*See also* Negro Cloth.

Old spinning house at Mount Ida, Talladega County, Alabama, 1935. (Library of Congress.)

## Spinning Cotton

George Fleming remembered the whirl and clang of spinning and weaving equipment to process cotton in South Carolina:

I don't know how many spinning wheels and looms and dem things Marse had, but he sho had lots of 'em. Dat business making cloth had lots to it and I don't know much 'bout it, but it was sort of dis way. Dey picked de seeds out of de cotton; den put de cotton in piles and carded it. Dey kept brushing it over and over on de cards till it was in lil' rolls. It was den ready fer de spinning wheels whar it was spun in thread. Dis was called de filling. I don't know much 'bout de warp, dat is de part dat run long ways.

Dem spinning wheels sho did go on de fly. Dey connected up wid de spindle and it go lots faster dan de wheel. Dey hold one end of de cotton roll wid de hand and 'tach de other to de spindle. It keep drawing and twisting de roll till it make a small thread. Sometimes dey would run de thread frum de spindle to a cornshuck or anything dat would serve de purpose. Dat was called de broach. Some of dem didn't go any further dan dat, dey had to make sech and sech broaches a day. Dis was deir task. Dat's de reason some of dem had to work atter dark, dat is, if dey didn't git de task done befo' dat.

Dey run de thread off de broach on to reels, and some of it was dyed on de reels. Dey made deir own dyes, too. Some of it was made frum copperas, and some frum barks and berries. Atter while, de thread was put back on de spinning wheel and wound on lil' old cane quills. It was den ready fer de looms. Don't know nothing, de looms—boom! boom! sho could travel. Dey put de quills, atter de thread was wound on dem, in de shettle and knocked it back and forth twixt de long threads what was on de beams. Can't see de thread fly out of dat shettle it come so fast. Dey sho could sheckle it through dar. Dey peddled dem looms, zip! zap! making de thread rise and drap while de shettle zoom twixt it. Hear dem looms booming all day long 'round de weaving shop. De weaving and spinning was done in de same place.

*Source:* George P. Rawick, ed. "South Carolina." *The American Slave: North Carolina and South Carolina Narratives*, Supp. Ser. 1, Vol. 11. Westport, CT: Greenwood Press, 1978.

## FURTHER READING

Jefferson, Thomas to Goodman Jeremiah, March 5, 1813. "'Site B': Online Archaeology Exhibit." Thomas Jefferson's Poplar Forest. At http://poplarforest.org/siteB/histdoctemplate.php?pick=March+5%2C+1813.

Vlach, John Michael. *Back of the Big House: The Architecture of Plantation Slavery*. Chapel Hill: University of North Carolina Press, 1993.

DEBRA A. REID

**SPRING HOUSES.** Spring houses provided cool storage for dairy products and **food** stuffs on plantations and farms across the nation, including the antebellum South. The structures were often brick or stone to retard rot due to the damp conditions. They were built into slopes over a spring and thus the spring's location, not the location of farm dwellings, dictated the location of the spring house. The water from the spring collected in a pool, and the steady flow in and out helped maintain a steady temperature. Built-in shelving on the walls, or planks set above the water, provided storage space.

Spring houses consolidated cool water to maintain consistently cooler temperatures. This proved critical when trying to prevent milk and processed cream from souring. Some large plantations specialized in dairying and built **dairies** to process milk, but most Southerners did not have the resources to invest in milk cattle, pasture, and labor to the degree required to specialize. Instead, most Southerners made due with spring houses to extend the life of perishable commodities.

Studies of Southern **food and foodways** indicate that Southerners generally, and slaves particularly, consumed few dairy products. Yet, spring houses made it possible for diversified Southern farms and smaller plantations to have milk, cream, butter, and cheese in small quantities.

Former slaves interviewed during the 1930s remembered spring houses on the plantations as rectangular buildings with a gable entrance.

FURTHER READING

Vlach, John Michael. *Back of the Big House: The Architecture of Plantation Slavery*. Chapel Hill: University of North Carolina Press, 1993.

DEBRA A. REID

**STEWS.** A stew is a combination of foods cooked in a liquid, producing a meal thicker than a soup with a rich stock or gravy. Many of the more complicated dishes enjoyed in the enslaved community were one-pot meals consisting of stews developed as a means to slowly cook **foods** on the hearth over the course of a work day in the fields, much in the way the slow cooker serves 21st-century families. Since enslaved households usually had few utensils, the stew prepared in one pot served as a convenient and expedient way to enjoy a variety of ingredients in one communal dish. The stews created by the enslaved community hearken to similar West and Central African traditions where the main meal of the day consisted of a stew consumed with a starch of some sort. Many of the popular Southern dishes—pepperpot (from the West Indies, Philadelphia, and the Chesapeake), **gumbo** (associated with the Lower Mississippi Valley), **okra** stew (from the Chesapeake and Carolina Low Country), **chicken** stewed with **yams** (as described by Mary Randolph (1762–1828) in *The Virginia Housewife*), burgoo (from Kentucky and the southern Ohio River valley), Brunswick stew (identified with Virginia, Georgia, and North Carolina)—have been connected through folk tradition in some way to an enslaved cook. Brunswick stew in particular was attributed to "Uncle" Jimmy Matthews from Virginia in 1828, who made a spicy stew from squirrel and other game bagged on his master's hunting trip. Common to these dishes were the savory elements of onion, hot peppers or pepper,

---

### Beef Stew

Former slave Charles Ball (ca. 1780–unknown) described the making of a beef stew near Camden, South Carolina, in the early 19th century:

> Each family, or mess, now sent its deputy, with a large wooden bowl in his hand . . . I went on the part of our family, and found that the meat dinner of this day was made up of the basket of tripe, and other offal, that I had prepared in the morning. The whole had been boiled in four great iron kettles, until the flesh had disappeared from the bones, which were broken in small pieces—a flitch of bacon, some green corn, squashes, tomatos, and onions had been added, together with other condiments, and the whole converted into about a hundred gallons of soup, of which I received in my bowl, for the use of our family, more than two gallons.

*Source:* Charles Ball. *Slavery in the United States: A Narrative of the Life and Adventures of Charles Ball.* New York: John S. Taylor, 1837. Documenting the American South Collection, University Library of the University of North Carolina at Chapel Hill. At http://docsouth.unc.edu/neh/ballslavery/menu.html.

---

okra as a thickener, and the occasional addition of tomatoes to create a richer sauce and gravy. Many stews included lima beans and other legumes as filler to absorb liquid and provide body. Cast-off meat, seafood, and aged chickens or beef usually provided the protein in these dishes. These stews were typically enjoyed with **rice**, **corn** mush, **hominy**, or various forms of corncake used to sop up the juices.

*See also* Cast Iron Pots; Cooks and Cooking; Yams and Sweet Potatoes.

FURTHER READING

Harris, Jessica B. *The Welcome Table: African American Heritage Cooking.* New York: Fireside, 1995.

Randolph, Mary. *The Virginia Housewife: With Historical Notes and Commentaries by Karen Hess.* Columbia: University of South Carolina Press, 1984.

MICHAEL W. TWITTY

**SUBFLOOR PITS.** Subfloor pits were dug by slaves to hide important items and have been found in late 17th- and 18th-century **slave quarters** in parts of the American South. The earliest appearance of these belowground pits was in the Chesapeake region of Virginia, where they begin to appear with regularity starting around 1680, coinciding with the increasing importation of Africans into that colony. Although subterranean pits have been found on Native American and Anglo-American sites from the 17th and 18th centuries, their regular appearance in high concentrations on slave quarter sites, particularly in Virginia, suggests they were an important cultural adaptation for the enslaved. Although subfloor pits are found in a few extant quarters, such as the Bremo Recess Quarter (ca. 1825) in Fluvanna County, Virginia, the vast majority of these pits exists only as archaeological evidence. Archaeologists have studied and debated the functions of subfloor pits since they were first discovered in the 1960s at Tutter's Neck in Williamsburg, Virginia. Explanations for how they were used include personal storage, **food** storage, and spiritual spaces.

## Locations

Only one 19th-century reference for the use of subfloor pits in Africa has been located, and thus it is likely that their use arose as a creolized tradition in Virginia largely in response to conditions of slavery, rather than arriving as an African tradition. Most pits to date have been located in Virginia, but they also have been found in Kentucky, Tennessee, Missouri, North Carolina, and Maryland. If extensive pit use began in Virginia as a response to enslavement, the subsequent geographic distribution of subfloor pits to other parts of the South appears to be an artifact of Virginia residents expanding westward during the early national period. Kentucky, Tennessee, and Missouri

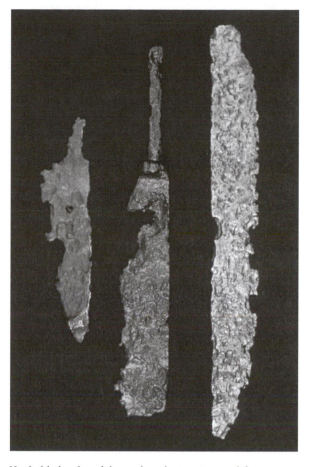

Knife blades found by archaeologists in a subfloor pit at Carter's Grove slave quarter, Williamsburg, Virginia. (The Colonial Williamsburg Foundation.)

were all destinations for Virginia settlers in search of new agricultural lands along the frontier, as well as for slaves who traveled overland to work these new plantations. Excavations of slave quarters in these states, as well as in eastern North Carolina, have revealed subfloor pits, suggesting that enslaved Virginians carried this cultural practice with them to these new areas. Subfloor pits also have been discovered in Nova Scotia at a late 18th-century black Loyalist site settled by former slaves from Virginia. Slave quarters in the lower South—South Carolina, Georgia, Mississippi, Alabama, and Florida—are virtually devoid of subfloor pits and their absence appears to be related to a combination of factors, including the different physical environments, slave demographics, and historical trajectories of the lower South.

## Physical Appearance

Subfloor pits began to appear with regularity in Virginia when slave importation began to increase toward the end of the 17th century and reached their highest peak of use in the 18th century. While some quarters contained only one or two pits, in others, they covered the available floor space: in a 384-square-foot building at Utopia Quarter

(1730–1750) in Williamsburg, 18 pits were cut through the clay underlying the building. The occurrence of multiple pits within a single structure was more typical of the first half of the 18th century, a period of heavy importation of slaves from West Africa. The occurrence of multiple pits in these structures is believed to be related to the practice of housing unrelated individuals together and the need for secure storage places for personal items and surplus food in these barracks-like living conditions.

Most subfloor pits were straight-sided, flat-bottomed holes cut through the packed clay floors typical of many slave quarters. A small percentage was upgraded with wood or brick floors, board linings, or even prefabricated boxes, which would have kept pit contents clean and dry and hindered rodent intrusions into pits containing foodstuffs. Linings and boxes also stabilized walls, which were prone to collapse in soil-floored structures. A few pits showed evidence of wooden dividers to create individual storage spaces or separate different foodstuffs.

Access to pits in buildings with wooden floors was through hinged trapdoors. In structures containing earthen floors, pits would have been covered with hewn boards that could be lifted away for access to the belowground space. Soil ledges near the tops of some pits suggest that the coverings were set flush with the soil floor. Pits tended to cluster along walls and in front of hearths, and protection from foot traffic was probably afforded by covering pits with tables, **beds**, or seating. Pits were particularly susceptible to damage from groundwater and rodents. At Williamsburg's 18th-century Rich Neck Quarter, pits showed extensive evidence of maintenance and repair, necessitated in part from groundwater undermining and collapsing walls. Pits became smaller and shallower over the 40-year occupation span at this dwelling, as residents learned that large, deep pits were more prone to damage.

**Functions**

After falling out of service, pits were filled with soil, ash, charcoal from cooking fires, broken dishes, animal bones, and other detritus of daily life at the quarter. These artifacts provide scholars with valuable clues to reconstructing physical aspects of enslaved life—material possessions, consumer behaviors, diet and subsistence strategies, and the creation of creole cultures, for example. Archaeologically, subfloor pits appear within the footprint or confines of former structures as soil stains cut into geologically deposited clay soils. Clear-cut functions for many subfloor pits have been difficult to determine, because the features were filled predominantly with soil and garbage not directly associated with their original use. Physical characteristics and spatial patterning of subfloor pits and ethnohistoric and documentary evidence and artifacts recovered from soil layers along the floor of the pits, which would be more likely to be deposited there as a result of original pit function, provide valuable clues for original pit functions. Archaeologists have explored several functions for these subfloor pits: as sources for clay, as personal storage units or "hidey holes" for stolen or valuable goods, as root cellars for the preservation of fruits and plant foods, and as places of spiritual significance.

*Clay Pits*

Some subfloor pits may have originally been dug to acquire clay for chinking log walls and chimneys. An 1850 issue of the *Southern Cultivator* reveals that "[m]any persons, in building negro houses, in order to get clay convenient for filling the hearth and for mortar, dig a hole under the floor." Log construction was a common building technique for 18th- and 19th-century slave houses in Virginia. Clay, readily available and cost-free, provided a degree of protection from drafts and wind-driven precipitation. Clay also was used in constructing and maintaining the stick-and-mud chimneys that remained common features on log and frame houses as late as the early 20th century. Holes originally dug for extracting clay may have been reshaped for use as subfloor pits.

### Storage Spaces or Hidey Holes

Another use for subfloor pits was for the storage of personal possessions such as **clothing**, adornment items, tools, eating utensils, or items crafted for sale. Archaeologists discovered 20 wine bottles resting on the floor of a subfloor pit at the Kingsmill Quarter (1750–1780) in Virginia. A late 18th-century pit at Carter's Grove plantation quarter near Williamsburg, Virginia, contained a group of objects interpreted as personal gear: cutlery, **buttons** and buckles from clothing, a **tobacco pipe**, and fire-making implements.

Subfloor pits provided effective storage units in the cramped confines of quarters, which, particularly before the mid-18th century, often were home to numbers of unrelated individuals. Not only did the pits make efficient use of space, they also were relatively secure from unauthorized access. It has been suggested the pits were used as safety deposit boxes to protect possessions from theft by other slaves. Because the ownership of each pit would be known by the quarter residents, the contents were protected from unauthorized entry. Other archaeologists believe that subterranean pits also were used for concealing ill-gotten gains, and documentary evidence from colonial Virginia indicates that the enslaved sometimes used subfloor pits in this fashion. William Henry Singleton (1835–1938), a runaway slave in eastern North Carolina, hid in a hearth front pit for three years to elude his captors.

### Food Storage

Hearth-front subfloor pits appear to have been used primarily for food storage, especially of the sweet potatoes that were a significant component of the diet of enslaved Virginians. Three 19th-century African American accounts, that of Frederick Douglass (ca. 1818–1895) in Maryland, Booker T. Washington in Virginia (1856–1915), and William Henry Singleton in North Carolina, recall the use of interior pits for storing sweet potatoes in slave quarters. Unlike most foods that require cool, moist conditions for optimal preservation, sweet potatoes are best stored in warmer, drier environments. Hearth-front pits may have benefited from ambient heat, maximizing potato preservation over the cold winter months. The preference for sweet potatoes among enslaved Virginians may have been related to the tuber's overall similarity to African **yams**, the primary dietary staple of the Niger Delta cultures brought to Virginia in large numbers in the 18th century. Fragmented sweet potatoes and starch granules typical of sweet potatoes have been recovered from the floor area of hearth-front pits at the 18th-century quarters in Virginia.

Overall, hearth-front pits were larger and deeper than pits found in other parts of the quarter. These pits also had a greater standardization of shapes and sizes with hearth-front pits, suggesting a specific use with "communal" implications, as opposed to individually created pits in other locations. The hearth was perceived as a communal space, and it is likely that pits located there served a communal function, such as food storage. Levels of repair and reconstruction on hearth-front pits were far greater than for other locations, with the continuing use and upkeep of these pits indicating the importance of this location. Maintenance needs for hearth-front pits in soil-floored structures may have been a function of greater foot traffic around these features, frequent access for adding or removing food, and damage from tunneling creatures, such as rats or moles, in search of a meal, all activities which would have accelerated the collapse of the clay walls. The hearth would be one of the areas with the highest level of foot traffic in the house, as people warmed themselves at the fire, prepared meals in inclement weather, or used its light for **sewing** or other tasks.

### Spiritual Spaces

Some subfloor pits were used in African-based spiritual practices as **shrines** to ancestors, deities, and other spirit forces. This interpretation derives from the religions of the Igbo and other West African cultures who were enslaved in colonial Virginia. In these cultures, the construction and maintenance of shrines are longstanding spiritual practices critical for honoring ancestors and deities, thus ensuring good fortune in health, harvest, and family well-being. The underground location of the pits kept shrines safe from prying eyes, and the clay into which the pits were dug was considered sacred, being the place where spiritual beings reside.

Shrines contain objects of spiritual significance, and daily offerings of food and drink are poured on these sacred spaces to ease communication with spirit forces. Items found placed in groups on the floors of some Virginia pits show distinct parallels with objects contained in West African shrines. At the Utopia Quarter, a shrine to the Igbo female water deity *Idemili* consisted of a group of white objects placed on an elevated sand platform on the bottom of the pit. Pollen analysis revealed that libations of wine had been poured over the fossil scallop **shells**, cow bone, and white clay **tobacco pipes** forming the shrine. The numbers, colors, and types of objects on this shrine, as well as its placement in the quarter at a point closest to the river, reveal that its creator possessed a sophisticated spiritual knowledge of this particular Igbo deity. Other shrines appear to be more creolized expressions of West African-based spiritual beliefs.

### Disappearance of Subfloor Pits

Over time, the number of subfloor pits appearing in slave quarters diminished, and they largely had fallen out of use by the end of the first quarter of the 19th century. Part of this decline was related to changing slave demographics; beginning in the second half of the 18th century, the formation of a Virginia-born creole slave society meant that more enslaved were living in houses occupied by family members. The need for private storage or a hidden spiritual space would have diminished in the cooperative environment of a family. Additionally, many enslaved converted to

Christianity during the Second Great Awakening of the early 19th century and may have become less reliant on West African-based spiritual traditions.

Changes in the architecture of Virginia slave quarters also may have led to a decline in subfloor pit use. Quarter size decreased in the second half of the 18th century as they became family-based housing rather than barracks for unrelated individuals. In the early 19th century, more quarters were being built with elevated wooden floors—a construction technique that made it more difficult to build and conceal these pits. Recent scholarship has suggested that the need for individual pits decreased as community and family cooperation and slave participation in the **market** economy made the need for surplus storage less critical. The need for food storage would have remained constant, however, and it is interesting to note that hearthfront pits were the last to disappear from quarters.

A subfloor pit may have gone through a complex use life—originally dug as a clay source, later used for storage of food or personal possessions, and ending as a convenient disposal place for garbage. Subfloor pits were used by the enslaved to transform their living spaces, and are symbols of individual and collective agency and strategies. They appear to have arisen as a response to enslavement—whether their creation stemmed from a need for food preservation, a desire for private space, a perceived spiritual need, or some other yet unknown factor.

*See also* Liquor.

FURTHER READING

Franklin, Maria. *An Archaeological Study of the Rich Neck Slave Quarter and Enslaved Domestic Life*. Williamsburg, VA: Colonial Williamsburg Foundation, 2004.

Hatch, Danny Brad. "Bottomless Pits: The Decline of Subfloor Pits and Rise of African American Consumerism in Virginia." MA thesis, College of William and Mary, 2009.

Kelso, William. *Kingsmill Plantations 1619–1800: Archaeology of Country Life in Colonial Virginia*. New York: Academic Press, 1984.

Kimmel, Richard. "Notes on the Use of Sub-Floor Pits as Root Cellars and Places of Concealment." *African American Archaeology* 7 (1993): 11–12.

Neiman, Fraser. "The Lost World of Monticello in Evolutionary Perspective." *Journal of Anthropological Research* 64, no. 2 (2008): 161–193.

Samford, Patricia M. *Subfloor Pits and the Archaeology of Slavery in Colonial Virginia*. Tuscaloosa: University of Alabama Press, 2007.

Young, Amy L. "Cellars and African-American Slave Sites: New Data from the Upland South." *Midcontinental Journal of Archaeology* 22, no. 1 (1997): 96–115; The African Diaspora Archaeology Network. At www.diaspora.uiuc.edu/background.html.

PATRICIA M. SAMFORD

**SUGAR.** Before the mid-19th century, white sugar was found only in the wealthiest households of Europe and the United States. The remainder of society used coarse, brown sugar and molasses (a thick, brown syrup) to sweeten their coffee, tea, and chocolate drinks, which also supplied a good, cheap source of energy (carbohydrates). Refined sugar was expensive because sugarcane cultivation and the production and refinement of the granulated sugar were complex and labor-intensive.

---

### Sugar Barrels

Ellen Betts from Louisiana reminisced about sugarcane and sugar:

Marse sho' turn over in his grave, did he know 'bout some dat 'olasses. Dem black boys don't care. I seen 'em pull rats out de sugar barrel, and dey taste de sugar and say, "Ain't nothin' wrong with dat sugar. It still sweet." One day a pert one pull a dead scorpion out from de syrup kettle. He jus' laught and say, "Marse don't want waste none dis syrup," he lick de syrup right off dat scorpion's body and legs.

Lawsy me, I seen thousands and thousands sugar barrels and kettles of syrup in my day. Lawd knows how much sugarcane old Marse have. To dem cuttin' de cane, it don't seem so much, but to dem what work hour in, hour out, dem sugarcane fields sho' stretch from one end of de earth to de other.

*Source:* "Born in Slavery: Slave Narratives from the Federal Writers' Project, 1936–1938," American Memory, Library of Congress. At http://memory.loc.gov/ammem/snhtml/.

---

Both granulated sugar and molasses are made from sugarcane. Sugarcane is part of the genus *Saccharum*, a family of tall, perennial, reed-like grasses indigenous to the tropical regions of southeastern Asia. The exact species of sugarcane used to produce sugar is known as *Saccharum officinarum*. Each sugarcane plant consists of multiple stalks, which range in height from 10 to 24 feet. The stalks of the plant are cylindrical and segmented; stalk diameters can reach two or more inches in size. Long, blade-like leaves grow over the entire stalk from the bands separating the segments. Cane juice is found only in the stalk of the plant. Cane leaves are cut off during the harvest and then either left in the field to decompose or used as animal feed. A flower or tassel forms on the top of the cane plant when the cane is ready to harvest.

From southeastern Asia, sugarcane cultivation spread throughout India and China before it was carried into Egypt and the Mediterranean region. It was introduced to Europe as a competitor with honey. Increased demand for sugar resulted in increased production as more land was dedicated to sugarcane cultivation. Sugarcane was introduced to the Americas by Christopher Columbus on his second trip to Hispaniola in 1493. By 1620, England and France were creating a plantation economy in the Caribbean based on the cultivation of sugarcane and the production of crystallized sugar and molasses. Transforming sugarcane into crystallized sugar and molasses was a labor-intensive endeavor. Able-bodied laborers were captured in Africa and then transported to the Caribbean and Brazil and, after the 1750s, to the sugar plantations in Louisiana. The captured Africans who survived the trans-Atlantic journey entered into a lifetime of enslavement and hard work.

On the sugar plantations, enslaved laborers were organized into gangs based on their age and their fitness level. Older individuals, handicapped laborers, and children were placed into a gang that undertook lighter tasks, like weeding and fertilizing the cane fields. The stronger laborers, both male and female, were placed into a gang and required to do the harder tasks, such as planting and cutting cane, digging irrigation ditches, and clearing the fields. Each gang was supervised by a **slave driver**, or overseer, who would use any means available to increase the productivity of the gang. These methods often included harsh physical punishment and the use of a **whip**. Gangs worked in shifts of 12 or more hours. When it was time for the cane to be harvested and processed, workdays would be longer. Longer workdays decreased the amount of time that the enslaved laborers could spend doing other activities, such as cultivating small plots of foodstuffs to supplement their meager **rations** or to sell at **market**.

Sugarcane was cultivated on large, monocrop plantations in the Caribbean, Louisiana, Florida, and northeastern South America. Attempts were made to grow cane in Georgia and South Carolina, but the short growing season resulted in low crop yields and made it more economical to grow **rice** and **cotton** in these areas. After clearing and leveling the fields, sugarcane cuttings were planted in linear furrows. Irrigation ditches, where needed, were hand dug by enslaved laborers to provide the crop with a constant supply of water. In Louisiana and Florida, the cane was harvested from October through December and only one crop was harvested per year to avoid losing the crops to an early frost. In more tropical areas, such as the Caribbean, two crops could be harvested per year. Because sugarcane is perennial, the planting of new cuttings was only undertaken every two to three years.

Sugar and molasses are produced from the juice of the sugarcane plants. The juice had to be extracted and processed within two days of cutting or else the juice would begin to ferment and spoil. During the sugar harvest, the crushing mill and boiling house would be working nonstop until all of the cane juice had been processed and sugar was settling in the molds. Enslaved laborers would cut the cane plants in the field using machetes. The cane would then be loaded onto ox carts or carried on the backs of the enslaved laborers to the mill. At the mill, the plant stalks were hand-fed into the crushing device, which consisted of three or four rollers. In the early decades of sugar production, the rollers were made of wood but eventually were replaced by metal rollers. Crushing of the cane produced cane juice and bagasse. The crushed plant remains were used to feed livestock or as fuel in the boiling house fires. The constantly moving rollers proved treacherous for many of the enslaved laborers who came into contact with them, resulting in lost or crushed fingers and hands.

Mills, in addition to boiling and pour houses, stood either on or near the sugar plantation. The mill, boiling house, and pour house were located adjacent to each other, with the mill preferably upslope of the boiling house. This positioning allowed for the cane juice to flow from the mill to the boiling house through a series of pipes and troughs. The types of crushing mills used in the sugar industry varied through time and by location. Some of the earliest mills were powered by animals: oxen, **horses**, or cattle. Animal-powered mills were the most common type found in the sugar-producing regions of the United States. When windmill technology spread throughout the Caribbean, many animal mills were replaced by windmills. However, not all areas were conducive for wind-powered mills. Windmills generally were used in areas with a strong and constant wind, such as some of the Lesser Antillean Islands in the Caribbean archipelago and along the northeastern coast of South America. Water-powered mills are present on some mountainous islands of the Caribbean and in parts of South America with ample sources of moving water. During the 19th century, steam engines began to be used in many sugar mills.

Once crushed, the cane juice would run from the mill to a settling vat in the boiling house through a series of pipes and troughs. In this vat, pieces of plant matter would settle out of the cane juice. In some locations, lime was added to the settling vat because the lime would cause the impurities, such as the plant material, to settle out of the cane juice. When enough juice was collected, the cane juice was then transferred into the first and largest boiling pot of a series of boiling pots. The boiling kettles were large **cast iron pots** called "coppers" or "pans." Four or more pans were aligned from largest to smallest in what was referred to as a "sugar train", or a "kettle train." The earliest configuration of the sugar train was known as a "Spanish train." In this system, four or more boiling coppers were lined up, each with its own source of heat, a small fire under each copper. This method produced good sugar, but it required a lot of fuel to maintain a fire under each individual copper. A more efficient sugar train was later developed, which consisted of five or more pans that shared a single heat source. A fire would be maintained adjacent to the smallest copper, while the chimney would have been located on the opposite end of the train next to the largest copper. A flue running under the pans would carry heat and smoke through the train to the chimney. This new system was called the "Jamaica train."

The fresh cane juice was first placed into the largest copper, called the *grande* in boiling houses of Louisiana. In this copper, the juice was brought to a boil to burn off some of the excess water. As the cane juice boiled, a skin, or film, collected on the surface. Using a skimmer, a large slotted spoon-like tool on a long wooden handle, enslaved workers would scrape the skin off the top of the boiling liquid. Some boiling houses saved the film by directing it through an overflow system of drains and pipes from the sugar train to vats where the substance would sit and ferment. After fermentation, this liquid would then be distilled to make a rough whiskey.

When the boiling cane juice reached a specific temperature in the first copper, it was then transferred to the next copper, which was slightly smaller. To transfer the boiling hot liquid, enslaved laborers used ladles to quickly scoop the juice from one copper to the next. The ladles, like the skimmers, were set on long handles and held up to a gallon of liquid. Transferring the cane juice between pans was a hot and dangerous job, undertaken by enslaved laborers. In the second copper, the liquid was again brought to a boil; the skin was skimmed off, and upon reaching a specific temperature, the liquid was transferred to the third copper. This third copper was smaller than the second one. The process continued again until the hot, syrupy liquid reached the final, and smallest, copper called the "strike pan," or the *batterie* in Louisiana. In the strike pan, the sugar began to crystallize. When the liquid reached a certain temperature and consistency, it was removed from the fire and ladled into molds.

Molds, like so many specific details of sugar production, varied depending on location and time period. Conical clay drip molds were used in some localities, while other sugar producers ladled the finished product into wooden barrels or boxes. Regardless of the type of container, all molds had to have a hole on the bottom. When the warm syrup was poured into the mold, the hole was plugged to prevent the hot syrup from running out the bottom. When the molds were filled, they were transferred and stored in the pour house for days or even weeks. During this period, the plug would be removed to allow the molasses to separate from the crystallized sugar. As the molasses separated, it would drip out of the hole in the mold and into a barrel placed under the mold. After the molasses settled out, a dark brown, unrefined sugar called "muscovado" would be left in the molds.

After all of the molasses drained from the sugar crystals, the muscovado sugar was then packed into barrels and shipped to sugar refineries. These refineries often were located close to the markets, so if the sugar was to be sold in London, England, then the muscovado sugar would be shipped to a refinery near London. In the refinery, the sugar would be reboiled and recrystallized numerous times until the desired whiteness was obtained.

The molasses would be placed into barrels and shipped to distilleries in Europe. Here, the molasses would be distilled into rum. The rum then entered into a large commercial network that connected Europe to the Caribbean and Africa. Rum played an integral part in a trade system commonly referred to as the Triangular Trade. European rum was sent to Africa where it was traded for enslaved laborers. The laborers were then shipped across the Atlantic Ocean to the sugar plantations in the Caribbean, the southern United States, and northern South America. Once in the sugar colonies, the enslaved laborers would be used to grow sugarcane and produce the sugar and molasses that kept the system running.

*See also* Liquor.

## FURTHER READING

Curtin, Philip D. *The Rise and Fall of the Plantation Complex: Essays in Atlantic History.* Cambridge: Cambridge University Press, 1990.

Deerr, Noel. *The History of Sugar.* Vols. 1 and 2. London: Chapman and Hall, 1949.

Follett, Richard. *The Sugar Masters: Planters and Slaves in Louisiana's Cane World, 1820–1860.* Baton Rouge: Louisiana State University Press, 2005.

Mintz, Sidney W. *Sweetness and Power: The Place of Sugar in Modern History.* New York: Penguin, 1985.

Moitt, Bernard, ed. *Sugar, Slavery, and Society: Perspectives on the Caribbean, India, the Mascarenes, and the United States.* Gainesville: University of Florida Press, 2004.

Van Hook, Andrew. *Sugar: Its Production, Technology, and Uses.* New York: Ronald Press Company, 1949.

AUDREY R. DAWSON

# T

**TABBY.** Tabby is a building material, a form of improvised concrete made by combining **shells** with lime, water, and sand. The mixture was common as a building material in colonial America and the Caribbean and was used well into the 19th century. During this time, many enslaved Africans in southeast North America lived in buildings that included tabby features, while other slaves employed in construction produced and applied the material in other buildings.

Making tabby was a labor-intensive but stable process. Workers would need to gather large numbers of seashells from ocean coasts and then burn them in a furnace to create lime, the bonding agent for the material. Some tabby mixes also might contain the ash remaining from the furnace fire, which also contributed to the mixture setting properly. The lime would then be combined with sand and water to form a base to which more loose shell pieces would be added. When used with small, finely ground shells, tabby can serve as a coarse plaster for sealing brick or timber construction and finishing roofs and floors. Tabby can also be combined with larger shells as well as gravel to form a more substantive building material used to make freestanding walls for small structures. In these cases, workers would pour tabby into wooden molds in successive layers, allowing each to dry before adding another. Tabby hardens into a whitish gray color, depending on the color of shells used in the mix.

The exact origins of tabby's use are unclear. Whatever its beginnings, by the 18th century, it was in use in both West Africa and the southeast American colonies. Some of the earliest uses of tabby were in the buildings of the Spanish colony of Florida. The material's name may have Hispanic origins as well, as suggested by the Spanish word *tapia,* meaning mud wall. One particular example of early Spanish tabby construction was the Castillo San Marcos fort in St. Augustine, Florida. Many African slaves worked on the construction of the fort, which had tabby plaster reinforcing stone walls, floors, roofs, and a gun-firing platform. Following the British siege of the fort in 1702, tabby's use as a building material spread to the British colonies north of Florida. The material became a favorite choice of Georgia's first governor, James Oglethorpe (1696–1785).

Many of the best surviving examples of tabby use can be found in existing slave cabins. A relatively cheap and simple material best suited for simple, sturdy structures,

Tabby construction in ruins of Kingsley plantation, Jacksonville, Florida. (Library of Congress.)

tabby made an ideal material for one-room **slave housing**. Relatively well insulated and water resistant, the walls would withstand rot and seepage, while remaining cooler in the summer. Excellent surviving examples of tabby cabins can be found at the Kingsley plantation in Jacksonville, Florida, and at the Drayton plantation and other sites in Beaufort County, South Carolina.

    ***See also*** Slave Quarters.

FURTHER READING

Adams, Denis. "Tabby: The Oyster Shell Concrete of the Lowcountry," Beaufort County Library. At www.beaufortcountylibrary.org/htdocs-sirsi/tabby.htm.
Merton, Ellis. *Georgia's Disputed Ruins*. Chapel Hill: University of North Carolina Press, 1937.

James Coltrain

**TAR, PITCH, AND TURPENTINE.** Slaves labored in a little-known aspect of Southern history in the production of tar, pitch, and turpentine, the so-called naval stores industry. These were essential commodities for waterproofing wooden sailing vessels in colonial times. To achieve independence from Baltic sources, the British government paid bounties to colonial producers from 1705 until the American

Revolution. The industry centered in the Carolinas because the long-leaf pine, native to the South, was the most prolific yielder of oleoresin.

Tar was the principal product, produced by gathering fragments of long-leaf pines from the ground, stacking them in a circular kiln 30 feet wide by 10 feet high, covering the kiln with green pine boughs and earth, and by controlled burning forcing out the resinous matter that was barreled for market.

During the first three decades of the 18th century, naval stores production centered in the region between North Carolina's Cape Fear River and Charleston, South Carolina. Planters used slaves productively in winter in preparing and burning tar kilns. Overproduction caused a reduction of bounties in 1729, and South Carolina planters accordingly shifted their labor force to **rice** and **indigo** cultivation. Tar became principally a North Carolina product, produced primarily by small white farmers who lived in the pine barrens and worked unassisted.

For a generation after the American Revolution, production of naval stores declined because of the loss of bounties and the introduction of **cotton**. In the 1830s, the industry had a remarkable revival based on the discovery of new uses for turpentine and more extensive use of slave labor. Crude turpentine, when distilled, yielded two valuable products: spirits of turpentine, which was used as an illuminant to replace whale oil and as a solvent in the new rubber industry; and rosin, a by-product used in the manufacture of fine soap and as a lubricant. Improvements in distilling in 1834 increased the yield, and the repeal of British tariffs on turpentine in 1846 boosted prices. By the 1850s, naval stores had emerged as the South's third-largest export crop.

With these inducements planters entered the business, buying or leasing thousands of acres of pine land, and using slave labor—either owned or hired from neighboring planters—to conduct large-scale operations. In the early 1850s as many as 5,000 laborers, not all slaves, were engaged in turpentine operations in North Carolina and perhaps three times that many were supported by the proceeds of the industry. In 1859–1860, 100 slaves on the James R. Grist plantation near Mobile, Alabama, produced more than 26,000 barrels of crude turpentine, yielding more than 3,000 barrels of spirits of turpentine and 15,000 barrels of rosin, worth about $70,000. By 1860, the total value of crude and distilled turpentine produced in the United States was almost $7.5 million, more than $5 million of which was produced in North Carolina. Derivative products brought the total value of the industry to almost $12 million.

In opening a turpentine plantation, a laborer was assigned a task of trees to contain approximately 10,000 boxes and occupying from 50 to 100 acres of land. From October to March, "boxers" were busy cutting elliptical holes in the base of the trees that would hold a quart of turpentine. Above the box the tree was "cornered" by removing two triangular chips to form a V face. The flow of resin into the box then began. From April to October "chippers" returned each 10 days to "chip" the face and reopen the wound to maintain the flow. "Dippers" visited the tree at intervals of two weeks to dip the turpentine from the box, using a flat, iron paddle. The turpentine was placed in wooden buckets that were emptied into barrels stationed throughout the woods. They were transported in two-wheeled carts to a distillery, located near a stream, for distillation into spirits of turpentine and rosin in the same manner in which whiskey was distilled. Nearby was a **cooperage** shop for making barrels. Boxing, coopering, and distilling were the most important aspects of the business, and each commanded a high wage. White distillers were always in demand, usually receiving $25 to $30 per month.

In 1860, a partnership of Grist and Stickney in eastern North Carolina hired 35 slaves from John W. Grist for turpentine production. Among these slaves were one distiller, an assistant distiller, two coopers for making barrels, 15 hands engaged in chipping, a driver, two wagoners—all men—and eight dippers, including four men and four women. In addition there were four small boys, three of whom helped about the still, and one who assisted about the house. There were a woman cook and two elderly women who sewed when able or, according to the contract, did "Nothing."

When slaves were hired, the owner usually specified that the slave should be furnished three suits of clothes, one of which was to be woolen, one pair of stockings, one hat and a **blanket**, one pair of **shoes**, "and Two if worked in Turpentine. . . . All to be well made." In the 1850s, the average price for hiring slaves for turpentine production was about $125 annually, plus board and **clothing**, but by 1860, the price had doubled.

Because of the skill of North Carolina slaves trained in turpentine operations, they sometimes were hired and transported to other parts of the state, even to Florida and Alabama, to open new turpentine plantations. Owners usually sought the consent of their slaves to be sent to another area to work turpentine before committing them to a planter.

Some planters encouraged their slaves to do good work by giving them an honorarium for a crop well attended or by giving them a task and paying for the additional work after the task had been completed. Some permitted them to build a tar kiln on their own time and to sell the tar.

The turpentine business was considered extremely favorable to health and long life. The pure air of the pine forest was considered salubrious for pulmonary diseases. Slaves engaged in turpentine operations were said to be healthier, happier, and more intelligent than those engaged in other pursuits. Turpentine plantation slaves worked as part of a production team, yet at an individual task, rather than in gang labor. This may have contributed to a sense of independence, responsibility, and greater contentment. One writer noted, "it is equally as healthy, and no set of hands have ever been known to willingly leave it and go back to **cotton**."

*See also* Clothing Allotments; Work Routines.

FURTHER READING

Crittenden, C. C. *The Commerce of North Carolina, 1763–1789*. New Haven, CT: Yale University Press, 1936.

Gray, Lewis C. *History of Agriculture in the Southern United States to 1860*. Washington, DC: Carnegie Institution of Washington, 1933.

Macleod, John. "The Tar and Turpentine Business of North Carolina." *Journal of Agriculture 2* (1846): 13–19.

Olmsted, Frederick Law. "A Journey in the Seaboard Slave States: With Remarks on Their Economy." (1856) Electronic Edition. Documenting the American South, University Library of the University of North Carolina at Chapel Hill. At http://docsouth.unc.edu/nc/olmsted/olmsted.html.

Perry, Percival. "The Naval Stores Industry in the Ante-bellum South, 1789–1861." PhD diss., Duke University, 1947.

PERCIVAL PERRY

**TEXTILES.** Essential to life, such as **clothing**, bedding, and items for storing seed and **food**, in antebellum America textiles constituted much of a household's wealth. Even after mass-produced textiles became available, most Southern homes continued to make some of the **cloth** they used. The magnitude of labor involved is hard to imagine. Because each adult required a bare minimum of 13 yards of cloth annually containing up to 90 miles of yarn, preparing the fiber, **spinning**, weaving, dyeing, knitting, and **sewing** were the perpetual burden of every household's female member, notwithstanding race or circumstances. Invalids, the elderly, and girls as young as six were expected to take part. Especially on smaller plantations, slaves and free white women typically labored together under the mistress's supervision, skill determining the role each played in making objects they all used. Antebellum Southern textiles thus present a rare example of slave–slave owner collaborative work.

Enslaved Africans would have found American attitudes about textiles to be familiar. Labor intensive, cloth was a precious commodity in both worlds. Professionals wove some types, whereas others were made at home. Custom and status dictated the kinds of cloth a person used and wore. Rituals demanded special symbol-embellished textiles. Although weavers strove for precision, and repeated motifs and balanced symmetry were the ideal, irregularities and mismatches were considered acceptable. Colors had similar meanings: red conveyed power, blue implied steadfastness and calm, and white, purity. Elites treasured bright European silks and Indian cottons, while blues, browns, and white predominated in most homes. But since **wool**, the most common American fiber, takes dye more readily than **cotton**, the most common African fiber, early American textiles were more likely to be multicolored than their African counterparts.

While attitudes about cloth were similar in both America and Africa, the textile-production methods Africans would encounter in bondage represented an abrupt change in technology, work flow, work space, and gender roles. The history of slave-made textiles thus reflects less a continuation of African craft traditions than a rapid, successful adoption of new materials and tools.

## Preparing the Fibers: Cleaning, Carding, Spinning, and Reeling

In both Africa and the American South, women prepared cotton fiber and spun the yarn. But while African women squeezed the seeds from each cotton boll by rolling it under a stick, in America, one adult (often male) or child fed quantities of cotton through a hand-operated gin (machine or "engine"). On plantations that could not afford a gin, women and children warmed the bolls to loosen the seeds and then picked the seeds out by hand.

### Cotton

In Africa, women flicked a bowstring over the cotton to fluff the fibers and then slowly made a relatively thick yarn using a portable, top-like drop spindle used while they stood or sat on the ground. In America, they rubbed the cotton between bristled paddles called "cards," to align the fibers, and rapidly spun a finer yarn with a foot-powered spinning wheel, used indoors while sitting on a chair or stool.

---

### Picking the Seeds Out of the Cotton

Sabe Rutledge, born in 1861 in South Carolina, recalled the work he did as a child to help process the cotton:

> . . . Mudder spin you know. . . . Have we chillun to sit by the fire place put the light-wood under—blaze up. We four chillun have to pick seed out the cotton. Mudder and Father tell you story to keep you eye open! Pick out cotton seed be we job every night in winter time—cept Sunday! When we grow bigger, Mudder make one card. One would spin and then Mudder go to knitting. Night time picking these cotton seed out; day time in winter getting wood!

*Source:* "Born in Slavery: Slave Narratives from the Federal Writers' Project, 1936–1938," American Memory, Library of Congress. At http://memory.loc.gov/ammem/snhtml/.

---

### *Wool*

Few enslaved Africans would have had been familiar with wool except as an imported accent in luxury textiles woven by men. But in America, wool was the most common fiber. Shearing the sheep appears to have been men's work, while women sorted the fleece according to quality, picked out debris, washed, combed and carded the wool, and spun it on a large standing wheel, walking back and forth to draw out the yarn and wind it onto **corn**-husk spindles often made by children.

### *Bast Fibers*

Bast fibers are the skeletons of plants like flax (*Linum usitatissimum*), jute (*Sida rhombifolia*), and caesarweed (*Urena lobata*). In America and Europe, flax was left to rot in trenches, pulverized with a brake and scutching knife, then drawn over progressively finer iron combs (hatchels) to extract long fibers that were spun into yarn on a foot-powered wheel. The longest fibers were reserved for the finest cloth, while the shorter fibers, called "tow," were used for rope, sacks, and clothing worn by laborers and slaves. Except for spinning, most of this work was done by men. Africans similarly processed jute and caesarweed and peeled strands from raphia palm (*Raphia regalis*) but spun these fibers on a drop spindle, twisted them together by hand, or used them individually.

In America, once the cotton, wool, or **linen** yarn was spun, it was wound into twisted bundles called hanks using an I-shaped stick (called a niddy-noddy). Commonly, female slaves were required to spin and wind a certain amount of yarn each night.

### Dyeing

To successfully absorb dye, the yarn had to be washed, rinsed, and usually simmered overnight in a chemical solution that made the dye stick to the fibers. This process, called "mordanting," was new to enslaved Africans, but they soon learned how to determine a mordant's strength and its effect on different fibers. Mordants could make

## Spinning, Weaving, and Dyeing

Josephine Bristow recalled textile production on her South Carolina plantation:

De people used to spin en weave, my Lord! Like today, it cloudy en rainy, dey couldn' work in de field en would have to spin dat day. Man, you would hear dat thing windin en I remember, I would stand dere en want to spin so bad, I never know what to do. Won' long fore I got to whe' I could use de shuttle en weave, too. I had a grandmother en when she would get to dat wheel, she sho know what she been doin. White folks used to give de colored people task to spin en I mean she could do dat spinnin. Yes'um, I here to tell you, dey would make de prettiest cloth in dat day en time. Old time people used to have a kind of dye dey called indigo en dey would color de cloth just as pretty as you ever did see.

*Source:* George P. Rawick, ed. *The American Slave: South Carolina Narratives,* Vol. 2. Westport, CT: Greenwood Press, 1972.

Adeline Willis's mother, enslaved in Georgia, was especially skilled at dying fabrics:

And my mother was one of the best dyers anywhere 'round, and I was too. I did make the most colors by mixing up all kinds of bark and leaves. I recollect the prettiest sort of a lilac color I made with maple bark and pine bark, not the outside pine bark, but that little thin skin that grows right down next to the tree—it was pretty, that color was.

*Source:* George P. Rawick, ed. *The American Slave: Georgia Narratives,* Vol. 13. Westport, CT: Greenwood Press, 1972.

George Coleman, formerly enslaved in Mississippi, was a weaver:

I milked the cows, 'tended the sheep and ran the loom in the weaving room. Lots of times I would weave at night. I could weave two and one half yards of cloth a day. We dyed the cloth with maple bark, Red Oak bark and copprice. The bark was boiled to make the dye. Red oak would make the cloth deep blue, so would maple bark, the copprice would make it yellow. Then I carried special messages to Mr. Dave when he'd be out on the plantation. The thread we used to weave the cloth was "soused" (meaning sized) and wound on a "skittle" (meaning shuttle) and hit with a "slay" (meaning sledge). The "skittle" was about sixteen inches long.

*Source:* George P. Rawick, ed. *The American Slave: Mississippi Narratives,* Supp. Ser. 1, Vol. 7, Part 2. Westport, CT: Greenwood Press, 1978.

Interior of weaving house, ca. 1821, showing remains of a cotton gin. The gin is thought to have been made locally in the 19th century by William Ellison, a free black carpenter and entrepreneur. Borough House, Stateburg, South Carolina. (Library of Congress.)

pokeberries dye pale pink or deep violet, and onion skins orange, yellow, or dark brown. Some dyes had to be purchased, but others were homemade, as were most mordants: rusty nails were soaked to produce copperas (ferrous sulfate), and alum came from stale urine (ammonia alum or chamber lye) or potash (potassium aluminum sulfate), made by evaporating water poured through wood ash. Because cotton and linen resisted dye, typically they were used in their natural state and were combined with dyed wool in lightweight, durable, and colorful fabrics called "linsey" and "jean."

To dye enough yarn for three pairs of socks or four yards of cloth, as much as a bushel of plant material had to be collected. Women and children pulverized leaves, berries, roots, nut hulls, bark and wood; soaked and boiled them; and strained this concentrated dye into a vat of water. Hanks of mordanted yarn were added, boiled and left to soak, and finally rinsed and dried.

*Indigo*

**Indigo**, a durable blue dye used in both Europe and Africa, uniquely bonds to any fiber through oxidation, turning blue as it contacts the air; the mordant, alum, is mixed with the dye. In America, slaves prepared indigo using not the methods of their ancestral homeland but those that Europeans had brought from India in the 16th century. Indigo plants were cut to the ground in June and August, loaded into a huge cypress vat, or, on a smaller scale, a pine barrel, covered with water, and left to ferment. The resulting greenish liquid was strained into another container and then stirred until blue dye granules settled on the bottom. These granules were scooped into sacks to drain and then spread into molds and cut into squares like bars of soap. Most American home dyeing with indigo was done by pulverizing one of these bars with madder root (*Rubia tinctorum*) in vinegar and then adding it to a vat of chamber lye and leaving it to stand for a week. A less noxious dye pot could be made by adding a solution of pulverized indigo, potash, and water to a pine barrel of water, copperas, and slaked lime, which was made by adding burned oyster shells to water.

The dyed hanks of yarn were next rewound into balls for knitting or onto spindles for weaving using a windmill-like device called a "weasel" or "swift." These spindles would be placed in a rack called a "scarn," and then simultaneously wrapped on a warping frame to measure out the cloth's long warp (vertical) yarns. Finally, hundreds of these yarns would be threaded individually by hand into heddles in the loom's

---

### Slave Mistress Directs the Cloth Production

Sarah Felder, born about 1853 in Mississippi, talked about the concerted efforts to produce textiles on her mistress's estate:

> Old Mistis work hard all de time. She hed a big room whar sum of de women was busy wid de cards, an' spinnin' an' de looms. Miss Vickey niver lowed de women ter rest. She med 'em wurk at night an' when it was rainin' she wus rite dar ter see dey wus wurkin'. She kep' de looms goin' an' made all kind uf pretty cloth, an' dey made "coverlets" jes as pretty as dey make 'em now. She made sum uf de wimmin git bark out uf de woods an' dye sum uf dat thread, an' it sho' made pritty coverlets. An' den she hed ter dye her thread ter make pants an' coats. She made de pants an' coats outen blue jeans [cloth]. She kep' sum uf de wimin sewin an' dey made mity fine things fur old Mistis an' her chilluns, an' dey made sum things fer us, but what we got wus made frum cloth spun dar at home, an' it niver wore out.

*Source:* George P. Rawick, ed. *The American Slave: Mississippi Narratives,* Supp. Ser. 1, Vol. 7, Part 2. Westport, CT: Greenwood Press, 1978.

---

comb-like reed, which lifted the yarns and determined the cloth's pattern. A 30-inch-wide linsey could contain up to 360 warp threads, each as much as 100 feet long.

## Weaving

In both Africa and America, most cloth was made by weaving, in solids, stripes, checks, and patterns that weavers named after historic events and everyday objects. The looms used and the gender of the weaver differed greatly, however.

In Africa, male weavers, regarded as professionals, sat on a stool before a portable, single- or double-harness loom, creating a very long strip of horizontally or vertically striped cloth 3 to 10 inches wide. When cut into segments and joined by the lengthwise edges to form a large panel that men wore like a toga, the overall effect was of a plaid or checked cloth with a decorative border along the bottom edge. Women wove for their own use, sitting on the ground before a portable, vertical loom that used sticks called swords rather than harnesses, creating a shorter strip of cloth about 20 inches wide in solid white, blue or brown checks, or stripes. This was cut in half and joined into a larger panel that women wore like a sarong.

In America, male weavers were usually professionals, while most women wove as part of their household duties. The only cloth woven exclusively by men was the jacquard coverlet, a bedcovering filled with realistic and symbolic images usually commissioned by women for their households. Both men and women used the bench loom. As big as a bed, it had a heavy frame and as many as four harnesses, was often located in an outbuilding, and produced cloth as wide as the weaver's arm span, up to 45 inches. Sometimes two or three panels were joined to form large cloths such as blankets and sheets, but most cloth was cut up and sewn into garments. Despite their unfamiliarity with this loom, enslaved African women readily adapted to it, and they and their descendants

Enslaved women spun yarn and wove textiles of many types. From *Sketchbook of Landscapes in the State of Virginia* by Lewis Miller, Virginia, 1853–1867, watercolor and ink on paper. (Abby Aldrich Rockefeller Folk Art Museum, The Colonial Williamsburg Foundation. Gift of Dr. and Mrs. Richard M. Kain in memory of George Hay Kain.)

became expert in using it to weave cloth as well as coverlets in the same patterns as their white counterparts. Many slave weavers also had other tasks; several former slaves recalled that house servants and cooks often did the weaving.

In a few instances, slaves were employed at textile mills. From 1846 until it was destroyed by fire in 1855, Florida's largest and most successful textile mill operated at Arcadia, north of Pensacola, where about 100 female slaves ages 15 to 20 used the latest power looms to weave as much as 1,300 yards of cotton cloth each day.

### Knitting and Crocheting

Knitting and crocheting were new crafts that enslaved Africans encountered in America. For needles, they might use what they could find, such as bone, wire, and sticks. Young female slaves learned to knit from their mothers and the mistress and from the age of six appear to have spent every free moment knitting for all who lived on the plantation. Girls were often required to knit a certain amount, such as a finger width, each day. Even the coarsest pair of work socks for slaves could contain more than 5,000 stitches using 200 yards of yarn.

### Sewing

Of secondary importance for most West African women, sewing well was a valuable skill in America. Because the sewing machine was not in widespread home use until the end of the Civil War, slave women joined fabric for clothing and household articles by hand, often using 20 tiny stitches per inch to create a durable, stress-resistant seam. Sewing also took the form of repairing garments with stitching alone (darning) or with patches, and embellishing with embroidery. However, most embroidery appears to have been done for the slave owner rather than for the slaves' own use, probably because of the time and materials required.

*See also* Negro Cloth.

FURTHER READING

Adrosko, Rita J., and Margaret Smith Furry. *Natural Dyes and Home Dyeing*. Mineola, NY: Dover, 1971.

"Born in Slavery: Slave Narratives from the Federal Writers' Project, 1936–1938," American Memory, Library of Congress. At http://memory.loc.gov/ammem/snhtml/.

Cannon, John F. M., Margaret J. Cannon, and Gretel Dalby-Quenet. *Dye Plants and Dyeing*. Portland, OR: Timber Press, 1994.

Channing, Marion L. *The Textile Tools of Colonial Homes*. New Bedford, MA: Reynolds-DeWalt Printing, 1969.

Foster, Helen Bradley. *New Raiments of Self: African American Clothing in the Antebellum South*. Oxford: Berg, 1997.

Gilfoy, Peggy Stoltz. *Patterns of Life: West African Strip-Weaving Traditions*. Washington, DC: Published for the National Museum of African Art by the Smithsonian Institution Press, 1987.

Kriger, Colleen E. *Cloth in West African History*. Lanham, MD: AltaMira Press, 2006.

MacRae, Ann Cameron. *Women at the Loom: Handweaving in Washington County, Tennessee, 1840–1860*. MA thesis, East Tennessee State University, 2001. At www.etd-submit.etsu.edu/etd/theses/available/etd-0330101-134816/unrestricted/MacRae0420.pdf.

Rucker, Brian. "Arcadia and Bagdad: Industrial Parks of Antebellum Florida." *Florida Historical Quarterly* 67, no. 2 (October 1988): 147–165.

Weissman, Judith Reiter, and Wendy Lavitt. *Labors of Love: America's Textiles and Needlework, 1650–1930*. New York: Knopf, 1987.

LEIGH FELLNER

**THUMB PIANOS.** The thumb piano is a uniquely Sub-Saharan African type of lamellophone that might have originated in Asia but was developed anew by African musicians. A handheld percussion instrument made of wood or **gourd**, it has the shape of a board, box, or bowl. Attached to the frame are metal or bamboo tongues, referred to as "lamellae," which the musician depresses or plucks with the thumbs and forefingers.

Many variations of the thumb piano are found throughout Sub-Saharan Africa; it is most often referred to as the "mbira," "kalimba," or "likembe." The earliest European description of the instrument was recorded in 1589 by Father Dos Santos (d. 1622), a Portuguese missionary, who said it produced a sweet and gentle harmony, and in the late 19th century, English explorer James Theodore Bent (1852–1897) called it decidedly melodious and likened it to a spinet. The instrument was and is still used for religious ceremonies as well as for secular activities and events.

In western Africa, ancient varieties had tongues made of bamboo. In Ghana, the instrument is referred to as the "mbila" or "sansa." In the eastern and central Africa, the tongues were made from iron or metal. *Kalimba* is the term for the instrument most often used by the Nsenga, Ngoni, Cewa, Nyungwe, and Chikunda societies in the Zambezi River basin; evidence suggests that the instrument has a more than 1,000-year history in that region. Shona societies in Zambia and Zimbabwe still have an especially rich tradition with their version of the kalimba, called the mbira. It is the largest of all the instrument's varieties in 21st-century Africa.

Enslaved Africans brought the thumb piano to the Caribbean and North and South America. In Brazil and other places, slave musicians developed it as the marimba, which is a much larger instrument, and in Cuba, the marímbula was born from the thumb piano. The marimba has played a central role in the development of jazz and modern Caribbean and Latin music, and a more modern lamellophone developed by the Yoruban people (Nigeria) resembles the Cuban marímbula.

FURTHER READING

Berliner, Paul. *The Soul of Mbira: Music and Traditions of the Shona People of Zimbabwe.* Chicago: University of Chicago Press, 1993.

Davies, Carole Boyce. "Kalimba." In *Encyclopedia of the African Diaspora: Origins, Experiences, and Culture*, Vol. 2, 602–603. Santa Barbara, CA: ABC-CLIO, 2008.

Montagu, Jeremy. "Mbira," Oxford Music Online. At www.oxfordmusiconline.com.

LINDA E. MERIANS

**TOBACCO.** The production of tobacco, a high-priced luxury item, was the focus of Chesapeake labor through most of the colonial era. Indeed, it was the labor-intensive nature of tobacco production that caused the colonies of Virginia and Maryland to adopt slavery as the most economically advantageous way of producing it. By the early decades of the 18th century, that human involvement was largely slave labor, especially on larger plantations. All the tedious manual work was implemented by enslaved workers, which sometimes included their participation in critical decision making.

The tobacco cycle began early each year with the burning of a nursery plot or "plant bed." For this, piles of brush, cut limbs, or old **corn** stalks were burned at the south-sloping edge of a fertile woodland. This slow-burning fire sterilized the soil surface, killing seeds, insects, and their eggs. When cool, the surface soil was mixed with the residual ash to make a smooth, fine bed for receiving the tiny seeds that were broadcast over it. The seeds, resembling ground coffee, were mixed with a carrying agent like talcum powder or sifted ash so that the seeds, in suspension, could be distributed over a given area of bed. The correct ratio of seed to bed size ensured adequate spacing to prevent competition and promote strong seedlings. The broadcast seed mixture was not covered, but rather tamped down using feet, and covered with brush when a late frost threatened the tender young plants. Seed beds were prepared and sown during the first three months of the new year.

During the germination and early growth of tobacco seedlings in the plant bed, the field that would receive them was prepared. Male and female slaves toiled together on tobacco plantations in gangs or groups, although by the end of the 18th century, more women than men worked in the fields, joined by young children of both sexes. Virgin or "new" ground, which was always preferred, had to be cleared of timber and large roots using felling axes, mattocks, and grubbing **hoes.**

Alternatively, trees could be girdled or "belted" by merely cutting through the bark and cambium to kill the standing tree and thus allow sunshine to reach the rich soil. If the field was already cleared, a heavy turning plow drawn by oxen or **horses** and a harrow to smooth the newly turned soil would be used. The next step in preparing the field was raising hills.

Tobacco was a "hoe-hill" Native American crop characterized by small mounds of earth that were drawn up for each tobacco plant to grow on. Such work was accomplished with a narrow or hilling hoe. Hills were raised three to six feet apart on a marked grid depending how good the soil was. On weaker soils, cattle manure might be incorporated into the hill to provide the high amount of nutrients good tobacco required.

Both field readiness and plant size, which was four to six inches tall, or "leaves the size of a shilling," had to converge on a rainy or wet day in the month of May for transplanting ("pitching") to commence. Young plants were drawn from the bed, placed in **baskets**, and taken to the field for placement in each hill using fingers, a small pointed stick or dibble. Only if dry conditions occurred immediately after transplantation, when the seedling was weakest, would water be carried to this field crop. Within three days, the wilted plants were normally standing.

Tobacco is a rather unique crop in that it is highly manipulated, being produced leaf by leaf like horticultural or garden crops but is grown on a field scale. Given the attention required, each laborer was able to produce only one to three acres of tobacco, as opposed to 5 to 10 acres of corn or **wheat** by hand. Its production is an art requiring judgment and experience more than technology or material input. Experienced slaves could make those critical decisions.

The next phase of tobacco production was to protect the plants from weed competition and the leaves from insect damage as they rapidly expanded. Weeds were "chopped" out using broad or weeding hoes, by advancing down the "alleys," which were the spaces between the rows of hills, as a work group or "gang." Singing and talking were common as stronger workers led the pace. Tobacco fields generally were kept cleaner than other crop fields. Any "ground worms," which fed at night and were

---

### Tobacco Fields

As an enslaved child, Simon Stokes worked in the Virginia tobacco fields:

Me sho' didn't like dat job, pickin' worms off de terbaccer plants; fo' our oberseer wuz de meanes old hound you'se eber seen, he hed hawk eyes fer seein' de worms on de terbaccer, so yo' sho' hed ter git dem all, or you'd habe ter bite all de worms dat yo' miss into, or git three lashes on yo' back wid his old lash, and dat wuz powfull bad, wusser dan bittin' de worms, fer yo' could bite right smart quick, and dat wuz all dat dar wuz ter it; but dem lashes done last a pow'full long time.

*Source:* George P. Rawick, ed. *The American Slave: Kansas, Kentucky, Maryland, Ohio, Virginia, and Tennessee Narratives*, Vol. 16. Westport, CT: Greenwood Press, 1972.

Colonial Williamsburg interpreter portrays an enslaved woman cultivating tobacco at Jamestown, Virginia. (The Colonial Williamsburg Foundation.)

located just beneath the soil surface near the plant, could damage or destroy young plants. They were to be destroyed, as were "horn worms," whose eggs were laid periodically on the undersurface of the leaves at night and also had to be found and destroyed. And "bud worms," found in the crown or top of the plant where the small new leaves emerge, similarly had to be eradicated. Worming and cultivating the crop constituted the most tedious and unpleasant aspects of tobacco crop management. This work required an individual to possess stamina during warm days plus a limber back and a sharp eye, rather than physical strength.

In June, the young plants began reproducing by forming a flower-budding stalk. This stalk was broken off down to the number of remaining leaves to be carried, 6 to 10 during the colonial period, depending on the quality of the soil. Henceforth, new leaves would not be generated, except by "suckering." Suckers formed between the main stalk and each selected leaf. They, too, were removed, like the top, to direct growth into the limited number of remaining leaves. The object was to produce as many large, heavy, and perfect leaves as possible. A few plants were left to naturally reproduce for future seeds.

In the Chesapeake Tidewater region, tobacco plants began to mature or ripen in late July or early August. Signs of ripeness included curling leaf edges and tips, yellow mottling throughout the leaf surface, and a drier feel and puffy appearance. Harvesting was accomplished by pushing a thin-bladed tobacco knife down the stalk to its base, effectively splitting the stalk in half lengthwise to expose the moist interior pith. The plant was severed at its base and turned upside down to prevent "sunburn" during the heat of the day. Either intense sun or the threat of rain limited the number of plants cut at one time. Two or three cutting cycles usually cleared the field.

After wilting to become flexible, the plants were gathered and heaped for a short "sweat," a heated prefermentation, before being draped over tobacco sticks. About 6 to 10 plants straddled a four-and-a-half-foot-long stick. Loaded sticks were temporarily hung on outdoor scaffolds and fences, or were taken directly into the tobacco barn (also called "tobacco house") to be hung for curing. Thus, tobacco's outdoor lifecycle came to an end.

Tobacco curing represented the climax of its production, where through physical and chemical transformation it changed into usable tobacco: brown or yellow, aromatic, valuable, and leather-like. Curing occurred through a reduction of moisture or drying, so the changing interior atmosphere of the well-ventilated barn was monitored in relation to the tobacco's location within the structure. Air that was too hot, moist, or still could adversely affect the cure. Therefore, the plants on the sticks as well as the sticks themselves were moved around within the barn to ensure even air circulation, a process called "regulating." If too hot, green plants could permanently turn a blue-green color and be ruined—a condition known as "house burn." If a weather system stalled, creating warm, moist, still air for more than two days, mold spores could begin reproducing, producing a white or black cast to the leaf. In this case, planters would close the barn and set small smokeless fires in the dirt floor to drive out the moisture and hopefully save the crop.

If all went well, the tobacco was fully transformed in four to six weeks. Now attention shifted toward securing the leaf for transit and meeting the desires of the buyers of the raw material: the manufacturing tobacconists of England and northern Europe.

When the leaf was fully cured with no green remaining anywhere, and when the atmosphere allowed the leaf to be in perfect "order," that is, not too dry and not too moist, the plants were taken down ("struck"), "bulked" or piled into a tight heap, and covered to preserve their condition. Throughout the next several months, cured tobacco plants were taken out of the bulk for further processing.

Cured flexible leaves were stripped from their stalks and sorted according to quality, and those of similar quality were tied into bundles or "hands" of five to seven leaves each. Again, this work was often done by slaves and required their judgment. Tied hands in turn were bulked and covered until all tobacco was so processed. This phase of selection, security, and presentation of the leaf could extend through the winter and early spring as moist weather conditions allowed. Packing the shipping cask or tobacco hogshead constituted the last critical operation on the plantation. By this time, a new seed bed already could have been burned and sown.

Whole-leaf tobacco was packed by enslaved workers into shipping casks called tobacco hogsheads. This packing process was called "prizing," a word meaning to pry or leverage something. In this case, it was cured tobacco, either tied into bundles or hands of five to seven leaves, or loose-stemmed tobacco leaves with their central ribs or spines removed. In both cases, the tobacco had to be in good order, case or condition, denoting correct moisture content. Leaves containing too much moisture could spoil or be crushed easier. Leaves too dry could shatter into flakes. Properly prized tobacco shipped more securely and at lower cost.

Tobacco was loaded into the casks ("barrels") in a tight, regular, and level manner by hand. A worker would first get into the empty cask and lay the hands or stemmed leaf halves lengthwise from one side of the cask to the other. Some overlapping and empty space filling might be required to ensure even raising and close density. The next layer of hands would run opposite, or perpendicular, to the first, with subsequent layers continuing this pattern so that a level surface was maintained. Radial or other regular patterns could be used as long as the tobacco was densely packed without "soft spots," and the mass remained level. Throughout this placement, the worker was using his body weight to compact the leaves. Indeed, such "foot packing" was the only force used through much of the 17th century. Once 12 inches or so of leaf was built up, the worker got out of the cask. A wooden disk called a "false head" was then placed over the tobacco to function as a pressure plate.

Although some planters used screw presses, like a large apple cider press, most used homemade lever presses to exert mechanical power for maximum compaction. This was little more than a long timber or prize beam where the larger end was fit into a rectangular mortise (hole) cut through a standing tree. The loose fit of these components allowed the beam to be raised and lowered from the opposite end. A large second-class lever was thus created.

A small, level, wooden platform was placed next to the tree on which the tobacco hogshead cask would stand. Following each loading of tobacco, the false head was set in place and a series of crossed wooden blocks were built up to the raised arm above. Two parallel and spaced blocks went over the head first, followed by two more set perpendicular, then two more the other way, and so on until the crib was formed and a physical connection to the beam was made.

With the heavy beam in a raised position, often achieved with a counterlever, the prize was ready to compact the tobacco further. At the opposite end of the beam hung a wooden pallet suspended from the beam end by ropes, like a swing. Heavy stones or any weighty objects were placed on this platform to exert pressure on the tobacco through the beam and cribbing. When the heavy pallet would descend no more, often the next day, the stones were tumbled off and the process repeated until no more tobacco would fit into the hogshead. James Wilson, a middling planter in Somerset County, Maryland, noted increments of 420, 175, 105, 120, 110, 115, and 35 pounds to finish his fourth hogshead weighing 1,080 pounds on April 21, 1773.

Planters tried to get as much tobacco as possible into each standard-size hogshead because shipping charges were calculated by size, not by weight. A tun (not a 2,000 pound ton) of shipping was four tobacco hogsheads, regardless of weight. But if a planter became greedy, he could damage the leaf by crushing it, causing it to become bruised or blackened, especially if it was prized in too high.

When completely filled, the permanent head or lid was nailed in place and braced tightly. The appropriately marked heavy hogshead was now ready to leave the plantation for the closest tobacco inspection warehouse, where officials of the local colonial government would open and inspect its contents for minimal quality. If it passed the quality check, its owner would receive a tobacco note that could be negotiated like money. The tobacco would remain safely in the warehouse until transferred to an awaiting tobacco ship sailing for England.

*See also* Cooperage; Tobacco Barns; Tobacco Factories; Tobacco Pipes.

FURTHER READING

Gray, Lewis Cecil. *History of Agriculture in the Southern United States to 1860.* 1933. Reprint, Gloucester, MA: Peter Smith, 1958.

Herndon, G. Melvin. *William Tatham and the Culture of Tobacco.* Coral Gables, FL: University of Miami Press, 1969.

Kulikoff, Alan. *Tobacco and Slaves*. Chapel Hill: University of North Carolina Press, 1986.

WAYNE RANDOLPH

**TOBACCO BARNS. Tobacco** barns were sites of a slave's seasonal **work routine**. Barns served the curing and stripping stages of processing tobacco; sometimes prizing—or packing—took place there too. Larger plantations that used the quarter system for agricultural work might have had numerous barns amid tobacco fields.

Planters and their slaves built tobacco barns for air-curing tobacco, using impermanent methods of construction. The 18th-century Chesapeake barn was often a 20- by 40-foot rectangle, with a simple gable roof, hole-set posts, dirt floor, and doors on the sides and ends. In tobacco barns, roof joists and collar beams tied only every other pair of rafters together, leaving the horizontal beams open as tier poles that held the short (about 4 foot long) sticks on which slaves hung the tobacco. The single-story height and simple ladders facilitated workers climbing up into the rafters to hang and remove the drying crop.

For tobacco varieties like Virginia, Orinoco, and Burley, slaves—women, men, and older children—cut whole plants, carted them to the barn, and used a spike or **nail** to fix each plant to a stick. Workers hung the sticks of tobacco in barns in late summer and for four to eight weeks adjusted the air moving through the barn by opening doors and vertical or horizontal vents in the barn siding. During extended rain or cold, slaves might have to spend hours in the barn keeping smudge pots or small fires smoldering, potentially dangerous work in a highly flammable environment. When the crop was cured, slaves took down the leaves so a few skilled workers—both women and men—could pull the fibrous stems from the softer leaf. The barn functioned merely as shelter for this process.

The adoption of flue curing in the early 19th century demanded changes to these barns, which needed to be airtight to maximize forced heat in an enclosed space. Flue-curing barns were small (as little as 16 by 16 feet), had a single door, and had a firebox built into the dirt floor with flues to carry the heat through the barn. During curing, slaves camped next to the barn day and night to stoke the fire through a small door to the firebox that opened low on an exterior wall. The discovery of "bright leaf" tobacco in Caswell County, North Carolina, in 1839 is attributed to an enslaved man named Stephen on the farm of Abisha Slade (1799–ca. 1870). Stephen fell asleep tending the fire, then stoked it high when he saw it was almost out. The burst of heat turned the leaves a bright golden color with an appealing flavor that became the hallmark of the Virginia–North Carolina Bright Leaf Belt. The bright leaf regions required smaller farms with fewer slaves. Slaves working in Bright Leaf tobacco picked the crop leaf by leaf, letting each plant maximize larger leaves. Workers used cord to string leaves on the sticks for hanging.

Beyond the seasonal cycle, slaves may have spent time in barns as alternative shelters or social spaces removed from regular living areas of the plantation.

*See also* Tobacco Factories; Tobacco Pipes.

FURTHER READING

Hart, John Fraser, and Eugene Cotton Mather. "The Character of Tobacco Barns and Their Role in the Tobacco Economy of the United States." *Annals of the Association of American Geographers* 51, no. 3 (September 1961): 274–293.

Ridout, Orlando V. "The Chesapeake Farm Buildings Survey." *Perspectives in Vernacular Architecture* 1 (1982): 137–149.

"Tobacco in Virginia," Virginia Places. At www.virginiaplaces.org/agriculture/tobacco.html.

SUSAN A. KERN

**TOBACCO FACTORIES.** While the early American South famously links slavery and **tobacco** in agricultural work, slave labor defined antebellum urban slavery in tobacco manufacturing centers.

During the colonial period, planters cured their tobacco and then sold it. Manufacturing the leaf into commercial products—ground for snuff or cut for pipe tobacco—happened overseas. Following the Revolution, small factories opened in the United States, primarily to process tobacco for pipe or cigar smoking, or for chewing. The use of slave labor in larger factories grew during the 1840s and 1850s as the discovery of Bright Leaf tobacco increased the popularity of smoking, and the improved transportation of canals and railroads made larger factories profitable.

Slaves in tobacco factories in cities like Richmond, Petersburg, Danville, or Lynchburg, Virginia, performed both heavy and skilled work. Much of the heavier male labor was in warehouses, offloading, opening, and unpacking the hogsheads used in shipping the crop. Slaves working as clerks marked, recorded, and managed the movement of the materials from warehouse to factory. Other workers—men, women, and children—carried the dried leaves to tables, where skilled workers sorted the leaves, stripped stems and foreign matter from the leaves, and cut leaves into shreds of tobacco. Other workers swept floors and carted trimmings from the work areas. Tobacco moved in bulk to shops where it was sold from jars on counters—consumer packaging was yet to come. Work in the factories was dusty, smelly, and dreadfully hot or cold depending on the season.

The use of slave labor in factories changed the face of slavery in urban areas. Richmond, Virginia, had 50 factories that illustrate the range of the enslaved factory experience. Factory work provided some stories of hard work and moral fortitude leading to escape from slavery, as in the case of Lott Cary (ca. 1780–1828), who worked as a shipping clerk in a Richmond warehouse. There he refined his reading skills and saved enough money to purchase freedom for himself and his family, ultimately putting his resources into the African Missionary Society and immigrating to Africa. Many other stories, however, recount harsher subjugation. During the 1850s and 1860s, one-half to two-thirds of slaves in factories were hired laborers and by 1860, more than 3,400 male slaves, more than half of Richmond's adult male slave population, worked in tobacco factories. Masters who hired out their slaves made money, as did factory owners, but factory work gave slaves access to wages as well. New black codes enacted in Richmond during the 1850s responded to white fears that black purchasing power meant gambling, prostitution, and other vices concentrated in black neighborhoods.

Other moralists decried hiring out and blamed urban factory work as undermining the slave system that already was balanced precariously on slaves in agricultural and domestic work.

After the Civil War, the story of freed blacks working in tobacco factories is but part of the urbanization of black labor and the rise of cigarette manufacturing and big corporations toward the end of the 19th century.

*See also* Cooperage; Slave Badges; Tobacco Barns; Tobacco Pipes.

FURTHER READING

Ashworth, John. *Slavery, Capitalism, and Politics in the Antebellum Republic.* New York: Cambridge University Press, 1995.

Documenting the American South Collection, University Library of the University of North Carolina at Chapel Hill. At http://docsouth.unc.edu.

Gurley, Ralph Randolph. *Life of Jehudi Ashmun, Late Colonial Agent in Liberia. With an Appendix, Containing Extracts from His Journal and Other Writings; With a Brief Sketch of the Life of The Rev. Lott Cary.* Washington, DC: James C. Dunn, 1835.

Robert, Joseph Clarke. *The Tobacco Kingdom: Plantation, Market, and Factory in Virginia and North Carolina, 1800–1860.* Durham: Duke University Press, 1938.

Schnittman, Suzanne. "Black Workers in Antebellum Richmond." In *Race, Class, and Community in Southern Labor History*, edited by Gary M. Fink and Merl E. Reed, 72–86. Tuscaloosa: University of Alabama Press, 1994.

SUSAN A. KERN

**TOBACCO PIPES. Tobacco** pipes played a role in the life and death of many enslaved workers in colonial and antebellum America. Slaves smoked tobacco in pipes, made their own pipes, and buried pipes with loved ones as **grave** goods. Additionally, the remains of tobacco pipes on both rural and urban sites offer archaeologists evidence of the spatial divisions of work and leisure activities that illustrate the social divisions between people in the past. Visitors to the colonial Chesapeake commented that both men and women, old and young, smoked tobacco while working and resting, although other evidence indicates that men tended to be the greater users of tobacco.

A tobacco pipe can be a simple device that requires only a vessel or bowl to hold dried plant matter and a stem through which smokers draw air into the mouth through the burning tobacco. Pipes can be cast or carved as a single piece of clay, wood, stone, metal, or other material or may be a composite, with different materials for the bowl, the stem, and decorative elements. The stem needs to be long enough to cool the smoke so it does not burn the smoker's lungs and, depending on the material of the bowl, provide a reasonably cool place to hold the pipe away from the burning bowl. Smoking a pipe requires a source of ignition for the material in the pipe bowl, such as a hot coal held with tongs or paper or wooden splints lit in a nearby flame.

Africans smoked plant material through pipes well before the Portuguese introduced tobacco from South America into the African continent in the 16th century, long before the rise of Atlantic slavery. Africans used pipes for smoking intoxicating substances as part of ritual, or as **medicine**, or simply for relaxation. Africans made pipes from carved wood, clay, and other material. In addition to single-user pipes,

Africans also made flat-bottomed pipes that could be set down among communal users, a form rarely seen outside of Africa or South America.

The most familiar 17th- and 18th-century pipes in European North America were molded, long-stemmed, white ball clay pipes made in English or Dutch factories. White clay pipes in the European fashion also were molded in America but not in the great numbers that European factories produced. The fragments of these fragile ceramic pipes show up on domestic sites of all economic and social classes. Additionally, **slave ships** carried quantities of pipes and gave their captives **rations** of tobacco during their crossing. By the late 18th century, whites made a distinction between fashionable pipes and "negro pipes," which they commented were shorter than European or English pipes.

Some pipes made from American red clays followed European styles, while others had the angular lines and scale of Native American pipe forms. The "Chesapeake Pipe Controversy" focuses on a group of pipes made with local red clays. These pipes bear decoration that many scholars attribute to Native Americans, whereas others see precedents in African art. The small number of pipes with decoration use dentate (toothed) lines to mark fields and depict quadruped animal forms, similar to designs in African, Native American, and European art. Because many of these pipes occur in contexts that predate the institutionalization of slavery, they may be associated with bound labor generally and a growing need for social groups to develop material culture that distinguishes them from others.

Stem pipes, also called penny pipes or Pamplin pipes, were common in antebellum America and echo a form familiar in Africa and Germany, where the pipe bowl and stem were separate pieces. The most famous manufacturer of these pipes was in Pamplin, Virginia, after 1860, although individuals produced pipes in this form before the mid-18th century. American stem pipes had a molded red clay bowl with a short stem or socket, into which the smoker inserted a fresh reed or other hollow tube to make a complete stem. The smoker then could replace the stem over and over and easily carry the reusable short, stout, ceramic bowl that was relatively strong compared with white ball clay pipes.

Another group of pipes was carved from stone, usually soft steatite or soapstone. Native Americans used this material for pipes during the late Woodland period (900–1600 CE) and continued using it after European contact. Slaves may have carved steatite into the pipes with small round bowls and short stems that are found on the **slave quarters** sites associated with Thomas Jefferson's (1743–1826) slaves at Poplar Forest and on Mulberry Row at Monticello, which lie near naturally occurring soapstone. Like other material culture associated with the enslaved, Chesapeake pipes and stone pipes prompt examination of the nature of exchange among Indians, blacks, and whites in colonial and early America.

By the 18th century, tobacco became synonymous with the Virginia colony and with African slavery. Tobacco manufacturers marked and advertised their product with labels that often depicted black slaves. On many of these labels, a slave, usually male, holds a long European clay pipe with one hand and holds an agricultural tool—a **hoe** or shovel—in his other hand and is posed in a field. The inefficiency of holding a long pipe means that he is not working, but the other tool he holds implies his labor. Other labels depict slaves working and a white man, presumably a planter or overseer, smoking as he watches over their work. A few other images of slaves or just-freed slaves show smoking while walking alongside a wagon or sitting and performing other labor, or in images satirizing the social dangers of city life.

Slaves clearly had access to tobacco for smoking. Tobacco may have been a **ration** given by their owners, while other tobacco may have been from plants they grew, dried, and ground themselves, with or without their owner's consent. Tobacco was part of slaves' alternative economy in many parts of America. Some slaves smoked while working; others smoked during leisure time. The dangers of lung and mouth cancer were not understood until the 20th century; in fact, European **medicine** based on balancing the body's humors associated smoker's phlegm with the healthy exchange of warm, dry smoke for moist, cold expectorant. While many critics commented on the unpleasant odor associated with smoking and the dependence of tobacco users on smoking, others celebrated its qualities as a relaxing, pleasant pastime that stimulated the taste buds. Because life expectancy was short, it is hard to know whether smoking further curtailed people's life spans in the 18th and 19th centuries.

One physical affect of pipe smoking that observers noted was damage to teeth. A 1772 *Virginia Gazette* advertisement for runaway couple Caesar and Kate highlighted the characteristic of "their Teeth somewhat worn with Pipes." Some who constantly clenched their pipes in their teeth wore perfect circular pipe facets into the softer enamel of the teeth where the harder ceramic pipe was held in the mouth. Archaeologists have seen this on both white and black individuals, both young and old, male and female.

The white clay pipes imported to early America were fragile, and the broken bits of stems and bowls have provided intriguing maps of their users' activities. In general, the diameters of the bores—or holes—in pipe stems decreased over time as pipe manufacturing technology improved and as wealthier smokers preferred pipes with longer stems that necessitated smaller bores. Concurrently, pipe manufacturers turned out cheaper pipes that became the smoking equipment for those who had fewer choices, such as indentured servants, slaves, or poor freeholders. Archaeologists use these two related patterns to date sites and to measure the relative spatial distribution of elite activity versus that of laborers. Some sites show that the working and living spaces of users of cheap pipes were segregated from users of expensive pipes well before the end of the 17th century. The spatial distribution of pipe smoking and work activities outside of elite houses and near outbuildings and work sites offers some of the best evidence of day-to-day work patterns.

Occasionally, slaves were buried with tobacco pipes tucked under arms or placed near the body. Both male and female deceased held unused pipes in burials in the Chesapeake, New York, and Barbados. Goods placed on top of **graves** may have included pipes as well as tobacco. Other grave goods included personal ornaments, such as **beads**, other intoxicants, such as **liquor**, or bottles or vessels.

For all the pipes and patterns that archaeologists find, the appeal of pipe smoking to slaves seems to have been the single goal of pleasure, or at the least, a distraction from the day-to-day demands of life.

***See also*** Colonoware; Tobacco Barns; Tobacco Factories.

FURTHER READING

Agbe-Davies, Anna S. "The Production and Consumption of Smoking Pipes along the Tobacco Coast." In *Smoking and Culture: The Archaeology of Tobacco Pipes in Eastern North*

*America*, edited by Sean M. Rafferty and Rob Mann, 273–304. Knoxville: University of Tennessee, 2004.

Emerson, Matthew C. "African Inspirations in a New World Art and Artifact: Decorated Tobacco Pipes from the Chesapeake." In *"I, Too, Am America": Archaeological Studies of African-American Life*, edited by Theresa A. Singleton, 47–82. Charlottesville: University Press of Virginia, 1999.

"Final Reports," African Burial Ground: Return to the Past to Build the Future. At www.africanburialground.gov/ABG_FinalReports.htm.

Handler, Jerome S. "Aspects of the Atlantic Slave Trade: Smoking Pipes, Tobacco, and the Middle Passage. In *African Diaspora Archaeology Newsletter* (June 2008). At www.diaspora.uiuc.edu/news0608/news0608.html#5.

Handler, Jerome S., and Michael L. Tuite, Jr. "The Atlantic Slave Trade and Slave Life in the Americas: A Visual Record," Virginia Foundation for the Humanities and University of Virginia. At http://hitchcock.itc.virginia.edu/Slavery/index.php.

Mouer, L. Daniel, Mary Ellen N. Hodges, et al. "Colonoware Pottery, Chesapeake Pipes, and 'Uncritical Assumptions.'" In *"I, Too, Am America": Archaeological Studies of African-American Life*, edited by Theresa A. Singleton, 83–115. Charlottesville: University Press of Virginia, 1999.

SUSAN A. KERN

**TOOLS.** *SEE* BLACKSMITH SHOPS; COOPERAGE; HOES; IRONWORK; MINES AND MINING; NAILS; WOODWORKING TOOLS; WRITING TOOLS.

**TWO ROOMS OVER TWO ROOMS HOUSES.** Two rooms over two rooms houses began to appear in the British North American colonies in the years immediately preceding the Revolutionary War. Small-scale slave owners and yeoman farmers paid to have these structures built, although slaves may have been employed to build them. Slaves working as cooks or wet nurses may have worked in the homes; skilled slaves may have frequented the home to consult with their masters or mistresses.

The structures represented a divergence from traditional, open floor plans associated with hall-and-parlor homes to a more closed and symmetrical floor plan. The new form was one room deep with a symmetrical façade and an interior composed of two rooms and a center hall on the first level and two rooms and a central hall on the second level. External chimneys on each end of the home completed the typical Southern "I-house."

The central hall funneled visitors into separate closed rooms. The new plan marked a shift from traditional communitarian ideals based on local exchange to a transcolonial awareness and unity. In fact, Southerners and Northerners were building similar houses by the start of the Revolution. Ironically, sectional distinction materialized after the war as Northerners built their houses but did not expect slaves to perform labor within them, while slaves served those who built the Southern I-house.

The basic form of two rooms over two rooms remained unchanged throughout the antebellum period, but stylistic influences, such as the Greek Revival, prompted antebellum Southerners to add porticoes to the front of the structure.

*See also* Cooking and Cooks; Nurseries and Nursemaids.

FURTHER READING

Glassie, Henry. *Folk Housing in Middle Virginia: A Structural Analysis of Historic Artifacts.* Knoxville: University of Tennessee Press, 1976.

Kniffen, Fred. "Folk Housing: Key to Diffusion." *Annals of the Association of American Geographers* 55, no. 4 (1965): 459–477.

DEBRA A. REID

# U

**UNDERGROUND RAILROAD.** The term "Underground Railroad" refers to a secretive, conspiratorial, and multifaceted effort to assist antebellum runaway slaves. By providing logistical assistance, transportation and finance, legal aid, and counterintelligence to blacks fleeing the South, Northern-based abolitionists helped fugitives keep running and avoid recapture. Northerners, who participated in the Underground Railroad as an open protest against the existence of slavery in their nation, have been the focal points of Underground Railroad studies for more than a century. Yet, thanks to expansive scholarship and fresh interpretations in the late 20th and early 21st centuries, the modern grasp of the Underground Railroad's history draws from a broader and much older history of anti-slavery behavior and activism.

Efforts of the newer scholarship attempt to reclaim the historical agency of the enslaved themselves and establish Southern communities as the locales of these events. In the 21st century, individual scholars and public historians, organizations, and institutions of varying scope now pursue interpretative, educational, and commemorative programs dedicated to the Underground Railroad and its related subject matter. Not so much refuting earlier pronouncements, this recontextualization affords Underground Railroad history a fuller place within the American freedom narrative.

## Resistance and Flight

According to one of the Underground Railroad's several origin legends, in the 1830s, Tice Davids, an enslaved African American man fleeing Kentucky, crossed the Ohio River with pursuers fast behind him. Swimming, he came ashore at Ripley, Ohio. His pursuers, arriving shortly thereafter, found no trace of him, and despite interrogation of local folk, deduced that Davids "must have gone off on an underground road." Whether the phrase actually was coined at that scene, by the 1840s, the term "Underground Railroad" had become part of the American lexicon.

Anti-slavery, as an impulse—personal and collective—is inarguably as old as the institution of slavery. It certainly was known to Americans from the introduction of slavery in the first decades of English settlement. Then, as later, enslaved people resisted their forced servitude. Among the most visible methods of resistance was to run away, or assist others in running. Indeed, when it surfaced, the Underground

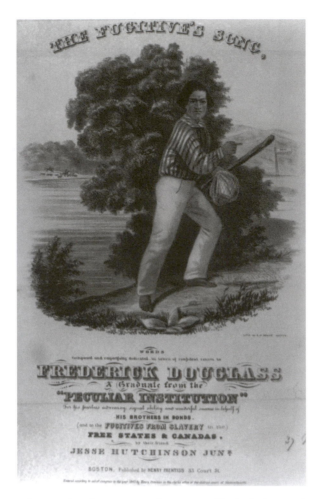

Sheet music cover illustrated with a portrait of prominent black abolitionist Frederick Douglass as a runaway slave. Douglass flees barefoot from two mounted pursuers who appear across the river behind him with their pack of dogs. Ahead, to the right, a signpost points toward New England. The cover's text states that "The Fugitive's Song" was "composed and respectfully dedicated, in token of confident esteem to Frederick Douglass (ca. 1818–1895). A graduate from the peculiar institution. For his fearless advocacy, signal ability and wonderful success in behalf of his brothers in bonds. (and to the fugitives from slavery in the) free states & Canadas by their friend Jesse Hutchinson Junr." As the illustration suggests, Douglass himself had escaped from slavery, fleeing in 1838 from Maryland to Massachusetts. The Douglass house in Rochester, New York, was a stop on the Underground Railroad. (Library of Congress.)

Railroad was not a path of escape, but rather a means of exploiting activities and activism already in place. What was new in the 19th century, and made the Underground Railroad possible, was the advent of "free states," a result of the American Revolution. Freedom was now a place on the map, and slaves began running North in the early 19th century. Slave flight in the antebellum era evolved into a major component of the national anti-slavery movement.

The methodology of the Underground Railroad as it emerged after 1800 involved two distinct stages: the escape from the plantation or other Southern slaveholding location and the move out of the geographic South altogether, and the engagement

---

### Escape to Freedom

Caroline Hammond's family escaped from slavery in Maryland to freedom in Pennsylvania via the Underground Railroad:

My father was a carpenter by trade, his services were much in demand. This gave him an opportunity to save money. Father often told me that he could save more than half of his income. He had plenty of work, doing repair and building, both for the white people and free colored people. Father paid Mr. Davidson for mother on the partial payment plan. He had paid up all but $40 on mother's account, when by accident Mr. Davidson was shot while ducking on the South River by one of the duck hunters, dying instantly.

Mrs. Davidson assumed full control of the farm and the slaves. When father wanted to pay off the balance due, $40.00, Mrs. Davidson refused to accept it, thus mother and I were to remain in slavery. Being a free man father had the privilege to go where he wanted to, provided he was endorsed by a white man who was known to the people and sheriffs, constables and officials of public conveyances. By bribery of the sheriff of Anne Arundel County father was given a passage to Baltimore for mother and me. On arriving in Baltimore, mother, father and I went to a white family on Ross Street—now Druid Hill Ave., where we were sheltered by the occupants, who were ardent supporters of the Underground Railroad.

A reward of $50.00 each was offered for my father, mother and me, one by Mrs. Davidson and the other by the Sheriff of Anne Arundel County. At this time the Hookstown Road was one of the main turnpikes into Baltimore. A Mr. Coleman whose brother-in-law lived in Pennsylvania, used a large covered wagon to transport merchandise from Baltimore to different villages along the turnpike to Hanover, Pa., where he lived. Mother and father and I were concealed in a large wagon drawn by six horses. On our way to Pennsylvania, we never alighted on the ground in any community or close to any settlement, fearful of being apprehended by people who were always looking for rewards.

*Source:* George P. Rawick, ed. *The American Slave: Kansas, Kentucky, Maryland, Ohio, Virginia, and Tennessee Narratives*, Vol. 16. Westport, CT: Greenwood Press, 1972.

---

of operatives and opportunities for coordinated assistance and escort to far Northern destinations. In the first stage, runaways made use of personal courage, intelligence, kinfolk, and social networks and often relieved slave owners and other whites of material resources as they made their break from the South. In the second stage, once escaped from the plantations and out of the South, runaways might reach willing strangers, like John Rankin (1793–1886) in Ripley, Ohio, or Levi Coffin (1798–1877) in Newport, Indiana, or others in Iowa, Michigan, Pennsylvania, and elsewhere. Runaways received **food**, shelter, information and first aid from these Northern

Underground Railroad operatives. After 1850, with the assistance of the Underground Railroad, many fugitives would press on toward Canada.

### Hubs and Destinations

Although national in impact, the Underground Railroad was not truly centralized. Several hubs may be identified, however. Along the Atlantic Seaboard, for example, runaways might connect with Underground Railroad operatives in eastern Pennsylvania, New Jersey, New York, and the New England states after they made their way out of Maryland, Delaware, Virginia, the Carolinas, or Georgia. Similarly, the Underground Railroad operations of western Pennsylvania, Ohio, Indiana, Illinois, Michigan, and points west and north aided fugitives from Kentucky and Tennessee, Alabama, and Mississippi. Although not traditionally viewed as part of the Underground Railroad, fugitives from slavery fled to Florida and even Mexico.

The terminology used by Northern operatives to coordinate their efforts borrowed heavily from the growing railroad industry; the Baltimore and Ohio Railroad was chartered in 1827, for example. Underground Railroad operatives were "agents"; the enslaved folk in their custody were "cargo" and "packages." The routes were "lines," the locations for rest and cover were "stations" with "station masters"; the leaders of Underground Railroad operations were "presidents," their financial supporters "stockholders." These, however, were terms of communications between Northerners and used on Northern soil. On the plantations, and in the South, from which the "cargo" came, these words would not have been recognized, nor likely would the phrase "Underground Railroad." Indeed, how exactly the Southern black population communicated is a source of some contention among scholars.

Not until the late 20th century did interpretations of the Underground Railroad shed light on Southern geographies. Several studies of slavery, flight, and the Underground Railroad now emphasize the process of getting away and of remaining at large in the Southern slaveholding locales through the agency of the enslaved and those who assisted them. Methods of preparation for flight—human and material resource considerations, identification of obstacles, and potential threats to success—are elements of Underground Railroad research that emerged in the late 20th century. Discussions of the Underground Railroad now consider the unintended but salutary aspects of the slaveholding cultures in the Upper South, including Kentucky, Tennessee, Virginia, Maryland, and the Carolinas. This, however, in no way devalues the traditional Underground Railroad narrative, which has its focus on processes and players who moved fugitives over great distances of Northern terrain toward a final destination.

### Underground Railroad in the 1850s: A Catalyst to War

The impact of the Underground Railroad's activities greatly contributed to the nation's increasing sectional divisions during the 1850s. Incendiary propaganda and intersectional violence marked the decade, all in the name of the slavery debate. While others talked and fought, the enslaved increasingly continued to run whenever possible. The Missouri Compromise of 1850, which greatly expanded the rights of slave owners to recover runaways across state lines, brought more difficult choices to the enslaved. With the law's enactment, Canada became the only true safe haven accessible to those who had already run north.

One of those Underground Railroad "conductors" who led runaways to Canada was Harriet Tubman (1822–1913), "the Moses of her people." Tubman began the work that made her the most recognizable figure in the history of the Underground Railroad in 1850, the year after she was assisted in fleeing North from Maryland. During the next decade, working with other Underground Railroad luminaries like Thomas Garrett (1789–1871) of Delaware, she executed perhaps a dozen missions back into Maryland, rescuing approximately 75 family, friends, and others.

Tubman's "extraction" approach to the Underground Railroad work was unique, for most other Underground Railroad operatives monitored and coordinated the arrival of runaways at their own doorstep. William Still (1821–1902) of Philadelphia, the son of a fugitive slave from Maryland and her free husband, was born in exile in New Jersey and spent most of the 1850s as the busiest "station master" on the Underground Railroad's eastern line. Still documented his work in a journal, which he published in 1872 as a record of liberation for some 800 runaways.

Much of the work of the Underground Railroad required secrecy and stealth, but detection could not always be avoided, and with detection often came violent confrontation. The 1850s began with the cry of murder in Christiana, Pennsylvania, when a group of four runaways, seeking refuge at the home of free African American William Parker, resisted capture and, in so doing, killed one of their pursuers, Maryland farmer Edward Gorsuch. By the mid-decade, abolitionists and anti-slavery activists routinely resorted to violence to free captured fugitives, like Anthony Burns (1834–1862) in Boston, where a U.S. Marshall was killed in the melee. The 1850s ended with the worst of all pro-slavery nightmares, as the abolitionist John Brown (1800–1859) attempted a racial Armageddon upon the South with his ill-fated rebellion at Harpers Ferry, Virginia. Slavery was the irrepressible question at the center of the debate. The stories of black attempts to be free—especially when freedom was thwarted, as with Burns—instilled more and more people with the idea that slavery in America had to be destroyed.

### The Underground Railroad and the World of a Slave

The Underground Railroad encompassed more than those who fled the South, or even those who assisted them in the North. The Underground Railroad also included those who remained in the South and played crucial roles. Abolitionist Frederick Douglass's own freedom, for example, was made possible by the participation of Isaac Rolls, a free black acquaintance who willingly committed a felony that, if discovered, surely would have sent him to prison, or to the **cotton** fields of the Deep South. Yet Rolls not only helped Douglass, but also never left Baltimore and likely helped others after Douglass. Tubman's efforts are even more indicative of the breadth of the conspiracy against slavery that supported Underground Railroad activities. Each of her heroic missions required the complicity and, thus, criminal involvement of the free and enslaved black community in the South, as well as that of some whites. Whereas others fled the South to take stands against slavery, as did the white abolitionist editor William Lloyd Garrison (1805–1879) in 1829, many remained and played willful, if only silent, roles acting mainly for the protection of family and friends as well as to the benefit of many more. Their stories, too, are part of the history of the Underground Railroad.

The Underground Railroad has been researched and written about for nearly 175 years, but much as yet is not fully understood. New scholarship does not so much challenge the views of the 19th-century, Northern-based, largely white chroniclers of their Underground Railroad, as much as reveal several aspects of Underground Railroad operations that were not acknowledged or that they simply could not recognize. Foremost among the arguments of current scholarship are the agency of the enslaved and the primacy of the Underground Railroad's Southern geography—that is, the plantation and the locales where flight began.

Thus, by connecting Northern-based supporters with blacks fleeing the U.S. South between approximately 1800 and the 1860s, the Underground Railroad represents a fundamental component of the 19th-century American historical narrative. It contextualizes the intersectional debate over slavery, the growing militancy of the antislavery versus pro-slavery debate, and the coming of the Civil War.

*See also* Abolition Imagery.

## FURTHER READING

Berlin, Ira. *Many Thousands Gone: The First Two Centuries of Slavery in North America.* Cambridge, MA: Belknap Press of Harvard University Press, 1998.

Blackett, R. J. M. *Building an Antislavery Wall: Black Americans in the Atlantic Abolitionist Movement, 1830–1860.* Baton Rouge: Louisiana State University Press, 1983.

Blight, David W., ed. *The Passages to Freedom: The Underground Railroad in History and Memory.* Washington, DC: Smithsonian Books, 2004.

Dillon, Merton L. *Slavery Attacked: Southern Slaves and Their Allies, 1619–1865.* Baton Rouge: Louisiana State University Press, 1990.

Franklin, John Hope, and Loren Schweninger. *Runaway Slaves: Rebels on the Plantation.* New York: Oxford University Press, 1999.

Frey, Sylvia R. *Water from the Rock: Black Resistance in a Revolutionary Age.* Princeton, NJ: Princeton University Press, 1991.

Menare Foundation. At www.menare.org/.

National Underground Railroad Freedom Center. At www.freedomcenter.org/.

"National Underground Railroad Network to Freedom," National Park Service. At www.nps.gov/history/Underground Railroad/.

Pathways to Freedom: Maryland and the Underground Railroad. At http://pathways.thinkport .org/flash_home.cfm.

Richards, Leonard L. *The Slave Power: The Free North and Southern Domination, 1780–1860.* Baton Rouge: Louisiana State University Press, 2000.

Routes: The Virtual Underground Railroad Experience. At www.undergroundrailroadexperience .cuny.edu/.

Stewart, James Brewer. *Holy Warriors: The Abolitionists and American Slavery.* New York: Hill and Wang, 1997.

DAVID TAFT TERRY

# W

**WATERMELONS.** The watermelon (*Citrullus vulgaris*), a fruit grown in **gardens** for its refreshing crimson meat, has long been associated with African Americans and their enslaved ancestors. The watermelon is originally an African domesticate and along with other melons was cultivated on both sides of the Atlantic during the era of trans-Atlantic slave trade. Although some varieties of watermelon came from Africa directly to the South, most forms traveled first through the West Indies via the Spanish and Portuguese, who in turn had received the watermelon from the Moors of northwestern Africa. Some of the earliest documentation for the fruit goes back to mid-17th century Massachusetts, where it was grown in the Bay Colony. In the South, the watermelon was not only valued for its sweet, juicy meat but also for its rind, which could be pickled, and its edible seeds. Such uses were carryovers from West and Central Africa, where the watermelon and other melons were prized for the multiple products that could be obtained from the plant.

The watermelons that would have come from West and Central Africa by way of **slave ships** may well include the Carolina Long watermelon, a dark-green-skinned, red-fleshed, oblong variety, cultivated for **market** and sold up and down the colonial Eastern seaboard. Other varieties that were grown in plantation fields, cabin gardens, and truck patches may have included a white-skinned variety known as the Bough that is now extinct and, in the antebellum period, a zigzag-striped variety known as the Georgia Rattlesnake that is still available. That the latter was grown and consumed by enslaved African Americans is attested to in several Federal Writers' Project narratives in the 1930s in which the variety is cited. From an early date, watermelons and muskmelons were grown in Maryland, Virginia, the Carolinas and Georgia and from there spread out with the migration to the Southwest. Their popularity as a food source for all of the South's ethnic groups was attested to by their cultivation in Creek and Cherokee villages, another possible connection to enslaved populations who sought refuge with these peoples during the 18th century.

As early as 1705, colonial historian Robert Beverly (ca. 1667–1722) of Virginia wrote of watermelon, "they are excellently good, and very pleasant to the taste, as also to the eye, having the rind of a lively green color, streaked and watered, the meat of a carnation and the seeds black and shining while it lies in the melon." In 1732 English

THE WATERMELON MARKET AT CHARLESTON, S. C.—From a Sketch by James E. Taylor.—See Page 198.

Watermelon market, Charleston, South Carolina. (Library of Congress.)

traveler William Hugh Grove noted, "chiefly of Watermelons which is green and bigg [*sic*] as a Pumpin [*sic*] (smooth not furrowed) They eat it as an apple." In Hanover County, Virginia, in the same area as the oldest known reference to enslaved African Americans growing collard greens and snap beans, Lieut. William Feltman remarked,

> This evening I had an invitation from Capt. Pierson to assist him in eating two water-melons, which were the best and finest I ever see. This country is full of them; they have large patches of two and three acres of them.

That these melons were likely expertly cared for by enslaved hands is hinted at by Philip Vickers Fithian (1747–1776), tutor for the children of Virginian Robert Carter III (1728–1804), who observed in 1774 at Carter's Nomini Hall plantation that Dadda Gumby, an elderly enslaved man born in Africa, rewarded him for giving him a list of his children and their ages by providing him with a watermelon. Indeed watermelon seeds have been found in the archaeological remains of several sites associated with slavery, including the Calvert House in Annapolis, Maryland, and at the House for Families at Mount Vernon in Virginia. Engineer William Tatham (1752–1819) wrote in 1800 that, in the Virginia piedmont, there were commodities "which are permitted (and generally confined by custom) to slaves," among these were "(sweet) potatoes, garden-stuff, pumpkins and melons." Squire, an enslaved master gardener at Monticello, was well known for the produce he sold the Jefferson family, which included both water- and muskmelons. "We had a watermelon patch," said former slave Henry Pettus of Arkansas, "and sometimes sold Dr. Palmer melons. He let us have a melon patch . . . our own to work. Mother worked in moonlight and at odd times. They give that to her extra. We helped her work it." Watermelons also were associated with cultivation by the elderly in the enslaved community. Planter Landon Carter (1710–1778), a member of one of Virginia's most prominent families, recorded in his diary, "I walkt [sic] out this evening to see how my very old and honest Slave Jack Lubber did to support life in his Extreme age; and I found him prudently working amongst his melon vines." Another enslaved Virginian, "Old Dick," was proud of the watermelons and **corn** he raised in his patch garden.

Watermelons were an especially precious fruit to have for the working person in the field. Ripening during the period of the hardest labor and highest heat of the Southern summer, watermelons provided much-needed water, sugars, and cooling juice during long, arduous days. The difficulty for enslaved people was that they often were not freely able to go get a watermelon during their workday and were not allowed to take them at will.

---

### Stealing Watermelons

Pharoah Jackson Chesney, a former slave from Tennessee, recalled the temptations of watermelons:

> It was a general weakness among slaves to steal, not that they always needed the things they took, but with some it seemed an impossibility to resist the temptation; but I know from a long experience that the negroes did not steal everything that was missed. There were thieves among the whites, and they generally managed to get out of being accused by charging it to the negroes on general principles. Personally, my greatest temptations were sweet potatoes in 'possum time, and the darkey's most delicious fruit, the watermelon. A watermelon patch was never any safer in Virginia or Tennessee, than an African cane patch from a drove of monkeys.
>
> We had, on our plantation near Clarksville, large watermelon patches, but it was big fun to swim the river over to Klipper's, and then if any of our master's melons were missed, it could not be traced to us. With these advantages, and the melons as an inducement, I, with some other boys, would make regular voyages across the Roanoke and Dan, when the sun was not shining; and paddle over two large melons apiece. The way we would manage the melons was to break off the stems rather long, tie a string to each of them, and swing them around our necks. When once in the water, they would float, and not be any weight much upon our necks in swimming.

*Source:* John Coram Webster. *Last of the Pioneers: Or, Old Times in East Tenn., Being the Life and Reminiscences of Pharoah Jackson Chesney (aged 120 years).* Knoxville, TN: S. B. Newman and Company, 1902.

Leonard Black, a formerly enslaved man from a Maryland **tobacco** plantation, observed that stealing watermelon to gain necessary refreshment was a crime to planters, punishable by severe force.

> One day, Eliza (a slave girl of his) and myself, went into the water-melon patch, procured a melon and ate it. We were compelled to this by the promptings of hunger, for the living had not altered since the death of Mr. Bradford. Eliza was about eighteen years of age. For that offence, our cruel master stripped us and tied us both up together, and whipped us till the blood ran down on the ground in a puddle.

It is possible that these punishments were related to the fact that watermelon patches were a source of extra money as the fruits were carted to market.

This heritage of controlling crucial refreshment was at the heart of the origin of a number of debilitating stereotypes and racist jokes centered on the watermelon. Well into the 20th century, cartoons, postcards, and folklore continued to make derisive comments about African Americans and watermelons. A "Sambo" or golliwog image, with an exaggerated grin eating half of a watermelon, was used in advertising to sell many products from the mid-19th well into the 20th centuries. These images prompted many African Americans to deemphasize their connection with the fruit and even hide the act of eating it in front of "mixed company." The watermelon stands alone as an enduring symbol of the connection between myth, reality, racism, and culinary folklore in the making of Southern identities during slavery.

*See also* Food and Foodways; Collards.

FURTHER READING

Greene, Wesley. "Gardening: Research: Melons and Cucumbers," Colonial Williamsburg. At www.history.org/history/cwland/resrch6.cfm.

Grime, William Ed. *Ethno-Botany of the Black Americans.* Algonac, MI: Reference Publications, 1979.

Morgan, Philip D. *Slave Counterpoint: Black Culture in the Eighteenth-Century Chesapeake and Lowcountry.* Chapel Hill: University of North Carolina Press, 1998.

Rawick, George P. *The American Slave: Kansas, Kentucky, Maryland, Ohio, Virginia, and Tennessee Narratives*, Vol. 16. Westport, CT: Greenwood Press, 1972.

Williams-Forson, Psyche. *Building Houses Out of Chicken Legs: Black Women, Food and Power.* Chapel Hill: University of North Carolina Press, 2006.

Wilson, Mary Tolford. "Peaceful Integration: The Owner's Adoption of His Slave's Food." *Journal of Negro History* 49, no. 2 (April 1964): 116–127.

MICHAEL W. TWITTY

**WEAPONS. *SEE* FIREARMS; MILITARY EQUIPMENT; WHIPS.**

**WHEAT.** European settlers introduced wheat to the North American colonies. English, Dutch, and German settlers transplanted their grain culture to Northern, mid-Atlantic, and Southern colonies while the French developed the first major grain

Blacks stacking wheat near Culpepper Courthouse, Virginia. Pencil drawing by Edwin Forbes, 1863. (Library of Congress.)

fields in the upper Mississippi River Valley. The infrastructure required to process and market wheat developed more slowly in the South than in other regions for various reasons. Still, wheat became an important cash and **food** crop in the South and continued as such through the antebellum period. Wheat growers did not require a slave labor force to prosper, but farmers and planters who raised wheat often also held slaves. Instead, slave labor became most associated with staple crops such as **tobacco**, **rice**, **indigo**, and **cotton**, crops that required more consistent or physically taxing labor. Wheat needed relatively little tending between planting and harvesting. Wheat farmers who did not hold slaves could have hired slaves only during the planting and harvesting seasons. Machines did not displace this slave labor because dependable reapers did not become available until the approach of the Civil War and the abolition of slavery, so wheat and slavery coexisted but did not become mutually dependent.

Different wheat varieties grew in Europe, but not all of these thrived in the soil and climate in North American colonies. Common or bread wheat, a hard winter wheat, and durum, a hard spring wheat, were hull-less varieties easily threshed and remained hardy over a wide range of temperature and rainfall levels. Bread wheat transplanted readily to various English, French, German, and Dutch colonies. In areas best suited to winter varieties, farmers planted during September or October and harvested during July and early August. In areas suited to spring varieties, farmers planted during March or April and harvested during the fall. Farmers experimented with both planting times, and in some areas, notably the fertile Mississippi River Valley, and in the alluvial lands in the Chesapeake, they double-cropped. Specific varieties mentioned in period sources include common English red wheat, Sicilian or forward white wheat,

Siberian wheat, and yellow-bearded wheat, among others. Each type yielded different types and colors of flour suitable for different breads and pastries.

Slaves had experience with grain cultivation and processing before arriving in the British North American colonies. Grains indigenous to Africa such as sorghum, Guinea corn, millet, African rice, and even an African variety of maize called "spiked Indian corn" constituted a major food group in slave diets. Many Africans may even have been familiar with American maize ("Indian **corn**") in their countries of origin, which was introduced by European mariners, missionaries, and slave traders. Slaves grew sorghum and then ground it along with red peas and various vegetables into starch-heavy porridges. Their knowledge of rice helped develop that industry in the coastal Carolinas, areas so wet that wheat rotted in the ground. Yet, early sources indicate that slaves did not appreciate the mush made from Indian corn or porridge made from oatmeal. Wheat porridge or wheat bread likely did not appeal to them, either, if they even had such foodstuffs available to them.

English colonists tried to replicate their foodways in a foreign land, and they planted "English graine" and "English wheat," a crop central to their cultural identity as Christians. Several factors caused Southern colonists to concentrate on other crops, but they remained committed to wheat bread as an ultimate goal for their tables. Although maize provided sustenance to many for a lifetime, in some instances, the European cultures pursued wheat flour until proper varieties, the production and marketing infrastructure, and transport systems helped them realize their goals.

European cultivation tools and practices changed little over centuries, and colonists brought these practices to the North American colonies. Farmers used horse- or ox-drawn plows and harrows to prepare the soil. Laborers hand seeded or "broadcast" the grain using one-half to one bushel per acre. A good reaper could cut, bind, and stack about three-quarters of an acre of wheat each day. Reaping entailed cutting the ripe wheat with a hand sickle, gathering the cut straw with intact heads into a sheaf, and then stacking the sheaves in the field to cure. After the grain cured in the field, laborers removed the grain to the threshing area. Threshing removed the ripe grain from the head with handheld wooden flails or by driving **horses** over the grain to trample the wheat from the head. By the late 1700s, Southerners began using mechanical threshing machines powered by animals on treadmills. These machines made it possible for farmers to process larger yields. Traditionally, laborers used winnowing **baskets** to separate the wheat from the chaff when yields were not too large, but fanning mills powered by hand or a treadmill came into use by the late 1700s as well.

Farmers stored grain in bins in barns, specially outfitted with tight-fitting boards to reduce loss and dissuade rodents from entering the cache. Some granaries, separate buildings dedicated to grain storage, survive, but these stand as evidence of the expanding trade in wheat during the early 1800s. African slaves likely had knowledge of traditional methods of cultivation and storage because of the importance of grains other than wheat in their homelands.

The precarious nature of early settlement in the Chesapeake prompted colonists to adopt native cultivation methods, girdling trees and planting higher yielding corn for food, and tobacco for **market**. Six acres of corn would produce the **rations** needed for a family or workforce of eight. Corn could grow in less-tilled soil and could be converted into a foodstuff for humans and stock with relatively little processing. Grains, particularly wheat, required more soil cultivation and an infrastructure for processing. Colonials grew wheat, processed it into flour and bread, and traded it between colonies and abroad. This prompted Parliament to enact, in 1689, the first "Corn Law." It limited imports of grain from the colonies if prices on the English market fell below a certain level. Southern investment in wheat, however, increased because it offered an alternative to tobacco monoculture and raised hope for local economic development that tobacco stymied.

A combination of factors made wheat more important as a cash crop by the early 1700s, despite the Corn Laws. The volatility of the tobacco market, declining tobacco yields due to soil exhaustion, and a ready market for wheat in the Atlantic prompted Southerners from Maryland to South Carolina to commit to wheat as a staple crop. Soon, the Chesapeake colonies, Virginia and Maryland, rivaled Pennsylvania as a grain exporter, with wheat and flour shipments going to non-English ports-of-call in defiance of mercantile laws. Ships hauled grain to southern Europe, particularly Spain and Portugal, and to the wine-producing islands of Madeira, Cape Verde, and the Azores as well as to the West Indies. Significant coastal trade occurred between colonies as well. South Carolina and New England colonies depended on wheat grown in the colonial breadbasket, Pennsylvania, as well as Maryland and Virginia, to realize their goal of preserving their culture, literally by consuming wheat bread.

Wheat trade in diverse markets fostered town, city, and port development along the southern coast between 1700 and 1800. Wheat had to be ground into flour to increase its value and facilitate transportation. In the Chesapeake, farmers found it more profitable to ship grain to the coast where mills ground it into flour for coastal trade or export. Entrepreneurs built grist mills, which expedited grain processing and marketing, but also facilitated town and city growth. The trade drew skilled artisans, both free and enslaved, to build grist mills, make barrels for the flour, and construct the harnesses, carts, and sloops adequate to haul the barrels. As a result, most slaves who worked with any aspect of wheat processing lived in town, not on the farm, and developed specialized skills not associated with planting or harvesting.

Wheat became increasingly important to the U.S. economy, and by the early 1800s, England tightened its Corn Laws, which remained in force until repealed in 1846, making it difficult for American grain to find a market in British ports. Wheat remained an important cash crop for Virginians and Marylanders, but slave labor concentrated more completely on cotton as a cash crop by the 1840s repeal. Furthermore, pests and fungal diseases proved particularly destructive to wheat in the eastern United States, and the Wheat Belt had moved into free states and territories of Illinois, Wisconsin, and beyond. Efforts to mechanize the grain harvest had shifted north and west as well, away from the Southern Wheat Belt and toward the expanding Northern market.

Southerners sought to profit from the grain trade as much as possible. During the early 18th century, innovation in agricultural methods imported from English sources appealed to Southerners transitioning from tobacco to wheat. Tradition dictated that land lie fallow for one season to rejuvenate the soil. Tobacco so depleted the soil, however, that the fallow period did not rejuvenate the soil and adequate manure could not be generated by plantations with stock ranging beyond fenced **yards**. The English agricultural reformer Jethro Tull (1674–1741) promoted a new crop rotation, including green manures and deep plowing, in an effort to rejuvenate soil long tilled. He included sketches of new machinery critical to his scientific methods, including a horse-drawn grain drill in his book, *The New Horse-Houghing Husbandry: An Essay on the Principles of Tillage and Nutrition*, published in 1733. George Washington (1732–1799) applied Tull's methods by the 1760s and corresponded with other scientific agriculturalists in England, specifically Arthur Young (1741–1820) who published *Annals of Agriculture* between 1784 and 1808. During 1785 and 1786, Washington had planted a variety of grains and grasses, including barley, clover, corn, flax, millet, oats, orchard grass, rye, spelt, timothy, and wheat.

French settlement along the Mississippi River in southern Illinois had a population consisting of one-third African- and American-born slaves and two-thirds French settlers by the early 1700s. The French adapted slavery to suit the open-field system of cereal-grain production and created such a successful operation that it continued despite the defeat and removal of French governance from the area as a result of the English victory in the French and Indian War in 1763. Despite the freeing of the slaves with Illinois statehood in 1818, 99-year indentures replaced lifetime enslavement and slaves remained bound to their French masters. The footprint of the open-field grain agricultural system remained into the late 19th century.

The open-field system as practiced in French Illinois included strips of arable land parceled among families, the use of stubble fields and fallow land for common pasture, the dedication of wasteland, that is, acreage too swampy, heavily wooded, hilly, or rocky to warrant cultivation to common pasture, and communal governance of agricultural land use. Farm families and their slaves lived in nuclear villages, thus preserving the rural community structure that had existed in Europe. The white and black communities bore the responsibility for maintaining the **fences** that enclosed the arable fields.

The French planted their wheat during the spring on the rich alluvial soils, even though the climate and soil away from the river bottom suited winter wheat best. Period sources recount the pilgrimage of masters and slaves from their village homes to the fields during mornings in April, with their plows, horses, and carts full of grain and other tools, and the reverse trip in the evening during the 8 to 10 days devoted to planting. Some enterprising residents even double-cropped, planting winter wheat in the ground from which they had just harvested their spring planting. This made it difficult for others to run their stock on stubble ground, so laborers, including slaves, would have to tend to cattle grazing on the strips of land they had the right to cultivate, while keeping the stock off of other farmers' strips. Grist mills powered by horses, or by wind or water, processed grain into flour for shipment to New Orleans, which developed as a major wheat port, with attendant specialized trades of barrel, cart, and sloop building to facilitate shipment.

Slaves in wheat-producing areas spent relatively little time working in wheat fields. In fact, a wheat farmer made a better economic decision to hire labor during planting and harvesting than to own a slave. Furthermore, wheat exceeded tobacco in profitability when using free labor, which led many to question the economic veracity of slavery as an institution, but slave owners with a slave population that naturally increased could farm tobacco profitably in the Chesapeake. Thus, wheat came to be increasingly associated with free labor as the debates about slavery intensified after the Revolutionary War. Some planters responded by building mills and working their slaves in grain processing. This developed an infrastructure for wheat processing and flour marketing inland.

Because of wheat's profitability without the use of enslaved laborers, many on Maryland's Eastern Shore freed slaves because retaining them did not make economic sense in a wheat economy. The freedmen became wage laborers or developed their own small farms supported by extended kinship networks that made it possible for them to remain in the state, according to the 1815 Virginia Manumission Act. Increased manumission generated debates in Virginia during 1831 about whether slavery should be abolished. Nat Turner's (1800–1831) rebellion on August 21, 1831, led to harsher slave laws, not abolition.

At about the same time the debate about abolishing slavery in Virginia took place and just before Nat Turner's rebellion, Cyrus McCormick (1809–1884) exhibited his father's mechanical reaper in late July 1831. Mechanizing harvesting would further reduce labor costs associated with the crop and remove the dependency on wage laborers at harvest. In this context, the reaper becomes a powerful statement for free labor. McCormick's leaving of Rockbridge County, Virginia, and establishment of the McCormick Harvesting Machine Company in Chicago in 1847 coincided with the migration of intense wheat production to the upper Midwest and Northern plains, but it also coincided with a shift in labor in the rural Midwest toward corn production. The shift in labor toward corn production increased the debate over the merits of slavery as an economic institution. Corn was a multiple-day staple, as were tobacco and cotton, while wheat was a few-day staple. Slave labor could be justified economically for multiple-day staples; wage labor was too expensive to hire to tend corn. Mechanization proved the answer, rather than slavery, for Midwestern farmers. The reaper, when perfected, could mow hay before and after cutting the grain crops. Machinery companies proliferated, developing and selling corn planters and cultivators to ease labor demands between April and July. Harvest corn proved less time-sensitive and occupied farm families from late fall into winter. Mechanization undermined the pro-slavery debate. The Civil War ultimately disarmed it. Wheat played a major role in the debate.

*See also* Gardens.

## FURTHER READING

Carr, Lois Green, Russell R. Menard, and Lorena S. Walsh. *Robert Cole's World: Agriculture and Society in Early Maryland.* Chapel Hill: University of North Carolina Press, 1991.

Earle, Carville. *Geographical Inquiry and American Historical Problems.* Stanford, CA: Stanford University Press, 1992.

Edelson, S. Max. *Plantation Enterprise in South Carolina.* Cambridge, MA: Harvard University Press, 2006.

Ekberg, Carl J. *French Roots in the Illinois Country: The Mississippi Frontier in Colonial Times.* Urbana: University of Illinois Press, 2000.

Gill, Harold B., Jr. "Wheat Culture in Colonial Virginia." *Agricultural History* 52, no. 3 (1978): 380–393.

Gray, Lewis C. *History of Agriculture in the Southern United States to 1860.* 2 vols. Gloucester, MA: Peter Smith, 1958.

Klingaman, David. "The Significance of Grain in the Development of the Tobacco Colonies." *Journal of Economic History* 29, no. 2 (1969): 268–278.

Klingaman, David. "Food Surpluses and Deficits in the American Colonies, 1768–1772." *Journal of Economic History* 31, no. 3 (1971): 553–569.

Nelson, Lynn A. *Pharsalia: An Environmental Biography of a Southern Plantation, 1780–1880.* Athens: University of Georgia Press, 2007.

"Washington and the New Agriculture." In "Introduction" to *The Diaries of George Washington.* 6 vols. Charlottesville: University Press of Virginia, 1976–1979. American Memory, Library of Congress. At http://memory.loc.gov/ammem/gwhtml/4gwintro.html.

DEBRA A. REID

**WHIPS.** Whipping became popular in the 19th century as the harsher punishments of the 17th and 18th centuries were discarded. When the whip was used in those centuries, both free persons and slaves felt its sting, and little, if any, regional differences existed in flogging slaves. Later, however, as slavery was confined to the South, whipping became a punishment that was largely restricted to slaves, both male and female, with the Deep South enacting harsher laws than those of the other slave states.

Few adult slaves had the good fortune to escape getting whipped during their lifetime. Sometimes the flogging was punishment for breaking a state code, a local code, or a plantation regulation; sometimes it was administered on general principle. For instance, the last slave out of the cabin to the fields in the morning might receive a lashing. Some masters used the whip to "break in" a young slave and to break the

"Virginian Luxuries," unidentified artist, New England, ca. 1825, oil on canvas. At right, a slaveholder or overseer raises a stick to whip an enslaved man; at left, a slaveholder or overseer forces his attentions on an enslaved woman. (Abby Aldrich Rockefeller Folk Art Museum, The Colonial Williamsburg Foundation.)

## Violent Punishments

Rebecca Jane Grant, enslaved in South Carolina, was whipped for refusing to call a small child "master."

Well, I was just a little girl about eight years old, staying in Beaufort at de Missus' house, polishing her brass and irons, and scrubbing her floors, when one morning she say to me, "Janie, take this note down to Mr. Wilcox Wholesale Store on Bay Street, and fetch me back de package de clerk gie (give) you."

I took de note. De man read it, and he say, "Uh-huh." Den he turn away and he come back wid a little package which I took back to de Missus.

She open it when I bring it in, and say, "Go upstairs, Miss!"

It was a raw cowhide strap bout two feet long, and she started to pourin' it on me all de way up stairs. I didn't know what she was whippin' me bout; but she pour it on, and she pour it on.

Turrectly she say, "You can't say 'Marse Henry', Miss? You can't say, 'Marse Henry'!"

"Yes'm. Yes'm. I kin say, 'Marse Henry'!"

Marse Henry was just a little boy bout three or four years old. Come bout halfway up to me. Wanted me to say Massa to him, a baby!

*Source:* George P. Rawick, ed. *The American Slave: South Carolina Narratives*, Vol. 2. Westport, CT: Greenwood Press, 1972.

As Rev. W. B. Allen described slave times in Georgia, both the whip and the paddle could deliver a horrendous beating that few enslaved individuals ever forgot:

One popular method of whipping a Negro was called the "Buck" and another was the "Rolling Jim." Throwing a Nigger into the "Buck" consisted in first stripping him (all Nigger whipping was applied to the bare body), making him squat and tying his hands between his knees to a stout stick run behind the bends of his knees. Then, the Nigger was pushed over and the performance begun. In the "Rolling Jim" system, a Nigger was stretched on his stomach at full length on a large log, about eight feet long. Into holes bored in each end of this log, wooden pegs were driven. The feet were securely tied to one set of these pegs—at one end of the log, and the hands to the pegs at the other end. The victim was then ready to be worked on.

Sometimes the "Buck" and the "Rolling Jim" candidates were flogged with a rawhide strap, and sometimes they were "persuaded" with a paddle. The rawhide cut the flesh and brought streams of blood. The paddle had holes in it which raised blisters. The muscular contortions of the Negro on the log caused it to sway—hence the name, "Rolling Jim."

Cruel masters and overseers, after "Bucking" and "Rolling Jimming" a Negro, would then rub salt and red pepper into his wounds, causing him to go into convulsions, developing fever, resulting frequently in a state of coma lasting for several days.

Most former slaves, like William McWhorter from Georgia, remembered the violent punishments they witnessed:

I ain't got no idee how many acres was in dat great big old plantation, but I'se heared 'em say Marse Joe had to keep from 30 to 40 slaves, not countin' chillun, to wuk dat part of it dat was cleared land. Dey told me, atter I was old enough to take it in, dat de overseer sho did drive dem slaves; dey had to be up and in de field 'fore sunup and he wuked 'em 'til slap, black dark. When dey got back to de big house, 'fore dey et supper, de overseer got out his big bull whip and beat de ones dat hadn't done to suit him durin' de day. He made 'em strip off deir clothes down to de waist, and evvywhar dat old bull whip struck it split de skin. Dat was awful, awful! Sometimes slaves dat had been beat and butchered up so bad by dat overseer man would run away, and next day Aunt Suke would be sho to go down to de spring to wash so she could leave some old clothes dar for 'em to git at night.

*Source:* George P. Rawick, ed. *The American Slave: Georgia Narratives,* Vol. 13. Westport, CT: Greenwood Press, 1972.

As Andrew Boone from North Carolina told it, the whip and paddle frequently were combined:

I saw a lot of slaves whupped an' I wus whupped myself. Dey whupped me wid de cat o' nine tails. It had nine lashes on it. Some of de slaves wus whupped wid a cobbin paddle. Dey had forty holes in 'em an' when you wus buckled to a barrel dey hit your naked flesh wid de paddle an' every whur dere wus a hole in de paddle it drawed a blister. When de whuppin' wid de paddle wus over, dey took de cat o' nine tails an' busted de blisters. By dis time de blood sometimes would be runnin' down dare heels. Den de next thing wus a wash in salt water strong enough to hold up an egg. Slaves wus punished dat way fer runnin' away an' sich.

*Source:* George P. Rawick, ed. *The American Slave: North Carolina Narratives,* Vol. 14. Westport, CT: Greenwood Press, 1972.

spirit of an insubordinate older slave. An Alabama slaveholder declared that slaves had to be whipped until they showed "submission and penitence." Moreover, whites generally believed that "whipping was the only thing that would do a Negro any good."

It seems that everywhere the slaves turned someone with a whip stood poised to beat them. The slaveholder, slaveholder's wife, overseer, and **slave driver** on the plantation; patrollers off the plantation; and jailers, constables, and other officials all were authorized to whip slaves. Jailers and constables who carried out court sentences also whipped unruly slaves for slaveholders who were reluctant to whip their own. Breaking a state or local code resulted in sentences of from 20 to 100 lashes, depending on the severity of the offense. In the case of a severe punishment of 500 lashes, the beating might be administered over several weeks to avoid killing the slave.

Breaking plantation regulations resulted in fewer lashes, usually about 15, although the number could be much higher. But chances of breaking those regulations were much greater than those of violating public codes because plantation regulations covered a multitude of transgressions. Slaves, in a sense, constantly walked through a punishment tinderbox: the marvel is that any escaped getting burned.

Several instruments were used to administer whippings, but the most common were the rawhide whip or cowhide whip, the leather strap, the cowhide paddle or "hot paddle," and the buckskin cracker whip. The rawhide whip caused lacerations; the others, allegedly, did not. These and other instruments usually were directed to the uncovered back of the slave who was immobilized during the whipping by being tied to a whipping post, a tree, stumps in the ground, or some other objects, or by being placed either in stocks or pillory.

The common practice was to administer the whippings publicly, this being the ultimate act of degradation. According to a slaveholder, "every Negro in this community regards a whipping in the market as the greatest disgrace which can befall them [sic]." This traumatic experience was exacerbated sometimes by rubbing salt in the raw flesh laid open by the flogging. A former slave in Missouri recalled that his master would "chain a nigger up to whip em and rub salt and pepper on him, like he said 'to season him up.'" This treatment was reserved for obstreperous slaves.

Whipping became the most commonly used form of punishment because it conveyed the slaveholder's message with the least amount of negative ramifications. Accordingly, the whip became the badge of a slaveholder's authority, through which slaveholders achieved discipline, deterrence, and degradation.

FURTHER READING

Bassett, John Spencer. *The Southern Plantation Overseer As Revealed in His Letters*. Northampton, MA: Printed for Smith College, 1925.

Stampp, Kenneth M. *The Peculiar Institution: Slavery in the Ante-Bellum South*. New York: Knopf, 1956.

Sydnor, Charles S. *Slavery in Mississippi*. New York: D. Appleton-Century Company, 1933.

Wade, Richard C. *Slavery in the Cities: The South, 1820–1860*. New York: Oxford University Press, 1964.

Yetman, Norman R., ed. *Life under the Peculiar Institution: Selections from the Slave Narrative Collection*. New York: Holt, Rinehart and Winston, 1970.

WHITTINGTON B. JOHNSON

**WOODWORKING TOOLS.** Planes, saws, turnscrews (screwdrivers), files, braces (drills), gouges, and rules were among the tools used by enslaved men who worked in wood, whether it was as a carpenter, cooper, cabinetmaker, housewright, sawyer (someone who saws logs into lumber, usually in a sawpit), or shipbuilder. In an era when buildings, ships, carts, and furniture all were made of wood, enslaved carpenters with the requisite knowledge and skill were highly valued both by their masters and were in a better position to make products that they could then sell for cash or for **barter goods**, or they even could hire themselves out.

Sawyers preparing timber that will be made into shingles, Montgomery County, Virginia. From *Sketchbook of Landscapes in the State of Virginia* by Lewis Miller, Virginia, 1853–1867, watercolor and ink on paper. (Abby Aldrich Rockefeller Folk Art Museum, The Colonial Williamsburg Foundation. Gift of Dr. and Mrs. Richard M. Kain in memory of George Hay Kain.)

The woodworking tools most commonly used in America throughout the 17th, 18th, and the first half of the 19th centuries came from England, which had a centuries-long tradition of toolmaking and an industrial system that produced high-quality tools at reasonable prices. The tools came to America via a sophisticated marketing system that started in the centers of English tool manufacturing—London, Birmingham, Lancashire, and Sheffield—and ended in the stores and tradeshops of North America and in the plantation workshops of slaveholders. Tools were American made, but these most often were made locally and did not have widespread distribution. It was not until the second quarter of the 19th century that the American tool manufacturing system begin to equal the products from England.

African American tool makers, free or enslaved, were extremely uncommon. The best known of these tool makers was Cesar Chelor (d. 1784), who was held by Francis Nicolson (1683–1753), generally recognized as America's first plane maker. Nicolson, who lived and worked in Wrentham, Massachusetts, had a flourishing plane-making business, and Chelor was working for Nicolson as early as 1736, when a "Negro," presumed to be Chelor, was listed on a Wrentham provisional tax list as belonging to Nicolson, who is not known to have owned any other slaves. Although still a slave in 1741, Chelor was admitted to membership in the town's Congregational church. Upon Nicolson's death in 1753, Chelor was set free by the terms of Nicolson's will, which directed that Chelor be given "his Bedstead [the frame], Bed & Beding [mattress, linens and blankets], his Chest and Cloathing, his Bench & common Bench-Tools." Chelor continued in the plane-making business. By all available evidence, Chelor was a successful businessman; at his death, he owned property valued at £88.2.0, including 23 shillings worth of **books** as well as "finished and unfinished" planes.

The tools that slaves used were supplied by their owners or, if they were hired out, their employers; they were not among the goods that both the enslaved and their masters considered to be the property of the slaves. In the 18th century, plantation owners like Thomas Jefferson (1743–1826) and George Washington (1732–1799) imported the tools used by their slaves and their paid employees directly from England. Those master cabinetmakers, coopers, and carpenters who owned or hired slaves purchased tools through agents in England or from nearby storekeepers. For example, Williamsburg, Virginia, shopkeeper John Greenhow advertised in 1771 that he sold "a large Assortment of Carpenters and Cabinet Makers Tools and Materials." In the 19th century, as American tool manufacture increased, the necessity to directly import tools from England decreased, although they continued to be imported and sold as part of the variety of tools available on the market. Craftsmen who had their own shops also acquired tools by **barter**, inheritance, secondhand purchase, or gift; many of these would have been used by slaves.

Besides the basic woodworking tools used by the enslaved, such as saws, chisels, gouges, planes, turnscrews, and files, they also used specialized forms of these tools. For example, those slaves who worked for a cabinetmaker and made furniture used veneer saws, turning chisels, or specially made planes for a specific type of furniture, whereas those who worked for coopers used drawknives, shaves, and froes specific to that work.

Slaveholders typically decided which enslaved boys would be taught a woodworking trade and, through a process similar to the apprenticeship experienced by free young men, they learned their trade over a number of years. Once taught the necessary skills and put to work, enslaved carpenters, coopers, sawyers, cabinetmakers, shipwrights, and housewrights were engaged in these trades for the rest of their working lives.

Because of the training and skill necessary to be a good craftsman, no matter what the area of specialization, enslaved woodworkers were among the most highly valued of bondsmen. Their skills were constantly in demand for construction and repair of buildings of all kinds, **cooperage**, **boats**, and furniture, and they used their skills to make things for themselves and their families, including **beds**, tables, chairs, and other furniture. They also made items that they sold for cash or traded for goods with their owners or storekeepers.

They could be easily hired out if necessary, earning money for their owners and, sometimes, for themselves. The U.S. Capitol was built, in part, by the hired labor of enslaved men, including sawyers, who were paid extra wages for overtime. They

---

### "Jack of All Trades" Slave Escapes

A notice that a highly skilled slave had run away was posted in the *Maryland Gazette*, Annapolis, May 24, 1759:

RAN away from Dumfries on Patowmack River, Virginia, in March last, a Mulatto Man Slave, named Dick (tho' it is probable he may now assume another) Country-born, about 35 Years of Age, a well-made slim Fellow, very active, is much addicted to Liquor, and when drunk, stammers in his Speech. Had on a good dark Bearskin Frock-Coat, and Cotton Breeches; but carried with him several other Cloaths. He is by Trade a compleat Wheelwright, and so much of a Smith, as to make the Nails, and shoe those he makes. He is likewise a good Cooper, Sawyer, and House-Carpenter, and has also been employed in small Craft by Water.

*Source:* Tom Costa. "The Geography of Slavery in Virginia." At www2.vcdh.virginia.edu/ saxon/servlet/SaxonServlet?source=/xml_docs/slavery/ads/md1759.xml&style=/xml_docs/ slavery/ads/display_ad.xsl&ad=m1759050001

---

removed the bark from logs with axes and then stood at either end of a pit saw—one end in the pit, one above—to saw the logs into boards that were then used in the building's construction. The boards were then turned into the lumber used by the hired slave carpenters who framed the building and the roof as well as the interior woodwork. The names of those who hired out their slaves are known, but the names of the enslaved are not and their work remains as proof of their skill with the tools of their trade.

FURTHER READING

Allen, William C. "History of Slave Laborers in the Construction of the United States Capitol." June 1, 2005. "Art, Artifacts, and Architecture," Office of the Clerk of the U.S. House of Representatives. At http://clerk.house.gov/art_history/art_artifacts/slave_labor_reportl.pdf.

Costa, Tom. "The Geography of Slavery in Virginia." At www2.vcdh.virginia.edu/gos/ index.html.

DeAvila, Richard T. "Ceasor Chelor and the World He Lived in." *The Chronicle of the Early American Industries Association* 46 (1993): 39–42, 91–97.

Gaynor, James M., and Nancy L. Hagedorn. *Tools: Working Wood in Eighteenth-Century America.* Williamsburg, VA: Colonial Williamsburg Foundation, 1993.

Salamon, R. A. *Dictionary of Woodworking Tools, c. 1700–1970, and Tools of Allied Trades.* Newtown, CT: Taunton Press, 1990.

MARTHA B. KATZ-HYMAN

**WOOL TEXTILES. Textiles** made from sheep's wool came in a wide variety of types and qualities. They included coarse materials worn by free laborers and the enslaved, expensive shiny glazed worsteds for upholstery, and beautifully finished broadcloth for men's suits. Woolens played an important role in the economies of Great Britain and the colonies of the American South. British woolens had been important manufacturing and trade commodities since the Middle Ages. Because British woolens were readily available and economical, American planters found it more cost-effective to devote resources to growing a single cash crop, rather than to produce woolen textiles. This was especially true in the Southern areas, where sheep were scarce.

Most of slaves' winter outerwear and **blankets** were wool. Because the textiles were often ordered by the hundreds of yards and tailored in bulk, the **clothing** of laborers on a plantation was often uniform in appearance. **Runaway slave advertisements** such as one published in the *Virginia Gazette* for December 13, 1770, describe runaway men dressed alike in "the common dress of field slaves." The woolens used most often by slaves included fustian, fear nothing (or fearnaught), duffil, kersey, and penniston, but the most prevalent were plains, cotton, and plaid.

The wool textile called "plain" or "plains" was woven in tabby (over one, under one) weave structure and finished with a fuzzy surface, or nap. The textile was woven a yard wide, often white in color, and described as being sturdy and comfortable for slaves' winter wear. Plains also came in colors such as blue and green. During the 18th century, undyed plains were often synonymous with the textiles called "**Negro cloth**," or "Negro cotton."

In the 18th century, Negro cloth was an inexpensive British napped woolen textile. By the second quarter of the 19th century, the manufacture of Negro cloth was well established in Rhode Island. The American version of the textile was made with cotton warps and woolen wefts. Advances in the technologies of cotton **spinning** and ginning, along with expansion of cotton plantations in the Southern states, made it cost-effective to substitute cotton for part of the wool in the American product.

Despite its confusing name, "cotton" often referred to a woolen fabric that was widely used for slaves' winter clothing and for blankets. Cotton was similar in appearance and use to plains. The name cotton probably stemmed from the napped or "cottoned" finish given to the substantial and warm woolen goods.

Just as "cotton" did not necessarily mean cotton fiber, so "plaid" did not always mean a patterned textile, as the term implies in the 21st century. A twilled wool fabric usually exported from Scotland, plaid came in white as well as checks. The textile was especially favored for cut-and-sewn fabric stockings or hose. Plaid hose worn by the enslaved were not necessarily checked or tartan designs; most often, plaid hose were unpatterned.

The wool textile known as cloth or broadcloth was a more expensive material that required considerable processing in its production. Broadcloth was woven in plain or tabby weave structure, deliberately and carefully shrunk in a process called fulling, napped to create a fuzzy surface, and finally shorn to even the nap and create an all-over mat texture. Because of the shrinking process, broadcloth did not ravel when cut. Broadcloth was used for **livery** suits of white and enslaved male servants in visible positions within the household. Livery suits typically were made in two contrasting colors taken from the family's coat of arms and trimmed with woven edgings called "livery lace." The finer grades of broadcloth also were made into expensive suits for gentry men and winter cloaks for men and women.

FURTHER READING

Baumgarten, Linda. "'Clothes for the People': Slave Clothing in Early Virginia." *Journal of Early Southern Decorative Arts* 14, no. 2 (November 1988): 26–70.

Baumgarten, Linda. "Plains, Plaid, and Cotton: Woolens for Slave Clothing." *Ars Textrina* 15 (1991): 203–222.

Baumgarten, Linda. "Common Dress, Clothing for Daily Life." In *What Clothes Reveal: The Language of Clothing in Colonial and Federal America,* edited by Linda Baumgarten, 106–139. New Haven, CT: Yale University Press, 2002.

Costa, Tom. "Virginia Runaways," Virginia Center for Visual History, University of Virginia. At http://people.uvawise.edu/runaways/index.html.

Montgomery, Florence. *Textiles in America, 1650–1870.* New York: W. W. Norton and Company, 1984, 2007.

Stachiw, Myron O. *"Negro Cloth": Northern Industry and Southern Slavery.* Boston: Merrimack Valley Textile Museum, 1981.

Windley, Lathan A., comp. *Runaway Slave Advertisements: A Documentary History from the 1730s to 1790.* 4 vols. Westport, CT: Greenwood Press, 1983.

LINDA BAUMGARTEN

**WORK ROUTINES.** Life for every young and adult enslaved individual revolved around work. Work for slaves began when they were young children and continued into old age. Whether on a small farm or larger plantation, hard, unrelenting labor, day in and day out, was the fate of most field slaves. Their day started and ended with the clang of the bell or the sound of a horn, sounded by the overseer or the slaveholder. More than one former slave, when interviewed by the Works Progress Administration's Federal Writers' Project in the 1930s, remembered working from dawn to dusk. As Dicey Thomas, interviewed in Arkansas, put it, "Long as you could see, you had to stay in the fields." Ellen Betts, a former Louisiana slave on a **sugar** plantation, recalled, "to dem dat work hour in, hour out, dem sugarcane fields sho' stretch from one end of the earth to de other." In the fields, men and women frequently worked side by side. Jennie Webb's pregnant mother worked in the fields in Mississippi and when her labor began, she attempted to rush back to the **slave quarters** for her baby's birth, but instead delivered on the path back from the fields. Failure to complete the work assignment in full usually resulted in some sort of punishment, frequently administered with the lash. Refusing to work by feigning illness or running away became the principal means by which many slaves resisted their enslavement.

Slaveholders and their overseer managers adopted different types of work arrangements and strategies for creating efficient workforces. In the antebellum period, various Southern agricultural journals published articles by planters that gave advice to their peers, outlining the efficiency of various arrangements, including the task system versus the gang system. The gang system required enslaved people to work cooperatively in groups and together complete large daily jobs like hoeing an entire field to prepare it for planting. On plantations, particularly the ones that grew crops like **tobacco**, sugarcane, or **cotton**, which placed heavy demands on laborers, slaves worked together in gangs, frequently under an enslaved overseer called a **slave driver**. On larger holdings, multiple gangs might be employed and gang members usually were selected for their physical abilities. Harsh punishment like whipping or flogging generally is associated with plantations that employed gang labor.

## Tasks

Rev. Silas Jackson described the work system divided by task on a Virginia plantation:

> In Virginia where I was, they raised tobacco, wheat, corn and farm products. I have had a taste of all the work on the farm, besides of digging and clearing up new ground to increase the acreage to the farm. We all had task work to do—men, women and boys. We began work on Monday and worked until Saturday. That day we were allowed to work for ourselves and to garden or to do extra work. When we could get work, or work on some one else's place, we got a pass from the overseer to go off the plantation, but to be back by nine o'clock on Saturday night or when cabin inspection was made. Some time we could earn as much as 50 cents a day, which we used to buy cakes, candies, or clothes.

*Source:* George P. Rawick, ed. *The American Slave: Kansas, Kentucky, Maryland, Ohio, Virginia, and Tennessee Narratives,* Vol. 16. Westport, CT: Greenwood Press, 1972.

Ben Horry recollected how the overseer punished his mother when she failed to complete her task as a slave in South Carolina:

> The worst thing I members was the colored oberseer. He was the one straight from Africa. He the boss over all the mens ad womens and if omans don't do all he say, he lay task on 'em they ain't able to do. My mother won't do all he say. When he say, "You go barn and stay till I come," she ain't do 'em. So he have it in for my mother and lay task on 'em she ain't able for do. Then for punishment my mother is take to the barn and strapped down on thing called the Pony. Hands spread like this and strapped to the floor and all two both she feet been tie like this. And she been give twenty five to fifty lashes till the blood flow. And my father and me stand right there and look and ain't able to lift a hand! Blood on floor in that rice barn when barn tear down by Hontingdon [A. M. Huntingdon].

*Source:* George P. Rawick, ed. *The American Slave: South Carolina Narratives,* Vol. 2. Westport, CT: Greenwood Press, 1972.

Under the task system, enslaved individuals would be assigned a daily task, and theoretically when it was completed, they were on their own time and free to do personal tasks. Naturally, the task system favored younger, stronger individuals who were able to do hard work efficiently. Fieldwork usually was measured in quarter- or half-acre units that made up the "task." Slaveholders came to believe that the task system encouraged slaves to be self-directed and therefore made them more motivated to complete their work. They needed less supervision, although the system probably worked better in situations in which enslaved individuals received their work assignments through direct personal contact with their owners. In some instances, slaves who exceeded their tasks or quotas sometimes were rewarded with incentives that ranged from extra time off to small amounts of money. Historians point out that the system did not permit slaves the kind of leisure time that modern Americans might imagine. Some slaveholders designed labor-intensive tasks that occupied entire days. In other cases, slaves who finished first often found themselves helping family members and others finish their tasks to avoid punishment. Although originally confined mostly to Low Country **rice** or Sea Island cotton plantations, the task system found widespread adoption by slavery's end in nearly every type of work environment that existed.

*See also* Bells and Horns; Whips.

FURTHER READING

Berlin, Ira, and Philip D. Morgan. *Cultivation and Culture: Labor and the Shaping of Slave Life in the Americas.* Charlottesville: University of Virginia Press, 1993.

Mellon, James ed. *Bullwhip Days: The Slaves Remember.* New York: Weidenfeld and Nicolson, 1988.

Morgan, Philip D. "Task and Gang Systems: The Organizing of Labor on New World Plantations." In *Work and Labor in Early America,* edited by Stephen Innes, 189–220. Chapel Hill: University of North Carolina Press, 1988.

KYM S. RICE

**WRITING TOOLS.** By the first quarter of the 19th century, most Southern states prohibited teaching slaves to read and write. Such laws were irregularly enforced, however, and enterprising slaves found ways to learn in spite of them. Historians estimate that approximately 10 percent of slaves were literate at the outbreak of the Civil War, and many more slaves at least observed reading and writing and understood the alphabet. They discovered literacy chiefly through its material accoutrements: the newspapers, **books**, slates, pens, ink, and paper that most slave owners tried to withhold. Slaves recognized the tools of writing as parts of the world of white people, but they frequently succeeded in appropriating them for their own.

Novelist Harriet Beecher Stowe's (1811–1896) depiction of *Uncle Tom's Cabin* (1852) character Uncle Tom using chalk and slate to compose a rough draft of a letter to his family might seem to be the Northern writer's projection of her children's education, but some slaves did have such experiences. Sam Aleckson, born a slave in South Carolina in 1852, was taught by his white owners, using a typical spelling book: "From this wonderful book we learned to read, write, and cipher, too. . . . We had slates, for those useful articles had not yet gone out of fashion." Indeed, archaeologists have excavated from **slave quarters** sites both slates, including some still bearing letters and numbers, and pencils. Clearly, many slaves apprehended, either because they received instruction from whites or because they cannily observed white children, the traditional means of learning to read and write in antebellum America. Little material evidence of slave literacy survives—quills and paper are less durable than graphite and slate—and most slaves had to do without the traditional tools, but slaves' testimony provides a fuller picture of their practices of writing.

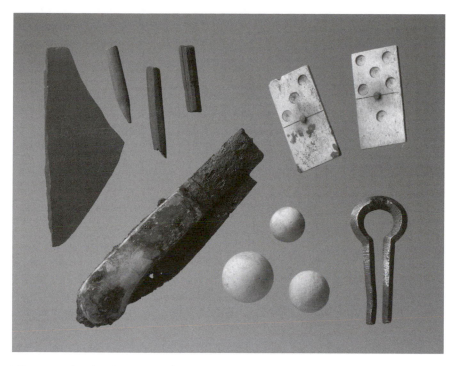

Writing tools, plus dominoes, marbles, and Jew's harp from Mulberry Row excavations at Thomas Jefferson's Monticello, Charlottesville, Virginia. (Monticello/Photograph by Edward Owen.)

Many **slave narratives**—those published in the 19th century as well as the oral histories gathered by the Federal Writers' Project in the 1930s—recount processes of literacy acquisition. In particular, former slaves described the things they used to learn to write. Enslaved African Americans labored in widely varying environments, and they adapted an equally wide array of material objects to their surreptitious projects of

---

### Writing Travel Passes

In Maryland, James Wiggins's father, who was literate, wrote out travel passes for other slaves:

> My father was a carpenter by trade, he was hired out to different farmers by Mr. Revell to repair and build barns, fences and houses. I have been told that my father could read and write. Once he was charged with writing passes for some slaves in the county, as a result of this he was given 15 lashes by the sheriff of the county, immediately afterwards he ran away, went to Philadelphia, where he died while working to save money to purchase mother's freedom, through a white Baptist minister in Baltimore.

*Source:* George P. Rawick, ed. *The American Slave: Kansas, Kentucky, Maryland, Ohio, Virginia, and Tennessee Narratives*, Vol. 16. Westport, CT: Greenwood Press, 1972.

---

self-education. Former slave and noted abolitionist Frederick Douglass (1818–1895) first learned to form letters from the markings on lumber in the shipyard where he worked in Maryland. Juan Manzano (1797–1854), a Cuban slave, studied the titles affixed to paintings on the walls of his owner's opulent home. Educator Booker T. Washington (1856–1915) first copied the figures written on barrels in a salt mine. Noah Davis (b. 1804) was apprenticed to a Fredericksburg, Virginia, shoemaker, and he studied the customers' names written on their boots.

Because of the legal and cultural opposition to African American literacy, slaves had to evade detection as they learned to write. Just as crucially, they struggled to acquire appropriate material implements. Peter Randolph (1825–1897), an enslaved Virginian, recalled, "I had no slate, so I used to write on the ground." In Missouri, William Wells Brown (1816–1884) likewise found convenient writing surfaces in the world around him. He also did not have a slate, but he did possess a piece of chalk, which he used to practice his letters on wooden **fences**. "All board fences within half a mile of where I lived," Brown remembered, "were marked over with some kind of figures I had made, in trying to learn how to write."

Other slaves managed to work with pen and paper, sometimes by salvaging the castoffs of slave owners, sometimes by crafting their own makeshift alternatives. Frederick Douglass, somewhat luckier than most slaves, had access to the used instructional materials of his owner's son; he furtively practiced his letters in the blank spaces of the white child's copybook. Solomon Northup (b. 1808), enslaved on a Louisiana plantation for more than 10 years in the 1840s, said that he "appropriated" a sheet of paper from his owner, and former Kentucky slave Henry Bibb (1815–1854) recalled in his 1849 narrative, "Whenever I got hold of an old letter that had been thrown away, or a piece of white paper, I would save it to write on." Manzano taught himself to write by tracing a "discarded sheet written in [his] master's hand." John M. Washington (1838–1918), a slave in Fredericksburg, Virginia, received a writing lesson from his uncle using a piece of wallpaper. Slaves who lived outside urban areas and had less contact with whites had to go to greater lengths. Multiple former slaves reported gathering feathers to use for quills and trying to produce their own ink. Northup and William Hayden made ink by boiling maple bark, and on Maryland's Eastern Shore, J. W. C. Pennington (1807–1870) made his ink from berries. An enslaved potter in South Carolina, David Drake, circumvented ink and paper altogether: he inscribed short poems into the clay of the pots he produced.

For those slaves who succeeded in becoming literate, pens and paper became part of their daily lives. Some slaves separated from their families by sale wrote letters to each other. Enslaved foremen charged to oversee distant plantations exchanged letters with their masters and kept records of the crops. Even for slaves who had not yet learned to write, paper could be an important part of how they manipulated the power relations of slavery. According to the former Missouri slave Henry Clay Bruce (1836–1902), many of the white men who composed slave patrols were illiterate, and slaves "would take a portion of a letter picked up and palm it off on them as a pass when arrested." Moses Roper (ca. 1815–1891), who escaped from slavery in Florida in 1835, did not know how to write, but he did understand the material properties of ink and paper. He showed a letter to a group of illiterate white men and tricked them into believing it proved he was free. Roper then covertly dipped the paper in a river to make the ink run, showed the ruined document to the same men, and enlisted their help in finding someone to write out a new copy—one that really did identify Roper as a free man. For Roper, as for all literate and marginally literate slaves, the materials of writing represented not just a medium for asserting themselves verbally but also a chance to gain purchase on the physical world of freedom.

*See also* Pottery.

FURTHER READING

Cornelius, Janet Duitsman. *"When I Can Read My Title Clear": Literacy, Slavery, and Religion in the Antebellum South*. Columbia: University of South Carolina Press, 1991.

Webber, Thomas L. *Deep Like the Rivers: Education in the Slave Quarter Community, 1831–1865*. New York: W. W. Norton, 1978.

Williams, Heather Andrea. *Self-Taught: African American Education in Slavery and Freedom*. Chapel Hill: University of North Carolina Press, 2005, pp. 7–29.

CHRISTOPHER HAGER

# Y

**YAMS AND SWEET POTATOES.** The sweet potato (*Ipomoea batatas*) is an edible tuber of the morning glory family indigenous to tropical America. It is different from the tropical yam (members of the family *Dioscorea*), but in American English the two words are often used interchangeably, partly because of the linguistic influence of enslaved Africans. The yam is indigenous to tropical Africa and Asia and was cultivated widely across West Africa during the period of the slave trade. The term "yam" has several origins. It is a verb (*nyam*) from the West Atlantic languages of Senegambia, such as Wolof, meaning "to taste" or "to eat." The term "nyambi" refers in Wolof to cassava, while a similar term is used by other groups for a wild edible root found in West Africa. It has been posited that the term "yam" was at one time applied to a white potato (*Solanum tuberosum*), named so by enslaved South Carolina African Americans who cultivated it in the early 18th century because it tasted similar to the yam with which they were familiar from Africa. For the people of the lower Guinea Coast (eastern Côte d'Ivoire to Cameroon), the yam was a traditional dietary staple of the belt of mixed-savanna and tropical rain forest between the hinterlands and the coast. For some groups, such as the Twi-speaking Akan of central and southern Ghana and the Igbo and Ibibio of southeastern Nigeria, the yam took on a spiritual and cultural meaning associated with its relationship with the Spirit of the Earth, usually a female deity, and the idea of demonstrable masculinity and social status by providing amply for one's family and community by successfully raising a yam crop. For enslaved Africans brought from these regions, no other **food** was as real and capable of providing sustenance as the yam. Just as bread was synonymous with eating and food in the Western world, the yam was its complement in West Africa. Exiled from their homes, the sweet potato filled that void.

African yams were brought to the Caribbean and South America during this time period, and one variety may have made it as far as South Carolina and Florida. Yams typically were stocked on **slave ships** as **rations** for the human cargo. In North America, enslaved Africans substituted different varieties of sweet potatoes for the true yam that was once the staple of their diet. Until about the 1760s, the term "potato" in the South was used primarily to describe the sweet potato. For enslaved African Americans it was the primary root crop and was essential to their diet. Some groups, including slaves from Central Africa, had already begun to significantly incorporate the sweet potato into their diet because of the introduction of the crop by the Portuguese.

Sweet potatoes were introduced to the colonial South via the Caribbean during the late 1600s. They quickly became a staple crop on most farms and plantations, with most chroniclers noting that the "white and red potatoes" were being grown in kitchen **gardens**. In southern Maryland, each slave garden had "at least sweet potatoes." English traveler William Hugh Grove stated in 1732 that enslaved Virginians grew "little Plats for [sweet] potatoes or [?] Indian pease [black-eyed peas] and Cimnells [pattypan squash]." He stated that "the potatoes are of the Barmudas kind fashion thick and short like a pear or long like a beet Root they are either white or red & Comonly rosted they are Sweet and over luscious best in a pye." Phillip Fithian (1747–1776), tutor for the children of Virginia planter Robert Carter III's (1728–1804) children at Nomini Hall on Virginia's Northern Neck, saw enslaved people preparing their provision **gardens** in April 1774, noting "they are digging up their small Lots of ground allow'd by their Master for Potatoes, Peas, etc." In both cases, sweet potatoes were interplanted with cowpeas to save space. Planters tended to oversee the planting of a diversity of tubers. At Tombee plantation, south of Charleston, South Carolina, multiple varieties, including Spanish, Leathercoats, Brimstones, and Redskins, were planted, each keeping the plantation in sweet potatoes for the better part of the year, with the red-skinned white-fleshed variety being "preferred by the Negroes." The sweet potato was not just valuable for its tubers but also for its leaves, which were eaten as a leafy green. Unbeknown to enslaved individuals, the sweet potato is high in beta-carotene, calcium, and iron and dietary fiber. In a diet based on **corn** and salted pork or **fish**, the sweet potato was nutritionally crucial.

The sweet potato had a number of culinary uses in the enslaved community. Sweet potatoes often were simply roasted in the ashes of the fire, sometimes covered by cabbage leaves to prevent burning. On other occasions, they were baked into loaves of sweet potato pone or cooked soft into puddings. These puddings later became the basis of sweet potato pie. In the Caribbean, sweetened potato puddings were developed by those enslaved workers forced to work at the **sugar** vats at night. In Mary Randolph's (1762–1828) cookbook, *The Virginia Housewife* (1824), sweet potatoes were also eaten stewed with **chickens** in an American version of an Igbo dish—chicken stew with yams.

The most celebrated Southern sweet potato dish was sweet potatoes roasted with opossum. About the same time of year that sweet potatoes had cured properly, the possums were fattened on persimmons and nuts. After they were captured and cleaned out, they were then butchered and roasted with sweet potatoes for a fall delicacy. Sometimes the sweet potato served as a garnish stuffed in the possum's mouth. It is possible that the sweet potato's starchy flavor toned down the gaminess of the dish.

So important was the sweet potato to the diet of enslaved Africans and African Americans that they cultivated other plants to serve as a substitute for its taste when the potato was unavailable. In Virginia, the striped cushaw, also known as the potato pumpkin or sweet potato pumpkin, was introduced from Jamaica and was quite popular with the enslaved population, according to Thomas Jefferson (1743–1826). He noted that it was used as a substitute at the time of the year that sweet potatoes were not normally available.

---

### Grandmother Betsey's Sweet Potatoes

The former slave and noted abolitionist Frederick Douglass (ca. 1818–1895) recalled his grandmother's green thumb in Maryland:

> She was a gardener as well as a fisherwoman, and remarkable for her success in keeping her seedling sweet potatoes through the months of winter, and easily got the reputation of being born to "good luck." In planting-time Grandmother Betsey was sent for in all directions, simply to place the seedling potatoes in the hills or drills; for superstition had it that her touch was needed to make them grow. This reputation was full of advantage to her and her grandchildren, for a good crop, after her planting for the neighbors, brought her a share of the harvest.

*Source:* Frederick Douglass. *Life and Times of Frederick Douglass: His Early Life as a Slave, His Escape from Bondage, and His Complete History to the Present Time.* Boston: DeWolfe & Fiske Co., 1892, http://docsouth.unc.edu/neh/dougl92/menu.html.

---

Sweet potatoes may have been stored in special storage areas in the floor of cabins in the **slave quarters**. Because the potatoes would be ruined if they froze, the hole was near the fire. The hidey hole or cuddy hole is a telltale marker of many slave quarters and was remembered fondly by formerly enslaved people reflecting on their past. The space doubled as both a cache for sweet potatoes and as the cabin's lockbox for personal items. Abolitionist Frederick Douglass recalled "the hole so strangely dug in front of the fire-place, beneath which grandmamma placed her sweet potatoes, to keep them from frost in winter, were full of interest to my childish observation."

Educator Booker T. Washington (1856–1915), originally from Franklin County, Virginia, liked to recall:

> There was no wooden floor in our cabin, the naked earth being used as a floor. In the center of the earthen floor there was a large, deep opening covered with boards, which was used as a place in which to store sweet potatoes during the winter. An impression of this potato-hole is very distinctly engraved upon my memory, because I recall that during the process of putting the potatoes in or taking them out I would often come into possession of one or two, which I roasted and thoroughly enjoyed.

Sweet potatoes could absorb some of the magical and spiritual associations surrounding yams and provided a means for enslaved families to create a semblance of personal space as well as continue a food tradition that linked them with their African roots. The sweet potato was the enslaved child's comfort food and left tactile memories of hot roasted potatoes or one jutting from the mouth of a possum or raccoon. Probably due to this influence, the sweet potato continues to be associated with the South and people of African descent and may account for their popularity in the 21st-century American diet.

***See also*** Subfloor Pits.

FURTHER READING

Chambers, Douglas Brent. "'He Gwine Sing He Country': Africans, Afro-Virginians, and the Development of Slave Culture in Virginia, 1610–1810." PhD diss., University of Virginia, 1996.

Douglass, Frederick. *Life and Times of Frederick Douglass: His Early Life as a Slave, His Escape from Bondage, and His Complete History to the Present Time.* Mineoloa, NY: Dover Publications, 2003.

Gamble, David. *The Wolof of Senegambia.* London: International African Institute, 1957.

Grime, William Ed. *Ethno-Botany of the Black Americans.* Algonac, MI: Reference Publications, 1979.

Hilliard, Sam Bowers. *Hog Meat and Hoecake: Food Supply in the Old South, 1840–1860.* Carbondale: Southern Illinois University Press, 1971.

McDaniel, George W. *Hearth and Home: Preserving a People's Culture.* Philadelphia: Temple University Press, 1982.

McLeod, Malcolm D. *The Asante.* London: Trustees of the British Museum by British Museum Publications, 1981.

Rosengarten, Theodore. *Tombee: Portrait of a Cotton Planter.* New York: Morrow, 1986.

Washington, Booker T. *Up from Slavery.* Oxford: Oxford University Press, 1995.

Weaver, William Woys. *Heirloom Vegetable Gardening.* New York: Henry Holt and Company, 1997.

MICHAEL W. TWITTY

**YARDS.** The yard, sometimes called a "service yard," was an essential feature on most plantation landscapes. Although mostly a work area, the yard represented a rare space for the convergence of whites and blacks. It typically lay at the rear of the slaveholder's dwelling and adjoined the work buildings. Reached through a back door or by walking around a building, it chiefly served as an outdoor extension of interior work space. Sometimes the yard was fenced or enclosed. The yard was dirt, rather than grass, and the dirt surface typically was swept smooth each day by **brooms**, likely a continuation of an African practice. Sweeping the yard was a task often assigned to children, as noted by Georgia Baker, who was 14 years old when slavery ended on Confederate Vice President Alexander Stephens's Georgia plantation where she was born. She remembered that she "swept yards, toted water to de field, and played round de house and yard wid de rest of de chillun."

The yard was the realm of enslaved individuals, usually women, who did laundry, washed dishes, cooked, repaired small items, and did other types of work there throughout most of the year but especially used it in good weather. White owners, particularly the plantation mistress, sometimes ventured out into the yard to give orders or supervise enslaved activities related to the Big House. Although the yard's location made it vulnerable to this type of white interference, it also functioned as a kind of staging area for activities by African Americans that related not just to work but also to precious leisure time. It also was a place where the enslaved community sometimes congregated together socially.

***See also*** Cooks and Cooking; Laundries.

FURTHER READING

Gundaker, Grey, and Judith McWillie, eds. *No Space Hidden: The Spirit of African American Yard Work*. Knoxville: University of Tennessee Press, 2005.

Mellon, James, ed. *Bullwhip Days: The Slaves Remember*. New York: Weidenfeld and Nicolson, 1988.

Vlach, John Michael. *Back of the Big House: The Architecture of Plantation Slavery*. Chapel Hill: University of North Carolina Press, 1993.

KYM S. RICE

# Selected Bibliography

Abrahams, Roger D. *Singing the Master: The Emergence of African American Culture in the Plantation South*. New York: Pantheon Books, 1992.

Baumgarten, Linda. "'Clothes for the People': Slave Clothing in Early Virginia." *Journal of Early Southern Decorative Arts* 14, no. 2 (1988): 27–70.

Baumgarten, Linda. *What Clothes Reveal: The Language of Clothing in Colonial and Federal America: The Colonial Williamsburg Collection*. Williamsburg, VA: Colonial Williamsburg Foundation, 2002.

Berlin, Ira. *Generations of Captivity: A History of African-American Slaves*. Cambridge, MA: Belknap Press, 2004.

Berlin, Ira. *Many Thousands Gone: The First Two Centuries of Slavery in North America*. Cambridge, MA: Belknap Press of Harvard University Press, 1998.

Berlin, Ira, Marc Favreau, and Steven F. Miller. *Remembering Slavery: African Americans Talk about Their Personal Experiences of Slavery and Freedom*. New York: New Press, 1998.

Blassingame, John W. *The Slave Community: Plantation Life in the Antebellum South*. New York: Oxford University Press, 1972.

Blassingame, John W. *Slave Testimony: Two Centuries of Letters, Speeches, Interviews, and Autobiographies*. Baton Rouge: Louisiana State University Press, 1977.

Blight, David, ed. *Passages to Freedom: The Underground Railroad in History and Memory*. Washington, DC: Smithsonian Books, 2004.

Bower, Anne L., ed. *African American Foodways: Explorations of History and Culture*. Urbana: University of Illinois Press, 2009.

Brown, Christopher Leslie, Philip D. Morgan, and the Gilder Lehrman Center for the Study of Slavery, Resistance, and Abolition. *Arming Slaves: From Classical Times to the Modern Age*. New Haven, CT: Yale University Press, 2006.

Campbell, Edward D. C., Jr., with Kym S. Rice, eds. *Before Freedom Came: African-American Life in the Antebellum South: To Accompany an Exhibition Organized by the Museum of the Confederacy*. Charlottesville: University Press of Virginia, 1991.

Caponi-Tabery, Gena. *Signifyin(g), Sanctifyin' & Slam Dunking: A Reader in African American Expressive Culture*. Amherst: University of Massachusetts Press, 1999.

Carey, Margret. *Beads and Beadwork of West and Central Africa*. Princes Risborough, England: Shire Publications, 1991.

Carney, Judith N. *Black Rice: The African Origins of Rice Cultivation in the Americas*. Cambridge, MA: Harvard University Press, 2001.

Carney, Judith, and Richard N. Rosomoff. *In the Shadow of Slavery: Africa's Botanical Legacy in the Atlantic World*. Berkeley: University of California Press, 2009.

Carter, Landon. *The Diary of Colonel Landon Carter of Sabine Hall, 1752–1778*. Edited by Jack P. Greene. Charlottesville: University Press of Virginia, 1965.

Cecelski, David S. *The Waterman's Song: Slavery and Freedom in Maritime North Carolina.* Chapel Hill: University of North Carolina Press, 2001.

Chambers, Douglas Brent. "'He Gwine Sing He Country': Africans, Afro-Virginians, and the Development of Slave Culture in Virginia, 1690–1810." PhD diss., University of Virginia, 1996.

Chireau, Yvonne Patricia. *Black Magic: Religion and the African American Conjuring Tradition.* Berkeley: University of California Press, 2003.

Cornelius, Janet Duitsman. *"When I Can Read My Title Clear": Literacy, Slavery, and Religion in the Antebellum South.* Columbia: University of South Carolina Press, 1991.

Covey, Herbert C., and Dwight Eisnach. *What the Slaves Ate: Recollections of African American Foods and Foodways from the Slave Narratives.* Santa Barbara, CA: Greenwood Press/ABC-CLIO, 2009.

Curtin, Philip. *The Rise and Fall of the Plantation Complex: Essays in Atlantic History.* 2nd ed. Cambridge: Cambridge University Press, 1999.

Dew, Charles B. *Bond of Iron: Master and Slave at Buffalo Forge.* New York: W.W. Norton, 1994.

Deyle, Steven. *Carry Me Back: The Domestic Slave Trade in American Life.* New York: Oxford University Press, 2005.

Doar, David. *Rice and Rice Planting in the South Carolina Low Country.* Charleston, SC: Charleston Museum, 1970.

Dubin, Lois Sherr. *The History of Beads: 30,000 B.C. to the Present.* Revised and expanded ed. New York: Abrams, 2009.

Edwards-Ingram, Ywone. "Medicating Slavery: Motherhood, Health Care, and Cultural Practices in the African Diaspora." PhD diss., College of William and Mary, 2005.

Egerton, Douglas R. *Death or Liberty: African Americans and Revolutionary America.* New York: Oxford University Press, 2009.

Ellis, Rex M. *The Birth of the Banjo.* Katonah, NY: Katonah Museum of Art, 2003.

Epstein, Dena J. *Sinful Tunes and Spirituals: Black Folk Music to the Civil War.* Urbana: University of Illinois Press, 1977.

Fennell, Christopher C. *Crossroads and Cosmologies: Diasporas and Ethnogenesis in the New World.* Gainesville: University Press of Florida, 2007.

Ferguson, Leland G. *Uncommon Ground: Archaeology and Early African America, 1650–1800.* Washington, DC: Smithsonian Institution Press, 1992.

Fett, Sharla M. *Working Cures: Healing, Health, and Power on Southern Slave Plantations.* Chapel Hill: University of North Carolina Press, 2002.

Fisch, Audrey. *The Cambridge Companion to the African American Slave Narrative.* Cambridge: Cambridge University Press, 2007.

Follett, Richard J. *The Sugar Masters: Planters and Slaves in Louisiana's Cane World, 1820–1860.* Baton Rouge: Louisiana State University Press, 2005.

Forman, Martha Ogle. *Plantation Life at Rose Hill: The Diaries of Martha Ogle Forman, 1814–1845.* Edited by W. Emerson Wilson. Wilmington: Historical Society of Delaware, 1976.

Foster, Helen Bradley. *New Raiments of Self: African American Clothing in the Antebellum South.* New York: Berg, 1997.

Foy, Charles R. "Seeking Freedom in the Atlantic World, 1713–1783." *Early American Studies: An Interdisciplinary Journal* 4, no. 1 (2006): 46–77.

Franklin, John Hope, and Alfred A. Moss. *From Slavery to Freedom: A History of African Americans.* 8th ed. New York: Knopf, 2002.

Franklin, John Hope, and Loren Schweninger. *Runaway Slaves: Rebels on the Plantation.* New York: Oxford University Press, 1999.

Fraser, Rebecca J. *Courtship and Love among the Enslaved in North Carolina.* Jackson: University Press of Mississippi, 2007.

Freedmen and Southern Society Project. *Freedom, a Documentary History of Emancipation, 1861–1867.* New York: Cambridge University Press, 1982.

Frey, Sylvia R., and Betty Wood. *Come Shouting to Zion: African American Protestantism in the American South and British Caribbean to 1830*. Chapel Hill: University of North Carolina Press, 1998.

Fry, Gladys-Marie. *Stitched from the Soul: Slave Quilts from the Antebellum South*. New York: Dutton Studio Books in association with the Museum of American Folk Art, 1990.

Gibbs, Patricia A. "Re-creating Hominy: The One-Pot Breakfast Food of the Gentry and Staple of Blacks and Poor Whites in the Early Chesapeake." In *Oxford Symposium on Food & Cookery 1988: The Cooking Pot; Proceedings*, 46–54. London: Prospect Books Ltd., 1989.

Greene, Harlan, Harry S. Hutchins, and Brian E Hutchins. *Slave Badges and the Slave-Hire System in Charleston, South Carolina, 1783–1865*. Jefferson, NC: McFarland, 2004.

Grime, William E. *Ethno-Botany of the Black Americans*. Algonac, MI: Reference Publications, 1976.

Gundaker, Grey, and Judith McWillie. *No Space Hidden: The Spirit of African American Yard Work*. Knoxville: University of Tennessee Press, 2005.

Gura, Philip F., and James F. Bollman. *America's Instrument: The Banjo in the Nineteenth Century*. Chapel Hill: University of North Carolina Press, 1999.

Hall, Gwendolyn Midlo. *Africans in Colonial Louisiana: The Development of Afro-Creole Culture in the Eighteenth Century*. Baton Rouge: Louisiana State University Press, 1992.

Handler, Jerome. "The Middle Passage and the Material Culture of Captive Africans." *Slavery & Abolition* 30, no. 1 (March 2009): 1–26.

Heath, Barbara J. *Hidden Lives: The Archaeology of Slave Life at Thomas Jefferson's Poplar Forest*. Charlottesville: University Press of Virginia, 1999.

Hess, Karen. *The Carolina Rice Kitchen: The African Connection*. Columbia: University of South Carolina Press, 1992.

Hilliard, Sam Bowers. *Hog Meat and Hoecake: Food Supply in the Old South*. Carbondale: Southern Illinois University Press, 1972.

Hodges, Graham Russell. *Root & Branch: African Americans in New York and East Jersey, 1613–1863*. Chapel Hill: University of North Carolina Press, 1999.

Hodges, Graham Russell, and Alan Edward Brown. *"Pretends to Be Free": Runaway Slave Advertisements from Colonial and Revolutionary New York and New Jersey*. New York: Garland, 1994.

Hudson, Larry E., Jr., ed. *Working Toward Freedom: Slave Society and Domestic Economy in the American South*. Rochester, NY: University of Rochester Press, 1994.

Hurmence, Belinda. *Before Freedom: 48 Oral Histories of Former North and South Carolina Slaves*. New York: Penguin Books, 1990.

Jefferson, Thomas, and Robert C. Baron. *The Garden and Farm Books of Thomas Jefferson*. Golden, CO: Fulcrum, 1987.

Johnson, Walter. *Soul by Soul: Life Inside the Antebellum Slave Market*. Cambridge, MA: Harvard University Press, 1999.

Joyner, Brian D. *African Reflections on the American Landscape: Identifying and Interpreting Africanisms*. Washington, DC: National Center for Cultural Resources, National Park Service, U.S. Department of the Interior, 2003.

Katz-Hyman, Martha. "'In the Middle of This Poverty Some Cups and a Teapot': The Furnishing of Slave Quarters at Colonial Williamsburg." In *The American Home: Material Culture, Domestic Space, and Family Life*, edited by Eleanor McD. Thompson, 197–216. Winterthur, DE: Henry Francis Du Pont Winterthur Museum, 1998.

King, Wilma. *Stolen Childhood: Slave Youth in Nineteenth-Century America*. Bloomington: Indiana University Press, 1995.

Koverman, Jill Beute, ed. *"I Made This Jar. . ." The Life and Works of the Enslaved African-American Potter, Dave*. Columbia: McKissick Museum, University of South Carolina, 1988.

Kulikoff, Allan. *Tobacco and Slaves: The Development of Southern Cultures in the Chesapeake, 1680–1800*. Chapel Hill: Published for the Institute of Early American History and Culture of Williamsburg, Virginia, by the University of North Carolina Press, 1986.

Leone, Mark P., and Gladys-Marie Fry. "Conjuring in the Big House Kitchen: An Interpretation of African American Belief Systems Based on the Uses of Archaeology and Folklore Sources." *Journal of American Folklore* 112, no. 445 (Summer 1999): 372–403.

Levine, Lawrence. *Black Culture and Black Consciousness: Afro-American Folk Thought from Slavery to Freedom.* New York: Oxford University Press, 1978.

Linn, Karen. *That Half-Barbaric Twang.* Urbana: University of Illinois Press, 1994.

Lounsbury, Carl. "The Structure of Justice: The Courthouses of Colonial Virginia." In *Perspectives in Vernacular Architecture, III,* edited by Thomas Carter and Bernard L. Herman, 214–226. Columbia: University of Missouri Press, 1989.

Lounsbury, Carl, and Vanessa Elizabeth Patrick. *An Illustrated Glossary of Early Southern Architecture and Landscape.* New York: Oxford University Press, 1994.

Malone, Jacqui. *Steppin' on the Blues: The Visible Rhythms of African American Dance.* Urbana: University of Illinois Press, 1996.

Margolin, Sam. "'And Freedom to the Slave': Anti-Slavery Ceramics, 1787–1865." In *Ceramics in America 2002,* edited by Robert E. Hunter, 80–109. Milwaukee, WI: Chipstone Foundation, 2002.

Martin, Ann Smart. *Buying into the World of Goods: Early Consumers in Backcountry Virginia.* Baltimore: Johns Hopkins University Press, 2008.

McDaniel, George W. *Hearth & Home: Preserving a People's Culture.* Philadelphia, PA: Temple University Press, 1982.

Medford, Edna Greene, ed. *The New York African Burial Ground: History, Final Report.* Washington, DC: Howard University, 2004. At http://www.africanburialground.gov/Final Reports/ABG_HistoryReportFinal_Tables.pdf.

Mintz, Sidney. *Sweetness and Power: The Place of Sugar in Modern History.* New York: Viking, 1985.

Morgan, Philip D. *Slave Counterpoint: Black Culture in the Eighteenth-Century Chesapeake and Lowcountry.* Chapel Hill: University of North Carolina Press, 1998.

Nichols, Elaine. *The Last Miles of the Way: African-American Homegoing Traditions, 1890–Present.* Columbia: South Carolina State Museum, 1989.

Olmert, Michael. *Kitchens, Smokehouses, and Privies: Outbuildings and the Architecture of Daily Life in the Eighteenth-Century Mid-Atlantic.* Ithaca, NY: Cornell University Press, 2009.

Opie, Frederick Douglass. *Hog & Hominy: Soul Food from Africa to America.* New York: Columbia University Press, 2008.

Orser, Charles E., Jr. *Race and the Archaeology of Identity.* Salt Lake City: University of Utah Press, 2001.

Otto, John Solomon. *Cannon's Point Plantation, 1794–1860: Living Conditions and Status Patterns in the Old South.* New York: Academic Press, 1984.

Perdue, Charles L., Thomas E Barden, Robert K Phillips, and Virginia Writers' Project. *Weevils in the Wheat: Interviews with Virginia Ex-Slaves.* Charlottesville: University Press of Virginia, 1976.

Pogue, Dennis. "The Domestic Architecture of Slavery at George Washington's Mount Vernon." *Winterthur Portfolio* 37, no. 1 (2002): 3–22.

Raboteau, Albert J. *Slave Religion: The "Invisible Institution" in the Antebellum South.* Updated ed. New York: Oxford University Press, 2004.

Rafferty, Sean, and Rob Mann, eds. *Smoking and Culture: The Archaeology of Tobacco Pipes in Eastern North America.* Knoxville: University of Tennessee Press, 2004.

Rawick, George P., ed. *The American Slave: A Composite Autobiography.* Westport, CT: Greenwood Press, 1972–1979.

Rediker, Marcus. *The Slave Ship.* New York: Viking, 2007.

Roberts, John Storm. *Black Music of Two Worlds: African, Caribbean, Latin, and African-American Traditions.* 2nd ed. New York: Schirmer Books, 1998.

Rose, Willie Lee Nichols. *A Documentary History of Slavery in North America.* Athens: University of Georgia Press, 1999.

Rosengarten, Dale, and the McKissick Museum. *Row Upon Row: Sea Grass Baskets of the South Carolina Lowcountry.* Columbia: McKissick Museum, University of South Carolina, 1986.

Rosengarten, Dale, Theodore Rosengarten, and Enid Schildkrout. *Grass Roots: African Origins of an American Art*. New York: Museum for African Art, 2008.

Ruppel, Timothy, Jessica Neuwirth, Mark P. Leone, and Gladys-Marie Fry. "Hidden in View: African Spiritual Spaces in North American Landscapes." *Antiquity* 77, no. 296 (June 2003): 321–336.

Samford, Patricia. *Subfloor Pits and the Archaeology of Slavery in Colonial Virginia*. Tuscaloosa: University of Alabama Press, 2007.

Schafer, Judith Kelleher. *Becoming Free, Remaining Free: Manumission and Enslavement in New Orleans, 1846–1862*. Baton Rouge: Louisiana State University, 2003.

Schwartz, Marie Jenkins. *Born in Bondage: Growing up Enslaved in the Antebellum South*. Cambridge, MA: Harvard University Press, 2000.

Singleton, Theresa A., ed. *"I, Too, Am America": Archaeological Studies of African-American Life*. Charlottesville: University Press of Virginia, 1999.

Smith, Billy G., and Richard Wojtowicz. *Blacks Who Stole Themselves: Advertisements for Runaways in the Pennsylvania Gazette, 1728–1790*. Philadelphia: University of Pennsylvania Press, 1989.

Smith, Julia Floyd. *Slavery and Rice Culture in Low Country Georgia, 1750–1860*. Knoxville: University of Tennessee Press, 1985.

Smith, Merrit Roe. *Harpers Ferry Armory and the New Technology: The Challenge of Change*. Ithaca, NY: Cornell University Press, 1977.

Sobel, Mechal. *The World They Made Together: Black and White Values in Eighteenth-Century Virginia*. Princeton, NJ: Princeton University Press, 1987.

Stachiw, Myron O. *Negro Cloth: Northern Industry & Southern Slavery*. North Andover, MA: Merrimack Valley Textile Museum, 1981.

Tadman, Michael. *Speculators and Slaves: Masters, Traders, and Slaves in the Old South*. Madison: University of Wisconsin Press, 1989.

Tate, Thad W. *The Negro in Eighteenth-Century Williamsburg*. Williamsburg: Colonial Williamsburg Foundation, distributed by the University Press of Virginia, 1965.

Taylor, Eric Robert. *If We Must Die: Shipboard Insurrections in the Era of the Atlantic Slave Trade*. Baton Rouge: Louisiana State University Press, 2006.

Thompson, Robert Farris. *Faces of the Gods: Art and Altars of Africa and the African Americas*. New York: Museum for African Art, 1993.

Thompson, Robert Farris. *Flash of the Spirit: African and Afro-American Art and Philosophy*. New York: Random House, 1983.

Tibbles, Anthony. *Transatlantic Slavery: Against Human Dignity*. 2nd ed. Liverpool, England: Liverpool University Press, 2006.

Todd, Leonard. *Carolina Clay: The Life and Legend of the Slave Potter Dave*. New York: W.W. Norton, 2008.

Trinkley, Michael, Debi Hacker, and Sarah Fick. *The African American Cemeteries of Petersburg, Virginia: Continuity and Change*. Columbia, SC: Chicora Foundation, 1999.

Upton, Dell, and John Michael Vlach, ed. *Common Places: Readings in American Vernacular Architecture*. Athens: University of Georgia Press, 1986.

U.S. Department of the Interior. *Places of Cultural Memory: African Reflections on the American Landscape: Conference Proceedings, May 9–12, 2001, Atlanta, Georgia*. Washington, DC: U.S. Department of the Interior, National Park Service, 2001.

Van Horne, John C. *Religious Philanthropy and Colonial Slavery: The American Correspondence of the Associates of Dr. Bray, 1717–1777*. Urbana: University of Illinois Press, 1985.

Vlach, John Michael. *Back of the Big House: The Architecture of Plantation Slavery*. Chapel Hill: University of North Carolina Press, 1993.

Vlach, John Michael. *By the Work of Their Hands: Studies in Afro-American Folklife*. Charlottesville: University of Virginia Press, 1991.

Vlach, John Michael. *Charleston Blacksmith: The Work of Philip Simmons*. Athens: University of Georgia Press, 1981.

Walsh, Lorena Seebach. *Motives of Honor, Pleasure, and Profit: Plantation Management in the Colonial Chesapeake, 1607–1763*. Chapel Hill: Published for the Omohundro Institute of Early American History and Culture, Williamsburg, Virginia, by the University of North Carolina Press, 2010.

Webber, Thomas L. *Deep like the Rivers: Education in the Slave Quarter Community, 1831–1865*. New York: Norton, 1978.

Weiner, Marli Frances. *Mistresses and Slaves: Plantation Women in South Carolina, 1830–1880*. Urbana: University of Illinois Press, 1998.

Westmacott, Richard. *African-American Gardens and Yards in the Rural South*. Knoxville: University of Tennessee Press, 1992.

White, Deborah Gray. *Ar'n't I a Woman?: Female Slaves in the Plantation South*. New York: Norton, 1985.

White, Shane, and Graham J. White. *Stylin': African American Expressive Culture from Its Beginnings to the Zoot Suit*. Ithaca, NY: Cornell University Press, 1998.

Whitman, T. Stephen. *The Price of Freedom: Slavery and Manumission in Baltimore and Early National Maryland*. Lexington: University Press of Kentucky, 1997.

Williams-Forson, Psyche A. *Building Houses Out of Chicken Legs: Black Women, Food, and Power*. Chapel Hill: University of North Carolina Press, 2006.

Wood, Marcus. *Blind Memory: Visual Representations of Slavery in England and America*. New York: Routledge, 2000.

Wood, Peter H. *Black Majority; Negroes in Colonial South Carolina from 1670 through the Stono Rebellion*. New York: Knopf, 1974.

Yellin, Jean Fagan, and John C. Van Horne. *The Abolitionist Sisterhood: Women's Political Culture in Antebellum America*. Ithaca, NY: Cornell University Press, 1994.

Yentsch, Anne E. *A Chesapeake Family and Their Slaves: A Study in Historical Archaeology*. New York: Cambridge University Press, 1994.

## WEB SITES

African Burial Ground. At www.africanburialground.gov/ABG_Main.htm.

"African Burial Ground National Monument," U.S. National Park Service. At www.nps.gov/afbg/index.htm.

*African Diaspora Archaeology Newsletter*, African Diaspora Archaeology Network. At www.diaspora.uiuc.edu/newsletter.html.

"The Bibliography of Slavery and World Slaving," Rector and Visitors of the University of Virginia. At www2.vcdh.virginia.edu/bib/index.php.

"Born in Slavery: Slave Narratives from the Federal Writers' Project, 1936–1938," American Memory, Library of Congress. At http://memory.loc.gov/ammem/snhtml/.

Costa, Tom. "The Geography of Slavery in Virginia." At www2.vcdh.virginia.edu/gos/.

Digital Archaeological Archive of Comparative Slavery, Thomas Jefferson Foundation. At www.daacs.org/.

Fellner, Leigh. "Betsy Ross Redux: The Underground Railroad 'Quilt Code.'" Hart Cottage Quilts. At www.ugrrquilt.hartcottagequilts.com.

"First-Person Narratives of the American South," Documenting the American South Collection, University Library of the University of North Carolina at Chapel Hill. At http://docsouth.unc.edu/fpn/.

Gibbs, Patricia A. "Slave Garden Plots and Poultry Yards," Colonial Williamsburg. At http://research.history.org/Historical_Research/Research_Themes/ThemeEnslave/SlaveGardens.cfm.

Handler, Jerome S., and Michael L. Tuite Jr. "The Atlantic Slave Trade and Slave Life in the Americas: A Visual Record," Virginia Foundation for the Humanities and University of Virginia. At http://hitchcock.itc.virginia.edu/ Slavery/index.php.

"Historic American Buildings Survey/Historic American Engineering Record/Historic American Landscapes Survey," American Memory, Library of Congress. At http://memory.loc.gov/ammem/collections/habs_haer/.

"The Making of African American Identity: Vol. I, 1500–1865," Primary Resources in U.S. History and Literature, Toolbox Library, National Humanities Center. At http://nationalhumanitiescenter.org/pds/maai/index.htm.

"Manuscript Collections Relating to Slavery," New York Historical Society. At https://www.nyhistory.org/slaverycollections/.

"National Underground Railroad: Network to Freedom," U.S. National Park Service. At www.nps.gov/history/ugrr/list.htm.

"North American Slave Narratives," Documenting the American South Collection, University Library of the University of North Carolina at Chapel Hill. At http://docsouth.unc.edu/neh/.

"Tobacco in Virginia," Virginia Places. At www.virginiaplaces.org/agriculture/tobacco.html.

# Index

Abd ar-Rahman. *See* Ibn Sori, Abdulrahman
*Abelmoschus esculentus*, 147, 359
abolition imagery, **17–23**, 18f, 19f, 91, 442,
    518f, 532f
abolitionism, 63–64. *See also* free produce
Abraham (silversmith, Charleston, SC), 458
accordions, **23–25**
"Act for the Gradual Abolition of Slavery"
    (New York), 26–27
Adams, Ezra, 134
Adams, William, 337
African American cooking traditions, 208.
    *See also* cooking and cooks; food and
    foodways
African background, of hair and hairstyles, 265
African Burial Ground (New York), 52, 53,
    204, 257, 421, 422
African Episcopal Church of St. Thomas
    (Philadelphia), 116
African Free School (AFS), **26–28**, 26f, 76
African Methodist Episcopal Church
    (Philadelphia), 116
African roots and Creole transformations,
    245–247
African traditions, 14, 69, 101, 158, 170; and
    food, 230; in music, 1–8
Afzelius, Adam, 272
agricultural outbuildings, 178. *See also* corn
    cribs; dairies; tobacco barns
Aiken-Rhett House (Charleston, SC), 282
Alabama, 36, 47, 55–56, 126, 161, 165, 276,
    285, 305f, 331, 379, 426, 463, 468,
    479f, 483, 495, 496, 520, 534
Alabama bed, 55
Aleckson, Sam, 542
Allen, Richard, 63, 116
Allen, Rev. W. B., 95, 533

American Anti-Slavery Society, 20
American Colonization Society (ACS), 63
Anderson, James, 350
Angel, Adam, 363
animal bones, 6, 29, 53, 76, 106, 209, 230,
    275, 484
animal traps, **29**
Antebellum South, slave furnishings in, 242–244
anti-slavery attitude, 343
anti-slavery imagery, 18f, 19f
*apo* (sacred pouch), 141
appraisers, of probate inventories, 311, 312
apprenticeship, 68, 74, 88, 146, 147, 151,
    187, 290, 313, 423, 459, 537
Arkansas, 47, 50, 161, 200, 202, 258, 410f,
    462; slave narratives from, 74, 132,
    198, 286, 296, 304, 309
Armfield, John, 19, 464, 465
armories, **30–33**. *See also* firearms; military
    equipment
arquebus, 221
"asafetida bags" (herbal bags), 143
auction advertisements, **33–36**
auction blocks, **37–38**, 87f, 375, 409, 411, 466
auction house, 34f

Baartman, Saarjite, 93
BaKongo, 104, 107, 138, 141, 142, 158, 159,
    160, 170, 214–217, 345, 351, 422, 429
balafons, **39**
Ball, Charles, 124, 133, 181, 224, 226, 247,
    319, 395, 482
Ball, Joseph, 55, 133, 242, 367
"bamboro" (Jew's harps), 293, 543
banjos, **40–43**, 55; banjar, 40f, 41, 42, 253;
    banza, 42; colonies, 41; from
    plantation to parlor, 42–43, 229f

barbecues, 370, 371, 372

barbers, 397

barefootedness, 425–426

barns, 155, 157, 164, 176, 332, 528. *See also* tobacco barns

barracks, 452, 484, 487. *See also* dormitories

barter goods, **44**

bartering, 44, 232

basil, 273

baskets and basket making, xv, **45–50**, 45f, 132, 133, 232, 243, 328, 456, 528; fish baskets, 29

bast fibers, 498

Baudelaire, Charles, 90

beads, xiii, **51–53**, 85, 105, 106, 217, 242 glass, 106

"beating" hominy, 155, 278, 279

Beckford, William, 228

beds, xiv, **54–57**, 72, 177, 239, 240, 242, 243

Beecher, Lyman, 62

beef, 206, 207, 208, 231

bell rack, 59–61, 59f

bells and horns, **57–61**; different perspectives, 61; manufacture, 57; other signals, 61; punishment, 59–61; resistance, 59; slaves disciplining each other, 59; time discipline and control, 58–59

"benefit of clergy" plea, 78

benevolent associations, **61–64** abolitionism, 63–64; benevolence, 62; and the black community, 63

Bennie (sesame) Soup, 417

Betts, Ellen, 488, 540

Beverly, Robert, 523

Bibb, Henry, 21, 64, 364, 544

Bible, xvi, 14, 27, **65–67**, 78, 249, 300, 301

Big Dipper, 253

"big dwelling." *See* double-pen houses

Big House, 47, 56, 58, 71, 81, 149, 177, 205, 239

Billings, Charles Howland Hammatt, 92

Black, Leonard, 375, 526

Black, Maggie, 403

black churches, diversity of, 115–117

blackface, 43, 93

blacksmithing, 46, 58, 350, 407

blacksmith shops, **68–70**, 349; African traditions, 69; iron production, 69–70

"Black Venus," 91

blankets, xiv, **70–72**, 120, 121, 122, 126, 242, 244, 311, 324, 361, 367, 387, 389, 410, 501, 537, 539

Blumenbach, Johann, 431

boats, 48, **72–73**, 246, 252, 353, 395, 411, 435, 537. *See also* canoes; ferries; slave ships

"boiling holes," 97

Bolton, James, 81, 224, 335

Bolzius, Johann, 393

bones, animal, 207f

Booker, Jim, 220

books, xvi, 66, 67, **73–76**, 145, 542. *See also* Bray schools; opening essay Literacy and Orality

Boone, Andrew, 534

Bost, W. L., 38

bottle trees, **76–77**

Boucher, Jonathan, 75

Bourne, George, 20

braids, varieties of, 269–270

Branagan, Thomas, 18

brands and branding, **77–78**, 199, 373, 432, 441

Bray, Thomas, 66, 75, 79

Bray schools, 75, **79–80**

Bremo Recess Quarter (Virginia), 66, 89, 483

Brewer, Jim, 25

Brice, Andy, 219

Bristow, Josephine, 498

*Brooks*, 475; same ship as *Brookes*, 18

brooms, 46, **80–83**, 132, 240, 241, 243, 550; making of, 80–81; rituals, 81–83

Brown, John, 32, 521

Brown, Sally, 304, 335

Brown, William Wells, 461, 544

"Brown Bess" (musket), 221. *See also* military equipment

Brown Fellowship Society (Charleston, SC), 63, 257

Bruce, Henry Clay, 544

Bruner, Peter, 279, 322

Bryan, Andrew, 117

Buffon, George, 430, 431

Bureau of Refugees, Freedmen, and Abandoned Lands. *See* Freemen's Bureau

burial associations, 257

burnishing colonoware, 137

Butler, Benjamin, 144

Butler, Isaiah, 60

Butler, Pierce, 336, 447

buttermilk, 175, 356, 394, 395

buttons, 52, 53, **83–85**, 85f, 106, 205, 209, 242, 251, 421, 427, 456, 485

"Buzzard Lope" dance, 82

cabins, 55, 56, 59, 81, 109, 135, 159, 176, 177, 188–190, 191f, 209, 239f, 240,

242, 243, 250, 252, 296, 297, 299, 307, 318, 323–325, 331–333, 336, 351, 356, 361, 363, 389, 421, 427–429, 448–451, 453, 456, 468, 471, 472, 493, 494, 523, 541, 549. *See also* subfloor pits

"calabash," 40, 42, 251–252, 253

California, 150, 343, 433

Campbell, Tunis, 233

"cane rows," 269

Cannon's Point Plantation, 207

canoes, **87–89**. *See also* boats; ferries

Carey, Mathew, 18, 91

caricatures, **89–94**, 90f, 267, 431f, 474f

carpenter shops, 180

Carter, George, 467

Carter, Landon, 44, 109, 118, 135, 227, 241, 319, 336, 366, 368, 397, 525

Carter, Robert "King," 368

Carter, Robert, III, 41, 100, 369, 426, 524, 548

Carter, Robert Wormeley, 189

Cary, Lott, 510

caskets. *See* coffins and caskets

cast iron pots, xiv, **94–99**, 96f, 149, 177, 241, 243, 278, 299, 317, 369, 374, 428, 490

catfish, 225, 226, 231

cauldrons, 97, 98, 175, 179

Cavendish, James, 441

Cawthorn, Cicely, 51, 394, 445

*Celia (a slave) v. Missouri* (1855), 167

cemeteries, **99–102**, 209. *See also* coffins and caskets; faunal remains; graves

chamber pots and privies, **102–104**, 136f

Chandler, Elizabeth Margaret, 18

Chandler, John, 379

Chandler, Thomas, 378, 379

Chaplin, Thomas B., 48

Charleston (South Carolina), 20, 30, 36, 38, 46, 47, 55, 61, 63, 66, 68, 75, 100, 127, 139, 146, 165, 189, 212, 247, 256, 257, 268, 282, 288, 321, 377, 390, 411, 415, 417, 423, 434–437, 453, 455, 457, 458, 466, 468, 471, 495, 548; ironwork in, 289–290

Charleston Neck (South Carolina), 435;

charms, xvii, 52, 53, **104–107**, 140, 142, 170, 205, 209, 248, 270, 272, 337, 346, 421, 428, 428f, 478. *See also* festishes; subfloor pits

cheese, 148, 169, 174–175, 481

Chelor, Cesar, 536, 537

Chesapeake region, 4, 5, 13, 53, 72, 109, 149, 158, 189, 209, 224, 226,

245, 247, 249, 252, 275, 276, 279, 359, 394, 395, 424, 430, 448, 450–452, 482, 504, 506, 509, 511–513, 527–530, 548

Chesapeake slave culture, 4, 5

Chesney, Pharoah Jackson, 525

Chesnut, Mary, 220

chicken houses/coops, 167, 178, 187

chickens, 44, 106, **108–111**, 132, 133, 141, 169, 177, 206, 207, 208, 211, 231, 262, 279, 319, 327, 332, 368, 373, 471, 481. *See also* cooking and cooks

children's dress, 126

Childs, Mary, 246

Chinn, Joseph, 133

Christianization of American slaves, 7, 74, 112–115, 138, 142, 158, 170, 194, 216, 255, 487. *See also* Bible; Bray schools; slave galleries

Christmas, 5, 164, 165, 169, 219, 261, 313, 318, 319, 320, 325, 364, 366, 396, 415; at the Big House, 329

churches and praise houses, **111–117**, 445; black churches, diversity of, 115–117; Christianization of American slaves, 112–115. *See also* benevolent associations; cemeteries

Church of England (Anglican Church), 26, 65, 75, 79, 80, 445

Civil War, 7, 13, 17, 22, 24, 30, 64, 66, 76, 93, 112, 116, 136, 137, 138, 146, 161, 173, 187, 197, 200, 341. *See also* contraband camps

Clark, Amos, 44

Clarke, Lillian, 395

clay pits, 484–485

clocks and watches, **117–118**. *See also* bells and horns

cloth, 106, **119–121**, 133, 141, 176, 180, 185, 186, 214, 244, 248, 254, 266, 267, 271, 285, 287, 288, 479f

clothes, washing, 304–305

clothing, xiv, 44, 62, 64, 84, 85, 106, 120, 123f, 143, 185, 206, 242, 303, 311–314, 315f, 316, 332, 356, 357, 366, 367, 389, 396, 398, 406, 407, 410, 421, 465, 479, 485. *See also* Negro cloth; textiles; wool

clothing allotments, 120, **121–122**

clothing and footwear, **123–128**; children's dress, 126; dressing up, 127–128; headgear, 127; resources for clothing, 123; rural slave dress, 125; shoes, 126–127; slave labor and clothing,

123–125; urban and house slave dress, 125
Cocke, Louisa Maxwell, 66
Coffin, Charles, 466
Coffin, Levi, 519
coffins and caskets, **128–129**. *See also* cemeteries; graves
coffles, 36, **129–131**, 129f, 410
Cohen, Jannie, 49
coins and currency, xvii, 52, 53, 91, 101, 105, 107, **131–134**, 142, 217, 259. *See also* shrines and spirit caches; subfloor pits
Coleman, George, 498
Coleman, Henry, 281, 384
collards, **134–135**, 208, 230, 248, 249, 396
Colleton, John, 415
Collins, Harriet, 272
colonial period and early republic, slave furnishings in, 240–242
colonization movement, 28, 63, 64, 199, 237
colonoware, 81, 102, 107, **135–139**, 136f, 159, 241, 375, 376
Congo-Angolan slaves, 212, 288
conjure bags, **140–143**
conjurer, 52, 104, 106, 115, 158, 159, 170, 209, 337
conjure/root-work system, 140, 158
Connecticut, 276, 346, 431f, 442
contraband camps, **143–146**; 144f
cooking and cooks, **146–150**, 147f. *See also* food and foodways
cooperage, **151–153**, 151f, 495, 537
Corbin, Gawen, 414
corn, 45, 47, 49, 56, 109, 132, 133, 147, **153–156**, 164, 185, 230, 246–248, 274, 275, 278f, 319, 334, 361, 366, 459, 504, 505, 525, 528, 530, 531, 548. *See also* corn cribs; rations
Corn Belt, 156
corn cribs, 154, 155, **156–157**, 178
corn husking/shucking, 6, 154, 155, 157, 279, 319, 389
Corn Laws (England), 529
cornrows, 269
cosmograms, 107, 138, **157–160**, 158f, 337, 346, 429. *See also* subfloor pits
cotton, 45, 56, 71, 122, 133, 141, **160–165**, 180, 236, 243, 249, 262, 268, 316, 347, 351, 352, 354, 377, 381, 387, 389, 395, 497, 498, 500, 502, 527, 529, 538. *See also* cloth
Cotton Belt, 276, 331
cotton gin, 35, 119, 500f

cotton plantations, 119, 120, 122, 124, 132, **160–165**, 161f, 177, 202, 231, 249
country dances, 4
country marks, 411–412
Couper, James Hamilton, 447
courthouses, 34, 37, **166–167**
"cow-collards," 135
cowrie shells, 52, 53
Craft, Ellen, 384, 461
Craft, William, 384
craft as a path to freedom, 459
Crawford, John, 439
credit accounts, xv, **168–169**, 368
creolization, 50, 245
*Crescentia cujete* ("gourd tree"), 251
Cresswell, Nicholas, 41
"cribbing," 157
crochet hooks, 419
crocheting, 502
Croghan, George, 41
crosses, **170–171**
Crow, Hugh, 371
croze, 152
Cruikshank, George, 90, 92
Cruikshank, Isaac, 474f
currency. *See* coins and currency
Custis, Mary Anna Randolph, 125, 151f
Cutts, Richard, 423
*Cypraea moneta* (cowrie shells), 52, 420
Cyrus, Shadrach, 425

dairies, **173–175**, 174f, 178, 481
dance and music, **1–8**; African legacies and the 18th century, 2–3; Evangelical transformation and the Ring Shout, 6–8; in everyday life, 5–6; regional foundations and historical development, 3–5; sources and stereotypes, 1–2
dancing, 24, 39, 40f, 41, 42, 83, 92, 93, 115, 157, 193, 218, 241, 253, 261, 369, 389
Daumier, Honoré, 90
Davenport, Charlie, 118, 318
"Dave the Potter" or "Dave the Slave." *See* Drake, David
Davids, Tice, 517
Davies, Rev. Samuel, 75, 76
Davies, Thomas, 378
Davis, Jefferson, 443
Davis, Noah, 544
Davis, Varina, 125
Davis, William Henry, 380
Dawson, Mollie, 85
Dawson, William, 75, 79

Deane, James V., 155, 279

Debow, James, 306

*Debows Review*, 396

deeds, 167, 309–310, 309f

Delany, Martin, 237

Delaware, 4, 29, 64, 200, 202, 236, 520, 521

Denmark Vesey conspiracy of 1822, 32, 66, 165, 377

Dennet, John, 247

dependencies, **176–181**. *See also* blacksmith shops; corn cribs; dairies, dormitories; dovecotes, kitchens, laundries; slave hospitals; spinning houses; tobacco barns

Diallo, Ayuba Suleiman. *See* Jallo, Job Ben Solomon

discipline, of slaves, 59. *See also* whips

Discus, Mark, 296

dishwashing tasks, 413

District of Columbia (Washington, DC), 19f, 20, 22, 52, 125, 131, 144, 197, 201, 305, 306, 313, 319, 327, 399, 464

Dobard, Raymond, 390–391

dogs, xiv, **181–183**, 182f, 223, 394, 439, 518f

dogtrot houses, **183–184**, 183f, 452. *See also* double-pen houses; two rooms over two rooms houses

Dolben Act, 475

dolls, 156, 185f, **184–188**, 209, 325, 337, 357, 429; doll play and slavery, 187–188; early black dolls in America, 185–187; in Europe and North America, 185. *See also* graves

domestic slave trade, 20, 21, 35, 36, 407, 463. *See also* coffles

dominoes, 543f

dormitories, 56, **188–190**, 242

double-pen houses, **191–192**, 191f, 452

Douglass, Frederick, 1, 225, 225, 320, 371, 390, 424, 461, 462, 485, 518f, 521, 544, 549

dovecotes, **192–193**, 193f

Drake, David, 137, 376f, 377, 378, 457

Drayton Hall (South Carolina), 48, 103, 330f, 494

drinking gourds, 252, 319, 367; "Follow the Drinking Gourd," 253

drivers, 59, 401, 404, 489, 496, 534, 540. *See also* slave drivers

drum (fish), 226

drummers, 340

drums, xii, 6, 40, 57, **193–195**, 250, 253, 255, 340, 478

Dunmore, Lord (Lt. Gov. John Murray), 32, 223, 340

duplexes, 452

Durant, Sylvia, 105

Durham, Marion J., 379

Durham, Tempie Herndon. *See* Herndon, Tempie

dyeing, 71, 125, 287, 288, 500–501

Edgefield potteries, 137, 376, 377, 378, 379, 457

Edwards, Doc, 68

eels, 225; eel pots, 29

Ellison, Ralph, 4

Elmore, Emanuel, 31

emancipation, vii, 22, 117, 128, 137, 144, 200, 273, 333, 424, 436, 437

Emancipation Proclamation, 22, 64, 144, **197–203**, 199f, 399; extending the promise of, 202–203; Lincoln, emancipation, and the beginning of Civil War, 200; Lincoln and, 200–202; Lincoln's early thoughts about emancipation and slavery, 197–200; reaction to, 202

embroidery. *See* sewing items and needlework

Emmett, Dan, 43

Eppes, Francis Wayles, 471

Equiano, Olaudah, 2, 238, 461

"Ethiopian Regiment" (Virginia), 340

"Ethiopian Serenaders," 24f

Evangelical transformation and the Ring Shout, 6–8

Evans, Lewis, 162

Evans, Philip, 474

Exchange Building (Charleston, SC), 466

Fairfax, Catherine, 271f

Falconbridge, Alexander, 475

Falls, Robert, 198

"farm quarters," 169, 450

faunal remains, **205–209**, 207f, 231; assemblages, 29, 149

Fayman, M. S., 451

Feaster, Gus, 266

feathers, 55, 140, 142, 192, 248, 361, 384, 544. *See also* charms; fetishes

Felder, Sarah, 266, 501

Felix, Archdeacon, 438

Feltman, William, 135, 248, 524

Female Anti-Slavery Society (Massachusetts and Pennsylvania), 64

Female Association for the Promoting the Manufacture and Use of Free Cotton (Philadelphia), 236
fences, **210–211**, 247, 250, 333, 363, 465, 469, 507, 530, 543, 544
ferries, 73, **211–213**. *See also* boats; canoes; shipyards
fetishes, 140, 142, **213–217**, 337. *See also* charms; gourds; graves; nails; subfloor pits
fiddles, 6, 23, 24, 25, 40, 42, 155, **218–220**, 219f, 244, 250, 251f, 260, 261
Finney, Charles, 62
firearms, **221–223**, 338–341, 339f; evolution of the musket, 221; restrictions on slave ownership of, 222–223; rifle, development of, 222; use and composition, 221–222. *See also* armories
First African Baptist Church, Richmond, 112f, 116; Savannah, 117
First Rhode Island Regiment, 340
fish, xv, 109, 147, 148, 149, 206, 207; migratory, 225; and shellfish, **224–226**, 231, 247, 262, 278, 280, 335, 353, 360, 367, 370, 393, 395, 396, 401, 548. *See also* fishing poles
Fisher, Abby, 233
fishing poles, **227**. *See also* nets and seines
Fithian, Philip Vickers, 41, 247, 524, 548
"flang-dang" tunes, 25
flatboats, 36, 73, 88, 411. *See also* boats
flax processing, 315
Fleming, George, 240, 318, 326, 480
Fletcher, William, 470
flintlocks, 221, 222, 340. *See also* armories
Florida, 4, 33, 47, 142, 194, 200, 202, 269, 340, 395, 470, 483, 489, 493, 502, 520
flutes, **228–229**, 229f; transverse, 228
"flutina" (accordion), 24
fly brushes. *See* punkahs and fly brushes
folklife and gardens, 249–250
food and foodways, **229–233**, 481
food storage, 241, 243, 483, 485–486
Forman, Martha Ogle, 70, 366
Forten, James, 327
Fort Monroe (Virginia), 144
Fort Mose (Florida), 194
Fourteenth Amendment, 203
Fox, Reuben, 60, 206
Franklin, Isaac, 464, 465
Franks, Pet, 246
Free African Society (Philadelphia), 63
Freedmen's Bureau, xvi, 76, 146, 348

freedom papers, **234–235**
freedom suits, 312
free produce, **235–237**, 236f
Fremont, John C., 200
French and Indian War, 190, 288, 460, 530
French horns, **238**
Frere, John, 133, 369
Fugitive Slave Act of 1850, 64, 144
fugitive slaves, 11, 17, 21, 64, 194, 199, 232, 235, 364, 390, 406, 517, 518f, 520, 521
Fulcher, Fannie, 132
furnishings, **239–244**, 239f, 454; in Antebellum South, 242–244; in colonial period and early republic, 240–242; early slave furnishings, 240; servants halls, 415. *See also* kitchens; slave housing; slave quarters

gang system, 118, 247, 540. *See also* task system
Garden, Rev. Alexander, 65, 75
gardens, 48, 76, 77, 135, 147, 148, 149, 154, 158, 164, 192, 206, 210, 226, 231, 232, 241, 243, **245–250**, 262, 273, 327, 335, 359, 365, 404, 471, 523, 548; African roots and Creole transformations, 245–247; and folklife, 249–250; and power, 249; form and function, 247–249. *See also* kitchens
garlic, 273
Garrett, Thomas, 521
Garrison, William Lloyd, 237, 521
*Gazette and Advertiser* (Charleston, SC), 46
Georgia, 3, 47–48, 74, 106, 136, 194, 200, 202, 223, 231, 239, 249, 258, 285, 286f, 319, 328f, 331, 376, 400, 423, 470, 481, 483, 489, 520, 523; slave narratives from, 51, 81, 95, 124, 132, 162, 181, 186, 224, 246, 252, 255, 304–305, 335, 355, 363, 384, 394, 425, 445, 456, 467, 472, 498, 533, 534. *See also* Low Country; Sea Islands
Georgia beds, 55–56, 243
"Georgia Feathers" (straw), 56
Georgia Rattlesnake (watermelon), 523
Georgia Sea Island. *See* Sea Islands
Glenny, Albert, 24
goat, 147, 173, 206
Gold Rush (California), 343
goobers. *See* peanuts
Goodman, Andrew, 50

Gordon, Joleen, 50

*Gossypium* (cotton), 160–161

gourds, 39, 76, 147, 228, 243, 246, 248, **250–253**, 251f, 319, 367, 416, 503. *See also* banjos; fiddles

gourd tree, 251

Grandy, Moses, 424

Grant, Rebecca Jane, 113, 533

graves, 170, 185, **254–258**, 325, 346, 511, 513; archaeological and bioanthropological studies, 257–258; burial associations, 257; magicoreligious beliefs, 257; rural and plantation burial grounds, 254–256; urban burial grounds and practices, 256–257; as shrines, 429. *See also* beads; bottle trees; cemeteries; charms; coffins and caskets; conjure bags; faunal remains; shells

Great Awakening, First (1730–1170), 111; Second (ca. 1790–1840), 7, 112, 487

Green, Allen, 47

"green seed" cotton, 161

Grew, Mary, 236

*gris-gris* (charm), 104, 140, 142. *See also* fetishes; shrines and spiritual caches

Gronniosaw, James Albert Ukasaw, 460–461

grotesque likenesses. *See* caricatures

Grove, William Hugh, 248, 278, 366, 393, 524, 548

guineas (coins), **259–260**, 259f

guitars, 23, 24, 472, **260–262**

Gullah (Geechee), xii, 29, 46, 47, 114, 138, 194, 213

gumbo, 110, 149, 208, 226, **262–263**, 359, 360, 481

guns, xiv, xvi, 22, 29, 30, 32, 206, 339, 341, 477. *See also* firearms

hair and hairstyles, **265–270**, 346, 384, 406, 421; African background, 265; bound heads in bondage, 265–269; braids, varieties of, 269–270. *See also* beads; caricatures; charms; dolls; headwraps, tignons, and kerchiefs; razors; ribbons

Haitian Revolution, 3, 146, 160, 223, 365, 373

hammer, 31, 180, 343, 349, 367. *See also* blacksmith shops; woodworking tools

Hammon, Briton, 460

Hammond, Caroline, 519

hand charms, 107. *See also* shrines and spirit caches

Harlem Renaissance, 93

Harper, Frances Ellen Watkins, 22, 237

Haynes, John, 47

headwraps, tignons, and kerchiefs, 127, **270–271**, 271f

Hearn, Lafcadio, 142

Hemings, John, 471

*Henrietta Marie*, xiii, 475

Henson, Josiah, 54

herbs, 230, 243, **271–274**, 262, 371. *See also* conjure bags; gardens; medicine

Herndon, Tempie, 71, 398

Herndon, Zack, 456

Heyrick, Elizabeth, 236

Heyward, DuBose, 268

Hicks, Elias, 236

"hiring out." *See* slave hiring

hoecakes, 156, 243, 274–275, **274–275**, 374, 395

hoes, 68, 69, 149, 243, 246, 274, **275–277**, 276f, 278, 367, 421, 504–505, 506f, 512

Hogarth, William, 90

hogs. *See* pigs and pork

"Holy Trinity" (gumbo seasoning), 262

homemade remedies, 335

Homer, Winslow, 253

homespun, 120, 124, 352, 389

hominy, 155–156, 177, **277–279**, 278f, 280, 370, 482

Hoodoo, 141, 170, 209, 337

Hoppin' John, **280**, 360

horns. *See* bells and horns

Horry, Ben, 366, 541

horses, 113, 132, 147, 178, 209, **281–283**, 282f

"Hottentot Venus." *See* Baartman, Saarjite

Hughes, Louis, 371, 372

Hunter, Gen. David, 200

Ibn Said, Omar, 300

Ibn Sori, Abdulrahman, 300

ice houses, 179, 180, 469

Illinois, 197, 198, 427, 520, 524, 530

indentured servants, 319

Indiana, 462, 520

Indian corn, 366, 528. *See also* corn

indigo, 119, 120, 125, 262, **285–288**, 286f, 389, 399, 495, 499, 500, 527

industrial slavery, 55, 242, 341, 450. *See also* mines and mining; slave-made objects

insurance policy, 91, 342, 476, 478

internal slave trade. *See* domestic slave trade

international slave trade, abolition of, 355

"intrastate" slave trade. *See* domestic slave trade

invisible institution. *See* churches and praise houses

Iowa, 519

iron production, 69–70, 455, 457

ironwork, ornamental, **288–291**; Charleston, 289–290; New Orleans, 290–291

Jackson, Andrew, 85, 106, 191f, 220, 327, 336, 415, 421

Jackson, Rev. Silas, 541

Jacobs, Harriet, 61, 125, 394, 462

Jallo, Job Ben Solomon, 300

"Jamaica train," 490

James, John, 133

Jamestown (Virginia), 160, 331, 343, 430, 506f

Jarbour, David, 459

Jefferson, Isaac, 350

Jefferson, Madison, 440

Jefferson, Thomas, xv, 12, 41, 103, 118, 147, 153, 175, 182, 233, 248, 249, 253, 273, 321, 323, 327, 328, 350, 359, 361, 365, 367, 382, 416, 426, 432, 449, 458, 465, 471, 479, 512, 537, 543, 548

Jew's harps, **293–294**, 543f

"Jim Crow," 43, 91

Jim Crow era, 93, 186, 203, 211, 213

"John Brown's Fort," 33

John Canoe (Jonkanu), 398

Johnson, Andrew, 146, 348

Johnson, Anthony, 430

Johnson, Ella, 468

Johnson, Mary, 23

Johnson, William, 260, 397

Jones, Absalom, 63, 116

Jones, Rev. Charles Colcock, Jr., 248

Jonkanu. *See* John Canoe

"jumping the broom," origins of, 82

*ka* (sacred bag), 141

kalimba. *See* thumb pianos

Kalm, Peter, 248, 359

Kansas-Nebraska Act, 197

Keckley, Elizabeth, 418

Kemble, Fanny, 270, 447

Kendall cotton, 70, 352

Kentucky, 38, 43, 142, 144, 150, 191, 200, 202, 210, 220, 222, 261, 364, 421, 431f, 481, 483, 520; slave narratives from, 279, 451

Kentucky rifle, 222

kerchiefs, 127, 266, 268, 269, **270–271**

Keswick Plantation (Powhatan County, VA), 189

Kimber, Edward, 367

King, Sylvia, 353

Kinney, Nicey, 252

kitchens, 54, 55, 58, 94, 135, 138, 179, 184, 189, 205, 243, **295–300**, 296f, 305f, 324, 332, 376, 378, 395, 402, 412, 413, 414, 418, 450, 453, 465, 472; aesthetics, 298–299; domestic's quarters, 297–298; furnishings, 298; home and workplace, 297; passageway, 298; plantation, 295–297; workspace, 299. *See also* cooking and cooks; dependencies

kneeling slave, 18

knitting, 27, 120, 180, 387, 418, 497, 498, 500, 501, 502

knitting needles, 419

Kongo peoples of West Africa, 76, 380. *See also* BaKango

"Koramanti flute," 228

Koran, 140, **300–301**

"Kuba cloth," 388

Lafar, John J., 436

Lafitte, Jean, 290

Lancasterian system of education, 27

Larkin, Julia, 124

laundries, 96f, 179, **303–306**, 305f, 453

Lawson, John, 135

lawsuits, 309, 312–313

Lay, Benjamin, 17–18

Lee, Jim, 378

Lee, Robert E., 24

legal documents, **306–314**; deeds, 309–310, 309f; indentures of apprenticeship, 313; lawsuits, 312–313; manumission, 314; probate inventories, 311–312; slave hiring, 313–314; wills, 310–311

*Leuden* (slave ship), 478

Levi Jordan Plantation (Brazoria, TX), 111, 159, 209, 217, 337, 351, 421, 429

Levington, Rev. William, 418f

Liele, George, 117

"Limpin' Susan," 280, 360

Lincoln, Abraham, 197, 199f; early thoughts about emancipation and slavery, 197–200; and Emancipation Proclamation, 200–202

Lincoln, Mary Todd, 125

linen, 54, 56, 98, 120, 122, 125, 179, 287, 303, 319, 321, 351, 361, 367, 368, 417, 479, 498, 500 linen textiles, **314–316**, 315f

linsey-woolsey, 125, 389, 500–501

Liot, Capt. Philippe, 477

liquor, xiv, xv, 44, 155, 157, 169, 298, **316–320**, 322, 513, 539

literacy and orality, **11–14**

livery, xiv, 84, 125, 185f, **320–321**, 322f, 367, 538

Locke, Alain, 93

locks and keys, 30, 69, 241, 249, 298, **322–323**, 454

lofts, 54, 56, 178, 192, 240, 243, 297, 299, **323–324**, 331, 447, 451, 453, 473; slave housing, 324; slave quarters, 323–324

log buildings, 332, 451. *See also* slave quarters

longrifle, 222

looms/weaving houses, 180, 479, 499, 500f, 501, 502

Louisiana, 3, 4, 25, 36, 38, 47, 59, 60, 73, 140, 142, 144, 160, 161, 164, 165, 176, 177, 191–194, 197, 200, 202, 207, 220, 223, 226, 231, 249, 258, 261, 262, 267, 268, 273, 285, 286, 288, 290, 306, 327, 331, 360, 381, 395, 410, 421, 441, 463, 489, 490, 540, 544; slave narrative from, 488

Low Country (Georgia and South Carolina), 3, 4, 7, 46, 47, 109, 136, 137, 138, 142, 159, 161, 189, 212, 217, 226, 227, 231, 245, 247, 248, 257, 276, 280, 288, 319, 359, 360, 380, 395, 396, 416, 426, 431, 481, 542

Lowell cloth, 352

"luck ball," 142

Lumpkin, Robert, 465

Lumpkin's Jail (Richmond, VA), 465, 468

Lundy, Benjamin, 236

Lusk, John, 220

MacIntosh, Susan, 132

magic, 106, 107, 115, 140, 158, 170, 257, 337, 344. *See also* Hoodoo

"maid dolls," 186

malnutrition, 11, 205, 334–335, 446

Mami Wati worship tradition, 346

"mammy" doll, 186. *See also* mirrors; water

Mandinka empire, 39

Manesty, Joseph, 475

Mann, Capt. Luke, 477

manumission, 62, 144, 234, 235, 309, 314, 424, 531. *See also* Emancipation Proclamation

Manzano, Juan, 544

Maryland, xvi, 35, 36, 38, 64, 107, 159, 200, 202, 223, 225, 235, 312, 319, 339, 343, 361, 410, 411, 421, 449f, 463, 483, 504, 508, 520–521, 529; Annapolis, 53, 160, 217, 369, 524; Baltimore, 68, 236, 249, 328, 350, 418f, 423, 464; slave narratives from, 133, 155, 224, 451, 519, 526, 543, 549

marbles, 107, 170, 244, **325–327**, 326f, 428, 543f

"market revolution," 62

markets, xv, 48, 73, 81, 88, 131, 133, 135, 138, 139, 206, 208, 211, 212, 225, 231, 232, 246, 247, 249, 311, 319, **327–328**, 333, 349, 362, 368, 369, 400, 404, 435, 453, 487, 489, 523, 524f, 526

Maroon communities, 194, 438

Martin, Rev. John Sella, 326

*Maryland Gazette* (Annapolis), 349

Mason, George, 319, 426

Massachusetts, 13, 32, 64, 224, 343, 420, 442, 518f, 523

master's house, 58, 178, 179, 181, **329–334**, 330f, 361, 453, 458

Mather, Cotton, 65, 442

Matthews, Susan, 186

McCormick, Cyrus, 531

McCree, Ed, 95

McIntire, Thomas, 56

McLeod Plantation (South Carolina), 100

McWhorter, William, 355, 368, 534

medicine, 101, 158, 170, 205, 208, 209, 247, 250, 254, 272, 319, **334–338**, 429, 478, 511, 513; in 19th century, 446. *See also* charms; conjure bags; cosmograms; fetishes; slave hospitals

Meekins, William, 397

Mercer, James, 368

Mexico, 237, 390, 520

Michigan, 150, 519, 520

military equipment, **338–341**, 339f. *See also* armories; firearms

milk, 173–175, 230, 252, 318, 356, 374, 481

Miller, Lewis, 35f, 129f, 383f, 499f, 536f

Miller, Philip, 365

mines and mining, 69, 242, **342–343**. *See also* slave-made objects

minkisi, 104, 141, 142, 159, 214–217. *See also* charms; subfloor pits

minstrels and minstrelsy, 1, 23, 42, 43, 93, 260

mirrors, **344–347**; European, 345

Mississippi, 25, 38, 47, 126, 143, 161, 165, 167, 200, 202, 213, 249, 261, 276, 331, 379, 381, 382f, 410, 421, 445, 463, 483, 520; Natchez, 102f, 103f, 382f, 465; slave narratives from, 60, 113, 118, 174, 206, 230, 246, 258, 266, 279, 318, 319, 472, 498, 501

Mississippi River, 36, 73, 191, 395, 497; Lower Mississippi Valley, 140, 42, 144, 145, 224, 245, 247, 262, 365

Missouri, 38, 75, 142, 144, 200, 202, 421, 427, 462, 483, 544; slave narratives from, 296, 304, 307

mixed-use buildings, 453. *See also* dependencies

moccasins, 126. *See also* shoes

Mohammed, Bilali, 300

mojo bags. *See* conjure bags

Monitorial System. *See* Lancasterian system

Monroe, James, 459

Montgomery, James, 442

Monticello, 14, 84, 103, 118, 148, 149, 182, 233, 249, 323, 350, 365, 382, 416, 421, 426, 449, 458, 471, 473, 512, 524, 543

Morland, George, 91

mortar, 278f, 499f

Morton, Samuel, 432

Mother Bethel African Methodist Episcopal Church (Philadelphia), 116

mothers and nurseries, 356

Mott, Lucretia, 236

Mount Vernon, 70, 84, 106, 146, 169, 182, 189, 190, 224, 225, 233, 241, 327, 353, 361, 414, 449, 471, 479, 524

Mueller, Mabel, 304

Mulberry Row, 103, 458, 512, 543

mules, 45f, 163, 177, 255, 281, **347–348**

Murray, John, Jr., 26

Museum of Early Southern Decorative Arts (MESDA), 455

music. *See* dance and music

musket, evolution of, 221. *See also* armories; military equipment

Muslims, 300, 319

mutton, 148, 206, 208, 370

nails, xvi, 31, 53, 77, 101, 106, 118, 129, 209, 210, 243, 289, 315, 318, 327, **349–351**, 500, 538. *See also* blacksmith shops; conjure bags; fetishes; medicine; shrines and spirit caches

Nebraska, 197

"necessary houses." *See* chamber pots and privies

needles, 205, 227, 419–420

needlework. *See* sewing items and needlework

Negro Act (South Carolina), 212

Negro cloth, 120, 122, 123, **351–352**, 389, 539

"Negroes' Vigil, The," 442

"Negro Jack," 133, 344, 369, 399. *See also* barter goods; credit accounts

"Negro shoes," 425. *See also* clothing and footwear

nesting boxes, 178

nets and seines, **353**. *See also* fish and shellfish; fishing poles

New Hampshire, 423

New Jersey, 190, 212, 363, 420, 520

New Mexico, 388

New Orleans, viii, 3, 24, 36, 37f, 38, 55, 68, 118, 127, 142, 146, 160, 194, 220, 247, 261, 385, 288, 289, 364, 411, 424, 427, 466, 467, 468, 530; ironwork in, 290–291

Newton, John, 475, 476

New York, 13, 21, 26, 28, 52, 53, 75, 79, 88, 106, 170, 187, 254, 273, 285, 339, 421, 513, 520

New York Manumission Society, 26, 27, 28, 75

Nicholas, Robert Carter, 79

Niemcewicz, Julian, 169, 241, 242, 361, 471

Nina Plantation (Louisiana), 207

nkisi, 159, 214–217, 337, 346. *See also* charms; fetishes; minkisi; subfloor pits

North Carolina, 4, 43, 46, 47, 74, 143, 159, 200, 202, 225, 249, 253, 273, 280, 365, 366, 369, 376f, 394, 395, 421, 424, 447, 455, 462, 463, 481, 483, 485, 495, 496, 509; slave narratives from, 38, 68, 71, 326, 534

Northup, Solomon, 5, 164, 165, 220, 544

nurseries and nurse maids, **354–358**

Oglethorpe, Gov. James, 493

Ohio, 42, 63, 389, 407, 462, 520

Ohio River, 213, 364, 413, 481, 517

Oklahoma, slave narrative from, 418

okra, 110, 147, 149, 226, 246, 248, 249, 262, 280, **359–360**, 481

"Old Plantation, The" (watercolor), 2f, 41, 83, 241, 253

Old Steve (slave), 441

Olmsted, Frederick Law, 323, 395, 469

open-hearth cooking, 97. *See also* cooking
and cooks; kitchens
orality. *See* literacy and orality
osnaburg, 316. *See also* oznaberg
Ottolenghe, Joseph, 66
oznaberg, 122, 125

pallets, xiv, 58, 156, 243, 324, 357, **361**,
367. *See also* beds
palm wine, 317, 319
Pamplin pipes, 512
Parker, Rev. Richard, 327
Parsons, Charles Grandison, 277
passageway, 298
passes, 213, 261, 325, **362–364**, 362f, 543
patrollers, 6, 59, 363, 364, 534
Patterson, Delicia, 361
Patterson, Orlando, xv
"patting juba," 6, 195, 374
peanuts, 230, 240, 248, **365**
*peculium*, xv
Pemberton, James, 443, 461
Pennsylvania, 47, 79, 116, 183, 222, 343,
414, 420, 529; slave narrative from,
519; Underground Railroad in,
519–521
Pennsylvania rifle, 222
Penny, James, xiii
penny pipes, 512
"people managers." *See* slave drivers
Percussion cap firing systems, 222
periagua, 87–88, 212. *See also* boats
personal objects, **366–370**
Petrie, Alexander, 458
Philadelphia Female Anti-Slavery Society,
64, 236
Pickersgill, Mary, 423
Pickett, Reverend, 378
pig houses, 178
pigs, 169, 178, 206, 207, 208, 232, 262, 395;
and pork, **370–373**
Pinckney, Eliza Lucas, 285
Pinkard, George, 41
pins, 49, 53, 77, 106, 227, 344, 370, 417,
419, 427. *See also* conjure bags
pirogue. *See* periagua
pitch, 129, **494–496**
pitch, musical, 3, 5, 40, 194
plantation fences, 211
"plantation formula," 92
poison, 142, 225, 273, 337, 338; "pizens,"
273
polyrhythm, 3, 194, 195
Poplar Forest, 249, 273, 323, 327, 512

pork, 110, 135, 149, 179, 205–208, 231,
233, 262, 274, 279, 280, 334, 336,
375, 378, 393–395, 548 pigs and,
**370–373**
pot likker, 356, 371, **374–375**, 416
pot-liquor, 135, 375. *See also* pot likker
pottery, 159, **375–379**, 376f; "Dave the
Slave," 377–378; face jugs, 378–379;
plantation, 377; production, 376–377.
*See also* colonoware; Drake, David;
slave-made objects
pounders, **380**
"pounding," 380
pounding rice, 380
praise houses. *See* churches and praise
houses
privies, 102–104, 102f, 103f, 334
prizing tobacco, 507, 509
probate inventories, xiv, 95, 303, 309,
311–312, 455, 458
products, buying and selling, 367. *See also*
barter goods; credit accounts; markets
Prosser, Gabriel, 13, 32, 223, 226, 373
punishment, of slaves, 59–61, 59f, 441f. *See
also* slave collars; slave drivers; slave
pens, slave jails, and slave markets
punkahs and fly brushes, **381–385**, 382f,
383f

Quaker slaveholders, 17
Quarls, Harre, 219
quarters. *See* slave quarters
"Quilt Code," 390
quilts, **387–391**
Qur'an. *See* Koran

Ralph, Atmar Jr, 434
Randolph, Mary, 359
Randolph, Peter, 544
Randolph, Thomas Mann, xv
Rankin, John, 519
rations, **393** rations as a matter of power,
396; regional variations, 395–396
razors, **396–397**
*Reales*, 107
resistance, 59
Revolutionary War, 350
Rhode Island, 63, 75, 352, 420, 539; First
Regiment (black Revolutionary War
troops), 340
ribbons, **398–399**
rice, 149, 231
Rice, Thomas Dartmouth, 43
rice and indigo cultivation, 495

rice and rice fields, **399–405**, 400f; daily life, 404; field system, 400–401; labor, 401–402; yearly cycle, 402–403

Rice Kingdom, 47

Richardson, Richard, 361

rifle, development of, 222. *See also* armories; military equipment

Ring Shout, 4, 6, 7, 8

ritual scarification, 406

Roberts, Robert, 233

Robinson, Tom, 198

rock fences, 210, 211

"Rolling Jim," 533

"rolls," 316

roofing materials, 451

root doctors, 337

"root-work" system, 140

Roper, Moses, 544

Rosboro, Al, 187

rum, 316

runaway slave advertisements, 41, 133, 220, **405–408**, 406f, 425, 455, 538

rural and plantation burial grounds, 254–256

rural slave dress, 125

rural slavery, 408

Rush, Benjamin, 431

Russell, Malinda, 233

Rutledge, Sabe, 498

Rutledge, Sarah, 280, 365

Saar, Betye, 93

"Sable Venus," 91

*Saccharum officinarum*, 488

sage tea, 273

sale notices, **409–411**, 410f

Santos, Fr. Dos, 503

Sarrazin, Jonathan, 458

Saturday-night dance, 6

scarification, 51, **411–412**

Schlereth, Thomas, xi

Schoepf, Johann David, 253, 366

scissors, 420

Scomp, Samuel, 118

"scraping cotton," 163

sculleries, **412–413**

Sea Islands (Georgia and South Carolina), xii, xvii, 29, 49, 82, 136, 194, 213, 248, 269, 280, 327, 348, 447, 542. *See also* basket and basket making

seines. *See* nets and seines

Sells, Abram, 105, 456

servants halls, **413** evolution, 413–414; function, 414–415

"service yard." *See* yards

sesame, **416–417**

sewing, 502; items and needlework, **417–420**, 418f

shackles, 131f

shellfish. *See* fish and shellfish

shelling, 155

shells, 209, **420–422**

Shepherd, Robert, 255, 468

shipwrights, 424

shipyards, **422–424**

shoes, 126–127, **424–426**, 426f

shotgun houses, **427**

"shout," 82

shrines and spirit caches, **427–429**, 428f. *See also* charms; fetishes; subfloor pits

shucking of corn, 154

"sick house," 447f

sick slaves, 336

Silver Bluff Baptist Church (Aiken County, SC), 115–116

Simpson, Ben, 130

sizing hoop, 152

skin, **430–433**, 431f. *See also* caricatures

Skipwith, Fulwar, 381

slave auction, 35f, 182f

slave badges, **434–437**, 435f; copper, 435

Slave Carrying Act of 1788, 475

slave cloth. *See* Negro cloth

Slave Coast, 259

slave collars, 59f, **438–442**, 441f

slave drivers, **442–444**, 540

slave galleries, **444–445**

slave hiring, 313–314, 334

slave hospitals, 336–337, **446–447**, 447f

slave housing, 324, **448**, 449f, 494f; construction and change, patterns of, 451–453; as creolized architecture, 454; terminology, 449; urban slave housing, 453. *See also* slave quarters

slave "intrapreneurship," 443

slave jails, 327, **463–468**

slave-made objects, 376f, **455**; in Charleston, SC, 458; craft as a path to freedom, 459; industrial slavery, 455, 457; plantation artisans, 457–458; training, 459

slave markets, **463–468**

slave narratives, 82, 457, **460–462**, 461f

slave pass, 364

slave pens, **463–468**, 463f, 464f

slave quarters, 6, 13, 47, 52, 54–59, 81, 84, 102, 113–115, 145, 149, 156, 159, 160, 164, 169, 176–178, 180, 182, 188, 189, 205–207, 217, 240–244, 248, 261, 263,

273, 278, 282, 297, 299, 308, 318, 319, 323–325, 327, 333, 334, 336, 344, 352, 357, 361, 367, 371, 387, 413, 448, 450–454, **468–473**, 482, 483–487, 512, 540, 542, 549

slave ships, 78, 91, 157, 393, 512, 523, 547, **473–478**, 474f

slave tags. *See* slave badges

slave traders, 35, 36, 37, 37, 52, 78, 127, 129, 140, 230, 409, 410, 411, 464, 465, 468, 528

Sloan, Hiram L., 307–309

Smalls, Robert, 438

Smith, Adam, 105

Smith, Jordan, 467

Smith, Paul, 81, 456, 472

smokehouses, 175, 179, 373, 394, 439, 453

smoothbore flintlock muskets, 221

Sneed, John, 227, 329

Snyder, Mariah, 352

soap, 303, 304, 305

sorghum, 80, 81, 246, 248, 250, 278, 317, 528

Sotterly slave cabin, 449f

"soul food," 205, 208, 373. *See also* food and foodways

South Carolina, 73, 136–138, 149, 159, 161, 182, 256, 267, 276, 339, 365, 399, 416, 429, 529; slave narratives from, 31, 46, 60, 105, 113, 134, 162, 187, 219, 240, 266, 281, 318, 326, 380, 403, 456, 480, 482, 498, 499, 533, 541; General Assembly, 213, 338

"Spanish train," 490

"spiked Indian corn," 528

spinning houses, 120, 180, **479–480**, 479f

spiritual spaces, 486

Spotswood, Gov. Alexander, 32, 455

spring houses, 174, 179, **481**

"square dances," 4

Squire (slave), 524

stables, 163, 176, 178, 180, 281, 282, 305, 332, 450, 453

Stanhope, Samuel, 431

Stanwood, Moody G., 23, 24f

Starke, R. O., 378

"Star Spangled Banner, The," 424

stealing, xv, 13, 77, 108, 164, 207, 298, 328, 373, 394, 525, 526. *See also* theft

Stedman, John Gabriel, 441

stews, 97, 109, 110, 134, 208, 230, 262, 278, 359, 360, 365, 380, 477, **481–482**, 548

Still, William, 22, 424, 521

Stodder, David, 423

Stokes, Simon, 505

Stone, William, 394

stone huts, 451

stonemasons, 211

Stone Rebellion/Uprising, 13, 32, 193, 223, 445

storage jar, 376f

Stothard, Thomas, 91

Stowe, Harriet Beecher, 269, 542

Strother, David Hunter, 147f

Stuart, James, 55

subfloor pits, 13, 52, 84f, 344, 421, 428, 428f, 429, 454, **482–487**, 483f; disappearance, 486–487; functions, 484–486; locations, 483; physical appearance, 483–484. *See also* charms; fetishes

sugar, xii, 35, 41, 59, 129, 133, 148, 149, 164, 177, 232, 236, 237, 246, 298, 334, 366, 396, 399, 400, 410, 443, 467, 540, 548, **487–491**

sugar plantations, 41, 59, 347, 400, 488, 489, 491, 540

Sweeney, Joel Walker, 43

sweet potatoes. *See* yams and sweet potatoes

tabby, 470, **493–494**, 494f

tar, **494–496**

task system, 88, 118, 247, 404, 540, 541

Tatham, William, 249, 524

Tayloe III, John, 305

Taylor, Emma, 186, 394

Taylor, Francis, 44, 133, 367, 368

Tennessee, viii, 47, 85, 107, 129f, 143, 150, 161, 167, 200, 210, 220, 223, 446, 407, 421, 483, 520; slave narratives from, 198, 525

terrapin, 206, 226; diamond back, 225

Terrill, J. W., 439

testator, 310, 311, 314

Texas, vii, 1, 23, 25, 47, 49, 58f, 111, 126, 159, 161, 171, 191, 200, 202, 209, 217, 219, 245, 249, 258, 272, 337, 351, 379, 395, 421, 427, 429, 470; slave narratives from, 85, 105, 108, 131, 141, 177, 186, 321, 329, 337, 352, 394, 439, 456s

textiles, **497–502**, 500f, 502f; dyeing, 498–500; bast fibers, 498; cotton, 497–498; dyeing, 498–500; indigo, 500–501; wool 498; fibers, preparing, 497–500; knitting and crocheting, 502; sewing, 502–503; weaving,

501–502. *See also* blankets; cloth; linen textiles; Negro cloth; sewing items and needlework

theft, xv, 78, 110, 111, 133, 178, 232, 319, 322, 323, 368, 393, 395, 454, 485. *See also* stealing

thimbles, 420

Thirteenth Amendment, 22, 33, 64, 203, 404

Thomas, Sarah, 230, 279

Thornton, James, 184

Thornton, Laura, 74, 132

thumb pianos, 250, **503–504**

Tidwell, Emma, 98, 286

tignons, 267, **270–271**, 365. *See also* hair and hairstyles

time discipline and control, 58–59. *See also* clocks and watches

Tims, J. T., 468

tobacco, xv, 4, 119, 129, 133, 152, 153, 169, 178, 220, 246, 247, 249, 275, 276f, 277, 410, 430, 443, 453, **504–508**, 506f, 527, 528, 529, 530, 531, 540, 541

tobacco barns, **509–510**

tobacco factories, **510–511**

tobacco hogsheads, 507

tobacco house. *See* tobacco barn

tobacco pipes, 158f, 429, 485, 486, **511–514**

Tobin, Jacqueline, 390–391

tomitudes, 187

Topsy Turvy dolls, 185–186, 187

Torrey, Jesse, 20

toys. *See* dolls; marbles

traps. *See* animal traps

trans-Atlantic slave trade, 51, 409. *See also* slave ships

travel pass, 362f, 364

Triangular Trade, 317, 319, 473, 491

Tschudi, Johann von, 433

Tubman, Harriet, 29, 390, 521

Tull, Jethro, 529–530

Turner, Joseph M. W., 91. *See also* Zong

Turner, Nat, 13, 32, 66, 165, 223, 373, 531

turnpike fences, 211

turpentine, **494–496**

two-room buildings, 297, 452, 453. *See also* dependencies

two rooms over two rooms houses, 184, **514–515**

Uncle Tom's Cabin, 92, 187, 269, 444, 542

Underground Railroad, 22, 117, 397, **517–522**, 518f; in 1850s, 520–521; husband destinations, 520; "Quilt Code," 390; resistance and flight, 517–520; and world of a slave, 521–522

Upson, Neal, 384

urban and house slave dress, 125

urban burial grounds and practices, 256–257. *See also* benevolent associations; cemeteries; coffins and caskets; churches and praise houses

urban slave housing, 55, 453. *See also* slave quarters

urban town houses, 333

Van Hook, John, 363

vaudeville, 43

Vesey, Denmark, 32, 66, 165, 377

vibraphone, 39

Vinson, Addie, 425

violence against black slaves, 432

violent punishments. *See* slave collars; slave drivers; whips

Virginia, 4, 13, 74, 78, 79, 159, 166, 225, 227, 241, 247, 273, 297, 338, 339, 371, 398–399, 429, 445, 482–483, 485–487, 548; slave narratives from, 372, 467, 505, 525, 539, 541

*Virginia Gazette* (Williamsburg), 350, 412, 471, 513, 538

*Virginia Housewife, The*, 110, 359, 481, 548

Virginia legislature, 116, 213

Virginia Manumission Act (1815), 531

Virginia Minstrels, 43

"Virginian Luxuries," 532f

Vodun, 140, 141, 160, 214, 217. *See also* Hoodoo

Voting Rights Act of 1867, 433

Wager, Ann, 79

"Waiter Carriers," 232. *See also* chickens; food and foodways

Walker, Alice, 93

Walker, Florence, 23

Walker, Jonathan, 78

Walker, Kara, 93

Walker, Robert, 459

Walpole, Sir Robert, 238

Ward, Samuel Ringgold, 237, 461

wash houses, 179. *See also* laundries

Washington, Aaron, 24

Washington, Booker T., 76, 110, 325, 383, 485, 544, 549

Washington, D.C. *See* District of Columbia

Washington, George, 70, 72, 109, 146, 169, 182, 189, 224, 227, 233, 241, 248,

282, 318, 320–321, 322f, 327, 340, 341, 347, 353, 361, 368, 369, 414, 449, 471, 479, 530, 537
Washington Navy Yard, 129, 395, 424
watches. *See* clocks and watches
water (as symbol), 14, 53, 77, 98, 101, 115, 159, 209, 267, 268, 333, 346, 376, 422, 429, 486. *See also* boats; canoes
watermelons, 91, 248, 249, 250, 325, **523–526**, 524f
Waud, A. R., 328f, 400f
Weathersby, David, 174
Weathersby, Foster, 130, 230, 472
Weathersby, Robert, 113
weaving, 124, 180, 352, 387, 418, 479, 480, 497, 500f, 501–502; weaving houses, 120, 180; weaving rooms, 297. *See also* textiles
Webb, Jennie, 540
Webb, William, 142
Wedgwood, Josiah, 18, 91
well houses, 179
West Virginia, 43
wheat, 4, 54, 132, 277, 366, 453, 505, **526–531**, 527f. *See also* cooperage; rations
Wheatley, Phillis, 11–12, 12f, 399
whips, 182f, **532–535**, 532f
white catfish. *See* fish
white-produced images of black life, 21
Whitlock, Bill, 43
Wiggins, James, 369, 543
wild Negroes, 193
Wilkes Street Pottery (Alexandria, VA), 459
Williams, Millie, 108
Williams, Ozella McDaniel, 390
Willis, Adeline, 498
wills, 235, 310–311, 314; executor, 311
Wilson, Wash, 141, 177
Wilson Pottery (Guadalupe, TX), 379
wine, 317, 318, 319, 429, 486. *See also* shrines and spirit caches

Winfrey, Oprah, 390
Winterbotham, Thomas, 478
Wisconsin, 529
Wood, Thomas Waterman, 253
Woodson, Willis, 321
Woodward, James, 459
woodworking tools, **535–538**, 536f. *See also* dependencies
wool, 54, 70, 71, 84, 119, 120, 122, 124, 182, 266, 303, 320, 351, 352, 367, 387, 389, 419, 479, 497, 498, 500. *See also* wool textiles
Woolman, John, 236
wool textiles, **538–540**
work routines, 428–429, **540–542**. *See also* gang system; task system
Works Progress Administration (WPA), vii, 25, 50, 98, 104, 126, 158, 187, 205, 242, 261, 369, 462, 540, 369, 457
Worsdale, James, 441
Wright, Henry, 162
writing tools, 13, **542–545**, 543f. *See also* African Free School; Bray schools
wrought iron, 78, 97, 276f, 289. *See also* blacksmith shops; nails

x-incised items, 217. *See also* charms; cosmograms; shrines and spirit caches; subfloor pits

Yale, Elihu, 441, 442
yams and sweet potatoes, 45f, 49, 109, 110, 147, 164, 246, 248, 249, 250, 380, 393, 481, 485, 524, 525, **547–550**
yards, 76, 77, 82, 178, 210, 299, 327, 333, 456, 529, **550–551**
*yowa. See* cosmograms

Zong, 91, 478

# About the Editors and Contributors

## EDITORS

**Martha B. Katz-Hyman** is an independent curator and consultant to museums on historic house furnishing and interpreting pre–Civil War African American material culture.

**Kym S. Rice** is the director of the Museum Studies Program at George Washington University and a long-time curator and consultant to museums on African American interpretation.

## CONTRIBUTORS

**Daniel K. Ackermann** is associate curator at the Museum of Southern Decorative Arts and the Old Salem Toy Museum Collections in Winston-Salem, North Carolina.

**Linda Baumgarten** is curator of textiles at the Colonial Williamsburg Foundation.

**Timothy E. Baumann** is curator of collections at the Glenn A. Black Laboratory of Archaeology, Indiana University.

**Andrew S. Bledsoe** is a doctoral candidate in history at Rice University.

**Antonio T. Bly** is assistant professor in the history department at Appalachian State University.

**Dana E. Byrd** is a doctoral candidate in the history of art at Yale University.

**Tammy K. Byron** is an assistant professor in the department of history at Dalton State College, Dalton, Georgia.

**Robin Campbell** is an independent scholar in Saratoga Springs, New York.

**Barbara G. Carson** is an independent scholar in Williamsburg, Virginia.

**Emily S. Clark** is a doctoral student in religion at Florida State University.

**James Coltrain** is a doctoral candidate in American history at Northwestern University.

**Audrey R. Dawson** is a principal investigator and project archaeologist at the South Carolina Institute of Archaeology and Anthropology at the University of South Carolina.

**Catherine E. Dean** is curator of collections at Preservation Virginia in Richmond.

**Kristen Baldwin Deathridge** is a doctoral candidate in public history at Middle Tennessee University.

**Kelley Deetz** is Ainsworth Visiting Professor of American Culture at Randolph College, Lynchburg, Virginia.

**Daniel C. Dillard** is a doctoral candidate in religion at Florida State University.

**Ywone Edwards-Ingram** is a staff archaeologist at the Colonial Williamsburg Foundation and teaches courses at the College of William and Mary.

**Rex Ellis** is Associate Director of the National Museum of African American History and Culture at the Smithsonian Institution in Washington, D.C.

**Christopher T. Espenshade** is an archaeologist with New South Associates in Greensboro, North Carolina.

**Chris Evans** teaches history at the University of Glamorgan, United Kingdom.

**Anne-Claire Faucquez** is a graduate student in the Département d'Etudes des Pays Anglophones at the Université Paris VIII, France.

**Leigh Fellner** is a quilt maker and independent quilt historian in Pensacola, Florida.

**Gretchen Goodell** is curator at Stratford Hall plantation in Stratford, Virginia.

**Harlan Greene** is director of Archival and Reference Services at the Avery Research Center, College of Charleston.

**Christopher Hager** is assistant professor of English at Trinity College in Hartford, Connecticut.

**Jonathan A. Hallman** is a journeyman cooper in the department of historic trades at Colonial Williamsburg.

**Fritz Hamer** is the chief curator of history at the South Carolina State Museum in Columbia.

**Susan Atherton Hanson** is principal of History Behind the Scenes, in Philadelphia.

**Martin Hardeman** is associate professor of history at Eastern Illinois University.

**John E. Harkins** is a member of the history department and school archivist at Memphis University School in Memphis, Tennessee.

**Juliette Harris** is the editor of *International Review of African American Art* at Hampton University Museum.

**Jurretta Jordan Heckscher** is a research specialist in the Digital Reference Section at the Library of Congress, Washington, D.C.

**Matt Hernando** is a doctoral student in history at Louisiana State University.

**Katie Hladky** is a doctoral student at Florida State University.

**Julie Holcomb** is a lecturer in museum studies at Baylor University.

**Daniel Hughes** is a doctoral candidate at the University of South Florida.

**Emilie Johnson** is a doctoral candidate in art and architectural history at the University of Virginia.

**Whittington B. Johnson** is professor emeritus in the Department of History at the University of Miami.

**Alexandra Jones** is a doctoral student in the department of anthropology at the University of California, Berkeley.

**Susan A. Kern** is a visiting assistant professor in the Lyon G. Tyler Department of History at the College of William and Mary.

**Katie Knowles** is a doctoral candidate in the department of history at Rice University.

**Jill Beute Koverman** is curator of collections at the McKissick Museum, University of South Carolina.

**Susan Kozel** is an adjunct instructor at Kean University and New Jersey community colleges.

**Lori Lee** is a doctoral candidate in anthropology at Syracuse University.

**Fred Lindsey** is an assistant professor of cultural studies at John F. Kennedy University.

**Barbara Magid** is an archaeologist and curator at the Alexandria Archaeology Museum in Virginia.

**Sam Margolin** is an independent scholar in Newport News, Virginia.

**Ann Smart Martin** is the Stanley and Polly Stone Professor and director of the Material Culture Program at the University of Wisconsin–Madison.

**Hugh B. Matternes** is a mortuary archaeologist and director of the cemetery studies program for New South Associates in Stone Mountain, Georgia.

**Maurie D. McInnis** is an associate professor of art history at the University of Virginia.

**Linda E. Merians** is an independent scholar in Forest Hills, New York.

**Hillary Murtha** is a doctoral candidate at the University of Delaware.

**Caryn E. Neumann** is a visiting assistant professor and special assistant to the dean for university relations, Miami University of Ohio.

**Neil L. Norman** is a visiting assistant professor in the department of anthropology at the College of William and Mary.

**Percival Perry** was professor emeritus of history at Wake Forest University.

**David Pleasant** is a musician and lecturer based in New York City, specializing in African American traditions.

**Laura Russell Purvis** is an independent scholar in Charlottesville, Virginia.

**Wayne Randolph** is a specialist in historic farming in the department of historic trades at Colonial Williamsburg.

**Debra A. Reid** is professor of history at Eastern Illinois University.

**Melissa Renn** is a research associate at the Fogg Museum of Art, Harvard University.

**Julie Richter** is a lecturer for the National Institute of American History and Democracy and the Lyon G. Tyler Department of History at the College of William and Mary.

**Julia Rose** is the director of the West Baton Rouge Museum in Louisiana.

**Dale Rosengarten** is a librarian in Special Collections at the Addlestone Library, College of Charleston.

**Linda H. Rowe** is an historian at Colonial Williamsburg.

**D. Al Saguto** is the master shoemaker in the department of historic trades at Colonial Williamsburg.

**Edward Salo** is a senior historian for Brockington and Associates in Norcross, Georgia.

**Patricia M. Samford** is director of the Maryland Archaeological Conservation Laboratory in St. Leonard, Maryland.

**Douglas W. Sanford** is professor and chair of the department of historic preservation at the University of Mary Washington.

**Marie Jenkins Schwartz** is chair and professor in the history department at the University of Rhode Island.

**Kenneth Schwarz** is master blacksmith in the department of historic trades at Colonial Williamsburg.

**Razika Touati Khelifa Senoussi** is a doctoral student in history at the University of Paris VIII.

**Jared Snyder** is an independent scholar in Rochester, Washington.

**Leni A. Sorensen** is African American research historian at the Thomas Jefferson Foundation–Monticello.

**Clif Stratton** is an instructor of history at Washington State University.

**Alice Taylor** is a postdoctoral fellow in history at the University of Toronto.

**David Taft Terry** is the executive director of the Reginald F. Lewis Museum of Maryland African American History and Culture in Baltimore.

**Mary V. Thompson** is research historian at George Washington's Mount Vernon Estate and Gardens, Alexandria, Virginia.

**Tony Tibbles** is emeritus Keeper of Slavery History for National Museums Liverpool, England.

**Michael Trinkley** is director of the Chicora Foundation in Columbia, South Carolina.

**Michael W. Twitty** is an independent scholar in Rockville, Maryland, who specializes in African American foodways.

**Wells Twombly II** is director of public history programs at Peralta Hacienda Historical Park in Oakland, California.

**John M. Vlach** is professor of American studies and folklife at George Washington University, Washington, D.C.

**Juliet E. K. Walker** is a professor of history at the University of Texas, Austin.

**T. Stephen Whitman** is associate professor emeritus in the department of history at Mount St. Mary's University, Emmitsburg, Maryland.

**Psyche Williams-Forson** is associate professor in the department of American studies at the University of Maryland, College Park.

**Peter H. Wood** is professor emeritus in the department of history at Duke University.

**Colin Woodward** is a project archivist in the department of manuscripts and archives at the Virginia Historical Society.

**Stacey L. Young** is an archaeologist with New South Associates in Columbia, South Carolina.